BRIEF EDITION

Computers:
Tools for an Information Age

BRIEF EDITION

Computers:
Tools for an Information Age

H. L. Capron

J. A. Johnson

Prentice Hall

Prentice Hall
Upper Saddle River
New Jersey, 07458

Library of Congress Cataloging-in-Publication Data

Capron, H. L.
    Computers: tools for an information age / H. L. Capron, J. A. Johnson—Brief ed.
        p. cm.
    Includes index.
    ISBN 0-13-091955-1
    1. Computers. 2. Microcomputers. I. Johnson, J. A. (James A.) II. Title.

QA76 .5 .C363 2002
004-dc21

                                                                        2001036124

Acquisitions Editor: Jodi McPherson
Publisher: Natalie E. Anderson
Managing Editor (Editorial): Monica Stipanov
Assistant Editor: Jennifer Cappello
Editorial Assistant: Mary Ann Broadnax
Developmental Editor: Rebecca Johnson
Media Project Manager: Cathleen Profitko
Senior Marketing Manager: Sharon Turkovich
Marketing Assistant: Jason Smith
Manager, Production: Gail deAcevedo Steier
Production Editor: Michael Reynolds
Production Assistant: Dianne Falcone
Permissions Supervisor: Suzanne Grappi
Associate Director, Manufacturing: Vincent Scelta
Design Manager: Patrica Smythe
Designer: Janet Slowik
Interior Design: Amanda Kavanagh
Illustrator (Interior): Precision Graphics
Cover Design and Illustration: Joseph Maas/Paragon 3
Manager, Print Production: Christy Mahon
Print Production Liaison: Ashley Scattergood
Composition: TECHBOOKS
Full-Service Project Management: TECHBOOKS
Printer/Binder: Banta/Manasha

Credits and acknowledgments borrowed from other sources and reproduced, with permission, in this textbook appear on pages 351–352.

10 9 8 7 6 5 4 3 2
ISBN 0-13-091955-1

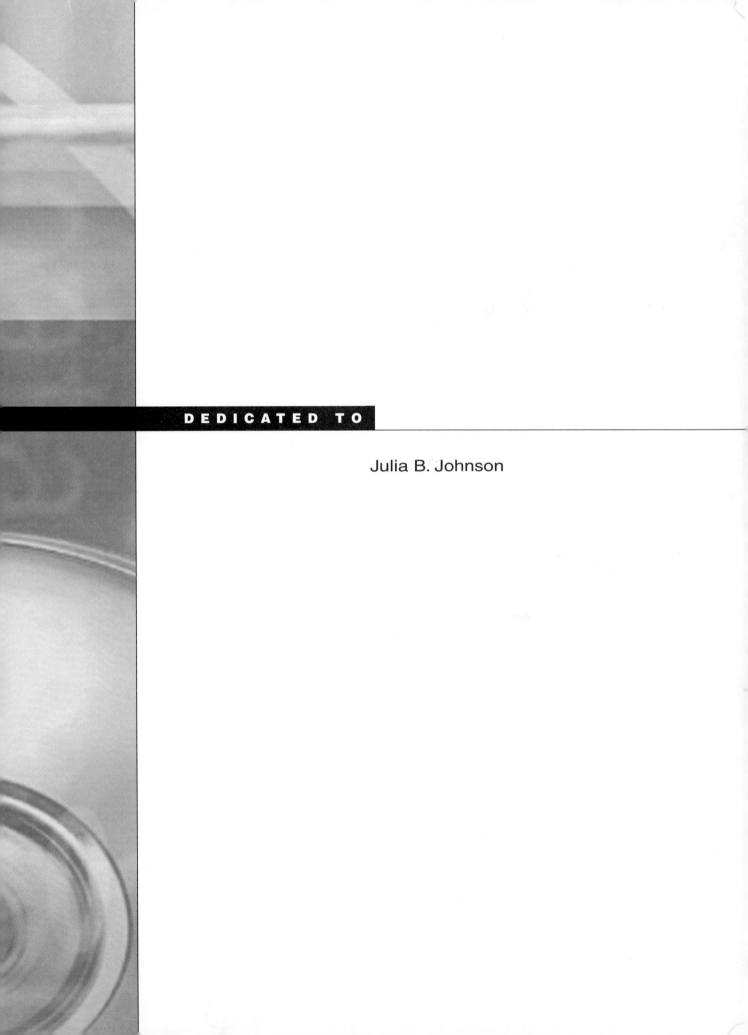

DEDICATED TO

Julia B. Johnson

BRIEF CONTENTS

CONTENTS

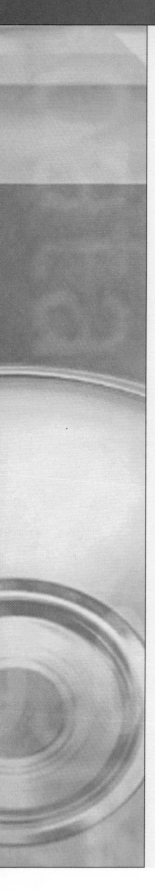

PREFACE

H. L. Capron, well-known and respected author of *Computers: Tools for an Information Age,* is joined by James A. Johnson to provide students with the most comprehensive, up-to-date introduction to computers. The seventh edition has new coverage on the latest in microcomputer operating systems, hardware, and e-commerce to ensure that students have the most current information as they learn about today's technology.

Connectivity is paramount in today's society. In this edition, the connectivity theme is integrated into several aspects of the book. Exploring the Internet is also simplified with an introduction in Chapter 1 and related materials in Chapters 8, 9, and in the Planet Internet features at the end of every chapter. In addition, Prentice Hall's Explore Generation IT Labs are included, free of charge, to give an interactive component to the course material.

FOCUS ON THE INTERNET

CHAPTER 1. Jump-start the text with an Introduction to the Internet in Chapter 1. Learn basic information about the Web, browsers, servers, and Internet protocol at the beginning and be able to use it throughout the course.

INTERNET CHAPTERS. The Internet is now covered in two different chapters so that you can read the Internet material you need, when you need it.

Chapter 8: "The Internet: A Resource for All of Us" explains the important aspects of Internet technology from URLs to links to search engines.

Chapter 9: "The Internet in Business: Corporations, Small Businesses, and Entrepreneurs" focuses on various aspects of business use of the Internet, particularly electronic commerce.

PLANET INTERNET. The Planet Internet feature offers a nontechnical look at various aspects of the World Wide Web in a two-page spread at the end of each chapter. Topics include places to start, global aspects of the Internet, FAQs, business, shopping, careers, privacy, multimedia, entertainment, resources, and Internet relay chat. Each Planet Internet suggests hands-on Internet exercises.

POCKET INTERNET. Students love the companion resource guide, "Pocket Internet: 4001 Sites." This popular pocket resource guide has been updated and expanded to include sites and even more disciplines.

DISTINCTIVE LEARNING FEATURES

MULTIMEDIA. Whether on CD-ROM or the Internet, multimedia continues to be a major newsmaker in the computer industry. Underlying CD-ROM technology and multimedia applications are described in Chapter 6.

ETHICS. In addition to the feature, "Focus on Ethics," that appears in each chapter, two major ethics categories are included: "Ethics and Software," "Ethics and Data."

OFFICE 2000. All screens for hands-on applications have been produced using Microsoft Office 2000®.

GETTING PRACTICAL. Various topics of practical interest to students, such as using the computer as a digital darkroom to produce semiprofessional pictures, caring for diskettes and CDs, and choosing an Internet service provider, are covered in the "Getting Practical" box in each chapter.

MAKING CONNECTIONS. Links people to computers. Topics include personalizing your desktop screen, buying a car on-line, updating software online, and Bluetooth communications.

MARGIN NOTES. To further engage the student, margin notes are placed throughout

the text. The margin notes extend the text material by highlighting interesting computer applications. Topics include chips that see, the networked home, cyberwarfare, and the wired campus.

BUYER'S GUIDE. Students and their families are making important economic decisions about the purchase of a computer for educational, personal, and business needs. This concise guide offers information to aid in hardware and software purchases.

MAKING MICROCHIPS GALLERY. The gallery text, supplemented by color photos, describes how microprocessors are made.

APPEALING WRITING STYLE. The authors' writing style is known to be student-friendly. More important, the material is presented with real-life examples. Each chapter begins with an engaging real-world vignette. Additional real-world examples are included throughout the chapter.

IN-TEXT LEARNING AIDS

Each chapter includes the following pedagogical support:

Learning Objectives at the beginning of each chapter provide key concepts for students.

Key terms appear in bold throughout the text.

A *Chapter Review* offers a summary of core concepts and key terms.

Critical Thinking Questions encourage students to discuss more thoroughly the information presented in each chapter.

The *Student Study Guide* offers objective questions that test comprehension of essential concepts.

Explore Generation IT Labs Icons prepare students in the interactive labs for hands-on experience from material covered in the chapter.

A *Glossary* and a comprehensive *Index* are included at the end of the text.

STUDENT LEARNING SUPPLEMENTS

Prentice Hall's Explore Generation IT Labs

The Explore IT labs offer students an interactive look at computer concepts. The labs are delivered both on the Web and on CD-ROM, allowing access in the classroom, the dorm, at home, and wherever computer and/or the Internet access is available.

EXPLORE GENERATION IT LABS have three key sections that encourage participation from students:

- *Introduction:* A multimedia exploration of the topic engages students and helps them fully understand the material presented in an interactive environment.

- *Explore:* Through further interaction and exploration of the material, students get a better understanding of the concepts in the lab.

- *Quiz:* Each lab includes a ten-question quiz that requires students to demonstrate an understanding of the concepts and material.

My PHLIP

My PHLIP is an on-line learning environment for instructors and students. Activities available through this Companion Web Site include:

- *On-line Study Guide*—self assessment exercises, including multiple choice, true/false, and fill-in-the-blank questions, with instant feedback at the click of a button.

- *Communication*—because learning does not occur in a vacuum, we have integrated several ways for students and faculty to communicate within this Companion Web Site.

Capron's Pocket Internet: 4001 Sites

On the professor's request, this pocket reference guide is included on with new orders of the student text. With over 4001 Internet sites, content is interesting and relevant to students. The sites are grouped by topic and include a number of disciplines such as animation, architecture, arts, best-hot-cool, finance and investing, career/jobs, computer science, cool companies, education, entertainment, entrepreneurs, financial aid, fitness and health, free stuff, and more.

INSTRUCTOR TEACHING SUPPLEMENTS

INSTRUCTOR'S MANUAL—A comprehensive manual and test bank provide the tools instructors need for easier class preparation.

INSTRUCTOR'S RESOURCES CD-ROM—This CD-ROM includes the Instructor's Manual and Test Bank in Microsoft Word and the Prentice-Hall Test Manager, along with PowerPoint presentation slides.

COMPUTER CHRONICLES VIDEOS—Through our partnership with *The Computer Chronicles* television series, we have compiled a video collection that features real-life computer stories and problems and how technology is changing.

WEBCT AND BLACKBOARD CONTENT—The custom-built distance learning course features all new and original interactive lectures, exercises, sample quizzes, and tests.

ACKNOWLEDGMENTS

Many people contributed to the success of this project. Although a single sentence hardly suffices, we would like to thank some of the key people. Rebecca Johnson, Senior Development Editor, provided invaluable guidance during the entire project, from planning the revisions for this edition to adjusting the final page layouts. Monica Stipanov, Managing Editor, kept everything on track during several changes in project personnel. Michael Reynolds, Production Editor, came on board mid-project and managed to bring all the elements together on schedule. Joseph Maas produced yet another outstanding cover design for this edition. Jerry and Nancy Reed provided updated material for the Planet Internet and Focus on Ethics features. Anthony Nowakowski provided end-of-chapter material for several chapters on very short notice. Dennis Egan (RPG) and Colin Archibald (Java) provided new sample programs for the Programming and Languages chapter. As you can see, this was truly a team effort.

We would also like to thank the following reviewers for their valuable input. Without them, our work would have been much more difficult.

Elise Bell, City College of San Francisco

David Glover, Glendale Community College

Philip Marshall, Darla Moore School of Business

Charles Hassett, Fort Hayes State University

Deborah Allen, Mercer University

Tom Hannah Jr., Ozarks Technical Community College

Scott Quinn, Portland Community College

Susan Sells, Witchita State University

Karen Willner, Saddleback Community College

Oren Johnson, Langston University

Deena Engel, New York University

Computers:
Tools for an Information Age

Computers: Tools for an Information Age

C H A P T E R 1

Learning Objectives

Describe the three fundamental characteristics of computers

Describe at least four areas of society in which computers are used

Identify the basic components of a computer system: input, processing, output, and storage

List some common input, output, and storage media

Distinguish data from information

Describe the significance of networking

Explain the significance of the Internet

Explain the various classifications of computers

or years Mike McDowell refused to buy a personal computer. The 38-year-old McDowell, owner of a 1200-acre farm in Wisconsin, told his disappointed children that they would just have to use the computers at school. The family simply could not justify the expense of a computer in the home. "If I buy a new tractor," he noted, "I can make the farm more profitable. But a computer? I just can't see it."

He can now. Mr. McDowell took a look at the new price tags. As personal computer prices ducked below $1000, they attracted a whole new audience of home users. In fact, more than half of new computers are purchased by first-time buyers. In addition, computers are continuing their winning ways: Almost 80 percent of computer buyers are "satisfied" or "very satisfied" with their computers.

Mr. McDowell ticks off the uses his family has found for the computer. He took a class at his local community college and learned to use spreadsheets, a kind of rows-and-columns report, to plan his crop planting and rotations. He uses the computer to send for weather and crop reports from agencies of the federal government. His wife favors e-mail, which lets her use the computer to send messages back and forth to her sisters in Duluth and Omaha. His teenage daughter, who wrote her high school reports using word processing, saved her summer job earnings to buy a laptop computer to take with her to college. Mr. McDowell now counts himself in the "very satisfied" category.

◀▶ **STEPPING OUT**

Your first steps toward joining the Information Age include understanding how we got to where we are today. Perhaps you recall from history books how the Industrial Age took its place in our world. In just a few decades, society accepted the dizzying introduction of electricity, telephones, radio, automobiles, and airplanes. However, the Information Age is evolving even more rapidly. It is likely to continue to evolve well into the twenty-first century.

Forging a Computer-Based Society

Traditional economics courses define the cornerstones of an economy as land, labor, and capital. Today we can add a fourth key economic element: information. As we evolve from an industrial to an information society, our jobs are changing from physical to mental labor. Just as people moved physically from farms to factories in the Industrial Age, so today people are shifting from muscle power to brain power in a new, computer-based society.

You are making your move, too, taking your first steps by signing up for this computer class and reading this book. But should you go further and get your own computer? We look next at some of the reasons why you might.

A Computer in Your Future

Computers have moved into every nook and cranny of our daily lives. Whether or not you personally know anything about it, you invoke computers when you make a bank withdrawal, when you buy groceries at the supermarket, and even when you drive your car. But should you have a computer at your personal disposal? The answer today is "probably." Although only a little more than half of Americans have personal computers in their homes, a much higher percentage use computers on the job. Almost any career in your future will involve a computer in some way.

In their homes people use various forms of computer technology for writing papers and memos, for keeping track of bank accounts, for communicating with friends and

Computers have moved into every nook and cranny of our daily lives.

People use their home computers to compose letters and memos, play games, and keep track of their finances.

associates, for accessing knowledge, for purchasing goods, for entertainment, and for so much more.

Computer Literacy for All

Why are you studying about computers? In addition to curiosity (and perhaps a course requirement), you probably recognize that it will not be easy to get through the rest of your life without knowing about computers. We offer a three-pronged definition of **computer literacy:**

- **Awareness.** As you study about computers, you will become aware of their importance, their versatility, and their pervasiveness in our society.

- **Knowledge.** You will learn what computers are and how they work. This requires learning some technical jargon, but do not worry—no one expects you to become a computer expert.

- **Interaction.** There is no better way to understand computers than through interacting with one. So being computer literate also means being able to use a computer for some simple applications.

Note that no part of this definition suggests that you must be able to create the instructions that tell a computer what to do. That would be akin to saying that anyone who plans to drive a car must first become an automotive engineer. Someone else can write the instructions for the computer; you simply use the instructions to get your work done. For example, an accountant might use a computer to prepare a report, a teenager to play a video game, or a construction worker to record data from the field.

Computers are characterized by speed, reliability, and storage capability.

► THE NATURE OF COMPUTERS

Every computer has three fundamental characteristics. Each characteristic has by-products that are just as important. The three fundamental characteristics are:

- **Speed.** Computers provide the processing speed essential to our fast-paced society. The quick service that we have come to expect—for bank withdrawals, stock quotes, telephone calls, and travel reservations, to name just a few—is made possible by computers. Businesses depend on the speedy processing that computers provide for everything from balancing ledgers to designing products.

- **Reliability.** Computers are extremely reliable. Of course, you might not think this from some of the stories you may have seen in the press about "computer errors." However, most errors supposedly made by computers are really human errors.

- **Storage Capability.** Computer systems can store tremendous amounts of data, which can be located and retrieved efficiently. The capability to store volumes of data is especially important in an information age.

These three characteristics—speed, reliability, and storage capability—have the following by-products:

- **Productivity.** When computers move into business offices, managers expect increased productivity as workers learn to use computers to do their jobs better and faster. Furthermore, jobs such as punching holes in metal or monitoring water levels can be more efficiently controlled by computers.

- **Decision making.** To make decisions, managers need to take into account financial, geographical, and logistical factors. The computer helps decision makers sort things out and make better choices.

- **Cost reduction.** Finally, because it improves productivity and aids decision making, the computer helps us hold down the costs of labor, energy, and paperwork. As a result, computers help to reduce the costs of goods and services in our economy.

Next we look at some of the ways in which we use computers to make the workday more productive and our personal lives more rewarding.

▶ WHERE COMPUTERS ARE USED

Computers can do just about anything imaginable, but they really excel in certain areas. This section lists some of the principal areas of computer use.

- **Education.** Most schools in the United States have computers available for use in the classroom, and some colleges require entering freshmen to bring their own. Many educators prefer learning by doing—an approach uniquely suited to the computer.

Most schools in the United States have computers in the classroom because many educators prefer the learning-by-doing method.

- **Graphics.** Business people make bar graphs and pie charts from tedious figures to convey information with far more impact than numbers alone convey. Architects use computer-generated graphics to experiment with possible exteriors and to give clients a visual walk-through of proposed buildings. Finally, a new kind of artist has emerged, one who uses computers to express his or her creativity.

- **Retailing.** Products from meats to magazines are packaged with zebra-striped bar codes that can be read by computer scanners at supermarket checkout stands to determine prices and help to manage inventory. Computers operate behind the scenes too; for example, this book was tracked from printer to warehouse to bookstore with the help of computers and the bar code on the back cover.

- **Energy.** Energy companies use computers to locate oil, coal, natural gas, and uranium. Electric companies use computers to monitor vast power networks. In addition, meter readers use handheld computers to record how much energy is used each month in homes and businesses.

- **Law enforcement.** Recent innovations in computerized law enforcement include national fingerprint files, a national file on the mode of operation of serial killers, and the computer modeling of DNA, which can be used to match traces from an alleged criminal's body, such as blood at a crime scene.

- **Transportation.** Computers are used in cars to monitor fluid levels, temperatures, and electrical systems. Computers also are used to help run rapid transit systems, load container ships, and track railroad cars across the country. The workers in an airport tower rely on computers to help monitor air traffic.

- **Money.** Computers speed up record keeping and allow banks to offer same-day services and even do-it-yourself banking over the phone. Computers have helped to fuel the cashless economy, enabling the widespread use of credit cards and instantaneous credit checks by banks and retailers.

Recent innovations in computerized law enforcement include national fingerprint files and computer modeling of DNA.

Air traffic controllers use computers to monitor and direct air traffic.

- **Agriculture.** Farmers use small computers to help with billing, crop information, cost per acre, feed combinations, and market price checks. Cattle ranchers can also use computers for information about livestock breeding and performance.

- **Government.** Among other tasks, the federal government uses computers to forecast weather, to manage parks, to process immigrants, to produce Social Security benefit checks, and—of course—to collect taxes. State and local governments also use computers routinely.

Cattle ranchers use computers for information about livestock breeding and performance.

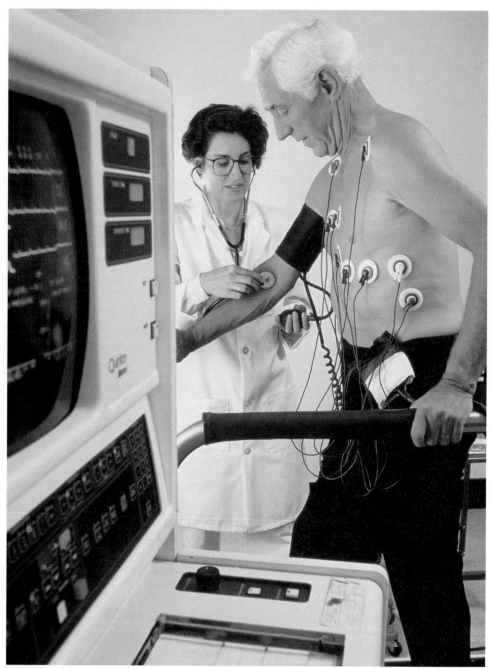

Doctors use computers to monitor the health of their patients and to make diagnoses.

- **The home.** People have computers in their homes, often justifying them as educational tools for their children. But that is only the beginning. Personal computers are being used at home to keep records, write letters, prepare budgets, draw pictures, publish newsletters, and connect with others.

- **Health and medicine.** Computers help to monitor the seriously ill in intensive care units and provide cross-sectional views of the body. Physicians can also use computers to assist in diagnoses; in fact, computers have been shown to correctly diagnose heart attacks more frequently than physicians do. If you are

This factory robot welds a new car under direction of the computer.

one of the thousands who suffer one miserable cold after another, you will be happy to know that computers have been able to map, in exquisite atomic detail, the structure of the human cold virus—the first step toward a cure for the common cold.

- **Robotics.** Computers have paved the way for robots to take over many of the jobs that are too unpleasant or too dangerous for humans, such as opening packages that are believed to contain bombs. Robots are best known for their work in factories, but they can do many other things, not the least of which is finding their way through the bloodstream.

- **The human connection.** Are computers cold and impersonal? The disabled do not think so; children, in particular, consider the computer their main education tool. Can the disabled walk again? Some can, with the help of computers. Can dancers and athletes improve their performance? Maybe they can, by using computers to monitor their movements. Can we learn more about our ethnic backgrounds and our cultural history with the aid of computers? Indeed we can.

- **The sciences.** Scientific researchers have long benefited from the high-speed capabilities of computers. Computers can simulate environments, emulate physical characteristics, and allow scientists to provide proofs in a cost-effective manner. Also, many mice—and other animals—have been spared since computer models have taken over their roles in research.

- **Connectivity.** One of the most popular uses of computers today is communicating with other people who have computers, whether for business or personal reasons. In addition, computers can give people the option of working at their homes instead of commuting to offices.

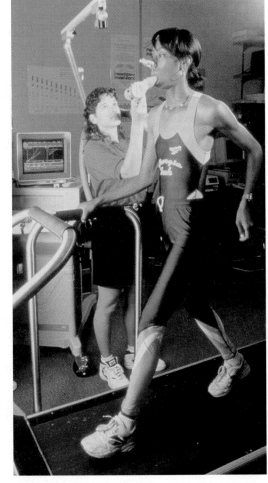

Athletes can use computers to assess and improve their physical performance.

● **Training.** It is much cheaper to teach aspiring pilots to fly in computerized training simulators than in real airplanes. Novice railroad engineers can also be given the experience of running a train with the help of a computerized device. Training simulations are relatively inexpensive and are always available on a one-to-one basis, making for very personal learning.

● **Paperwork.** In some ways the computer contributes to paper use by adding to the amount of junk mail you find in your mailbox. However, in many ways it cuts down on paper handling. Using a computer, for example, you might type several drafts of a term paper before printing anything. Computerized record keeping and ordering have also made paperwork more efficient.

Computers are all around us. You have been exposed to computer hype, computer advertisements, and computer headlines. You have interacted with computers in your everyday life—at the grocery store, your school, the library, and more. You know more about computers than you think you do. The beginnings of computer literacy are already apparent.

Have It Your Way

Have it your way exactly. The name of the new movement is *mass customization,* and the computer makes it possible.

Companies with millions of customers are starting to build products designed just for you. The woman in the photo is being measured for a pair of Levi jeans, which will be cut to fit her body. But clothes are just the beginning. You can buy a Dell computer made to your exact specifications. You can also buy eyeglasses molded to fit your face, CDs with music tracks you select, cosmetics mixed to match your skin tone, or a specially designed Barbie doll. Although these are massmarketed goods, they can be uniquely tailored to the customers who buy them.

►■ THE BIG PICTURE

A computer system has three main components: hardware, software, and people. The equipment associated with a computer system is called **hardware.** A set of instructions called **software** tells the hardware what to do. People, however, are the most important component of a computer system—people use the power of the computer for some purpose.

Software is also referred to as programs. To be more specific, a **program** is a set of step-by-step instructions that directs the computer to do the required tasks and produce the desired results. A **computer programmer** is a person who writes programs. **Users** are people who purchase and use computer software. In business, users are often called **end-users** because they are at the end of the "computer line," actually making use of the computer's capabilities.

This chapter examines hardware. The chapter looks at the big picture; therefore many of the terms introduced in this chapter are discussed only briefly here. Subsequent chapters will define the various parts of a computer system in greater detail.

►■ HARDWARE: THE BASIC COMPONENTS OF A COMPUTER

What is a computer? A 6-year-old called a computer "radio, movies, and television combined!" A 10-year-old described a computer as "a television set you can talk to." The 10-year-old's definition is closer but still does not recognize the computer as a machine that has the power to make changes. A **computer** is a machine that can be programmed to accept **data** (*input*), process it into useful **information** (*output*), and store it away (in a *secondary storage* device) for safekeeping or later reuse. The processing of input to output is directed by the software but performed by the hardware, the subject of this chapter.

To function, a computer system requires four main aspects of data handling: input, processing, output, and storage (Figure 1-1). The hardware responsible for these four areas is as follows:

● *Input devices* accept data or commands in a form that the computer can use; they send the data or commands to the processing unit.

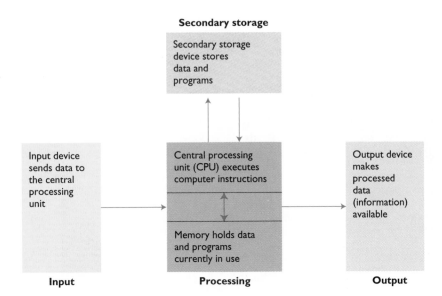

Secondary storage

Secondary storage device stores data and programs

Input device sends data to the central processing unit

Central processing unit (CPU) executes computer instructions

Memory holds data and programs currently in use

Output device makes processed data (information) available

Input   **Processing**   **Output**

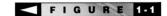

◄ F I G U R E 1-1

The four primary components of a computer system.

To function, a computer system requires input, processing, output, and storage.

- *The processor,* more formally known as the *central processing unit* (*CPU*), has electronic circuitry that manipulates input data into the information people want. The central processing unit actually executes computer instructions.

- *Output devices* show people the processed data—information—in understandable and usable form.

- *Storage* usually means *secondary storage,* which consists of secondary storage devices such as disk—hard disk or diskettes or some other kind of disk—that can store data and programs outside of the computer itself. These devices supplement *memory* or *primary storage,* which can hold data and programs only temporarily.

Before looking at each of these hardware aspects, consider them in terms of what you would find on a personal computer.

HARDWARE.

Prentice Hall
EXPLORE Generation **it**

► YOUR PERSONAL COMPUTER HARDWARE

Let us look at the hardware of a personal computer. Suppose you want to do word processing on a personal computer, using the hardware shown in Figure 1-2. Word processing software allows you to input data such as an essay, save it, revise and resave it, and print it whenever you wish. The *input* device, in this case, is a keyboard, which you use to key in—type—the original essay and any subsequent changes to it. You will also probably use the mouse as an input device. All computers, large and small, must have a *central processing unit,* so yours does too—it is within the personal computer housing. The central processing unit uses the word processing software to accept the data you input through the keyboard. Processed data from your personal computer is usually *output* in two forms: on a screen and by a printer. As you key in the essay on the keyboard, it appears on the screen in front of you. After you have examined the essay on the screen, made changes, and determined that you are satisfied with the result, you can print the essay on the printer. Your *secondary storage device,* as shown in Figure 1-2, which stores the essay until it is needed again, will probably be a hard disk or diskette. For reasons of convenience and speed, you are more likely to store your data—the essay—on a hard disk than on a diskette. (However, if you are using someone else's computer, such as a school computer, you will probably keep your own files on your own diskette.)

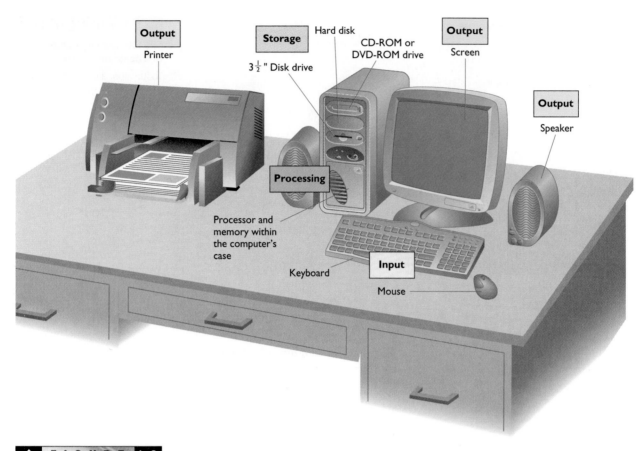

△ FIGURE 1·2

A personal computer system.

In this personal computer system, the input devices are a keyboard and a mouse. The input devices feed data to the central processing unit, which is inside the computer case, the vertical box to the left of the screen. The output devices in this example are the screen, the printer, and the speakers. The secondary storage devices are a hard drive, a 3½-inch disk drive, and a CD-ROM or DVD-ROM drive, all contained within the computer case. This popular configuration, with the case standing on end, is called a minitower.

Next is a general tour of the hardware needed for input, processing, output, and storage. These same components make up all computer systems, whether small, medium, or large.

Input: What Goes In

Input is the data that you put into the computer system for processing. Here are some common ways of feeding input data into the system:

- *Typing* on a **keyboard** (Figure 1-3a). The keys on a computer keyboard are arranged in much the same way as those on a typewriter. The computer responds to what you enter; that is, it "echoes" what you type by displaying it on the screen in front of you.

- *Pointing* with a **mouse** (Figure 1-3a). A mouse is a device that is moved by hand over a flat surface. As the ball on its underside rotates, the mouse movement causes corresponding movement of a pointer on the computer screen. Pressing buttons on the mouse lets you select commands.

- *Scanning* with a **wand reader, bar code reader, flatbed scanner,** or **sheet-fed scanner.** Wand and bar code readers, which you have seen used by clerks in retail

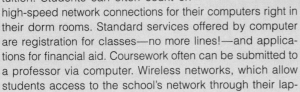

stores, use laser beams to read special letters, numbers, or symbols such as the black-and-white bar codes found on many products (Figure 1-3b). Flatbed or sheet-fed scanners are used to scan pictures or printed documents into your computer.

An input device may be part of a terminal. The simplest **terminal** includes a keyboard as the input device, a screen display for output, and some method of connection to a computer. For example, operators taking orders over the phone for a mail-order house would probably use terminals to input orders and send them to be processed by a large computer. You can input data into a computer in many other interesting ways, including by writing, speaking, pointing, or even just looking at the data.

(a)

(b)

▲ **F I G U R E** **1-3**

Input devices.

(a) The keyboard is the most widely used input device, though the mouse has become increasingly popular. Movement of the mouse on a flat surface causes corresponding movement of a pointer on the screen. (b) The information contained in the bar code on this package of green beans is scanned into the computer.

The Processor and Memory: Data Manipulation

In a computer the processor is the center of activity. The **processor,** as has already been noted, is also called the **central processing unit (CPU).** The central processing unit consists of electronic circuits that interpret and execute program instructions as well as communicating with the input, output, and storage devices.

It is the central processing unit that actually transforms data into information. **Data** is the raw material to be processed by a computer, such as grades in a class, touchdowns scored, or light and dark areas in a photograph. Processed data becomes **information**—data that is organized, meaningful, and useful. In school, for instance, an instructor could enter various student scores (data), which could be processed to produce final grades and perhaps a class average (information). Note that the instructor's final grade information could, in turn, become the data for the school's student records system, which would produce grade reports and GPAs as its information. Data that is perhaps uninteresting on its own may become very interesting once it is converted to information. The raw facts (data) about your finances, such as a paycheck or a donation to charity or a medical bill, may not be captivating individually, but together these and other items can be processed to produce the refund or amount you owe on your income tax return (information).

Computer **memory,** also known as **primary storage,** is closely related to the central processing unit but separate and distinct from it. Memory holds the data after it is input into the system and before it is processed; also, memory holds the data after it has been processed but before it has been released to the output device. In addition, memory holds the programs (computer instructions) needed by the central processing unit. Memory can hold data only temporarily because memory requires a continuous flow of electric current; if the current is interrupted, the data is lost.

Output: What Comes Out

Output—the result produced by the central processing unit—is, of course, a computer's whole reason for being. Output is usable information—that is, raw input data that has been processed by the computer into information. Common forms of output are text, numbers, graphics, and even sounds. Text output, for example, might be the letters and memos prepared by office workers using word processing software. Other workers may be more interested in numbers, such as those found in formulas, schedules, and budgets. In many cases numbers can be understood more easily when output is in the form of graphics.

The most common output devices are computer screens and printers. A **screen,** or **monitor,** can vary in its form of display, producing text, numbers, symbols, art, photographs, and even video, in full color (Figure 1-4a). **Printers** produce printed reports as instructed by a computer program (Figure 1-4b). Many printers, particularly those associated with personal computers, can print in color.

You can produce output from a computer in other ways, including film, voice, and music.

Secondary Storage

Secondary storage provides additional storage separate from memory. Recall that memory holds data and programs only temporarily; therefore there is a need for secondary storage. The most common secondary storage media for personal computers are magnetic disks. A **magnetic disk** can be a diskette or a hard disk. A **diskette** usually consists of a flexible magnetic disk 3½ inches in diameter, enclosed in a plastic case (Figure 1-5a). **Hard disks** have more storage capacity than diskettes and also offer much faster access to the data they hold. On large computer systems, hard disks are often contained in disk packs. Disk data is read by **disk drives.** Most personal computers have a built-in hard disk and a drive that reads diskettes. **Optical**

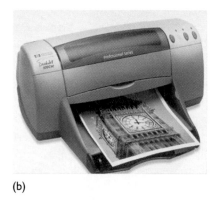

(b)

Output devices.

Monitors and printers are two types of output devices. (a) This monitor can display text or the colorful graphics shown here. (b) This ink-jet printer is used to produce high-quality text and graphics output.

(a)

disk drives, such as **CD-ROM**s and **DVD-ROM**s, use a laser beam to read large volumes of data relatively inexpensively (Figure 1-5b).

Magnetic tape is a storage medium that is used primarily with large computer systems, though some personal computers also use this form of secondary storage. This tape usually comes on a cartridge and is similar to tape that is played on a tape recorder. Magnetic tape cartridges are inserted in a **tape drive** when the data on them need to be read by the computer system or when new data is to be written on the tape. Magnetic tape is usually used for backup purposes—for "data insurance"— because tape is inexpensive. The chapter on storage presents more detailed information about storage media, notably alternative types of disk storage.

The Complete Hardware System

The hardware devices that are attached to the computer are called peripheral equipment. **Peripheral equipment** includes all input, output, and secondary storage

(a)

(b)

Secondary storage devices.

(a) A 3¹/₂-inch diskette is being inserted into a disk drive. (b) Optical disks can hold enormous amounts of data: text, music, graphics—even video and movies.

Like people who have boats or cameras, computer owners are tempted to buy the latest gadget. There are many from which to choose, some new, neat, and nifty—and some more useful than others.

For greater flexibility, check out a wireless keyboard or mouse, which works well as long as it is within direct line of sight of the computer. For everyday computer comfort, consider gel-based wrist rests for your keyboard and mouse pad. To reduce neck strain, get a document holder that attaches to the side of your monitor. While you are at it, you can reduce

eyestrain by attaching a magnifier to the screen itself.

If you prefer to say what you think instead of writing it, you can purchase a microphone and accompanying software to accept your voice input. Road warriors can buy practical laptop cases, with lots of padding and pockets for accessories. Webcams enable you to send video images across the Internet. If music and gaming are a big part of your computer life, you could invest in the very best: surround-sound speakers with a separate subwoofer.

devices. In most personal computers, the CPU and disk drives are all contained in the same housing, a metal case; the keyboard, mouse, and monitor are separate.

In larger computer systems, however, the input, processing, output, and storage functions may be in separate rooms, separate buildings, or even separate countries. For example, data may be input on terminals at a branch bank and then transmitted to the central processing unit at the bank's headquarters. The information produced by the central processing unit may then be transmitted to the international offices, where it is printed out. Meanwhile, disks with stored data may be kept at the bank headquarters, and duplicate data may be kept on disk or tape in a warehouse across town for safekeeping.

Although the equipment may vary widely from the simplest computer to the most powerful, by and large the four elements of a computer system remain the same: input, processing, output, and storage. These basic components are supplemented by hardware that can make computers much more useful, giving them the ability to connect to one another.

BUILDING A NETWORK.

Prentice Hall
EXPLORE Generation **it**

  N E T W O R K I N G

Many organizations find that their needs are best served by a **network,** a system that uses communications equipment to connect computers and their resources. Resources include printers and hard disks and even software and data. In one type of network, a **local area network (LAN),** personal computers in an office are connected together so that users can communicate with one another. Users can operate their personal computers independently or in cooperation with other computers to exchange data and share resources. The networking process can be much more complex; we will describe how large computers can be involved in networks in the chapter on networking.

Individual users in homes or offices have joined the trend to connectivity by hooking up their personal computers, usually via telephone lines, to other computers. Users who connect their computers to other computers via the phone lines must use a hardware device called a **modem** as a go-between to reconcile the inherent differences between computers and the phone system. From their own homes, users can connect to all sorts of computer-based services, performing such tasks as getting stock quotes, making airline reservations, and shopping for videotapes. An important

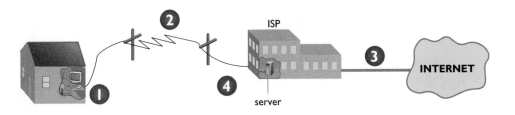

◄ F I G U R E 1·6

The Internet.

(1) At his or her own computer, a user accesses the ISP's server computer, (2) probably over the phone line. (3) The server computer communicates with the Internet, perhaps passing on e-mail messages or requests for certain Web sites and picking up responses. (4) Incoming messages, e-mail, or requested Internet information is returned to the original requesting computer. This back-and-forth communication goes on as long as the user wishes to remain connected to the Internet.

INTERNET AND THE WWW.

Prentice Hall
EXPLORE Generation **it**

service for individuals is **electronic mail,** or **e-mail,** which lets people send and receive messages via computer.

Whether the user is operating in a business capacity or simply exploring the options, a popular conduit for connectivity is the Internet.

► THE INTERNET

The **Internet,** sometimes called simply "the Net," is the largest and most far-flung network system of them all, connecting users worldwide. Surprisingly, the Internet is not really a single network but a loosely organized collection of thousands of networks. Many people are astonished to discover that no one owns the Internet. It has no central headquarters, no centrally offered services, and no comprehensive index to tell you what information is available.

Originally developed by the U.S. government, the Internet connects libraries, college campuses, research labs, government organizations, businesses, and any other organization or individual who has the capacity to hook up.

Getting Connected

How are all kinds of different computers able to communicate with one another? To access the Internet, a user's computer must connect to a type of computer called a **server.** Each server uses the same special software called **TCP/IP** (for **Transmission Control Protocol/Internet Protocol);** it is this standard that allows different types of computers to communicate with each other (Figure 1-6). The supplier of the server computer, often called an **Internet service provider (ISP),** charges a fee, usually monthly, that either covers unlimited access or is based on the amount of service provided. Once a user has chosen a service provider, he or she will be furnished with the information needed to connect to the server and, from there, to the Internet.

Getting Around

Since the Internet did not begin as a commercial customer-pleasing package, it did not initially offer attractive options for finding information. Most of the information was text-only, and the arcane commands needed to find it were invoked only by a hardy and determined few. Furthermore, the vast sea of information, including news and trivia, can seem an overwhelming challenge to navigate. As both the Internet user population and the types and amount of available information grew, new ways were developed to tour the Internet.

The most attractive method used to move around the Internet is called *browsing.* Using a program called a **browser,** you can use a mouse to point and click on screen text or pictures to explore the Internet, particularly the **World Wide Web (WWW or the Web),** an Internet subset of text, images, and sounds linked together to allow users to peruse related topics. Each different location on the Web is called a **Web site** or, more commonly, just a **site.** You may have heard the term **home page;** this is just the main page of a Web site.

The Internet is an important and complex topic. Although it is easy to use once you know how, there is much to learn about its use and its place in the world of computers. This opening chapter merely scratches the surface. More detailed information can be found in specific chapters devoted to the Internet. In addition, this book has a two-page spread, called "Planet Internet," at the end of each chapter, giving examples of some aspect of the Internet. The more generic topic of connectivity is discussed in the feature "Making Connections," offered in each chapter of the book.

Move Over, Kid

Computers in business? Of course. Computers for youngsters? Certainly. But senior citizens are the fastest-growing group of computer users. Furthermore, the average senior spends about twice as much time per month at a personal computer as the average teenage user spends. This is partly because many seniors have more discretionary income and more time on their hands than teenagers do.

The majority of seniors say that they were drawn to computers because they did not want to be left behind. They flock to classes, both private and public. Many senior students use their new word processing skills to write memoirs for their grandchildren. Others monitor their investments, research their family genealogy, create greeting cards, or even begin postretirement businesses.

► CLASSIFICATION OF COMPUTERS

Computers come in sizes from tiny to monstrous, in both appearance and power. The size of a computer that a person or an organization needs depends on the computing requirements. Clearly, the National Weather Service, keeping watch on the weather fronts of many continents, has requirements that are different from those of a car dealer's service department that is trying to keep track of its parts inventory. And the requirements of both of them are different from the needs of a salesperson using a small notebook computer to record client orders or those of a student writing a paper. Although we will describe categories of computers here, keep in mind that computers do not fall too readily into groups of distinct islands; the reality is blurry and over-lapping—and changing all the time.

Personal Computers

Most often called **personal computers,** or just **PCs,** desktop computers are occasionally known as **microcomputers** or sometimes **home computers.** Personal computers now fall into categories; most are low-end functional computers (sometimes ungallantly referred to as "cheap PCs") or else fully powered personal computers. A third category of upper-end PCs, called **workstations,** is used by specialized workers such as engineers, financial traders, and graphic designers. Workstations are small enough to fit on a desktop but approach the power of a mainframe.

Most users choose between personal computers in the first two categories: less expensive or more expensive. For many years PCs were offered only in the fully powered state-of-the-art category and cost upwards of $2000, enough to make some home buyers hesitate. But now, for a few hundred dollars, anyone can own a personal computer. At the low end, a cheap PC has less of everything: a slower and less powerful microprocessor, less memory, a smaller and less crisp screen, less hard drive space, and fewer software choices. Nevertheless, cheap PCs perform primary functions more than adequately. Customers who want a computer mainly for basic applications such as word processing, personal finance, record keeping, simple games, and access to the Internet are usually happy with computers at the low end.

There are, of course, people who should buy the more expensive, cutting-edge computers. You will want all the computer you can get if you plan to spend a lot of time on graphic images, heavy-duty calculations, programming, and—above all—action-oriented arcade games.

A variation on the personal computer is the **net computer,** or **net box,** a limited piece of hardware with a central processing unit and minimal memory, offered with Internet access in mind. The net computer hooks up to the Internet via a telephone line. In the office, keyboards and monitors are provided. In the home, people can use a net computer with the television set as the computer screen and a keyboard as an optional add-on. (The best-known consumer net computer is the WebTV®.) Most net computers have no disk storage at all. The original idea behind this un-PC was simplicity and low price. However, net computers have faltered in the marketplace, mainly because cheap PCs have cut into their territory.

Notebook Computers

Notebook computers are lightweight (often under six pounds) and portable. Travelers use them to get work done while on the move in trains and airplanes, consultants load their analytical software on them to take to client locations, and salespeople use them as presentation tools (Figure 1-7). Somewhat larger and heavier versions of these computers are known as laptops and can be used as desktop replacements for those with only occasional portability requirements.

The memory and storage capacity of notebook computers today can compete with those of desktop computers. Notebooks have a hard disk drive and most accept diskettes, so it is easy to move data from one computer to another. Many offer a CD-ROM or DVD-ROM drive. Furthermore, notebooks can run most available software. Notebooks are not as inexpensive as their size might suggest; they carry a price tag

◄ **F I G U R E 1-7**

Notebook computer.

This woman can get some work done in a convenient place away from the office.

greater than that of a full-size personal computer with the same features. However, like other technology, notebook computers are getting faster, lighter, and more feature-rich.

Smaller Still: Handheld Computers

A handheld computer called a **personal digital assistant (PDA)** can be used to keep track of appointments and other business information, such as customer names and orders. PDAs are also called pen-based computers because, with the use of a penlike stylus, they can accept handwritten input directly on a touch-sensitive screen. Many PDAs offer multiple functions, including wireless e-mail and fax capabilities (Figure 1-8). The **Pocket PC** is a handheld computer with slightly more power than a PDA. In addition to the functions performed by a PDA, the Pocket PC can also run stripped-down versions of PC productivity software such as word processing and spreadsheets.

Users of handhelds are often clipboard-carrying workers, such as parcel delivery drivers and meter readers. Other potential users are workers who cannot easily use a notebook computer because they are on their feet all day: nurses, sales representatives, real estate agents, and insurance adjusters. But the biggest group of users is found right in the office; these users like the fact that this convenient device can keep their lives organized.

Mainframes

In the jargon of the computer trade, large computers are called **mainframes.** Mainframes are capable of processing data at very high speeds—billions of instructions per second—and have access to billions of characters of data. The price of these large systems can vary from several hundred thousand to many millions of dollars. With that kind of price tag, you will not buy a mainframe for just any purpose. Their principal use is for processing vast amounts of data quickly, so some of the obvious customers are banks, insurance companies, and manufacturers. But this list is not all-inclusive; other types of customers are large mail-order houses, airlines with sophisticated reservation systems, government accounting services, aerospace companies doing complex aircraft design, and the like. As you can tell from these examples of mainframe applications, a key characteristic of large computers is that they are designed for multiple users. For example, many reservations clerks could be accessing the same computer at the same time to make reservations for waiting customers.

► **FIGURE 1-8**

PDAs

Personal digital assistants can be used to keep track of appointments and other business information, such as customer names and orders.

As computer users have marched inexorably toward personal computers and networking, pundits have erroneously predicted the demise of mainframes. But "big iron," the affectionate nickname for these computers, is proving to be hardy and versatile. More recent uses include helping large businesses carry out critical applications such as running automated teller machines and delivering e-mail. Thus the mainframe has taken on the coloration of a server and is often referred to as a server. On the Internet, where computers of all stripes can coexist and even work in concert, vast data stores are being kept on large servers. The large server—the mainframe—is still the most reliable way to manage vast amounts of data. As an example, national retailer L.L. Bean is using an IBM mainframe system to offer its entire catalog of merchandise on the Internet.

Supercomputers

The mightiest computers—and, of course, the most expensive—are known as **supercomputers.** Supercomputers are also the fastest: They can process trillions of instructions per second. Supercomputers can be found in mainstream activities as varied as stock analysis, automobile design, special effects for movies, and even sophisticated artwork. However, for many years supercomputer customers were an exclusive group: agencies of the federal government. The federal government uses supercomputers for tasks that require mammoth data manipulation, such as worldwide weather forecasting and weapons research (Figure 1-9).

This chapter has taken a rather expansive look at computer hardware. However, hardware by itself is just an empty shell. Software is the ingredient that gives value to the computer.

Typically, the machine's innards are housed in a titanium alloy case, about 20 times as strong as the plastic that is generally used in conventional notebooks. The keyboard is sealed to prevent liquid from seeping into the internal circuitry, and all external connections are dust-resistant. The disk drives are mounted in a shock-absorbing gel compound.

So who needs all this hardiness? The military, for openers. Also, construction engineers, oil rig managers, and anyone else whose center of operations is based on sand, water, or ice.

◄ **FIGURE 1-9**

A Cray Supercomputer.

Supercomputers are the most expensive and fastest computers, processing trillions of instructions per second.

CHAPTER REVIEW

 Summary and Key Terms

- **Computer literacy** has three components: an awareness of the importance, versatility, and pervasiveness of computers in society; knowledge of what computers are and how they work; and the capability of interacting with a computer to use simple applications.

- Every computer has three fundamental characteristics: speed, reliability, and a large storage capability. Through these characteristics computers increase productivity, aid in decision making, and reduce costs.

- The equipment associated with a computer system is called **hardware.** The **programs,** or step-by-step instructions that run the machines, are called **software.** **Computer programmers** write programs for **users,** or **end-users**—people who purchase and use computer software.

- A **computer** is a machine that can be programmed to process **data** (input) into useful **information** (output). A computer system comprises four main aspects of data handling—input, processing, output, and storage.

- **Input** is data to be accepted into the computer. Common input devices are the **keyboard;** a **mouse,** which translates movements of a ball on a flat surface to actions on the screen; a **wand reader** or **bar code reader,** which uses laser beams to read special letters, numbers, or symbols such as the zebra-striped bar codes on products: and a **flatbed** or **sheet-fed scanner,** used to scan photos or documents into the computer.

- A **terminal** includes an input device, such as a keyboard or wand reader; an output device, usually a televisionlike screen; and a connection to the main computer.

- The **processor,** or **central processing unit (CPU),** processes raw **data** into meaningful, useful **information.** The CPU interprets and executes program instructions and communicates with the input, output, and storage devices. **Memory,** or **primary storage,** is related to the central processing unit but is separate and distinct from it. Memory holds the input data before processing and also holds the processed data after processing until the data is released to the output device.

- **Output,** which is raw data processed into usable information, is usually in the form of words, numbers, and graphics. Users can see output displayed on a **screen,** or **monitor,** and use **printers** to display output on paper.

- **Secondary storage** provides additional storage space separate from memory. The most common secondary storage devices are **magnetic disks.** Magnetic disks are **diskettes,** usually 3½ inches in diameter, or **hard disks.** Hard disks on large systems are contained in a disk pack. Hard disks hold more data and offer faster access than diskettes do. Disk data are read and written by **disk drives. Optical disk drives,** such as **CD-ROMs** and **DVD-ROMs,** use a laser beam to read large volumes of data. **Magnetic tape** comes on reels or in cartridges and is primarily used for backup purposes. Magnetic tape is mounted on a **tape drive.**

- **Peripheral equipment** includes all the input, output, and secondary storage devices that are attached to a computer. Some peripheral equipment may be built into one physical unit, as in many personal computers, or contained in separate units, as in many large computer systems. Often organizations use a **network** of personal computers, which allows users to operate independently or in cooperation with other computers, exchanging data and sharing resources. Such a setup is called a **local area network (LAN).**

- Users who connect their computers via the phone lines must use a hardware device called a **modem** to reconcile the inherent differences between computers and the phone system. Individuals use networking for a variety of purposes, especially **electronic mail,** or **e-mail.**

- The **Internet,** sometimes called simply "the Net," connects users worldwide. To access the Internet, a user's computer must connect to a type of computer called a **server,** which has special software called **TCP/IP** (for **Transmission Control Protocol/Internet Protocol**) that allows different types of computers to communicate with one another. The supplier of the server computer, often called an **Internet service provider (ISP),** charges a fee that either covers unlimited access or is based on the amount of service provided.

- With software called a **browser,** a user can manipulate a mouse to point and click on screen text or pictures to explore the Internet, particularly the **World Wide Web (WWW** or **the Web),** an Internet subset of text, images, and sounds linked together to allow users to view related topics. Each different location on the Web is called a **Web site** or, more commonly, just a **site.** A **home page** is the main page of a Web site.

- Desktop computers are called **personal computers (PCs), microcomputers,** or sometimes **home computers. Workstations** combine the compactness of a desktop computer with power that approaching that of a mainframe. Lower-priced PCs are sometimes called "cheap PCs." A **net computer,** or **net box,** is a limited machine that has had difficulty competing with cheap PCs. **Notebook** computers are small portable computers; somewhat larger, heavier versions are called **laptop** computers.

- **Personal digital assistants (PDAs),** also called pen-based computers, are handheld computers that allow users to keep track of appointments and other information. **Pocket PCs** add the capability of running stripped-down versions of some desktop software.

- Large computers called **mainframes** are used by businesses such as banks, airlines, and manufacturers to process very large amounts of data quickly. The most powerful and expensive computers are called **supercomputers.**

► Critical Thinking Questions

1. Consider the hardware used for input, processing, output, and storage for personal computers. Most personal computer systems come configured in a standard way, but you may find differences in how you would use that equipment.
   a. Input: You would probably use a keyboard to input data. For what purposes would you use a mouse?
   b. Output: You would, of course, have a screen. After the computer itself, the biggest expense is the printer. Can you imagine getting along without a printer?
   c. Is a 3½-inch diskette drive sufficient? Why would a hard disk be of value to you? Why might you want a CD-ROM or DVD-ROM drive?

2. Discuss this statement: "I see myself using word processing to prepare term papers and the Internet to do research. Other than that, I doubt if I would have any use for computers during my college years."

3. Are you considering a particular career? Discuss how computers are used, or could be used, in that field.

▶ Student Study Guide

Multiple Choice

1. The central processing unit is an example of
   a. software
   b. hardware
   c. a program
   d. an output unit

2. Additional data and programs not being used by the processor are stored in
   a. secondary storage
   b. output units
   c. input units
   d. the CPU

3. Step-by-step instructions that run the computer are
   a. hardware
   b. CPUs
   c. documents
   d. software

4. Which of the following is not necessary to be considered computer literate?
   a. knowledge of what computers are and how they work
   b. the ability to write the instructions that direct a computer
   c. an awareness of the computer's importance, versatility, and pervasiveness in society
   d. the ability to interact with computers using simple applications

5. Desktop and personal computers are also known as
   a. microcomputers
   b. mainframes
   c. supercomputers
   d. peripheral equipment

6. The raw material to be processed by a computer is called
   a. a program
   b. software
   c. data
   d. information

7. A home page is part of a(n)
   a. terminal
   b. Web site
   c. NC
   d. LAN

8. A bar code reader is an example of a(n)
   a. processing device
   b. input device
   c. storage device
   d. output device

9. The computer to which a user's computer connects in order to access the Internet is called a
   a. server
   b. supercomputer
   c. notebook
   d. PDA

10. Printers and screens are common forms of
    a. input units
    b. storage units
    c. output units
    d. processing units

11. The unit that transforms data into information is the
    a. CPU
    b. disk drive
    c. bar code reader
    d. wand reader

12. The device that reconciles the differences between computers and phones is the
    a. TCP/IP
    b. LAN
    c. wand reader
    d. modem

13. PDA stands for
    a. protocol disk administrator
    c. primary digital assistant
    b. processor digital add-on
    d. personal digital assistant

14. An example of peripheral equipment is the
    a. CPU
    b. printer
    c. spreadsheet
    d. microcomputer

15. A computer that interacts with a television set is the
    a. desktop computer
    b. net computer
    c. supercomputer
    d. PDA

16. Software used to access the World Wide Web is called
    a. a browser
    b. Web
    c. a server
    d. e-mail

17. Which of the following is not one of the three fundamental characteristics of a computer?
    a. high cost
    c. reliability
    b. speed
    d. storage capability

18. Another name for memory is
    a. secondary storage
    b. primary storage
    c. disk storage
    d. tape storage

19. Which is not a computer classification?
    a. maxicomputer
    b. microcomputer
    c. notebook computer
    d. mainframe

20. A Web site may be found on the
    a. PDA
    b. WWW
    c. TCP/IP
    d. CPU

21. An input device that translates the motions of a ball rolled on a flat surface to the screen is a
    a. wand reader
    b. bar code reader
    c. keyboard
    d. mouse

22. Computer users who are not computer professionals are sometimes called
    a. librarians
    b. information officers
    c. peripheral users
    d. end-users

23. The most powerful computers are
    a. super PCs
    b. supermainframes
    c. supercomputers
    d. workstations

24. Raw data is processed by the computer into
    a. number sheets
    b. paragraphs
    c. updates
    d. information

25. Laser beam technology is used for
    a. terminals
    b. keyboards
    c. optical disks
    d. magnetic tape

True/False

T F 1. The processor is also called the central processing unit, or CPU.
T F 2. Secondary storage units contain the instructions and data to be used immediately by the processor.
T F 3. A home page is the main page of a Web site.
T F 4. Two secondary storage media are magnetic disks and magnetic tape.
T F 5. A diskette holds more data than a hard disk does.
T F 6. PDAs accept handwritten data on a screen.
T F 7. The most powerful personal computers are known as supercomputers.
T F 8. An Internet service provider provides Internet connections to its customers.
T F 9. Processed data is called information.
T F 10. The Internet is a subset of the World Wide Web.
T F 11. A modem is the hardware device that is the go-between for computers and telephones.
T F 12. Secondary storage is another name for memory.
T F 13. The most powerful personal computer is the workstation.
T F 14. TCP/IP is hardware that connects to the Internet.
T F 15. These computers are arranged from least powerful to most powerful: microcomputer, mainframe, supercomputer.

T F 16. The Internet is an example of a peripheral device.

T F 17. The best-selling personal computer is the net computer.

T F 18. A LAN is usually set up between two cities.

T F 19. Magnetic tape is most often used for backup purposes.

T F 20. Most mistakes that are blamed on the computer are actually caused by human errors.

T F 21. Most users use supercomputers to access the Internet.

T F 22. A modem is used to accept handwritten input on a pen-based computer.

T F 23. A notebook computer is a small, portable computer.

T F 24. A location on the World Wide Web is called a site.

T F 25. Another name for workstation is personal digital assistant.

Fill-In

1. The four general components of a computer are
   a. _____
   b. _____
   c. _____
   d. _____

2. The part of the Internet that is noted for images and sound is the _____.

3. After data is input into the system but before it is processed, it is held in _____.

4. Magnetic tape cartridges are inserted into a(n) _____ when their data is to be read by the computer system.

5. The input, output, and secondary storage devices attached to a computer are collectively known as _____.

6. Large computers in the computer industry are called _____.

7. Lightweight PCs that fit in a briefcase are called _____.

8. The term used for raw material read into a computer for processing is _____.

9. People who purchase and use software are called _____.

10. A hardware device that is the intermediary between a computer and the phone system is the _____.

11. The computer that must be accessed to reach the Internet is called the _____.

12. A(n) _____ provides its customers access to a server that connects to the Internet.

13. CPU stands for _____.

14. Three input devices mentioned in the chapter are
    a. _____
    b. _____
    c. _____

15. Another name for a microcomputer is _____.

16. TCP/IP stands for _____.

17. Messages sent via computer are called _____.

18. A(n) _____ is a handheld computer that keeps track of appointments.

19. The opening screen on a Web site is called the _____.

20. LAN stands for _____.

▶ Answers

Multiple Choice

1. b	8. b	15. b	22. d
2. a	9. a	16. a	23. c
3. d	10. c	17. a	24. d
4. b	11. a	18. b	25. c
5. a	12. d	19. a	
6. c	13. d	20. b	
7. b	14. b	21. d	

True/False

1. T	8. T	15. T	22. F
2. F	9. T	16. F	23. T
3. T	10. F	17. F	24. T
4. T	11. T	18. F	25. F
5. F	12. F	19. T	
6. T	13. T	20. T	
7. F	14. F	21. F	

Fill-In

1. a. input unit
   b. processor
   c. output unit
   d. storage unit
2. World Wide Web (or just the Web)
3. memory (or primary storage)
4. tape drive
5. peripheral equipment
6. mainframes
7. notebook computers
8. data
9. users, or end-users
10. modem
11. server
12. Internet service provider, or ISP
13. central processing unit
14. keyboard, mouse, wand reader, or bar code reader
15. personal computer (or home computer)
16. Transmission Control Protocol/Internet Protocol
17. electronic mail (or e-mail)
18. Internet service provider
19. home page
20. local area network

Planet Internet

What is it All About?

First, just what is the Internet?

The Internet is a meta-network—it's a network made up from a loosely organized global collection of other networks. It's millions of computers. It's technology, protocols, software, servers, routers, and human organizations. This text explains a lot of that. But that's not how most citizens of Planet Internet view the Internet most of the time.

For anyone with a computer and appropriate software today, the "Net" represents a source of news, images, conversation, shopping, music, video, entertainment, and controversy. When you connect your personal computer to another computer—a "server"—across the Internet, you're part of the largest and least-regulated information exchange on the planet.

Why is the Internet so important?

The Internet is powerful, it's pervasive, and it's still evolving.

You can reach more information from your computer desktop than is contained in most libraries. Increasingly, the Internet is like television—it's everywhere and it's always on. And, like TV, the ready access to the Internet afforded by personal computers, Internet appliances, shopping mall kiosks, palm-tops, and mobile phones is already changing our lives and our lifestyles.

Maybe the most exciting thing about the Internet is that it is always changing. Of course, the technology we use to get to the Net improves at an amazing pace, but perhaps more dramatic is the incidence of new cultural, legal, and ethical issues posed by the quick, cheap, and unchecked exchange of ideas across traditionl boundaries. Issues of intellectual property, free speech, individual rights, contracts, liability, morality, and taste abound on the Net.

When you use the Net, you enjoy, you learn, and you confront new, technology-driven variants of age-old problems. What could be more exciting than that?

Why should I use the Internet?

The one answer that applies to everyone is that you don't dare risk being left behind. Futurists predict that networking of some kind will be as necessary to work and to living as technologies such as the telephone or computers. After that, the answer to this question depends on you. Are you curious? Would you like to connect with people around the world? Would you like an amazing library at your finger-

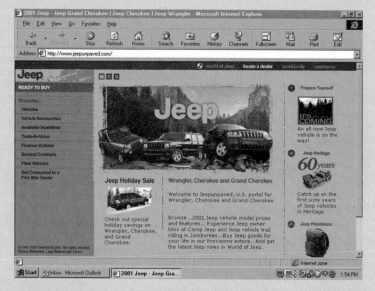

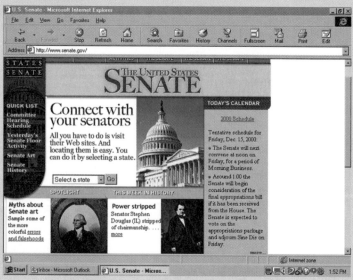

tips? Would you like the convenience of finding out about almost anything current—political events, the weather, the score of your favorite team's ball game, the verdict of a court case—by typing at the keyboard? Do you plan to buy a car in the near future? The Internet offers informative sites describing cars, such as the Jeep site shown here. Need some information on what your U.S. senators are up to? The Senate site shown here is a good place to begin.

Is this going to cost money?

Maybe. Free Internet access is common in schools and libraries and other government organizations. Your employer may offer free access. If you want to hook up from your own personal computer, the required software is probably free, but you will have to pay some sort of monthly charge to the company providing the physical connection.

Ok, how can I be an informed consumer of the Internet?

You can learn, you can experiment, and you can think critically.

This text is one way of learning about the Internet. The Planet Internet features that follow this one each address a specific aspect of the Internet. You can learn about e-shopping, on-line chats, security and hackers, computer games and entertainment, Web programming languages, privacy, and other topics in these features.

There's nothing quite so informative as trying things out yourself. Use the links provided in this section and in many other places in the text to explore the Web. If you want an easy start, try the structured activities at the end of each Planet Internet. If you're feeling more adventurous, use the free-form activities. If you already know your way around portions of the Net, you may enjoy the challenge of the advanced activities.

Finally, you can apply what you already know, what you learn here, and your own culture and beliefs to critically examine what goes on in Planet Internet. Sure, the Internet is about technology, but it's also about people and ideas. As you learn more about how things are on the Net, ask yourself, "Is this how things should be?" Some of the Focus on Ethics features in each chapter can help highlight the implications of the Net for your beliefs and your ideals.

Welcome to Planet Internet. Enjoy.

Internet Exercises:

At the end of the Planet Internets, three exercises are suggested. The first exercise is structured since it's based on using links provided at the publisher's Web site. Use the URL supplied here to get started. If you are feeling a little daring try the free-form exercise, where we make suggestions but no guarantees. If you are fairly familiar with the Web, try the advanced exercise.

1. **Structured exercise.** Begin by browsing to the Web site for this text at http://www.pren hall.com/capron. What information and assistance are offered on these pages? Examine the materials on the Web site for at least two chapters. First, find a chapter topic with which you are reasonably familiar. Then look at the study materials available for a chapter addressing a topic that is mostly new to you. Try to list two features or links you think you will find useful and why.

2. **Free-form exercise.** What on-line assistance is available to you from your school, your lab, or your instructor? Does your institution provide Internet access as part of your student fees? If so, what type of access and support does your school provide? Does your instructor have a Web site? If so, what resources are available (e.g., syllabus, class notes, FAQs, links to other sites)? Do you have access to a lab where you can use the types of software discussed in your text? Be sure to ask your instructor if you have difficulty finding the answers to these questions.

3. **Advanced exercise.** Investigate and speculate on the future of Internet access. What Internet-capable devices are available now? What new devices are being planned for the future? Which devices would be most relevant to a typical student at your school? Why? You may find it helpful to begin with http://www.pren hall.com/capron and follow the links to TechTV and on-line technology publications such as Salon, Wired, Slashdot, and Forbes to begin your research.

Planet Internet

Operating Systems:
Software in the Background

Operating Systems:
Software in the Background

CHAPTER 2

LEARNING OBJECTIVES

Describe the functions of an operating system

Explain the basics of a personal computer operating system

Describe the advantages of a graphical operating system

Differentiate among different versions of Microsoft Windows

Explain the need for network operating systems

Describe the methods of resource allocation on large computers

Describe the differences among multiprocessing, multiprogramming, and time-sharing

Explain the principles of memory management

List several functions that are typically performed by utility programs

When Linda Ronquillo was taking a night class in applications software at a community college four years ago, she did not have to worry much about the operating system, the necessary software in the background. The college personal computers were on a network that managed all the computers. As Linda sat down to begin work, the computer screen showed a menu of numbered choices reflecting the software packages available: WordPerfect, Microsoft Word, Microsoft Excel, and so forth. At the bottom of the screen, Linda was instructed to type the number of her chosen selection; if she typed 1, for example, the system put her into WordPerfect. Linda did have to learn operating system commands to prepare her own diskettes and save data on them so that she could take her work with her, but she had little other contact with the operating system.

On the job as a supervisor for a small airport freight company, Linda needed to use word processing, spreadsheets, and database software packages on her personal computer. But no one had set up a menu shortcut there; with a little advice from colleagues, she learned what she needed to know about the operating system MS-DOS. She learned, among other things, to execute the software she needed to use and to take care of her data files, copying files from one disk to another and sometimes renaming or deleting them. She eventually felt fairly comfortable with her operating system knowledge.

Two months later, Linda was informed by the company personal computer manager that the company's three personal computers were going to be switched to Microsoft Windows Me, an operating system that included a user-friendly interface. Despite assurances that the new system would be colorful and easy to use, Linda was less than thrilled to be making another change. But she didn't say so. She knew that being a computer user meant being willing to adjust to change. So Linda learned to use a mouse and mastered icons, overlapping windows, pull-down menus, and other mysteries.

Approximately six months later, Linda took a job at another, larger airline freight company. Part of the reason she was hired was her response to the revelation that the new company used Windows 2000, which she knew was yet another operating system. Linda said, "Oh, I have learned several systems. It shouldn't be any problem learning another." She was right, of course. In fact, she had little trouble switching to the new operating system.

► OPERATING SYSTEMS: HIDDEN SOFTWARE

When a brand-new computer comes off the factory assembly line, it can do nothing. The hardware needs software to make it work. Part of the story is the applications software, such as word processing or spreadsheet software, that allows users to perform useful work. This type of software will be discussed in the next chapter. But applications software cannot communicate directly with the hardware, so the operating system software serves as an intermediary between the applications software and the hardware. An **operating system** is a set of programs that lies between applications software and the hardware; it is the fundamental software that controls access to all other hardware and software resources. Figure 2-1 illustrates this concept. Incidentally, the term **systems software** is often used interchangeably with *operating system*, but systems software means all programs related to coordinating computer operations. Systems software includes the operating system but also includes programming language translators and a variety of utility programs.

Note that we said that an operating system is a set of programs. The most important program in the operating system, the program that manages the operating system, is the **kernel**, most of which remains in memory and is therefore referred to as *resident*. The kernel controls the entire operating system and loads into memory other operating system programs (called *nonresident*) from disk storage only as needed (Figure 2-2).

No matter what operating system is being used, when the computer is turned on, the kernel will be loaded from the hard drive into the computer's memory, thus making it available for use. This process of loading the operating system into memory is

OPERATING SYSTEMS

Prentice Hall
EXPLORE Generation **it**

► **F I G U R E 2-1**

A conceptual diagram of an operating system.

Closest to the user are applications programs, software that helps a user to compute a payroll or play a game or write a report. The operating system is the set of programs between the applications programs and the hardware.

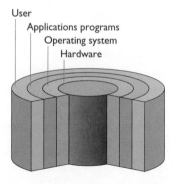

User
Applications programs
Operating system
Hardware

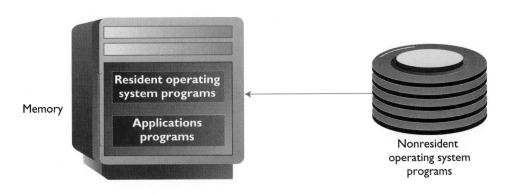

Retrieving operating system programs from disk.

The kernel of the operating system is resident in memory and calls in nonresident operating system programs from the disk as needed.

called *bootstrapping*, or **booting,** the system. The word "booting" is used because, figuratively speaking, the operating system pulls itself up by its own bootstraps. When the computer is turned on, a small program stored in a ROM chip performs some internal hardware component tests, then loads the kernel from the hard disk.

An operating system has three main functions: (1) managing the computer's resources, such as the central processing unit, memory, disk drives, and printers; (2) establishing a user interface; and (3) executing and providing services for applications software. Keep in mind, however, that much of the work of an operating system is hidden from the user; many necessary tasks are performed behind the scenes. In particular, the first listed function—managing the computer's resources—is taken care of without the user being aware of the details. Furthermore, all input and output operations, although invoked by an applications program, are actually carried out by the operating system.

Although many of its functions are hidden from view, you will have to communicate directly with the operating system to begin using an applications software package and to perform various housekeeping tasks. This communication occurs through the operating system's **user interface,** which determines how the user interacts with the operating system. The two basic forms of user interfaces are the command-line interface and the graphical user interface (GUI). The command-line interface is text-based and requires you to type in complete operating system commands. MS-DOS, Unix, Linux, and many large-computer operating systems use a command-line interface, as you will see in the following pages. GUIs use visual images and menus to allow users to enter commands. Windows and Mac OS use GUIs. Some installations of Linux and Unix are set up to offer a GUI.

Operating systems for large computers must keep track of several programs from several users, all running in the same time frame. We will examine the inherent complexities of such systems later in the chapter. For now, we focus on the interaction between a single user and a personal computer operating system.

► OPERATING SYSTEMS FOR PERSONAL COMPUTERS

If you browse the software offerings at a retail store, you will generally find the software grouped according to the platform on which the software can run. The term **platform** refers to a combination of computer hardware and operating system software. The most common microcomputer platform today consists of some version of Microsoft Windows running on an Intel-based PC, often referred to as *Wintel* for short. Generally, applications software—word processing, spreadsheets, games, whatever—can run on just one platform. Just as you cannot place a Nissan engine in a Ford truck and expect it to run, you cannot take a version of WordPerfect that was designed to run on a computer using the Wintel platform and run it on an Apple

FOCUS ON ETHICS **Bugs and Back Doors: Who Is Responsible?**

Operating systems, like all software, are far from perfect. In fact, because of their complexity and demanding performance requirements, they probably have more defects than common application programs do. Suppose you are a programmer and you discover a serious software bug in a widely used operating system. Imagine further that this bug could allow an attacker to read or alter sensitive files on many computers. Weigh the following possible actions and decide which one you think is most practical and ethically sound.

1. Keep quiet about the bug. Maybe it will get fixed in a new release, and at least you aren't helping potential hackers by publicizing it.
2. Contact the manufacturer and describe the bug. Ask them to fix the bug in the next release but realize that they may give it a low priority.
3. Contact a popular computer magazine and describe the nature of the bug, hoping that publication of the problem will pressure the manufacturer to fix it immediately but knowing that publicity about it might help potential exploiters of the bug.

Macintosh using the Mac OS operating system. Software makers must decide for which platform to write an applications software package, although some make versions of their software for more than one platform.

Most users do not set out to buy an operating system; they want computers and the applications software to make them useful. However, since the operating system determines what software is available for a given computer, users must at least be aware of their own computer's operating system.

Although operating systems differ, many of their basic functions are similar. Let us examine some of the basic functions of operating systems by examining MS-DOS.

A BRIEF LOOK AT MS-DOS

The MS-DOS operating system employs a command-line user interface. When a computer using MS-DOS (often called just DOS, rhyming with "boss") is booted, the screen is blank except for the characters C:\> appearing in the upper left corner. The C:\ refers to the disk drive; the > is a **prompt,** a signal that the system is prompting you to do something. At this point, you must give some instruction, or command, to the operating system. Although the prompt is the only visible result of booting the system, DOS also provides the basic software that coordinates the computer's hardware components and a set of programs that lets you perform the many computer tasks you need to do. To execute a given DOS program, you must type a **command,** a name that invokes a specific DOS program. Some typical tasks that you can perform with DOS commands are listing the files on a disk, copying files from one disk to another, and erasing files from a disk. Figure 2-3 gives some examples of MS-DOS commands. As you can see, these are not the easiest commands to remember.

FIGURE 2-3

MS-DOS commands.

C:\>FORMAT A: Prepares an unformatted diskette on drive A: for use.

C:\>DIR A: Lists the files on the diskette in drive A: (DIR stands for directory)

C:\>COPY MRKTDATA.SUM A: Copies file MRKTDATA.SUM on drive C to Drive A.

C:\>DEL A:SALESRPT.TXT Deletes file SALESRPT.TXT from drive A:

C:\>RENAME MRKTDATA.SUM SSDATA.CHT Renames the file MRKTDATA.SUM on drive C: to SSDATA.CHT

Command-line interfaces have the reputation of being very user-unfriendly and have been largely replaced by GUIs. However, if you wish, you can still execute DOS commands from within Windows, Microsoft's GUI operating system.

► MICROSOFT WINDOWS

Today there is another—most say better—way to interact with the computer's operating system. **Microsoft Windows**—Windows for short—uses a colorful graphics interface that, among other things, eases access to the operating system. Microsoft Windows defines the operating environment standard for computers with Intel processors. Most new personal computers come with Windows already installed.

A Windows Overview

The feature that makes Windows so easy to use is a **graphical user interface (GUI,** pronounced "goo-ee"), in which users work with on-screen pictures called **icons** and with **menus** rather than keyed-in commands (see Figure 2-4). Clicking the icons or menu items activates a command or function. The menus in Figure 2-5 are called **pull-down menus** because they appear to pull down like a window shade from the original selection on the menu bar. Some menus, called **pop-up menus,** originate from a selection at the bottom of the screen or when the right mouse button is clicked. Icons and menus allow pointing and clicking with a mouse, an approach that can make computer use fast, easy, and intuitive.

Windows started out as an **operating environment** for MS-DOS, another layer added to separate the operating system from the user. This layer is often called the **shell** because it forms a "coating," with icons and menus, over the operating system.

Windows is now a family of operating systems, with three branches serving different users. The branch serving the home/consumer market is often referred to as

◄ **F I G U R E 2·4**

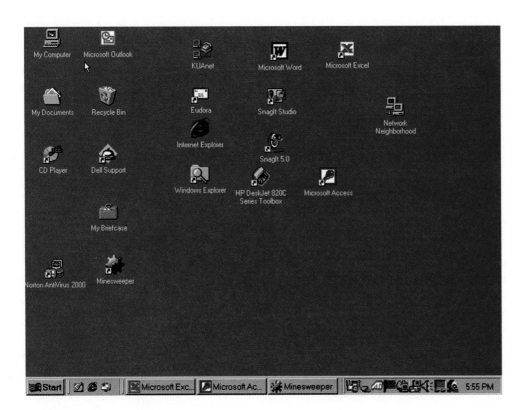

A typical Windows desktop display.

The icons represent programs, which can be run by double-clicking the corresponding icon. The taskbar across the bottom of the screen contains the Start button on the left, which can be clicked to show a pop-up menu with various options, including shutting down. Next are three clickable icons for (left to right) returning to the desktop, Internet Explorer, and Outlook Express. Next are the buttons representing active application programs; here Microsoft Excel, Microsoft Access, and Minesweeper (a game) are shown. The set of icons on the right represent various system functions. For example, the speaker icon is used to control your speaker volume. Finally, the rightmost entry is the system time; if you rest your mouse pointer on it, the day and date appear.

Windows menus.

This screen from Microsoft Word illustrates Windows menus. Here, the user has clicked the Insert choice on the menu bar to get a drop-down menu. Note the little triangular arrowhead to the right of the Picture option; this indicates that a submenu will be displayed if this option is highlighted. The submenu shown presents a series of locations from which a picture may be inserted into a Word document.

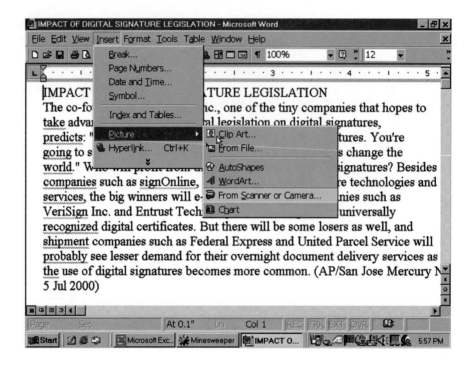

Introducing Mr. Gates

Anyone who has not figured out what the trend is for operating systems has missed the heavy press coverage of billionaire Bill Gates, the founder of Microsoft Corporation, the largest software company in the world. Mr. Gates has graced the covers of *Time, Fortune,* and any other news magazine you could name. Each time he is interviewed, Mr. Gates makes a pitch for his vision of the future, which features, among other things, Microsoft Windows.

Windows 9x and consists of a series of versions called Windows 95, Windows 98, and Windows Millennium Edition (Me). For the corporate market the two most recent versions are Windows NT and Windows 2000. The newest member of the Windows family, Windows XP, is designed to replace both Windows Me and Windows 2000, serving both the consumer and corporate markets with a single product. Finally, Windows CE has been introduced for pocket computers and Internet appliances. All of these are discussed next.

Windows 95 and 98

Beginning with **Windows 95,** Windows is no longer a shell; it is a self-contained operating system and therefore requires no preinstalled DOS. However, DOS commands are still available. **Windows 98** is a variation on Windows 95 and has much the same screen look.

Windows features a Start button in the lower left-hand corner (refer to Figure 2-4). From this button you can conveniently find a program or a file. Programs can also be invoked—started—by double-clicking an icon on the desktop, the Windows opening screen. Figure 2-4 shows a number of program icons on the desktop area. Perhaps the greatest convenience, as you can see in Figure 2-4, is the taskbar along the bottom of the screen, which contains an array of buttons for the programs that are currently in use. You can click from program to program as easily as changing channels on your TV. Windows allows longer file names of up to 255 characters (MS-DOS and Windows 3.1, the shell version of Windows, permitted only eight).

Anyone who has added a new component, perhaps a modem or a sound card, to an existing computer knows that it must be configured into the system, a process that may involve some software and even hardware manipulations. Windows supports **Plug and Play,** a concept that lets the computer configure itself when a new component is added. For Plug and Play to work, hardware components must also feature the Plug and Play standard. Once a peripheral is built to the Plug and Play standard, a user can install it simply by plugging it in and turning on the computer. Windows recognizes that the new device has been added and proceeds to configure it.

A Windows technology called **object linking and embedding (OLE**—wonderfully pronounced "oh-lay") lets you embed or link one document to another. For instance, you can embed a spreadsheet within a report created in a word processing program that supports OLE. When you click the spreadsheet to modify it, you will be taken to the program that you used to create the spreadsheet.

Features added by Windows 98 include the following:

● **Internet/intranet browsing capabilities.** Microsoft's browser, Internet Explorer, is included with Windows. In fact, Windows itself has been made to look more like a browser.

● **Support for state-of-the-art hardware.** This includes support for digital video disk (DVD) and the latest multimedia components. DVD and multimedia are described in the chapter on storage.

● **Support for huge disk drives.** Everyone wants more disk space, and multigigabyte drives provide an answer. Support for high-capacity drives is provided in Windows in the form of tables that can handle the sizes of today's hard drives.

● **TV viewer and broadcast ability.** A broadcast-enabled computer blends television with new forms of information and entertainment. It blurs the line between television, Web pages, and computer content. It also enables the reception of broadcast Web pages and other live data feeds, such as across-the-screen news headlines and stock quotes.

● **Wizards.** Windows lets users accomplish various tasks by using "wizards," step-by-step software tools that make tasks more user-friendly (Figure 2-6).

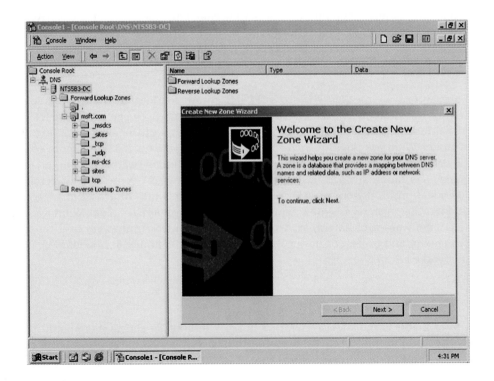

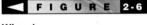

Wizards.

Wizards are easy-to-use, step-by-step software tools that make tasks more user-friendly.

Further, Windows 98 includes technologies to help reduce the cost of owning and maintaining a personal computer. Other features include improved backup, improved interfaces with other software, new and improved networking features, and increased security. Finally, Windows 98 includes an improved Dr. Watson, which provides technical information about the computer when it suffers a general protection fault, commonly called a crash.

Windows Me

The newest member of the Windows 9x family is **Windows Millennium Edition (Windows Me).** It is built on the same code base as both Windows 95 and Windows 98 and has a similar look and feel. The major features added in this version include the following:

● **Multimedia support.** Windows Media Player 7 now includes a jukebox and music database controls and allows you to record music CDs as digital files. Windows Movie Maker provides basic video editing capabilities on your PC. Windows Image Acquisition provides additional support for manipulating scanner and digital camera images.

● **Reliability features.** Anyone who has accidentally overwritten key system files while installing new software will appreciate the System File Protection feature. If any system files are accidentally deleted or overwritten with out-of-date versions, the System File Protection feature will automatically restore them the next time you boot the system. An AutoUpdate function automatically checks appropriate sites on the Internet for updates to installed system and application software. A system restore feature lets you return to an earlier system configuration if the addition of hardware or software disrupts your system's settings. Finally, a Help Center contains a variety of problem-solving tools to help users troubleshoot their systems.

● **Home network support.** As the number of homes with multiple PCs increases, the demand for home networking grows. Windows Me includes the Home Networking Wizard to guide the user through the often confusing process of interconnecting multiple computers and peripherals. On this network, multiple users can share a single Internet connection.

Windows NT

The operating system called **Windows NT** (NT stands for "new technology") is meant mostly for corporate, networked environments. Version 4.0, the last with the NT designation, looks exactly like Windows 98 and runs most of the same software that runs under Windows 98. But beneath the surface, Windows NT is far more robust and heavy-duty. It has been engineered for stability and, as befits a networked environment, has much stronger security features. Windows NT comes in two versions: NT Workstation, designed for individual users on a network, and NT Server, a network operating system. Because Windows NT lacks support for older Windows and MS-DOS software and hardware, is more complex to learn and use, and requires more memory and processor power than the Windows 9x family, it is seldom used on nonnetworked PCs.

Windows 2000

Windows 2000 is the latest generation in the Windows NT series. As such, it maintains the stability and security features that are NT's hallmark and incorporates Windows 98's ease of setup and hardware awareness. As with Windows NT, there are

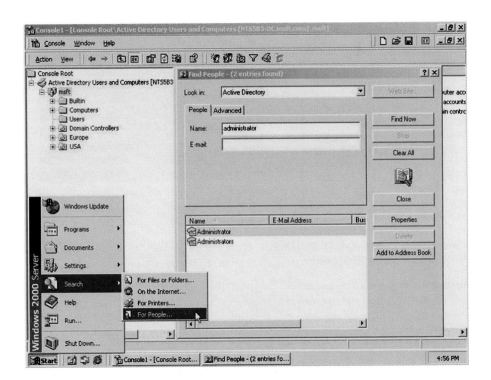

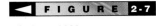

Windows 2000.

Windows 2000, the latest generation in the Windows NT series, maintains the stability and security features of Windows NT and includes support for Windows 98's file structure, Plug and Play features, and better support for laptops.

two versions: Windows 2000 for network servers and Windows 2000 Professional for individual users. Microsoft originally intended that Windows 2000 would be the convergence of the 9x and NT series, providing a single operating system for both home and corporate users (Figure 2-7). However, Window 2000's complexity and heavy demand for computer resources convinced Microsoft to update the Windows 9x home user series with a newer version (Windows Me, discussed above) and delay the convergence for another software generation.

The most noticeable new feature of Windows 2000 is that it knows who you are. One computer can serve many people. Once you identify yourself, it will immediately reconfigure to your preferences. It personalizes the Start menu so that the programs you use most frequently are visible and others are hidden. A particularly attractive feature is the self-healing applications software: If you accidentally delete a necessary component, Windows will automatically restore it. Other improvements over Windows NT include support for the Windows 98 file structure, Plug and Play features, and much better support for laptops.

Windows XP

Windows XP, the latest generation of Windows, brings Microsoft's consumer and corporate operating systems together into a single product. It incorporates and extends the consumer-oriented features of Windows Me into the stable, dependable Windows 2000 environment. Windows XP versions fall into two categories, network server and desktop computer. There are three versions for network servers, based on network complexity. Two additional versions are designed for desktop computers. The Professional Client version is aimed toward business users connected to corporate networks and includes features for file encryption, remote desktop access, and dual processor support. New features in the Personal Client consumer-oriented version include:

● **Improved user interface.** The desktop appears much cleaner and uncluttered. Most icons have been replaced with entries in a redesigned Start menu. Any desk-

► **FIGURE 2-8**

Windows CE on the Pocket PC.

Windows CE includes an interactive scheduling calendar, an address book for contacts, electronic mail, and Web browsing.

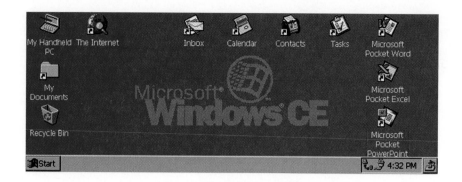

top shortcuts that haven't been used recently will be placed into a separate folder by the Desktop Cleanup Wizard.

● **Improved multimedia support.** Support for digital media, such as MP3 music and digital still and video cameras, has been integrated into the operating system. Much plug-in software is no longer required.

● **More extensive personalization.** A feature called Visual Styles allows the user to customize the appearance of many Windows components. What's more, applications written to the new standards will automatically take on the same appearance.

● **Multiple user support.** Since many home computers have more than one user, Windows XP allows multiple users to be logged on at the same time. One user can walk away leaving applications running, come back later and resume work with all applications still active. During that time, other users can log on, then leave their own applications running. A child can be assigned a limited use configuration that restricts what can be done on the computer.

Windows CE

Windows CE (CE stands for "consumer electronics") is a Windows-based modular operating system designed for the embedded system and Internet appliance market. Its most noticeable use is as the operating system for the Pocket PCs being produced by Hewlett-Packard, Compaq, and others (see Figure 2-8). Windows CE is a subset of Windows, scaled back to work with less memory on smaller screens and without much, if any, file storage. **Embedded systems** are computing devices that are integrated into other products. Embedded systems powered by Windows CE are currently being used in such diverse products as industrial controllers, robots, office equipment, cameras, telephones, home entertainment devices, and automobile navigation systems. In addition to giving all these devices a familiar Windows-like interface, Windows CE provides one other important feature: Internet connectivity. In the eyes of many, almost everything electronic will be connected to the Internet in the not-too-distant future.

► MAC OS

Apple's Macintosh operating system **(Mac OS)** was introduced along with the Macintosh microcomputer in 1984. It had the first commercially successful graphical user interface and quickly gained a reputation for user-friendliness. Based on concepts developed at Xerox's PARC research center in Palo Alto, California, the Mac OS GUI has served as a model for most of the graphical interfaces that have been developed since then. Still considered by many to be easier to use than Windows, Mac OS

GETTING PRACTICAL | Accessibility Options

Long hours staring at the computer screen can be hard on the eyes. As shown here, Windows offers the option of enlarged letters and high-contrast colors.

Improved visibility is only part of the story. The Accessibility Options icon, found in the control panel, offers aids for seeing, hearing, and touching. For example, a hearing-impaired individual can elect to have any computer sound show up as a visual indicator on the screen. Furthermore, spoken words can be seen as screen captions.

An option called StickyKeys permits keys that normally must be pressed at the same time to invoke a command, such as Ctrl-Alt-Del, to be

pressed separately but still achieve the same effect. Another option, handy for anyone who has a habit of inadvertently pressing the Caps Lock key, is to sound a beep whenever the Caps Lock, Num Lock, or Scroll Lock key is pressed. Mouse movements can also be replaced by using the arrow keys on the numeric keypad.

X (X is the Roman numeral for 10) contains enhancements in multimedia support and multitasking—the ability to do several things at once. See Figure 2-9 for an illustration of the Mac OS X desktop.

► UNIX

Unix, a multiuser time-sharing operating system, was developed in 1971 by Ken Thompson and Dennis Ritchie at AT&T's Bell Laboratories for use on its DEC minicomputers. In the late 1970s Bell gave Unix away to many colleges and universities, and students became accustomed to using it. Consequently, when many of

◄ **FIGURE 2-9**

Mac OS X.

The Mac OS interface has served as a model for most of the graphical interfaces available today. Still considered by many to be easier to use than Windows, Mac OS X contains enhancements in multimedia support and multitasking.

these school's graduates entered the work force, they began agitating for the acceptance of Unix in industry, thus producing what is known as the "Unix graduate" phenomenon.

At its basic level, Unix is a character-based system with a command-line user interface. In contrast to the operating systems we have discussed up to this point, Unix is not tied to any specific family of processors. It will run on just about every type of computer available, from microcomputers to mainframes, from any manufacturer. No one company controls Unix, and several versions are available. These versions are similar enough that an experienced Unix user would be comfortable with any of them, but there are some software compatibility problems. The main reason that you need to be aware of Unix is that it is the primary operating system in use on Internet servers today.

► LINUX

In 1991 Linus Torvalds, a student at the University of Helsinki in Finland, created the kernel of a Unix-like operating system named **Linux.** He made the source code available to the public free of charge, under a concept known as **open-source** software. Users can download Linux for free, make any changes they wish, and freely distribute copies. The only restriction is that any changes they make must be freely available to the public.

Currently, most PC systems come with Windows preinstalled; if you would like to use Linux, you must install it yourself. Although the Linux code may be downloaded for free from the Internet, installing it is a complex task suitable only for the most advanced users. Several companies have packaged the Linux code with an installation program, documentation, customer support, and a number of utilities and application packages. These packages, know as distributions, make it easier for a typical user to install and use Linux and are relatively inexpensive (less than $50). Since Linux itself uses a command-line inerface, most distributions also provide a GUI that the user can install. Many users install Linux in a **dual-boot** configuration with Windows; that is, when you boot the system, you choose which operating system will be loaded (Figure 2-10).

► FIGURE 2-10

Linux.

Linux is the fastest-growing operating system for Intel-based computers. Linux includes all the respected features of UNIX and it's free.

Linux has several advantages over Windows. Windows users accustomed to the occasional system crash will be happy to learn that Linux is extremely stable—it rarely ever crashes. Also, Linux users form a close-knit community. If you have a problem or question, posting it on the Internet will almost always result in a quick, accurate answer from Linux experts who are happy to share their knowledge. Finally, if the operating system should somehow become corrupted, reinstallation of Linux is a much simpler task than reinstalling Windows.

The biggest disadvantage of Linux is the relative scarcity of applications. Although a number of applications have become available, many under the same open-source concept as Linux itself, the numbers are still far fewer than for Windows. As Linux gains acceptance, this disparity may disappear.

► OPERATING SYSTEMS FOR NETWORKS

An extension of operating systems for personal computers is a **network operating system (NOS),** which is designed to let computers on a network share resources such as hard disks and printers. A NOS is similar to a standard operating system but includes special features for handling network functions. Our earlier discussion of Windows 2000 described the workstation version; the server version of Windows 2000 is one example of a network operating system. Novell NetWare is another example. In addition to resource sharing, a NOS supports data security (does this user have the right to that data?), troubleshooting (oops, computer XYZ on the network failed to receive a message intended for it), and administrative control (track the online hours and track the number of messages to and from each computer).

In a client/server relationship, parts of the NOS (mostly file access and management programs) run on the server computer, while other NOS components, such as software that permits requests to the server and messages to other computers, run on the client (user) computers. In addition, each of the client computers has its own operating system, such as Windows Me.

One of the network operating system's main tasks is to make the resources appear as though they are running from the client's computer. Whether issuing commands, running applications software, or sending jobs to a printer, the role of a NOS is to make the desired services appear to be local to that client computer. The whole point of a client/server system is to provide expanded services to individual users at their own networked computers; the network operating system is the software that makes it possible.

► OPERATING SYSTEMS FOR LARGE COMPUTERS

Large computers—mainframes—have been around about twice as long as personal computers. Those big computers are usually owned by businesses and universities, which make them available to many users. So, unlike the scenario with which you may be familiar—one person per personal computer at a time—a large computer is used by many people at once. This presents special problems, which must be addressed by the operating system.

Computer users often have questions when they first realize that their program is "in there" with all those other programs. At any given moment, which program gets the CPU? If several programs are in memory at the same time, what keeps the programs from getting mixed up with one another? How is storage handled when several programs may want to get data from disk or send processed data to disk at the same time? Why doesn't printer output from several programs get all jumbled up? The oper-

---

The Technology Spiral

Many people wonder whether the constant upgrading of both hardware and operating systems is really necessary. After all, if what you've got works for you, why should you have to buy new stuff? The short answer is: You don't. But there is an interesting dynamic at work here. Technological advances in hardware make it possible for manufacturers to offer more powerful systems at a lower price. At the same time, competition leads software developers to add more features to their products. This increased functionality requires the faster processors, larger memory capacity, and bigger hard drives on the newer systems. Frequently, this new software just will not function well on an older computer that has, relatively speaking, limited capacity. Consumers can resist new software for just so long. In particular, if they cling too long to an older operating system, they will find that no applications software is being written for it. There are several stopgap measures: adding memory, adding a hard drive, upgrading the microprocessor. But most people eventually buy the new computer, one with the capacity to handle all the new software. And then the cycle begins again.

ating system anticipates these problems and takes care of them behind the scenes so that users can share the computer's resources without worrying about how it is done.

► RESOURCE ALLOCATION

Notice that the questions above all address sharing problems, that is, multiple users sharing the CPU, memory, storage, and the printer. Shared resources are said to be allocated. **Resource allocation** is the process of assigning computer resources to certain programs for their use. Those same resources are deallocated—released—when the program using them is finished, and then they are reallocated elsewhere.

Sharing the Central Processing Unit

Since most computers have a single central processing unit, all programs running on the computer must share it. The sharing process is controlled by the operating system. Two approaches to sharing are multiprogramming and time-sharing. But first, let us distinguish multiprogramming from multiprocessing. **Multiprocessing** refers to the use of a powerful computer with multiple CPUs so that multiple programs can run simultaneously, each using its own processor.

MULTIPROGRAMMING   If there is only one central processing unit (the usual case), it is not physically possible for more than one program to use it at the same time. **Multiprogramming** means that two or more programs are being executed in the same time frame, that is, **concurrently,** on a computer. What this really means is that the programs are taking turns; one program runs for a while, and then another one runs. The key word here is *concurrently* as opposed to *simultaneously*. One program could be using the CPU while another does something else, such as sending output to the printer. Concurrent processing means that two or more programs are using the central processing unit in the same time frame—during the same minute, for instance—but not exactly at the same instant. In other words, concurrent processing allows one program to use one resource while another program uses another resource; this gives the illusion of simultaneous processing. As a result, there is less idle time for the computer system's resources. Concurrent processing is effective because CPU speeds are many times faster than input/output speeds. During the time it takes a disk drive to perform a read instruction for one program, for example, the central processing unit can execute thousands or even tens of thousands of calculation instructions for another program.

Multiprogramming is **event-driven.** This means that programs share resources based on events that take place in the programs. Normally, a program is allowed to complete a certain activity (event), such as a calculation, before relinquishing the resource (the central processing unit, in this example) to another program that is waiting for it.

The operating system implements multiprogramming through a system of interrupts. An **interrupt** is a signal that causes normal program processing to be suspended temporarily. Suppose, for example, that several programs are running on a large computer, two of them being a payroll program and an inventory management program. When the payroll program needs to read the next employee record, that program is interrupted—or, in a sense, interrupts itself—while the operating system takes over to do the actual reading. Once the read operation has begun and the payroll program is waiting for the results, the operating system may allocate the CPU to the inventory program to do some calculations. When the read operation is completed, another interrupt is generated. The operating system suspends the inventory program, determines the reason for the interrupt—completion of the payroll program's read operation in this case—and then determines which program gets to resume using the CPU. That determination may be based on priorities—the program with the highest priority goes next—or on which has been waiting the longest.

The point of this discussion is not to clarify which program does what when. Rather, it is to show that shared resources are being managed by the operating system in the background. Although it may appear to the user that a program is being run continuously from start to finish, in fact it is constantly being interrupted. This process is not without cost—the operating system does use some of the CPU resources itself—but the overall effect is much more efficient use of the CPU.

In large computer systems, programs that run in an event-driven multiprogramming environment are usually batch programs that don't require user input. Typical examples are programs for payroll, accounts receivable, and sales and marketing analysis. If any interactive programs are running, they can be given the highest priority so that the users won't have to wait.

TIME-SHARING   A special case of multiprogramming, **time-sharing** is usually **time-driven** rather than event-driven. A common approach is to give each user a **time slice**—a fraction of a second—during which the computer works on a single user's tasks. However, the operating system does not wait for completion of an event; at the end of the time slice—that is, when time is up—the resources are taken away from that user and given to someone else. This is hardly noticeable to the user: When you are sitting before a terminal in a time-sharing system, the computer's response time will be quite short—fractions of a second—and it may seem as if you have the computer to yourself.

Response time is the time between your typed computer request and the computer's reply. Even if you are working on a calculation and the operating system interrupts it, sending you to the end of the line until other users have had their turns, you may not notice that you have been deprived of service. Not all computer systems give ideal service all the time, however; if a computer system is trying to serve too many users at the same time, response time may slow down noticeably.

Typical time-sharing applications are those with many users, each of whom has a series of brief, randomly occurring actions; examples include credit checking, point-of-sale systems, and airline reservation systems. Each of these systems has many users, perhaps hundreds, who need to share the system resources.

Sharing Memory

What if you have a very large program for which it might be difficult to find space in memory? Or what if several programs are competing for space in memory? These questions are related to memory management. **Memory management** is the process of allocating memory to programs and of keeping the programs in memory separate from one another.

There are many methods of memory management. Some systems simply divide memory into separate areas, each of which can hold a program. The problem is how to know how big the areas, sometimes called **partitions** or **regions,** should be; at least one of them should be large enough to hold the largest anticipated program. Some systems use memory areas that are not of a fixed size; that is, the sizes can change to meet the needs of the current assortment of programs. In either case, whether the areas are of a fixed or variable size, there is a problem with unused memory between programs. When these memory spaces are too small to be used, space is wasted.

FOREGROUND AND BACKGROUND   Large all-purpose computers often divide their memory into foreground and background areas. The **foreground** is generally for programs that have higher priority and therefore receive more CPU time. A typical foreground program is in a time-sharing environment, with the user at a terminal awaiting response. That is, a foreground program is interactive, with the CPU often unused while the user is entering the next request. Thus there is CPU time available for the waiting background programs. The **background,** as the name implies, is for programs with less pressing schedules and therefore lower priorities and less CPU time. Typical background programs are batch programs in a multiprogramming environment. Foreground programs are given privileged status—more turns for the central processing unit and other resources—and background programs take whatever they need that is not currently in use by another program. Lists of programs waiting to run are kept in **queues** suitable to their job class.

VIRTUAL STORAGE   Many computer systems manage memory by using a technique called **virtual storage** (also called **virtual memory**). The virtual storage concept means that the programs currently being executed are stored on disk and portions of these programs are brought into memory as needed. Since only one part of a program can be executing at any given time, the parts that are not currently needed are left on the disk. Since only part of the program is in memory at any given time, the amount of memory needed is minimized. Memory, in this case, is considered to be **real storage,** while the secondary storage (hard disk, most likely) holding the rest of the program is considered virtual storage.

Virtual storage can be implemented in a variety of ways. Consider the paging method, for example. Suppose you have a very large program, which means that there will be difficulty in finding space for it in the computer's shared memory. If your program is divided into small pieces, it will be easier to find places to put those pieces. This is essentially what paging does. **Paging** is the process of dividing a program into equal-size pieces called **pages** and storing them in equal-size memory spaces called **page frames.** All pages and page frames are the same fixed size, typically 2 kilobytes (KB) or 4 KB. The pages are stored in memory in *noncontiguous* locations—locations that are not necessarily next to each other (Figure 2-11).

Even though the pages are not right next to each other in memory, the operating system is able to keep track of them. It does this by using a **page table,** which, like an index, lists each page that is part of the program and the corresponding beginning memory address where it has been placed. The operating system does require CPU time to control paging. If too large a portion of available CPU time is spent performing this paging, very little is left over to actually execute user programs. This situation, called **thrashing,** can be eliminated by running fewer programs concurrently or by adding additional memory.

MEMORY PROTECTION   In a multiprogramming environment it is theoretically possible for the computer, while executing one program, to destroy or modify another program by transferring to the wrong memory locations. That is, without protection, one program might accidentally hop into the middle of another, causing destruction of data and general chaos. This, of course, is not permitted. To avoid this problem, the operating system confines each program to certain defined limits in memory. If a program inadvertently attempts to enter some memory area outside its limits, the operating system terminates the execution of that program. This process of keeping one program from straying into another is called **memory protection.**

► **F I G U R E 2-11**

Virtual storage.

In this illustration, three programs (A, B, and C) are currently running. All three programs in virtual storage are divided in to standard-sized segments called pages. Primary memory, referred to as real storage, is divided into the same sized segments called page frames. As pages of each program are needed for execution, they are copied from virtual storage into available pages frames. If all the page frames are full, the system will copy the contents of the least recently used page frame back to virtual storage to make room for the new page.

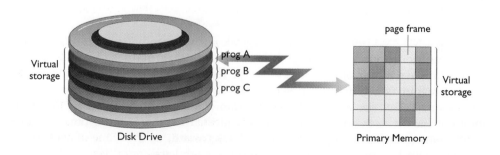

Sharing Storage Resources

The operating system keeps track of which file is where and responds to commands to manipulate files. But the situation is complicated by the possibility that more than one user may want to read or write a record from the same disk pack at the same time. Again, it is the operating system that keeps track of the input and output requests and processes them, usually in the order in which they were received. Any program instruction to read or write a record is routed to the operating system, which processes the request and then returns control to the program.

Sharing Printing Resources

Suppose half a dozen programs are active but the computer has only one printer. If all programs took turns printing out their output a line or two at a time, interspersed with the output of other programs, the resulting printed report would be worthless. To get around this problem, a process called **spooling** is used: Each program writes onto a disk each line that is to be printed. Or, to be more accurate, the program "thinks" that it is writing the line to the printer, but the operating system intercepts the line and sends it instead to a disk file. When the program finishes printing, the disk file is placed into a queue to be printed when the printer becomes available.

Spooling also addresses the problem of relatively slow printer speeds. Writing a record to disk is much faster than writing that same record to a printer. A program therefore completes execution more quickly if records to be printed are written temporarily to disk. The actual printing can be done at some later time, after the program has completed execution. Some large installations use a separate (usually smaller) computer dedicated exclusively to the printing of spooled files; some print lengthy reports during off-hours or overnight so that smaller, more immediate jobs can use the printer during the day.

Utility Programs

Most of the resource allocation tasks just described are done by the operating system without user involvement. For example, activities such as paging and spooling go on without explicit commands from users. But the operating system can also perform explicit services at the request of the user.

Why reinvent the wheel? Duplication of effort is what **utility programs,** or just **utilities,** are supposed to avoid. Such programs perform many secondary chores, such as backing up and restoring files, compressing files and entire hard disks, locating files, and ferreting out computer viruses. As we have noted, strictly speaking, these utilities are considered part of the system software but not part of the operating system. Some utilities are packaged with operating systems; others can be purchased separately. A few typical utilities are described below.

FILE MANAGER   Most storage devices can store large numbers of files. Imagine how difficult it would be to locate a single file among thousands of files on your hard drive. The **file manager** utility allows you to store your files in a hierarchical directory structure that is organized in a way that makes sense to you. A **directory** is a named area in storage that can contain files and other directories. For example, you might have a directory called Word Processing, in which you plan to store the files that you create with your word processor. You could then create a subdirectory named School within the Word Processing directory for all your schoolwork. Within the School directory you might create individual subdirectories for each of your classes. Incidentally, the newer versions of Windows refer to directories as *folders.*

In addition to enabling you to create this directory structure, the file manager also provides the capability to display lists of files in directories; to copy, move, rename, and delete files; and to format and copy diskettes. Figure 2-12 shows a dis-

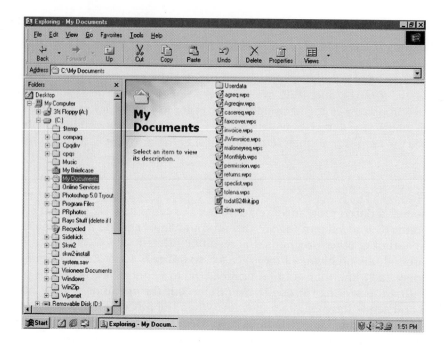

FIGURE 2-12

Windows Explorer.

Windows Explorer is the file manager utility that is part of the Windows operating system. The left screen panel shows the systems device and folder structure; the right panel shows the contents of the selected folder.

play from Windows Explorer, the file manager that comes with the Windows operating system.

BACKUP AND RESTORE Backing up files involves making duplicate copies and storing them in a safe place, in case anything happens to the originals. **Backup and restore** utilities allow you to make backups of entire hard drives or of selected directories. These backups could be made to diskettes but are normally stored on high-capacity media such as CD or tape (see Chapter 6, "Storage and Multimedia: The Facts and More," for more detail on these devices). Since the utility creates the backup files in a specialized format to minimize space requirements, the copies must be processed by the restore routine before you can use them. Rudimentary backup and restore utilities accompany most operating systems, but more capable utilities are provided with tape and CD devices or can be purchased separately.

FIGURE 2-13

WinZip®.

Winzip® is one of the best-known file compression utilities.

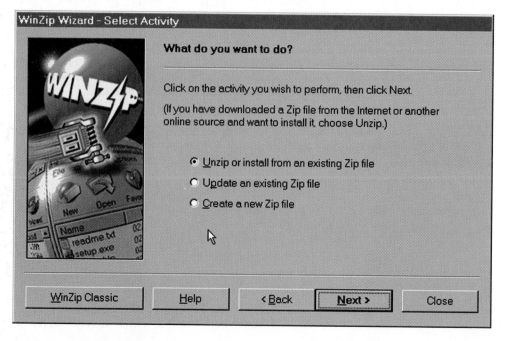

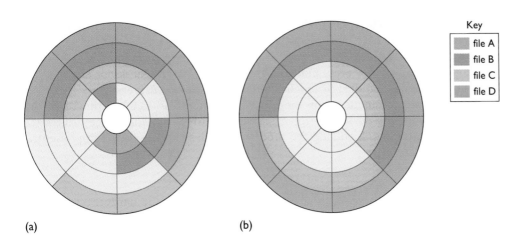

Key

file A
file B
file C
file D

Disk defragmentation.

(a) Before defragmentation, portions of files are scattered over the disk surface, slowing access. (b) After defragmentation, each file is stored in a contiguous group of sectors.

(a)   (b)

FILE COMPRESSION A **file compression** utility reduces the amount of space required by a file. Compressed files take up less space on disk and also take less time to transmit across communication lines. Many files available for downloading from the Internet are in compressed format and must be uncompressed into their original form before they can be used. PKZIP™ and WinZip® are two popular file compression utilities (Figure 2-13).

DEFRAGMENTER When the operating system is looking for space in which to store a file, it cannot always find enough space in one place on the disk. It often has to store portions of a file in noncontiguous, or separated, disk locations. When this happens, the file is fragmented. Although this process makes efficient use of disk space, it slows down access to the file. If a lot of files are fragmented, the effect on system performance can be very noticeable. A **disk defragmenter** utility will reorganize the files on the disk so that all files are stored in contiguous locations. Windows' defragmenter utility is called, not surprisingly, Disk Defragmenter (Figure 2-14).

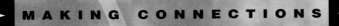
► M A K I N G   C O N N E C T I O N S ◄ **Personalizing Your Windows Desktop**

Many users quickly become bored with the standard plain blue Windows desktop. Windows does provide a few simple alternatives, such as clouds and red blocks, but much more creative options are available for free on the Internet. Windows uses the term "wallpaper" to refer to an image used for the desktop background. An Internet search on the term "wallpaper" will turn up thousands of sites providing free images in many categories, including scenery, celebrities, sports, commercial products, abstract art, and just about anything else you can imagine.

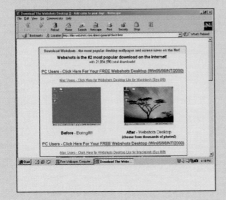

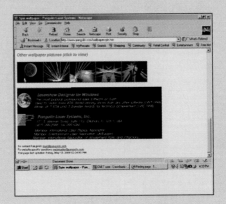

DEVICE DRIVERS   The commands necessary to print a line on one manufacturer's laser printer are much different from the commands necessary to print the same line on another manufacturer's ink-jet printer. An operating system cannot possibly know the proper commands for every model of every type of peripheral device on the market. This problem is handled by small utilities called **device drivers.** A device driver accepts standard commands from the operating system and converts them into the proper format for the device it supports. Manufacturers provide device drivers for each of their products. Installing the product includes copying the appropriate driver(s) to your hard drive.

▲

This chapter has discussed the software used to control the hardware and allow you to interact with the computer. In the next chapter, we will look at the software that you use to accomplish useful tasks, such as creating reports, keeping track of expenses, and coordinating group projects.

CHAPTER REVIEW

▶ **Summary and Key Terms**

- An **operating system** is a set of programs that lies between applications software and the computer hardware. **Systems software** means all programs related to coordinating computer operations, including the operating system, programming language translators, and service programs.

- The **kernel,** most of which remains in memory, is called *resident.* The kernel controls the entire operating system and loads into memory *nonresident* operating system programs from disk storage as needed.

- Loading the operating system into memory is called **booting** the system.

- An operating system has three main functions (1) managing the computer's resources, such as the central processing unit, memory, disk drives, and printers; (2) establishing a user interface; and (3) executing and providing services for applications software.

- The user communicates with the operating system through the **user interface.**

- A **platform** is a combination of computer hardware and operating system software that determines which applications users can run on their systems.

- The > in "C:\>" is a **prompt,** a signal that the system is waiting for you to give an instruction to the computer. To execute a given DOS program, a user must type a **command,** a name that invokes a specific DOS program.

- A key product is **Microsoft Windows,** software with a colorful **graphical user interface (GUI).** Windows offers on-screen pictures called **icons** and lists called **menus;** both encourage pointing and clicking with a mouse, an approach that can make computer use faster and easier. **Pull-down menus** pull down like a window shade from a selection on the menu bar. **Pop-up menus** originate from a selection at the bottom of the screen or when the right mouse button is clicked. Early versions of Windows were merely a layer of software over the operating system, called an **operating environment** or **shell.**

- Microsoft **Windows 95** is a true operating system, not a shell. A key feature is **Plug and Play,** a concept that lets the computer configure itself when a new component is added. A Windows technology called **object linking and embedding (OLE)** lets you embed or link one document with another. **Windows 98** is built on the same code base as Windows 95 and has a similar look and user interaction. In particular, Windows 98 incorporates Internet Explorer, a Web browser, into the operating system. **Windows Me** is the latest in the Win 9x series.

- **Windows NT** (for "new technology") is meant mostly for corporate, networked environments. It looks exactly like Windows 95 but has been engineered for stability and has much stronger security features. **Windows 2000** is the latest generation in the NT series.

- **Windows CE** (for "consumer electronics") is a Windows-based modular operating system for **embedded systems** (systems built into other products) and other new digital appliances.

- The **Mac OS,** introduced with Apple's Macintosh computer in 1984, had the first generally available GUI. Its latest version, Mac OS X, is still considered to be the easiest to use for beginners.

- **Unix** is a multiuser, timesharing operating system that runs on all types of computers. It is the primary operating system used on Internet servers today.

- **Linux** is a Unix-like operating system available under the **open-source** concept, which means that it is freely available and not under control of any one company. Many users install Linux in a **dual-boot** system, allowing them to choose between Windows and Linux each time they boot their PC.

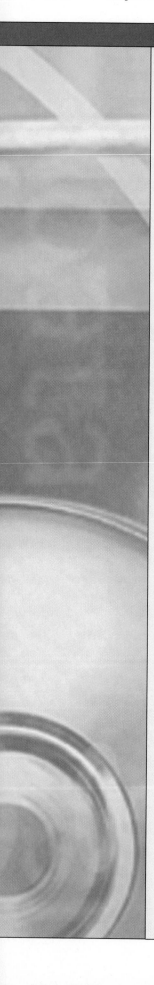

- A **network operating system (NOS)** is designed to let computers on a network share resources such as hard disks and printers. A NOS supports resource sharing, data security, troubleshooting, and administrative control. Parts of the NOS run on the server computer, while other NOS components run on the client computers.

- **Resource allocation** is the process of assigning computer resources to certain programs for their use.

- **Multiprocessing** means that a computer with more than one central processing unit can run multiple programs simultaneously, each using its own processor.

- **Multiprogramming** is running two or more programs in the same time frame, **concurrently,** on the same computer. Multiprogramming is **event-driven,** meaning that one program is allowed to use a particular resource (such as the central processing unit) to complete a certain activity (event) before relinquishing the resource to another program. In multiprogramming, the operating system uses **interrupts,** which are signals that temporarily suspend the execution of individual programs.

- **Time-sharing** is a special case of multiprogramming in which several people use one computer at the same time. Time-sharing is **time-driven**—each user is given a **time slice** in which the computer works on that user's tasks before moving on to another user's tasks. **Response time** is the time between the user's typed computer request and the computer's reply.

- **Memory management** is the process of allocating memory to programs and of keeping the programs in memory separate from each other. Some systems simply divide memory into separate areas, sometimes called **partitions** or **regions,** each of which can hold a program. Large all-purpose computers often divide memory into a **foreground** area for programs with higher priority and a **background** area for programs with lower priority. Programs waiting to be run are kept on the disk in **queues.**

- In the **virtual storage** (or **virtual memory**) technique of memory management, part of the application program is stored on disk and is brought into memory only when needed for execution. Memory is considered **real storage;** the secondary storage holding the rest of the program is considered virtual storage.

- Virtual storage can be implemented in several ways, one of which is paging. **Paging** divides a program into equal-size pieces **(pages)** that fit exactly into corresponding noncontiguous memory spaces **(page frames).** The operating system keeps track of page locations using an indexlike **page table. Thrashing** occurs when the CPU spends all its time swapping pages in and out of real memory.

- In multiprogramming, **memory protection** is an operating system process that defines the limits of each program in memory, thus preventing programs from accidentally destroying or modifying one another.

- **Spooling** writes each file to be printed temporarily onto a disk instead of printing it immediately. When this spooling process is complete, all the appropriate files from a particular program can be printed intact.

- **Utility programs (utilities)** are programs that perform many common tasks for users. Examples include **file managers** to organize and manage disk files in a **directory** structure, **backup and restore** utilities to facilitate making file backups, **file compression** utilities to reduce the amount of space required by files, **disk defragmenters** to relocate disk files into contiguous locations, and **device drivers** to allow the operating system to communicate with peripherals.

► Critical Thinking Questions

1. How would your access to computers be affected if there were no operating systems?

2. How do you explain the rapid acceptance of Microsoft Windows?

3. Which of these kinds of operating systems might you expect to use in your career: Personal computer operating system? Large computer operating system? Network operating system? All of these? Will it depend on the type of job you have?

► STUDENT STUDY GUIDE

Multiple Choice

1. An operating system is a
   a. set of users
   b. set of programs
   c. form of time-sharing
   d. kernel program

2. In multiprogramming, two or more programs can be executed
   a. by optimizing compilers
   b. simultaneously
   c. with two computers
   d. concurrently

3. Time-sharing of resources by users is usually
   a. based on time slices
   b. event-driven
   c. based on input
   d. operated by spooling

4. Management of an operating system is handled by
   a. an interpreter
   b. utility programs
   c. the kernel program
   d. the CPU

5. The process of allocating main memory to programs and keeping the programs in memory separate from one another is called
   a. memory protection
   b. virtual storage
   c. memory management
   d. real storage

6. The Windows version that is especially designed for strong stability and security is
   a. DOS
   b. 3.1
   c. Me
   d. 2000

7. The technique in shared systems that avoids mixing printout from several programs is
   a. paging
   b. slicing
   c. queuing
   d. spooling

8. The technique whereby part of the program is stored on disk and is brought into memory for execution as needed is called
   a. memory allocation
   b. virtual storage
   c. interrupts
   d. prioritized memory

9. Part of a NOS runs on client computers, and part of it runs on the
   a. page frame
   b. page table
   c. server
   d. host

10. Another name for an operating environment is a
    a. page
    b. shell
    c. layer
    d. supervisor

11. Loading the operating system into a personal computer is called
    a. booting
    b. interrupting
    c. prompting
    d. paging

12. Which one of the following uses graphical icons?
    a. command-line interface
    b. utility program
    c. page
    d. GUI

13. In multiprogramming, the process of confining each program to certain defined limits in memory is called
    a. spooling
    b. program scheduling
    c. time-sharing
    d. memory protection

14. The corresponding memory spaces for pages are called
    a. page utilities
    b. page blocks
    c. page frames
    d. page modules

15. The time between the user's request and the computer's reply is
    a. concurrent time
    b. allocation time
    c. response time
    d. event time

16. An on-screen picture that represents an object, such as a program or file, is a(n)
    a. page
    b. icon
    c. NOS
    d. spool

17. Running programs with more than one CPU is called
    a. interrupting
    b. multiprocessing
    c. embedding
    d. multiprogramming

18. The memory area for programs with highest priority is the
    a. frame
    b. page table
    c. foreground
    d. background

19. Lists of programs waiting to be run are in
    a. page frames
    b. shells
    c. the background
    d. queues

20. System programs that handle common user tasks are called
    a. pull-down menus
    b. supervisors
    c. pages
    d. utilities

21. The signal that the computer is awaiting a command from the user is a(n)
    a. prompt
    b. event
    c. time slice
    d. interrupt

22. The term NOS refers to
    a. memory management techniques
    b. virtual storage
    c. the booting process
    d. an operating system for a network

23. The combination of hardware and operating system for which an application program is written is called a(n)
    a. shell
    b. interrupt
    c. platform
    d. operating environment

24. The main program in an operating system is the
    a. kernel
    b. file manager
    c. directory
    d. NOS

25. Which of the following is an operating system designed for embedded systems?
    a. Windows Me
    b. Mac OS X
    c. MS-DOS
    d. Windows CE

True/False

T F 1. A DOS program is invoked by issuing a command.

T F 2. The most important program in an operating system is the kernel program.

T F 3. Multiprogramming means that two or more programs can run simultaneously.

T F 4. Time-sharing is effective because input/output speeds are so much faster than CPU speeds.

T F 5. Resource allocation means that a given program has exclusive use of computer resources.

T F 6. Background programs are usually batch programs.

T F 7. Virtual storage is a technique of memory management that appears to provide users with more memory space than is actually the case.

T F 8. Windows employs a graphical user interface.

T F 9. In a network operating system, some functions are performed by the server and others by the client computers.

T F 10. Shell is another name for page.

T F 11. An operating system includes system software, programming language translators, and service programs.

T F 12. Utility programs avoid duplication of effort.

T F 13. In a given memory system, all page frames are the same size.

T F 14. Virtual memory is another name for virtual storage.

T F 15. Loading the operating system into memory is called booting.

T F 16. An interrupt causes a program to stop temporarily.

T F 17. Portions of a NOS reside on both client and server computers.

T F 18. Paging divides a program into pieces of various sizes to fit in the available memory spaces.

T F 19. Response time is the elapsed time for program execution.

T F 20. OLE lets a user link from one program to another.

T F 21. Multiprocessing is simultaneous processing.

T F 22. The shared resources that the operating system manages include the CPU, memory, storage devices, and the printer.

T F 23. Multiprogramming is one approach to sharing the CPU.

T F 24. All operating system programs must be in memory during the time an application program is running.

T F 25. A knowledgeable user can interact directly with the hardware without invoking the operating system.

T F 26. A typical time-sharing application is processing payroll checks.

T F 27. Open-source software is freely available but may not be modified by the user.

T F 28. A prompt is used in a command-line interface and indicates that the operating system is waiting for the user to enter an instruction.

T F 29. Unix is a multiuser time-sharing operating system that is available for most computers.

T F 30. Interactive programs would most likely be assigned to background memory.

Fill-In

1. NOS stands for _____.

2. The operating system program that remains resident in memory is the _____.

3. The term used for the time between a user's request at the terminal and the computer's reply is _____.

4. The type of system that lets two or more programs execute concurrently is ____.

5. What are the program pieces called in the virtual storage technique of paging? What are the corresponding memory spaces called?
   a. _____
   b. _____

6. Simultaneous processing of more than one program using more than one processor is called _____.

7. Another name for partition is _____.

8. High-priority programs usually operate in this part of memory: _____

9. The process of assigning computer resources to certain programs for their use is called _____.

10. The operating system keeps track of page locations by using a _____.

11. The process that an operating system uses to avoid interspersing the printout from several programs is called _____.

12. A program that overlays the operating system to provide a more friendly environment is the _____.

13. In time-sharing, each user is given a unit of time called a _____.

14. OLE stands for _____.

15. A utility that reorganizes disk files into contiguous storage locations is the ____.

16. Loading the operating system into memory is called _____.

17. Time-sharing is time driven but multiprogramming is _____ driven.

18. The situation that occurs when the CPU spends all its time swapping pages into and out of real memory is _____.

19. A utility that translates operating system commands into instructions that operate a peripheral is a _____.

20. GUI stands for _____.

21. In multiprogramming, a condition that temporarily suspends program execution is an _____.

22. Keeping programs in memory separate is called _____.

23. A utility that reduces the amount of space required to store a file is a _____.

24. A Unix-like operating system that is available under the open-source concept is

   _____.

25. A Windows feature that automatically configures new hardware is known as

   _____.

► ANSWERS

Multiple Choice

1. b	8. b	15. c	22. d
2. d	9. c	16. b	23. c
3. a	10. b	17. b	24. a
4. c	11. a	18. c	25. d
5. c	12. d	19. d	
6. d	13. d	20. d	
7. d	14. c	21. a	

True/False

1. T	9. T	17. T	25. F
2. T	10. F	18. F	26. F
3. F	11. T	19. F	27. F
4. F	12. T	20. T	28. T
5. F	13. T	21. T	29. T
6. T	14. T	22. T	30. F
7. T	15. T	23. T	
8. T	16. T	24. F	

Fill-In

1. network operating system
2. kernel program
3. response time
4. multiprogramming
5. a. pages
   b. page frames
6. multiprocessing
7. region
8. foreground
9. resource allocation
10. page table
11. spooling
12. operating environment (or shell)
13. time slice
14. object linking and embedding
15. disk defragmenter
16. booting
17. event
18. thrashing
19. device driver
20. graphical user interface
21. interrupt
22. memory protection
23. file compression program
24. Linux
25. Plug and Play

Planet Internet

Jumping-off Points

How Do I Start?

Briefly, to get started, you need an URL for the Web. Translation: You need a starting address ("URL" stands for "Uniform Resource Locator") to find a site on the subset of the Internet called the World Wide Web, also called *WWW* or just *the Web.* You can read more detailed information about URLs and the Web, and most important, *links,* in Chapter 8.

Where Do I Find a URL?

An URL is often pretty messy—a long string of letters and symbols. No one likes to type URLs, and, what's more, there is a good chance of making an error. Fortunately, you rarely have to type an URL because, once started, you can click your mouse on links— icons or highlighted text—to move from site to site on the Internet.

The publisher of this book has set up this URL for our readers:

http://www.prenhall.com/capron

Once you use this URL to reach the publisher's site, you will find links—colored and/or underlined text—to all other sites mentioned in this and other chapters. Simply click the desired link. Because everything on the Internet, including URLs, is subject to change, we supply here the publisher's URL, which will not change.

What Other Starting Points Are There?

Keep in mind that, unlike a commercial product, the Internet is not owned or managed by anyone. One consequence of this is that there is no master table of contents or index for the Internet. However, several organizations have produced ordered lists that can be used as a helpful starting place. Users often favor one or more of these as comprehensive starting places: Yahoo!, Alta Vista, Netscape, Magellan, and Excite.

Each of these sites has a set of major categories, and each major category has links of its own, as do

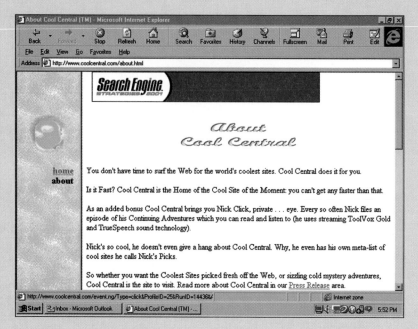

the topics at the next level, and so on. Major categories typically include careers, computers, business, politics, education, society, kids, shopping, travel, magazines, recreation, government, events, science, sports, health, reference, and family. Most major starting sites also include special lists of new and "hot" sites. You could hang around for literally days, burrowing deeper and deeper, just from a starting point such as Yahoo!

Favorites.

Many sites make no attempt to be comprehensive but instead list their own favorites, sites they consider to be of high quality. The Lycos Top 50 site lists the hot search topics for the past week. Examples of other sites that offer special lists are Internet Tonight's "The Big List" and Netscape. The Cool Central site offers the Cool Site of the Week, of the Day, and of the Hour, and, for the attention-deficient, the Cool Site of the Moment. Remember that the links for all of these sites can be found at the publisher's site. Just point and click and go to any of the listed sites. A good starting point for the technologically-inclined is SlashDot, which bills itself as "News for Nerds."

But I Need to Get to the Web First.

Yes. To use the Web, you need a browser, special software devoted to managing access to the Web. You can get general information about browsers in Chapter 8, but you will need to ask your instructor, lab personnel, or a designated employee how to use the Web browser at your location. If you are using a browser that you acquired for your personal computer or have access to the Internet via some online service, then these suppliers will provide instructions.

Internet Exercises:

At the end of most Planet Internet features, three exercises are suggested. The first exercise is structured, since it's based on using links provided on the publisher's Web Site. Use the URL supplied here to get started. If you are feeling a little adventurous, try the free-form exercise, in which we make suggestions but not guarantees. If you are fairly familiar with the Web, try the advanced exercise.

1. **Structured exercise.** Go to the URL http://www.prenhall.com/capron. Link to the Yahoo! Site, and then link to the list of new sites. From there, choose two places to link to. Write a brief evaluation of the sites to share with classmates, friends, or family, using such criteria as overall ease of use, quantity and quality of information, availability of information about the privacy policy, contact person, and key features of the site.

2. **Free-form exercise.** Using the same URL, choose a site that lists favorites. Then go to several sites they recommend? (choose a site) Write a brief evaluation of the site to share with classmates, friends, or family, using such criteria as overall ease of use, quantity and quality of information, availability of information about the privacy policy, contact person, and key features of the site.

3. **Advanced exercise.** Find a page for a hobby or recreational interest of your own that serves as the jumping-off point to many other pages, including shopping information, FAQs, chat rooms, and so on. Follow two or three links from this page and total up the number of links from there. Write a brief report to share with classmates, friends, or family on the features of this Web site. For example, the Knitting page in About—The Human Internet's Hobbies section, includes basic information about knitting, free patterns, information about charity projects, discussion groups, and a host of other topics.

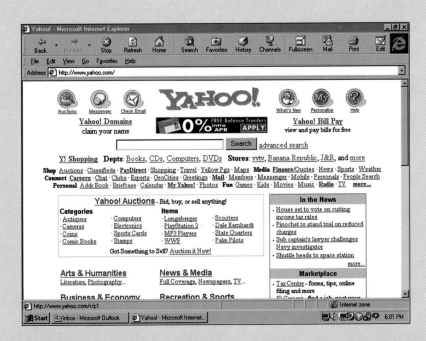

Planet Internet

Applications Software:
Getting the Work Done

Applications Software:
Getting the Work Done

C H A P T E R

LEARNING OBJECTIVES

Distinguish between operating systems and applications software

List the various methods by which individuals and businesses acquire software

List and briefly describe various types of task-oriented software

Identify the kinds of software that are available for both large and small businesses

Discuss ethical issues associated with software

Describe the functions of various computer professionals

fter her first year in college, Anita Jefferson got a summer job in the resort town of Friday Harbor. She waited tables for both the noon and evening shifts at a small family-owned restaurant. Her wages were supplemented nicely by generous tips from tourists. An accounting major, Anita would have preferred a job in a business office, but at least her summer income would make a significant dent in her upcoming tuition.

As it turned out, Anita's summer was more valuable than she expected. When the owners learned that Anita had taken introductory computer and accounting classes during her first two semesters, they asked her whether she would be willing to help them out in the office for a few hours several mornings a week. She readily agreed, figuring not only that the extra money would come in handy, but also that the experience would look good on her résumé.

Her first project was to design a "Specials of the Day" menu insert. By studying the software manuals and Help files, she learned how to add graphics, color, and attractive typefaces—fonts—to the basic typed information, resulting in an eye-catching insert design. The owners were able to easily enter the current specials each morning and print the inserts for lunch and dinner on their ink-jet printer.

Anita completed several other office projects that summer, but the one of which she was proudest was a detailed analysis of the cost to produce each of the restaurant's entrées. She used spreadsheet software to list the cost and amount of the basic ingredients in each entrée, along with its preparation time. She used the built-in charting feature to develop a chart that visually compared each menu item's cost with its price. The owners could easily see which dishes were most profitable and adjust prices as necessary. What's more, as ingredient costs changed, simple numeric entries on the spreadsheet automatically updated the charts, allowing the owners to decide quickly if price changes were necessary.

Application Software

Prentice Hall
EXPLORE Generation **it**

▶ APPLICATIONS SOFTWARE: GETTING THE WORK DONE

When people think about computers, they usually think about machines. The tapping on the keyboard, the rumble of whirling disk drives, the changing flashes of color on a computer screen—these are the attention getters. However, it is really the software—the planned, step-by-step set of instructions required to turn data into information—that makes a computer useful.

Generally speaking, software can be categorized as systems software or applications software. Chapter 2 dealt with systems software. This chapter covers **applications software,** software that users *apply* to real-world tasks. It can be used to solve a particular problem or to perform a particular task—to keep track of store inventory, design a car engine, draft the minutes of the PTA meeting, or play a game of solitaire. We will discuss both software that individuals use to accomplish personal tasks and software that is used to run businesses.

Applications Software

Applications software may be either custom or packaged. Many large organizations pay **computer programmers**—people who design, write, test, and implement software—to write **custom software,** software that is specifically tailored to their needs. Custom software for the tasks of a large organization may be extremely complex and take a lot of time—possibly years—to write.

The average person is most likely to deal with software for personal computers, called **packaged software** or **commercial software.** This software is literally packaged in a container of some sort, usually a box or folder, and is sold in stores or through catalogs or Web sites. Some commercial software is available for downloading (for a fee, of course) on the Internet. Packaged software for personal computers often comes in a box that is as colorful as that of a board game. Inside the box you will find one or more CDs or DVDs holding the software and, usually, an instruction manual, also referred to as documentation (Figure 3-1). Note, however, that some packaged software has little written **documentation;** the information about the software is mostly stored on CD or DVD with the software for handy future reference. Documentation for software downloaded on the Internet is usually contained in an accompanying file.

Large organizations also purchase and use an assortment of commercial software. They may buy some of the same software that you might buy, although they probably buy it from a distributor or directly from the publisher. They also are likely to consider purchasing software for major applications such as payroll and personnel management. This software is purchased directly from the software publisher for tens, or even hundreds, of thousands of dollars. The factors that determine whether an organization buys or custom-makes its software will be discussed in Chapter 15, "Systems Analysis and Design: The Big Picture."

Packaged software.

Each of the colorful software packages shown here includes one or more disks containing the software and at least a minimal instruction manual, or documentation, describing how to use the software.

Although it is not possible to tell you how to use a specific software package, we can say, in general, that you begin by installing the software on your computer. This usually involves inserting the CD-ROM or DVD-ROM into the drive, then following the instructions that appear on your screen. Complex packages, such as a full-featured database system or word processor, often provide numerous installation options for advanced users. Luckily, there is almost always a standard installation that the beginner can choose. During installation the setup process copies some or all of the new software to the hard disk drive. Some software may require the CD-ROM to be in the drive whenever the software is used. Once the software is installed, you can click its icon, its picture image on the screen, or type an instruction—command—to get the program started.

A great assortment of software is available to help you with a variety of tasks—writing papers, preparing budgets, storing and retrieving information, drawing graphs, playing games, and much more. This wonderful array of software is what makes computers so useful.

Most personal computer software is designed to be **user-friendly.** The term "user-friendly" has become a cliché, but it still conveys meaning. It usually means that the software is supposed to be easy—perhaps even intuitive—for a beginner to use or that the software can be used with a minimum of training and documentation.

But What Would I Use It For?

New computer owners soon discover a little secret: The box is only the beginning. Although they may have agonized for months over their hardware choice, they are often uncertain as to how to proceed when purchasing software. The most common pattern for a new user is to start out with some standard software packages, such as word processing and other basic applications, that are preinstalled by the computer manufacturer. Later, this base may be expanded as the user becomes aware of what software is available. The needs of different people will be met with different software. Here are two real-life scenarios.

Kristin Bjornson is a private detective who, using a computer, runs her business from her home. Her computer came with word processing software plus some CD-ROMs holding an encyclopedia, a "family doctor" reference program, and several

Tax preparation software.

This software simplifies preparation of tax returns.

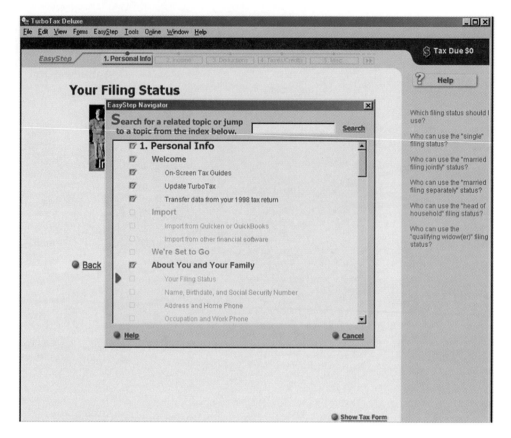

games. Kristin's primary interest in the software was focused on business information and certain public files on the Internet. She selected an Internet service provider and used software supplied by the provider. She also prepared her income taxes using a question-and-answer tax preparation program (Figure 3-2). Over the next year, Kristin purchased other software that was unrelated to business applications: software to help her plan and record her aerobic workouts, a program to help her son study for the Scholastic Assessment Tests, and a combination game/book called *Happy and Max* for her six-year-old.

As a second example, consider Max Prentiss, whose first job as an apprentice carpenter did not involve computers. But Max made a computer one of his first acquisitions. He subsequently purchased various software: software containing an atlas and quotations; an on-screen version of The Far Side calendar; and an all-in-one package that included software for a personal phone book, home budget planning, and home repair. But he eventually focused on the large *National Geographic* map images available on CD-ROM (Figure 3-3).

The point of these stories is that different people want different software applications. You have only to stroll through a few aisles of software racks to appreciate the variety of software available. Whether you want to learn to type, tour a museum, build a deck, or perhaps try such crazy-but-real titles as *Internet for Cats* or the sci-fi thriller called *I Have No Mouth, and I Must Scream,* someone offers the software.

ACQUIRING SOFTWARE   Sometimes software is free. Software is called **freeware** if its author chooses to provide it free to all. However, freeware is copyrighted—that is, the author retains legal ownership and may place restrictions on its use. Uncopyrighted software, called **public domain software,** may be used, or even altered, without restriction. Software developed by universities and research institutions using government grants is usually in the public domain.

Open-source software is a variation of freeware. A freeware program is normally distributed in a machine-readable format that is unreadable by humans. You can

▲ **FIGURE 3-3**

Images from CD-ROM software.

These images are from a *National Geographic* CD-ROM of maps that have been featured in the magazine.

use it, but even if you know how to write programs, you can't make changes to it. The developers of open-source software, however, make the source code available, which means that programmers can understand how it works and modify it. More and more commercial-quality software is being made available under the open-source concept, especially software designed to run under the Linux operating system.

Shareware is a category of software that is often confused with freeware. Like freeware, it is freely distributed, but only for a trial period. The understanding is that if you like it enough to continue using it, you will pay a nominal fee to register it with the author. Many authors add incentives such as free documentation, support, and/or updates to encourage people to register.

The software that people use most often, packaged software such as word processing or spreadsheet software, sometimes called *commercial software,* is probably both copyrighted and at least somewhat costly. This kind of software must not be copied without permission from the manufacturer. In fact, software manufacturers call making illegal copies of commercial software **software piracy** and pursue miscreants to the full extent of the law.

What is the best way to purchase commercial software? The small retail software store has all but disappeared because the price of software has declined too much to provide an acceptable profit margin. So software has moved to the warehouse stores and to mail-order houses, each with thousands of software titles. The high sales volume makes up for slim per-unit profits. From the individual consumer's point of view, the lower prices and convenient one-stop shopping are significant advantages. However, the consumer does pay a price: Warehouse stores and mail-order houses are seldom able to provide the assistance that the smaller retail stores formerly provided. College students have another option—their college bookstore. In order to encourage students to become familiar with their products, many software publishers make their most popular products available through college bookstores at deep discounts.

An organization, in contrast to individual users, must take a different approach in acquiring software. Most organizations—such as businesses, governments, and nonprofit agencies—have computers, and their users, of course, need software. Although software publishers' policies vary, several options are usually available. If an organization is going to install the software on individual computers, it might be able to arrange a volume discount for the required number of packages. Alternatively, the organization could purchase a **site license,** which allows the software to be installed either on all its computers or on a specific number of computers, depending on the license terms. The customer agrees to keep track of who uses the software and takes responsibility for copying and distributing the software and manuals to its own per-

---

FOCUS ON ETHICS   Any Guarantees?

Most software packages are covered by "shrink-wrap licenses." This means that consumers can't read the terms of the warranty or guarantee until after the product is purchased and opened, or even until after the software is installed—and many vendors will not accept returns of opened software. These licenses contain language shielding the vendor from all claims other than those arising from physical defects in the CD. Recently, Congress and the courts have moved to make these licenses more enforceable and to allow software manufacturers the right to change the terms of the license after purchase.

Read the shrink-wrap license that came with some software that you or your school purchased. What remedies does the license give you if the product doesn't work or if it damages your computer? Now read the warranty from an inexpensive electronic device, say a VCR, CD player, or TV. What similarities and differences do you see?

Software corporations argue that they need the protective terms of the shrink-wrap licenses to shield them from frivolous lawsuits. Consumer advocates assert that consumers need recourse if the product doesn't work as advertised. How would you balance these competing claims?

sonnel. Incidentally, if you work for a large corporation, check with your employer before you buy a copy of the expensive software you use at the office. Under some license agreements, employees are allowed to use the same software at home.

Organizations with local area networks often install a network version of widely used software such as word processing on the network's server computer. Thus the software is available to users connected to the network without the necessity of installing the software on each user's computer. In this case the license fee may be based on the total number of users on the network or may provide for a maximum number of concurrent users.

Another software movement is gaining in popularity: **electronic software distribution.** Never mind the trip to the store. You can get freeware, shareware, and even commercial software from the Internet. One common scenario is to download copyrighted software free from the manufacturer for a trial period. When you use the software, you will be encouraged to go back online and register (pay with a credit card); unregistered software often disables itself automatically after a given time period, such as 21 days. In addition, many online vendors offer a wide range of popular business and consumer software for download, with payment by a secure method. In the not-so-distant future, users will not need to purchase software but will be able merely to download it temporarily from a vendor via the Internet for a per-use rental fee.

Application service providers provide an alternative method of delivering applications via the Internet. An **application service provider (ASP)** is a company that sets up and maintains application software on its own systems and makes the software available to its customers over the Internet. By using an ASP for its applications, a business can avoid the expenses involved in installing and maintaining its own applications. According to some estimates, the cost of renting a major enterprisewide application such as a human resources package can be as much as 30% less than the cost of buying, deploying, and supporting it in-house.

Disney Magic
New users sometimes worry that a computer will be used mostly for games. Surveys show that about 70 percent of personal computer users happily admit that they play games—at least a little—almost daily. In fact, entertainment is a perfectly valid use of a personal computer in the home. But the entertainment need not be limited to games. There are many types of entertainment packages.

Here is an example: Disney's *Magic Artist* software lets young children have fun coloring Disney images—and learn a bit at the same time. For instance, children can use a mouse to select images and apply different tools—such as pen, paintbrush, chalk, and spray paint—to color the image. They can also resize, flip, and rotate images. They can combine images with backgrounds and even, if they wish, add music.

► SOME TASK-ORIENTED SOFTWARE

Most users, whether at home or in business, are drawn to task-oriented software, sometimes called *productivity software*, that can make their work faster and their lives easier. The major categories of task-oriented software are word processing (including desktop publishing), spreadsheets, database management, graphics, and communications. Office suites and integrated packages offer some combination of these categories in a single package. A brief description of each category follows. Later chapters will discuss each category in detail.

Word Processing/Desktop Publishing

Word processing is the most widely used personal computer software. Business people use word processing for memos, reports, correspondence, minutes of meetings, and anything else that someone can think of to type. Users in a home environment type term papers, letters, journals, movie logs, and much more. Word processing software lets you create, edit, format, store, and print text and graphics in one document. Since you can store on disk the memo or document you typed, you can retrieve it another time, change it, reprint it, or do whatever you like with it. Unchanged parts of the stored document do not need to be retyped; the whole revised document can be reprinted as if new.

As the number of features in word processing packages has grown, word processing has crossed the border into desktop publishing territory. **Desktop publishing** packages are usually better than word processing packages at meeting high-level publishing needs, especially when it comes to typesetting and color reproduction.

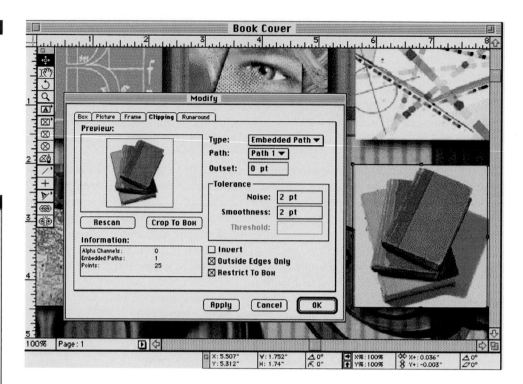

▶ **F I G U R E 3-4**

Desktop publishing.
Desktop publishing packages meet high-level publishing needs related to typesetting and color reproduction.

The Killer App

In computing, the term "killer app," short for "killer application," refers to an application that is so compelling that everyone must have the underlying technology so that they can use the application. The first electronic spreadsheet program, named VisiCalc was the first killer app for the microcomputer. Almost immediately, what had been viewed as a toy was now a must-have for everyone whose job required manipulating numbers. By one estimate in 1981, over one half of all Apple IIs sold between 1979 and 1981 were purchased solely to run VisiCalc.

One other example of a killer app is the combination of the browser with the World Wide Web. Until these appeared in the early 1990s, Internet use was mostly limited to scientists, researchers, and computer geeks using text-based communications. Almost everyone is familiar with what has happened with the Internet since then!

Many magazines and newspapers today rely heavily on desktop publishing software (Figure 3-4). Businesses use it to produce professional-looking newsletters, reports, and brochures—both to improve internal communication and to make a better impression on the outside world.

Electronic Spreadsheets

Spreadsheets, made up of columns and rows of numbers, have been used as business tools for centuries (Figure 3-5). A manual spreadsheet can be tedious to prepare, and when there are changes, a considerable amount of calculation may need to be redone. An **electronic spreadsheet** is still a spreadsheet, but the computer does the work. In particular, spreadsheet software automatically recalculates the results when a number is changed. For example, if one chore of a spreadsheet is to calculate distance based on rate and time, a change in the rate would automatically cause a new calculation so that the distance would change too. This capability lets business people try different combinations of numbers and obtain the results quickly. The ability to ask, **"What if . . . ?"** and then immediately see the results on the computer before actually committing resources helps business people make better, faster decisions.

What about spreadsheet software for the user at home? The ability to enter combinations of numbers in a meaningful way—such as different combinations of down payments and interest rates for the purchase of a home—gives users a financial view that they could not readily produce on their own. Users at home employ spreadsheets for everything from preparing budgets to figuring out whether to take a new job to tracking their progress at the gym.

Database Management

Software used for **database management**—the management of a collection of interrelated facts—handles data in several ways. The software can store data, update it, manipulate it, retrieve it, report it in a variety of views, and print it in as many forms.

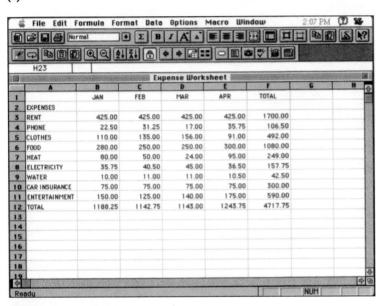

EXPENSES	JANUARY	FEBRUARY	MARCH	APRIL	TOTAL
RENT	425.00	425.00	425.00	425.00	1700.00
PHONE	22.50	31.25	17.00	35.75	106.50
CLOTHES	110.00	135.00	156.00	91.00	492.00
FOOD	280.00	250.00	250.00	300.00	1080.00
HEAT	80.00	50.00	24.00	95.00	249.00
ELECTRICITY	35.75	40.50	45.00	36.50	157.75
WATER	10.00	11.00	11.00	10.50	42.50
CAR INSURANCE	75.00	75.00	75.00	75.00	300.00
ENTERTAINMENT	150.00	125.00	140.00	175.00	590.00
TOTAL	1188.25	1142.75	1143.00	1243.75	4717.75

(a)

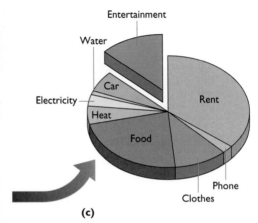

(c)

(b)

▲ **F I G U R E 3-5**

A simple expense spreadsheet.

(a) This paper-and-pencil expense sheet is a typical spreadsheet of rows and columns. You have to do the calculations to fill in the totals. (b) This screen shows the same information on a computer spreadsheet program, which does the calculations for you. (c) The spreadsheet program can also present the expenses graphically in the form of a pie chart.

By the time the data is in the reporting stage—given to a user in a useful form—it has become information. A concert promoter, for example, can store and change data about upcoming concert dates, seating, ticket prices, and sales. After this is done, the promoter can use the software to retrieve information, such as the number of tickets sold in each price range or the percentage of tickets sold on the day of the concert.

Database software can be useful for anyone who must keep track of a large number of related facts. Consider crime detection, which involves a process of elimination—a tedious task. Tedious work, however, is often the kind the computer does best. Once data is entered into a database, searching by computer is possible. Consider these examples: Which criminals use a particular mode of operation? Which criminals are associates of this suspect? Does license plate number AXB221 refer to a stolen car? One particularly successful crime detection database applica-

▶ **FIGURE** 3-6

Crime Detection.

Fingerprint-matching systems can match crime-scene fingerprints with computer-stored fingerprints.

▶ **FIGURE** 3-7

Presentations.

Presentation graphics packages allow business people to easily develop professional-looking "slide show" presentations containing high-quality graphics, audio, and video.

tion is a fingerprint-matching system, which can match crime scene fingerprints with computer-stored fingerprints (Figure 3-6).

Home users can apply database software to any situation in which they want to retrieve stored data in a variety of ways. For example, one hobbyist stores data about her coin collection. She can retrieve information from the coin database by country, date, value, or size. Another user, an amateur genealogist, stores data on the lives and relationships of hundreds of ancestors. He can easily retrieve biographical data by branch of the family tree, country of birth, or any other criterion.

Graphics

It might seem unnecessary to show **graphics** to business people when standard computer printouts of numbers are readily available. However, graphs, maps, and charts can help people compare data, spot trends more easily, and make decisions more quickly. In addition, visual information is usually more compelling than a page of numbers. **Presentation graphics** packages allow business people to easily develop professional-looking "slide show" presentations containing high-quality graphics, audio, and video (Figure 3-7). A salesperson attempting to sell a new piece of machinery to a factory manager might list the features of the product using text displays, show cost/benefit projections on charts, include a video clip of the product in operation, and present audio/video testimonials from satisfied customers.

The most pleasing use of graphics software is the work produced by **graphic artists,** people who have both artistic ability and the skills to use sophisticated graphics software to express their ideas. Artists use software as a tool of their craft to produce stunning computer art.

Communications

From the viewpoint of an individual with a personal computer at home, **communications** means—in simple terms—that he or she can hook the computer up to a phone line and communicate with the computer at the office, access data stored in another computer in another location, or send a message to a friend or family member. The most likely way for such a user to connect to others is via the Internet. A user needs software called a **browser** to access Web sites and other parts of the Internet (Figure 3-8). A browser may be a stand-alone software package or it may be

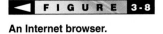

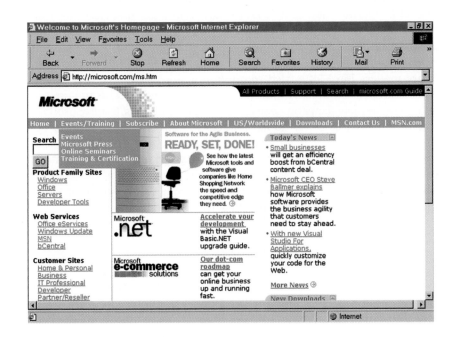

◄ **F I G U R E 3-8**

An Internet browser.

This screen shows Microsoft's home page displayed using Microsoft's Internet Explorer browser.

included as part of other software offerings. Internet access is described in more detail in subsequent chapters.

Although the Internet is heavily used by both individuals and businesses, organizations—mostly business, government, and academic organizations—were major users of communications software long before the Internet was in the mainstream. Consider weather forecasting. Some businesses, such as agriculture, amusement parks, and ski areas, are so dependent on the weather that they need constantly updated information. Various services offer analysis of live weather data, including air pressure, fog, rain, and wind direction and speed.

For a totally different type of communications application, consider the stock exchange. Stock portfolios can be managed by software that takes quotations over communication lines directly from established market monitors such as Dow Jones. The software keeps records and offers quick and accurate investment advice. And, of course, the stock exchange itself is a veritable beehive of computers, all communicating with one another and with remote computers that can provide current information.

Office Suites

Since most people need to use the kinds of task-oriented software just described, some choose to buy a **suite**—a group of basic software applications designed to work together. The phrase "work together" is the key. If you buy word processing software from one manufacturer and a spreadsheet package from another, you may run into difficulties transferring data from one to the other. Using suite software, however, means that you can easily build a spreadsheet and then move it into a report you are preparing using word processing. Another advantage of suites is that the various applications have the same "look and feel"—the same buttons, menus, and overall appearance. Once you learn one application, the rest are easy. Finally, the cost of a suite is much less than the combined costs of the individual packages.

Many inexpensive personal computers come with an **integrated application** that combines basic word processing, spreadsheet, and graphics capabilities in a single program. An integrated program is easier to learn and use than a suite, but even moderately sophisticated users may quickly outgrow its limitations. The next step up, whether you are a professional working from home, a small business owner, or just a hobbyist, includes suites containing more sophisticated versions of these applications and additional software types, such as database management and Web page design. In fact, one of the most common office applications of suites is mail merge, in which certain names and addresses from a database are used on letters prepared by using word processing. Two or three software makers have dominated the suite market for years and continue to offer software upgrades—newer, presumably better versions.

Software makers have long tried to outdo one another by offering software with myriad seldom-used features. However, they have recently begun to take a different approach. Vendors now focus on ease of use and on throwing in nifty programs such as personal time organizers, to-do list makers, e-mail programs, and—best of all—access to the Internet.

The do-everything programs, of course, need significant amounts of memory and also require a lot of disk space, so be sure that the requirements listed on the software box fit your hardware. The good news, however, is that competition continues to heat up the price wars, causing the prices of these packages to fall.

▶ BUSINESS SOFTWARE

We have already mentioned that many large organizations often hire their own programmers to write custom software. The Boeing Company, for example, will not find software to plan the electrical wiring of an airplane among off-the-rack packages. However, not all of a company's software need be custom-made. Many companies use standard packages for standard tasks such as payroll and accounts receivable. Furthermore, some software vendors specialize in a certain "vertical" slice of the business community, serving similar customers such as plumbers or accountants.

Vertical Market Software

Software that is written especially for a particular type of business, such as a dentist's office or a drugstore, is called **vertical market software.** This user-oriented software usually presents options with a series of easy-to-follow screens that minimize the training needed. Often, the vendor includes the software as part of a complete package that also includes hardware, installation, training, and support. This all-in-one approach appeals to business owners who often have limited computer expertise.

An auto repair shop is a good example of a business that can make use of vertical market software. Designed in conjunction with people who understand the auto repair business, the comprehensive software for an auto shop can prepare work orders, process sales transactions, produce invoices, evaluate sales and profits, track parts inventories, print reorder reports, and update the customer mailing list.

Software for Workgroups

If you work on a project with a group of people, it is likely that you will use software especially made for that scenario. **Groupware,** also called **collaborative software,** can be defined generally as any kind of software that lets a group of people share information or track information together. Using that general definition, some people might say that electronic mail is a form of groupware. But simply sending data back and forth by e-mail has inherent limitations for collaboration,

---

GETTING PRACTICAL | Computer User Groups

You have started your own business and even have a computer to keep track of things. The knowledge you have from your computer classes sustains you, but you wish you had some ongoing source for help and even enrichment. Unfortunately, the very people who could be helped the most—new users—often don't even know that user groups exist. User groups are run by volunteers with minimum funds and thus have little money to advertise.

There are hundreds of user groups; some focus on a particular type of computer, such as the Apple Macintosh, or a particular software package, such as *Microsoft Excel,*

and some cover all aspects of computing. Typically, a group meets once a month to share ideas and knowledge and also publishes a newsletter. In addition, many general computing groups have subgroups called special interest groups (SIGs) that focus on a single topic, such as graphics or a particular software package.

Some people have the impression that user groups are for the die-hard techie, but anyone is welcome to join. Just show up at a meeting, pay your (nominal) dues, and you belong. Interested? You can probably find out about local user groups at local computer stores or the library.

the most obvious being confusion if there are more than two group members. To work together effectively on a project, the data being used must be in a central place that can be accessed and changed by anyone working on the project. That central place is a database, or databases, on disk. Having the data in just one place eliminates the old problem of separate and possibly different versions of the same project.

A popular groupware package called *Notes* combines electronic mail, networking, scheduling, and database technology (Figure 3-9). Using such groupware, business people can work with one another and share knowledge or expertise unbounded by factors such as distance or time zone differences. *Notes* can be installed on all computers on the network.

Groupware is most often used by a team for a specific project. A classic example is a bid prepared by Price Waterhouse, an accounting firm, for a consulting contract. They had just a few days to put together a complex proposal, and the four people who needed to write it were in three different states. They were able to work together using their computers and *Notes,* which permitted a four-way dialog on-screen. They also extracted key components of the proposal from existing company databases, including the résumés of company experts, and borrowed passages from similar successful proposals.

Getting Software Help at Work: The Information Center

More often than not, a worker in an office has a computer on his or her desk. It is just a matter of time until that user needs help. If personal computer users compared

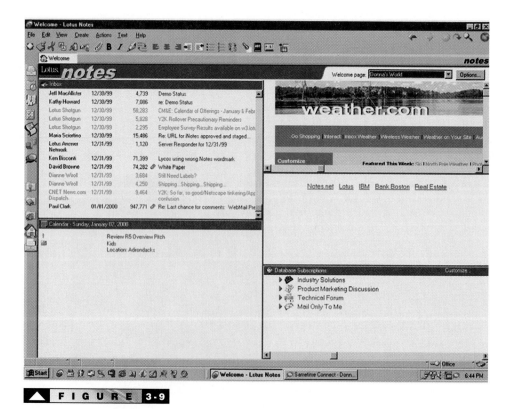

▲ **F I G U R E 3-9**

Notes.

These screens are from a groupware package called *Notes.* Groupware lets workers use the computer to collaborate on a project.

notes, they would probably find that their experiences are similar. The experience of budget analyst Manuela Lopez is typical. She was given her own personal computer so that she could analyze financial data. She learned to use a popular spreadsheet program. She soon thought about branching out with other software products. She wanted a statistics software package but was not sure which one was appropriate or how to get it. She saw that a colleague was using a database management program but had no idea how to use it herself. Most of all, Manuela believed that her productivity would increase significantly if she knew how to use the software to access certain data in the corporate data files.

The company **information center,** often called simply the **help desk,** is one solution to these kinds of needs. Although no two centers are alike, all information centers are devoted exclusively to giving users service. Information center staff usually offer help with software selection, software training, and, if appropriate, access to corporate computer systems. They may also perform software and hardware installation and updating, as well as troubleshooting services when problems arise.

Software for a Small Business

Suppose that, as a fledgling entrepreneur with some computer savvy, your ambition is to be as competitive as one personal computer will let you be. You are not alone. Two interesting statistics are that more than half of U.S. workers would like to own their own businesses and that the number of home-office workers is increasing by 5 percent a year. Savvy entrepreneurs realize that a computer is a major asset in running the business, even at the very start. The software industry has responded to this need with various packages that come under the generic heading of **small office/home office,** or **SOHO** for short (Figure 3-10).

You know that you cannot afford expensive software, but you also know that there is an abundance of moderately priced software that can enhance all aspects of your business. A look through any store display of software packages will reveal many that are aimed at small businesses, from marketing strategy software to software for handling mailing lists.

The following basic list is presented according to business functions—things that you will want to be able to do. The computer can help.

● **Accounting.** Totaling the bottom line must be the number one priority for any business. If you are truly on your own or have just one or two employees, you may

Working at Home.
The number of home-office workers is increasing by 5 percent a year. The software industry has responded with various packages that come under the generic heading of small office/home office, or SOHO for short.

be able to get by with simple spreadsheet software to work up a ledger and balance sheet and generate basic invoices and payroll worksheets. Larger operations can consider a complete accounting package, which produces profit-and-loss statements, balance sheets, cash flow reports, and tax summaries. Most packages will also write and print checks, and some have payroll capability.

- **Writing and advertising.** Word processing is an obvious choice because you will need to write memos and the like. Desktop publishing can be a real boon to a small business, letting you design and produce advertisements, flyers, and even your own letterhead stationery, business forms, and business cards. A big advantage of publishing your own advertisements or flyers is that you can print small quantities and start anew as your business evolves. Finally, you may think it worthwhile to publish your own newsletter for customers.

- **Customer service.** Customer service is a byword throughout the business world, but the personal touch is especially important in a small business. Database software can be useful here. Suppose, for example, that you run a pet-grooming service. You surely want to keep track of each customer by address and so forth for billing and advertising purposes. But this is just the beginning. Why not store data about each pet too? Think how impressed the customer on the phone will be when you recall that Sadie is a standard poodle, seven years old, and that it is time for her to have her booster shots.

- **Keeping up and making contacts.** Even if you have only one computer, you can still be networked to the outside world. Business connections are available in many forms from dozens of sites on the Internet.

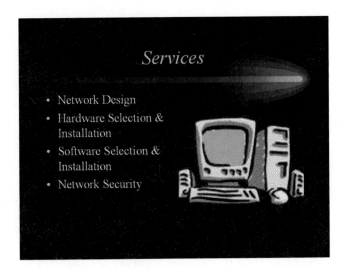

▲ **FIGURE 3-11**

A computer-produced presentation.

Shown here are just two of the screens that Carol Tracy uses when making a presentation about her business. She was able to prepare them quickly using graphics software (Microsoft PowerPoint). She can show the screens directly with a projector connected to a computer or have them converted to conventional slides or transparencies.

- **Making sales pitches.** If your business depends on pitching your product or service in some formal way, presentation software can help you create colorful demonstrations that are the equivalent of an electronic slide show. Presentation software is designed for regular people, not artists, so putting together a slick sequence of text and graphics is remarkably simple (Figure 3-11).

Finally, consider an all-in-one software package that is specifically designed to help you get your home office organized. This is a variation on the suites described earlier but is geared specifically to the small business. If you are on your own, you need the organizational skills of a secretary, the research skills of a librarian, the accounting skills of a bookkeeper, and the experience of someone who has done it before. Comprehensive SOHO packages address all these needs, providing a searchable library of resources, a legal guide, and a tax guide. The packages also include collections of business documents for every situation, from asset depreciation to press releases. Such packages also typically offer links to useful business and government sites on the Internet.

► ETHICS AND APPLICATION SOFTWARE

The most sizzling ethics issue related to software is the acquisition and use of illegal software copies, the software piracy that we mentioned earlier. Lamentations by both business and the computer industry are so persistent and so loud that we are devoting a separate section to this issue.

Have you ever copied a friend's music CD or tape onto your own blank tape? Many people do so without much thought. It is also possible to photocopy a book. Both acts are clearly illegal, but there is much more fuss over illegal software copying than over copying music or books. Why is this? Well, to begin with, few of us are likely to undertake the laborious task of reproducing a Stephen King novel on a copy machine. The other part of the issue is money. A pirated copy of a top 20 CD will set the recording company—and the artist—back just a few dollars. But pirated software may be valued at hundreds of dollars. The problem of stolen software has grown right along with the personal computer industry.

Software publishers have traditionally turned a blind eye toward individual pirating, since prosecution would be time-consuming and expensive, and most of those making illegal copies wouldn't have purchased the software anyway. However, a number of recent cases have involved pirating within small and medium-sized businesses, often with the knowledge and participation of management. In the typical scenario, a company might buy two or three legitimate copies of a software package, then make and distribute copies to dozens, or even hundreds, of employees. This type of piracy costs the software industry significant amounts of money. Counterfeiting is another type of piracy that results in large financial losses. Large numbers of CD-ROMs or DVD-ROMs are copied and packaged to resemble the real thing, then sold in flea markets or small stores for much less than the regular price. While much of this type of piracy occurs overseas, some copies find their way into U.S. and European markets. Two software industry organizations, the Business Software Alliance and the Software & Information Industry Association, actively pursue and prosecute software pirates worldwide.

OK If I Copy That Software?

Consider this incident. Bill Huston got his computer education at a local community college. One of his courses taught him how to use software on personal computers. He had access to a great variety of copyrighted software in the college computer lab. After graduating, he got a job at a local museum, where he used database software on a personal computer to catalog museum wares. He also had his own computer at home.

One day Bill stopped back at the college and ran into a former instructor. After greetings were exchanged, she asked him why he had happened to drop by. "Oh," he said, "I just came by to make some copies of software." He wasn't kidding. Neither was the instructor, who, after she caught her breath, replied, "You can't do that. It's illegal." Bill was miffed, saying, "But I can't afford it!" The instructor immediately alerted the computer lab. As a result of this encounter, the staff strengthened policies on software use and increased the vigilance of lab personnel. In effect, schools must protect themselves from people who lack ethics or are unaware of the law.

There are many people like Bill. He did not think in terms of stealing anything; he just wanted to make copies for himself. But as the software industry is quick to point out, unauthorized copying is stealing because the software makers do not get the revenues to which they are entitled. If Bill had used illegally copied software at his place of work, his employer could have been at risk for litigation.

Why Those Extra Copies?

Copying software is not always a dirty trick—there are lots of legitimate reasons for copying. To begin with, after paying several hundred dollars for a piece of software, you will definitely want to make a backup copy in case of disk failure or accident. You probably want to copy the program onto a hard disk and use it, more conveniently, from there. Software publishers have no trouble with these types of copying. But thousands of computer users copy software for another reason: to get the program without paying for it. This is clearly unethical and illegal.

► COMPUTERS AND PEOPLE

These first few chapters have described hardware, software, and data, but the most important element in a computer system is people. Anyone who is nervous about a takeover by computers will be relieved to know that computers will never amount to much without people—the people who help to make the system work and the people for whom the work is done.

Computers and You, the User

As we noted earlier, computer users have come to be called just *users,* a nickname that has persisted for years. Whereas once computer users were an elite breed—highly educated scientists, research-and-development engineers, government planners—today the population of users has broadened considerably. This expansion is due partly to user-friendly software for both work and personal use and partly to the availability of small, low-cost personal computers. There is every likelihood that all of us will be computer users, even if our levels of sophistication vary.

Computer People

Many organizations have a department called **Management Information Systems (MIS)** or **Computer Information Systems (CIS), Computing Services, Information Services,** or **Information Technology (IT).** Whatever it is called, this department is made up of the people who are responsible for the organization's computer resources. Large organizations, such as universities, government agencies, and corporations, keep much of the institution's data in computer files: research data, engineering drawings, marketing strategy, student records, accounts receivable, accounts payable, sales figures, manufacturing specifications, transportation plans, and so forth. The people who maintain the data are the same people who provide service to the users: the computer professionals. Let us touch on the essential personnel required to run large computer systems.

Data entry operators prepare data for processing, usually by keying it in a machine-readable format. **Computer operators** monitor the computer systems, review procedures, keep peripheral equipment running, and make backup copies of data. **Librarians** catalog the processed disks and tapes and keep them secure.

Computer programmers, as we noted earlier, design, write, test, implement, and maintain the programs that process data on the computer system; they also maintain and update the programs. **Systems analysts** are knowledgeable in the programming area but have broader responsibilities. They plan and design entire computer systems, not just individual programs. Systems analysts maintain a working relationship with both programmers and the users in the organization. The analysts work closely with the users to plan new systems that will meet the users' needs. A professional called a **network manager,** implements and maintains the organization's network(s). The department manager, often called the **chief information officer (CIO),** must understand more than just computer technology. This person must understand the goals and operations of the entire organization and be able to make strategic decisions.

These are some standard jobs and standard titles. There are many others, most notably those associated with creation and maintenance of Internet sites; these will be discussed in detail in the Internet chapters.

▲

These opening chapters have painted a picture with a broad brush. Now it is time to get down to details. The next chapters describe hardware in more detail.

CHAPTER REVIEW

► Summary and Key Terms

- Software is the planned, step-by-step set of instructions required to turn data into information. **Applications software** can be used to solve a particular problem or to perform a particular task. Applications software may be either custom-designed or packaged.

- **Computer programmers** are people who design, write, test, and implement software. Organizations may pay computer programmers to write **custom software,** software that is specifically tailored to their needs.

- **Packaged software,** also called **commercial software,** is packaged in a container of some sort, usually a box or folder, and is sold in stores or catalogs. Inside the box is one or more disks holding the software and perhaps an instruction manual, also referred to as **documentation.**

- The term **user-friendly** means that the software is supposed to be easy for a beginner to use or that the software can be used with a minimum of training.

- **Freeware** is software for which there is no fee. **Public domain software** is uncopyrighted and therefore may be used or altered without restriction.

- **Open-source software** is freely distributed in a format that allows programmers to make changes to it.

- **Shareware** is freely distributed; the user is expected to register and pay a nominal fee to use it past a free trial period.

- Commercial software is copyrighted, costs money, and must not be copied without permission from the manufacturer. Making illegal copies of commercial software is called **software piracy** and is punishable under the law.

- A **site license** permits an organization, for a fee, to distribute copies of a software product to its employees. **Electronic software distribution** means that a user can pay to download the software—move it from another computer to the user's computer.

- An **application service provider (ASP)** is a company that sets up and maintains applications software on its own systems and makes the software available for its customers to use over the Internet.

- **Word processing** software lets you create, edit, format, store, and print text and graphics in one document. It is those three words in the middle—edit, format, and store—that reveal the difference between word processing and plain typing. **Desktop publishing** packages meet high-level publishing needs to produce professional-looking newsletters, reports, and brochures.

- An **electronic spreadsheet,** made up of columns and rows of numbers, automatically recalculates the results when a number is changed. This capability lets business people try different combinations of **"what if . . ."** numbers and obtain the results quickly.

- **Database management** software manages a collection of interrelated facts. The software can store data, update it, manipulate it, retrieve it, report it in a variety of views, and print it in as many forms.

- **Graphics** software allows users to manipulate images. **Presentation graphics** software can produce graphs, maps, and charts and can help people compare data, spot trends more easily, and make decisions more quickly. **Graphic artists** use graphics software to express their ideas visually.

- **Communications** software allows computers to communicate with each other via phone lines or other means. A **browser** is software that is used to access the Internet.

- A **suite** is a group of basic software designed to work together. A typical suite application is mail merge, in which certain names and addresses from a database are applied to letters prepared using word processing. An **integrated application** combines basic word processing, spreadsheet, and graphics capabilities in a single program.

- Software that is written especially for a particular type of business is called **vertical market software.**

- **Groupware,** also called **collaborative software,** is any kind of software that lets a group of people share information or track information together.

- The company **information center,** or **help desk,** is devoted to giving users help with software selection, software training, and, if appropriate, access to corporate computer systems.

- Software designed for small businesses is termed **SOHO,** for **small office/home office.**

- Many organizations have a department called **Management Information Systems (MIS), Computer Information Systems (CIS), Computing Services, Information Services,** or **Information Technology (IT).** This department is made up of the people who are responsible for the organization's computer resources.

- **Data entry operators** prepare data for processing, usually by keying it in a machine-readable format. **Computer operators** monitor the computer systems, review procedures, and keep peripheral equipment running. **Librarians** catalog the processed disks and tapes and keep them secure. Computer programmers design, write, test, and implement the programs that process data on the computer system; they also maintain and update the programs.

- **Systems analysts** are knowledgeable in the programming area but have broader responsibilities; they plan and design not just individual programs but entire computer systems. A professional called a **network manager** implements and maintains the organization's network(s). The department manager, often called the **chief information officer (CIO),** must understand computer technology as well as the goals and operations of the entire organization.

◀ Critical Thinking Questions

1. Consider these firms. What uses would each have for computer software? Mention as many possibilities as you can.
   a. Security Southwestern Bank, a major regional bank with several branches
   b. Azure Design, a small graphic design company that produces posters, covers, and other artwork
   c. Checkerboard Taxi Service, whose central office manages a fleet of 160 cabs that operate in an urban area
   d. Gillick College, a private college that has automated all student services, including registration, financial aid, and testing

2. If you have, or will have, a computer of your own, how will you get software for it?

3. How does software piracy affect individual users? How does it affect businesses?

4. Several common office applications are often integrated together and sold as a "suite" of products. Based on your major, or intended major, explain how you would professionally use each of the following software applications.
   a. word processing
   b. spreadsheet
   c. database
   d. presentation

5. Although they are not as popular as the task-oriented software typically found in office suites, there are many career-specific applications that are routinely used by professionals. Identify and describe how you would use a software application that is specific to your major or intended major. To find this information you may wish to visit a department computer lab, talk to an instructor who teaches courses in the major, or look at the literature related to the major.

6. Identify the Internet browser that you use most often, and describe the features that you use most frequently. What additional functionality would you like to see added to the browser?

7. Some high-end computer systems now include a DVD-R (DVD "burner"). Even though there is also room for a conventional DVD-ROM ("player"), they are not included. Why do you think that both drives are not sold with the same computer?

8. Business and institutions frequently purchase site licenses for their software applications. What are the advantages and disadvantages of using this method to purchase software? Does your institution use licensed software and is student home use of software applications included in the agreement? (It is on some campuses!)

9. Go to your institution's computing services and interview some of the computer personnel. Describe their title, duties, and educational/ professional preparation.

10. Explain the differences between the operating system software discussed in Chapter 2 and the applications software discussed in this chapter. Include the names of two specific operating systems and the names of two specific software applications.

11. Explain why some software companies will allow you to download their software from the Internet, install it on your computer, and run it for an initial trial period without having to pay for it. As a consumer, what do you think about this method of distributing and selling software?

12. Do any of your instructors use presentation software in their classroom lectures or demonstrations? If they do, then explain why you like or dislike their use of this software.

► STUDENT STUDY GUIDE

Multiple Choice

1. A computer professional who writes and tests software is called a(n)
   a. programmer
   b. systems analyst
   c. librarian
   d. operator

2. Step-by-step instructions that run the computer are called
   a. hardware
   b. CPUs
   c. documents
   d. programs

3. CIS stands for
   a. Computer Internet System
   b. Commercial Internet System
   c. Collaborative Information Systems
   d. Computer Information Systems

4. Which of the following terms is not a description of a type of software?
   a. custom
   b. freeware
   c. download
   d. collaborative

5. The department within an organization that is designed to help users with software is the
   a. browser
   b. SOHO
   c. information center
   d. network

6. Software that is written especially for a single type of business is called
   a. freeware
   b. word processing
   c. shareware
   d. vertical market software

7. Making illegal copies of copyrighted software is called
   a. software piracy
   b. browsing
   c. collaboration
   d. electronic distribution

8. Software that allows the production of professional newsletters and reports is called
   a. database management
   b. groupware
   c. spreadsheet
   d. desktop publishing

9. The type of software that can store, update, manipulate, and retrieve data is called
   a. desktop publishing
   b. spreadsheet
   c. database management
   d. graphics

10. Another name for commercial software is
   a. secondary software
   b. packaged software
   c. systems software
   d. peripheral software

11. CIO stands for
   a. Channeled Input Output
   b. Chief Information Officer
   c. Computer Integrated Operation
   d. Complete Interactive Object

12. Pie charts are typically created by using which of the following?
   a. word processing software
   b. browser software
   c. database software
   d. presentation software

13. A record of personal finances is best maintained by using which of the following?
   a. word processing software
   b. spreadsheet software
   c. database software
   d. presentation software

14. Information about a coin collection is best kept by using which of the following?
   a. word processing software
   b. spreadsheet software
   c. database software
   d. presentation software

15. The type of software used for collaborative efforts is
    a. vertical market software
    b. user-friendly software
    c. groupware software
    d. electronic distribution software

16. Documentation for software applications can be found
    a. on CD-ROM or DVD/ROM
    b. on the Internet
    c. printed in hard copy form
    d. all of the above

17. E-mail means
    a. easy mail
    b. enhanced mail
    c. effortless mail
    d. none of the above

18. A tax preparation program would be an example of
    a. groupware software
    b. communications software
    c. desktop publishing software
    d. none of the above

19. SIG stands for
    a. Special Interest Group
    b. Spreadsheet Integrated Graphics
    c. Symbolic Icon Generator
    d. Standardized Information Generator

20. Which application is **not** typically included in an office suite?
    a. word processor
    b. spreadsheet
    c. antivirus
    d. database

True/False

T F 1. A browser is software that is used to access the Internet.

T F 2. Making illegal copies of copyrighted software is called software piracy.

T F 3. Users must purchase a license to use open-source software.

T F 4. Workers using groupware must be physically in the same office.

T F 5. Software documentation may be printed or may be included as part of the software.

T F 6. The operating system is an example of applications software.

T F 7. The term "user-friendly" refers to a special kind of computer.

T F 8. Custom software is specially tailored to user needs.

T F 9. Word processing is a type of task-oriented software.

T F 10. Desktop publishing software is used to manage numbers in columns and rows.

T F 11. The person who plans new systems is the network manager.

T F 12. Another name for groupware is SOHO.

T F 13. Copyrighted software is in the public domain.

T F 14. An advantage of groupware is the ability to collaborate with others.

T F 15. A site license entitles an individual to use freeware.

T F 16. As long as you paid for a software application, you are allowed to give copies of it to others.

T F 17. A systems analyst designs and maintains computer networks.

T F 18. A help disk is a place where you can call for assistance with hardware and software problems.

T F 19. You are legally required to pay for shareware.

T F 20. Most applications suites can be installed by using just two or three floppy disks.

Fill-In

1. A group of software applications designed to work together is called a(n) _____.

2. What kind of software presents numbers in columns and rows? _____

3. SOHO stands for _____.

4. The term for collaborative software is _____.

5. The general name for software that can be used to solve a problem or perform a task is _____.

6. Software that is written for a particular type of business is called _____.

7. _____ software is freely distributed and can be altered by the programmer.

8. The department within an organization that is dedicated to giving software help is the _____.

9. A(n) _____ is a company that sets up and maintains application software on its own systems and makes the software available to its customers over the Internet.

10. A(n) _____ is a single program that has word processing, spreadsheet, and graphics capabilities.

11. In a computer center, _____ catalog the processed disks and tapes and keep them secure.

12. _____ prepare data for processing, usually by keying it in a machine-readable format.

13. _____ is software for which there is no fee.

14. People who design, write, test, and implement software are called _____.

15. Spreadsheets are helpful because of their ability to answer _____ questions.

16. An instruction manual for using the software is also referred to as _____.

17. VisiCalc was the first highly successful _____.

18. _____ software can produce graphs, maps, and charts.

19. A(n) _____ is software that is used to access the Internet.

20. _____ is used most often by a group of people who need to share information or track information together.

► ANSWERS

Multiple Choice

1. a	6. d	11. b	16. d
2. d	7. a	12. b	17. d
3. d	8. d	13. b	18. d
4. c	9. c	14. c	19. a
5. c	10. b	15. c	20. c

True/False

1. T	6. F	11. F	16. F
2. T	7. F	12. F	17. F
3. F	8. T	13. F	18. T
4. F	9. T	14. T	19. T
5. T	10. F	15. F	20. F

Fill-In

1. suite
2. spreadsheet
3. small office/home office
4. groupware
5. applications software
6. vertical market software
7. open-source
8. information center or help desk
9. application service provider (ASP)
10. integrated program
11. librarians
12. Data entry operators
13. Freeware
14. computer programmers
15. "what if"
16. documentation
17. spreadsheet
18. Presentation graphics
19. browser
20. Groupware

Planet Internet

Web Games

"While it is nice to win a game, losing is a part of life. All squadron members should have a firm grasp of this reality." (From a game clan's "Squadron Code of Conduct".)

You know the stereotype of the computer gamer: a lone, pasty-complexioned, geeky guy, locked in his dimly lit room, obsessively blasting away at imaginary enemies, or wrapped up in a medieval fantasy world of dragons, elves, and aliens. Enter the Internet. He's still pasty, he's still obsessive, and, yes, he's still likely a guy, but he's no longer alone, and he's definitely not confined to his room anymore.

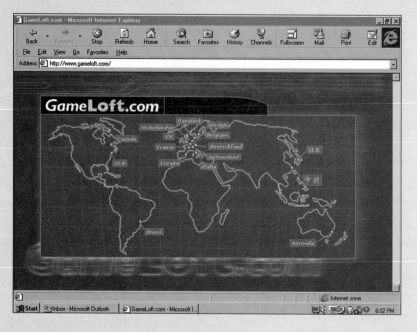

Ever since Doom loosed the First Person Shooter on the Web, online, interactive play with and against other players has become a permanent part of the gaming landscape. Doom's boom has passed, but its wildly successful successor Quake still offers the opportunity to pit your hardened space marine against the talents of thousands of other players scattered around the world.

Most games aren't online yet, but manufacturers such as Sony and Sega are building high-speed Internet connectivity into the next generation of their gaming machines.

What drives gamers (and game developers) onto the Net? One thing is competition. For all the highly-touted artificial intelligence that is carefully programmed into robotics game opponents, nothing yet beats a real human for skillful competition and challenging game play.

Despite their highly competitive (and sometimes downright gory) nature, online games can also foster cooperation and socializing. Many gamers organize into clans, and some games—most notably Starsiege Tribes—have been specifically designed to support team play. To join a clan, players might have to pass an audition of sorts in which they demonstrate proficient game play. Clans have their own membership, bylaws, customs, jargon and leadership; in many ways they mirror (or parody) teams in the real world.

The real-time communication abilities that are built into the latest online games allow textual and spoken dialog among team members, and some games even feature voice-over narration "shoutcasts" to provide blow-by-blow coverage and color commentary. Gamers can personalize their players with "skins" that replace the default appearance of their character with a picture of themselves, or another person, real or imaginary. (In election years players clad in the skins of candidates are not unheard of.)

Although online gamers can be widely separated (Tribes is hosted on servers in the United States, the United Kingdom, Asia, and Russia), the urge to actually meet the members of your own and others' clans has spawned a new trend: the LAN party. For a LAN party all you need is a local area network—preferably a very fast one—a lot of computers, and some dedicated gamers. Everyone sits in the same building at his or her PC, playing against opponents only a few feet, instead of a world, away. One Quake-based LAN party recently drew over a thousand participants, and featured video projection screens and gigabit Internet connections.

Even if you're not drawn to computer gaming, you should be aware that computer entertainment, and games in particular, are one of the driving forces behind computer hardware innovation. After all, you don't think all those folks bought 1000-megahertz machines with those 3D graphics cards exclusively for spreadsheets, did you?

Internet Exercises:

1. **Structured exercise.** Starting with www.prenhall.com/capron, browse some of the online gaming links provided. Find out what computer hardware and software are required to run one of the games you find described there.

2. **Free-form exercise.** Watch someone playing an online game or try to play one yourself. How does this experience compare to playing a game alone on a PC, or at an arcade?

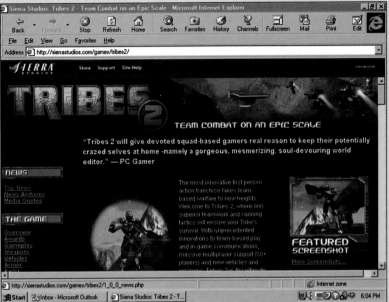

3. **Advanced exercise.** Visit the Web page of one or more game clans. Report on what you find there as if you were an anthropologist. What customs, rules, and jargon did you find? How would you describe the culture of this online gaming community?

The Central Processing Unit:
What Goes on Inside the Computer

The Central Processing Unit:
What Goes on Inside the Computer

CHAPTER 4

LEARNING OBJECTIVES

Identify the components of the central processing unit and explain how they work together and interact with memory

Describe how program instructions are executed by the computer

Explain how data is represented in the computer

Describe how the computer finds instructions and data

Describe the components of a microcomputer system unit's motherboard

List the measures of computer processing speed and explain the approaches that increase speed

Mark Ong, who hoped to be a scriptwriter, planned a double major in creative writing and drama. In the summer before he entered college, he took a job as an intern editorial assistant, where he first used word processing. He decided that it would be helpful to have a personal computer of his own when he went to college in the fall. But he felt unsure of how to make a purchase. In fact, he felt that he did not even know what questions to ask. He discussed this with an office colleague, who casually noted that any computer setup comes with the "standard stuff"—processor, keyboard, mouse, screen, disk drives—and that all Mark had to do was go to a computer store and pick one that fit his price range. Mark was not satisfied with this approach, especially in light of the advertisements he had seen in the local newspaper and in computer magazines.

Most advertisements displayed photos of personal computers, accompanied by cryptic descriptions of the total hardware package. A typical ad was worded this way: Pentium 4, 1.5GHz, 128MB RAM, 512KB cache, 1.44MB diskette drive, 16x DVD-ROM, 40GB hard drive. The price for this particular machine was pretty hefty—over $1800. Mark noticed that the ads for machines with lower numbers—for example, only 1.0GHz—also had lower price tags. Similarly, higher numbers meant higher price tags. Although he did recognize the disk drives, he had no idea what the other items were or why the numbers mattered. Clearly, there was more to a purchasing decision than selecting a system with the "standard stuff."

Mark tore out some of the ads and went to a nearby computer store. After asking a lot of questions, he learned that Pentium III is a microprocessor type, that "GHz" stands for "gigahertz" and is a measurement of the microprocessor's speed, that RAM is the computer's memory, that cache is a kind of handy storage place for frequently used data and software instructions, and that "GB" is an abbreviation for "gigabytes," a measurement of storage size for the hard disk. Most important, Mark learned that the number variations mattered because they were factors in determining the computer's capacity and speed.

Many buyers do select their personal computer system merely on the basis of a sales pitch and price range. Those people could argue, with some justification, that they do not need to know all the computer buzzwords, any more than they need to know the technical details of their television sets or sound systems. They know that they do not have to understand a computer's innards to put it to work.

But there are rewards for those who want to dig a little deeper and learn a little more. Although this chapter is not designed to help you purchase a computer, it does provide some background information and gives you the foundation on which future computer knowledge can be built.

HARDWARE.

EXPLORE Generation **it**

 ## THE CENTRAL PROCESSING UNIT

The computer does its primary work in a part of the machine we cannot see: a control center that converts data input to information output. This control center, called the **central processing unit (CPU),** is a highly complex, extensive set of electronic circuitry that executes stored program instructions. All computers, large and small, must have at least one central processing unit. As Figure 4-1 shows, the central processing unit consists of two parts: the *control unit* and the *arithmetic/logic unit.* Each part has a specific function.

Before examining the control unit and the arithmetic/logic unit in detail, consider data storage and its relationship to the central processing unit. Computers use two major types of storage: primary storage and secondary storage. The CPU interacts closely with primary storage, or memory, referring to it for both instructions and data. For this reason this chapter will discuss memory in the context of the central processing unit. Technically, however, memory is not part of the CPU.

Memory holds data only temporarily, while a program is working directly with it. Secondary storage holds permanent or semipermanent data on some external medium, such as a disk, until it is needed for processing by the computer. Since the physical attributes of secondary storage devices determine how data is organized on them, secondary storage and data organization will be discussed together in the chapter on storage.

Now let us consider the components of the central processing unit.

The Control Unit

The **control unit** contains circuitry that uses electrical signals to direct the entire computer system to carry out, or execute, stored program instructions. Like an orchestra leader, the control unit does not execute program instructions; rather, it directs other parts of the system to do so. The control unit must communicate with both the arithmetic/logic unit and memory.

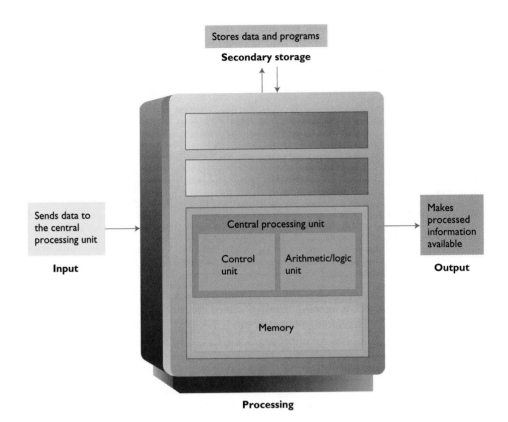

Input

Sends data to the central processing unit

Processing

Secondary storage

Stores data and programs

Central processing unit

Control unit

Arithmetic/logic unit

Memory

Output

Makes processed information available

◄ **F I G U R E** **4-1**

The central processing unit.

The two parts of the central processing unit are the control unit and the arithmetic/logic unit. Memory holds data and instructions temporarily while the program they are part of is being executed. The CPU interacts closely with memory, referring to it for both instructions and data.

The Arithmetic/Logic Unit

The **arithmetic/logic unit (ALU)** contains the electronic circuitry that executes all arithmetic and logical operations.

The arithmetic/logic unit can perform four kinds of **arithmetic operations,** or mathematical calculations: addition, subtraction, multiplication, and division. As its name implies, the arithmetic/logic unit also performs **logical operations,** or comparisons. The unit can compare numbers, letters, or special characters to test the conditions described below. The computer can then take action based on whether the test produces a true or false result. This is a very important capability. It is by comparing that a computer is able to tell, for instance, whether there are unfilled seats on airplanes, whether charge card customers have exceeded their credit limits, or whether one candidate for Congress has more votes than another.

Logical operations can test for three conditions:

- **Equal-to condition.** In a test for the **equal-to condition,** the arithmetic/logic unit compares two values to determine if they are equal. For example, if the number of tickets sold equals the number of seats in the auditorium, then the concert is declared sold out.

- **Less-than condition.** To test for the **less-than condition,** the computer compares two values to determine if the first is less than the second. For example, if the number of speeding tickets on a driver's record is less than three, then the insurance rate is $425; otherwise, the rate is $500.

- **Greater-than condition.** In testing for the **greater-than condition,** the computer determines if the first value is greater than the second. For example, if the hours a person worked this week are greater than 40, then the program should multiply every extra hour by 1½ times the usual hourly wage to compute overtime pay.

In addition to these three basic conditions, the computer can test for less-than-or-equal-to, greater-than-or-equal-to, and less-than-or-greater-than conditions. Note that less-than-or-greater-than is the same as **not-equal-to.**

The symbols that programmers use to tell the computer which type of comparison to perform are called **relational operators.** The most common relational operators are the equal sign (=), the less-than symbol (<), and the greater-than symbol (>).

Registers: Temporary Storage Areas

Registers are special-purpose, high-speed, temporary storage areas for instructions or data. They are not a part of memory; rather, they are special additional storage locations located within the CPU itself that offer the advantage of speed. Registers work under the direction of the control unit to accept, hold, and transfer instructions or data and perform arithmetic or logical comparisons at high speed. The control unit uses a register the way a store owner uses a cash register—as a temporary, convenient place to store what is used in transactions.

Special-purpose registers have specific tasks, such as holding the instruction that is currently being executed or keeping track of where the next instruction to be executed is stored in memory. (Each storage location in memory is identified by an address, just as each house on a street has an address.) Some CPU designs include general-purpose registers, which the control unit can use for different tasks, as required.

Consider registers in the context of all the means of storage discussed so far. Registers hold data that is immediately related to the operation being executed. Memory is used to store data that will be used in the near future. Secondary storage holds data that may be needed later in the same program execution or perhaps at some more remote time in the future.

Now let us look at how a payroll program, for example, uses all three types of storage. Suppose the program is about to calculate an employee's gross pay by multiplying the hours worked by the rate of pay. The control unit has placed a copy of the data representing the hours worked and the data for the rate of pay in their respective registers. Other data related to that employee's salary calculation—overtime hours, bonuses, deductions, and so forth—is waiting nearby in memory. The data for other employees is available in secondary storage. As the computer finishes calculations for one employee, the data for the next employee is brought from secondary storage into memory and eventually into the registers.

▶ MEMORY

Memory is also known as **primary storage, primary memory, main storage, internal storage,** and **main memory;** people in computer circles use all these terms interchangeably. Manufacturers often use the term **RAM,** which stands for random-access memory. Memory is the part of the computer that holds data and instructions for processing. Although closely associated with the central processing unit, memory is separate from it. Memory stores program instructions or data only as long as the program they pertain to is in operation. Keeping these items in memory when the program is not running is not feasible for these reasons:

- Most types of memory store items only while the computer is turned on; data is lost when the machine is turned off.

- If more than one program is running at once (usually the case on large computers and sometimes on small computers), a single program cannot lay exclusive claim to memory. There may not be room in memory to hold all the processed data.

- Secondary storage is more cost-effective than memory for storing large amounts of data.

The CPU cannot process data from an input device or disk directly; the data must first be available in memory. How do data and instructions get from an input or storage device into memory? The control unit sends them. Likewise, when the time is right, the control unit sends these items from memory to the arithmetic/logic unit, where an arithmetic operation or logical operation is performed. After being processed, the result is sent to memory, where it is held until it is ready to be released—sent—to an output or storage device.

The chief characteristic of memory is that it allows very fast access to instructions and data, no matter where the items are within it. A discussion of the physical components of memory—memory chips—appears later in this chapter.

► HOW THE CPU EXECUTES PROGRAM INSTRUCTIONS

Let us examine the way in which the central processing unit, in association with memory, executes one instruction in a computer program. Many personal computers can execute instructions in less than one millionth of a second, whereas the speed demons known as supercomputers can execute instructions in less than one trillionth of a second.

Before an instruction can be executed, program instructions and data must be placed into memory from an input device or a secondary storage device. As Figure 4-2

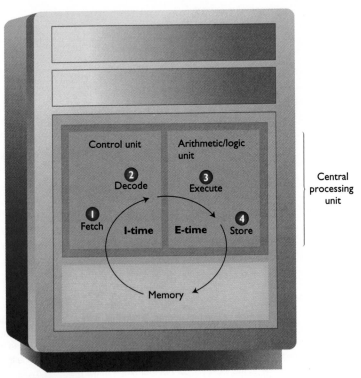

▲ **FIGURE 4-2**

The machine cycle.

Program instructions and data are brought into memory from an external source, either an input device or a secondary storage medium. The machine cycle executes instructions one at a time, as described in the text.

shows, once the necessary data and instruction are in memory, the central processing unit performs the following four steps for each instruction:

1. The control unit fetches (gets) the instruction from memory and puts it into a register.

2. The control unit decodes the instruction (decides what it means) and determines the memory location of the data required. These first two steps together are called instruction time, or **I-time.**

3. The control unit moves the data from memory to registers in the arithmetic/logic unit. The arithmetic/logic unit executes the arithmetic or logical instruction. That is, the ALU is given control and performs the actual operation on the data.

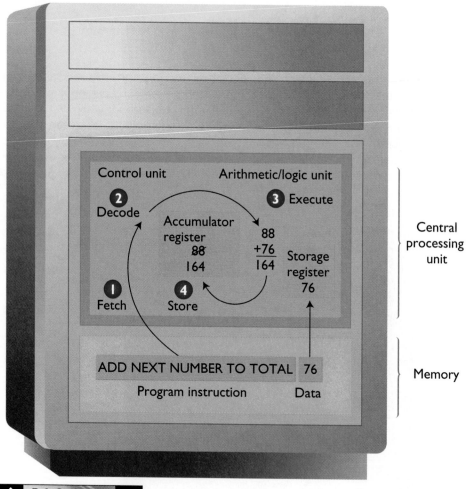

▲ F I G U R E **4·3**

The machine cycle in action.

Suppose a program must find the average of five test scores. To do this, it must total the five scores and then divide the result by five. The program would begin by setting the total to 0; it then would add each of the five numbers, one at a time, to the total. Suppose the scores are 88, 76, 91, 83, and 87. In this figure the total has been set to 0, and then 88, the first test score, has been added to it. Now examine the machine cycle as it adds the next number, 76, to the total. Follow the four steps in the machine cycle. (1) Fetch: The control unit fetches the instruction from memory. (2) Decode: The control unit decodes the ADD instruction. It determines that addition must take place and gives instructions for the next number (76) to be placed in a register for this purpose. The total so far (88) is already in a register. (3) Execute: The next number (76) is placed into the register, and the ALU does the addition, increasing the total to 164. (4) Store: In this case the ALU stores the new total in the register instead of in memory, since more numbers still need to be added to it. When the new total (164) is placed in the register, it displaces the old total (88).

4. The control unit stores the result of this operation in memory or in a register. Steps 3 and 4 together are called execution time, or **E-time.**

The control unit eventually directs memory to send the result to an output device or a secondary storage device. The combination of I-time and E-time is called the **machine cycle.** Figure 4-3 shows an instruction going through the machine cycle.

Each central processing unit has an internal **system clock** that produces pulses at a fixed rate to synchronize all computer operations. Note that this is not the clock that the computer uses to keep track of the date and time—that's a separate chip. A single program instruction may be made up of a substantial number of subinstructions, each of which must take at least one machine cycle. Each type of central processing unit is designed to understand a specific group of instructions—such as ADD or MOVE—called the **instruction set.** Just as there are many different languages that people understand, so too are there many different instruction sets that different types of CPUs understand.

►■ STORAGE LOCATIONS AND ADDRESSES: HOW THE CONTROL UNIT FINDS INSTRUCTIONS AND DATA

It is one thing to have instructions and data somewhere in memory and quite another for the control unit to be able to find them. How does it do this?

The location in memory for each instruction and each piece of data is identified by an address. That is, each location has an address number, like the mailboxes in front of an apartment house. And, like the mailboxes, the address numbers of the locations remain the same, but the contents (instructions and data) of the locations may change. That is, new instructions or new data may be placed in the locations when the old contents no longer need to be stored in memory. Unlike a mailbox, however, a memory location can hold only one instruction or piece of data at a time. When a new instruction or piece of data is placed in a memory location, that location's prior contents are destroyed.

Figure 4-4 shows how a program manipulates data in memory. A payroll program, for example, may give instructions to put the rate of pay in location 3 and the number of hours worked in location 6. To compute the employee's salary, then, instructions tell the computer to multiply the data in location 3 by the data in location 6 and move the result to location 8. The choice of locations is arbitrary—any locations that are not already spoken for can be used. Programmers using programming languages, however, do not have to worry about the actual address numbers, because each data address is referred to by a name. The name is called a **symbolic address.** In this example, the symbolic address names are Rate, Hours, and Salary.

►■ DATA REPRESENTATION: ON/OFF

BINARY REPRESENTATION.

Prentice Hall
EXPLORE Generation **it**

We are accustomed to thinking of computers as complex mechanisms, but the fact is that these machines basically know only two things: on and off. This two-state on/off system is called a **binary system.** Using the two states—which can be represented by electricity turned on or off—the computer can construct sophisticated ways of representing data.

Let us look at one way in which the two states can be used to represent data. Whereas the decimal number system has a base of 10 (with the ten digits 0, 1, 2, 3, 4, 5, 6, 7, 8, and 9), the binary system has a base of 2. This means it contains only two digits, 0 and 1, which correspond to the two states off and on. Combinations of 0s and 1s represent larger numbers (Figure 4-5).

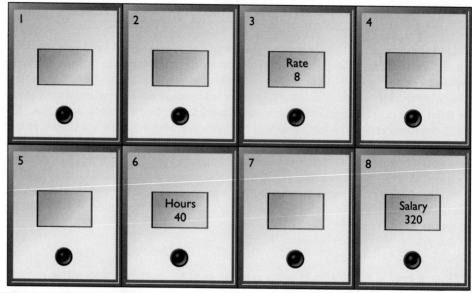

▲ **F I G U R E 4-4**

Addresses are like mailboxes.

The addresses of memory locations are like the identifying numbers on apartment house mailboxes. Suppose you want to compute someone's salary as the number of hours multiplied by the rate of pay. Rate ($8) goes in memory location 3, hours (40) in location 6, and the computed salary ($8 × 40 hours, or $320) in location 8. Therefore the addresses are 3, 6, and 8, but the contents are $8, 40, and $320, respectively. Note that the program instructions are to multiply the contents of location 3 by the contents of location 6 and move the result to location 8. (A computer language used by a programmer would use some kind of symbolic name for each location, such as Rate or Pay-Rate instead of the number 3.) The data items are the actual contents—what is stored in each location.

BINARY EQUIVALENT OF DECIMAL NUMBERS 0–15	
Decimal	**Binary**
0	0000
1	0001
2	0010
3	0011
4	0100
5	0101
6	0110
7	0111
8	1000
9	1001
10	1010
11	1011
12	1100
13	1101
14	1110
15	1111

▲ **F I G U R E 4-5**

Decimal and binary equivalents.

Seeing numbers from different systems side by side clarifies the patterns of progression. The two numbers in each row have the same value; they are simply expressed differently in different number systems.

Bits, Bytes, and Words

Each 0 or 1 in the binary system is called a **bit** (for *binary digit*). The bit is the basic unit for storing data in computer memory: 0 means off, 1 means on. Notice that since a bit is always either on or off, a bit in computer memory is always storing some kind of data—it can never be empty.

Since single bits by themselves cannot store all the numbers, letters, and special characters (such as $ and ?) that a computer must process, the bits are put together in a group called a **byte** (pronounced "bite"). Most computers today are designed to use 8-bit bytes. For text data, each byte usually stores one character of data—a letter, digit, or special character.

Computer manufacturers express the capacity of memory and storage in terms of the number of bytes they contain. The number of bytes can be expressed as **kilobytes.** "Kilo" represents 2 to the tenth power (2^{10}), or 1024. Kilobyte is abbreviated **KB,** or simply **K.** A kilobyte is 1024 bytes. In an older computer, a memory of 640K means that the computer can store 640×1024, or 655,360, bytes. Memory capacity today is stated in terms of **megabytes.** One megabyte, abbreviated **MB,** means roughly one million bytes. Personal computer memory may be 128MB and more. With secondary storage devices, manufacturers express capacity in terms of **gigabytes** (abbreviated **GB**)—billions of bytes. Also, mainframe memories are measured in gigabytes. Secondary storage systems on mainframes and networks often have **terabytes (TB)**—trillions of bytes of storage capacity. Figure 4-6 summarizes the terms used to specify memory and storage sizes.

A computer **word,** typically the size of a register, is defined as the number of bits that the CPU processes as a unit. The length of a word varies by CPU. Generally, the larger the word, the more powerful the computer. There was a time when word size alone could classify a computer. Word lengths have varied from 8 bits for very early personal computers to 32 or 64 bits for most personal computers today.

Coding Schemes

As we noted, a byte—a collection of bits—can represent a character of data. But just what particular set of bits is equivalent to which character? In theory we could each make up our own definitions, declaring certain bit patterns to represent certain characters. Needless to say, this would be about as practical as each person speaking his or her own special language. Since we need to communicate with the computer and with each other, it is appropriate that we use a common scheme for data representation. That is, there must be agreement on which groups of bits represent which characters.

Since each byte contains 8 bits, each of which can hold a 1 or 0, there are $2^8 =$ 256 possible combinations of 1s and 0s in a byte. A **coding scheme** (or just **code**) assigns each one of those combinations to a specific character. The **ASCII** (pronounced "as-kee") code, which stands for American Standard Code for Information Interchange, is the most widely used code; it is used on virtually all personal computers and on many larger systems. An earlier version of ASCII used a 7-bit byte and could represent only 128 characters. Another code, **Extended Binary Coded**

Term	Abbreviation	Approximate Number of Bytes	Exact Number of Bytes
Kilobyte	K (or KB)	one thousand	1,024
Megabyte	MB	one million	1,048,576
Gigabyte	GB	one billion	1,073,741,824
Terabyte	TB	one trillion	1,099,511,627,776

 **FIGURE 4-6**

Storage sizes.

This table gives the terminology used to specify primary memory and secondary storage capacities.

▶ **F I G U R E** 4-7

The ASCII and EBCDIC codes.

(a) Shown are the ASCII and EBCDIC binary representations for selected characters. This is not the complete code; many characters are missing, such as lowercase letters and punctuation marks. The binary representations are in two columns of 4 bits each to improve readability.

Character	ASCII	EBCDIC
0	0011 0000	1111 0000
1	0011 0001	1111 0001
2	0011 0010	1111 0010
3	0011 0011	1111 0011
4	0011 0100	1111 0100
5	0011 0101	1111 0101
6	0011 0110	1111 0110
7	0011 0111	1111 0111
8	0011 1000	1111 1000
9	0011 1001	1111 1001
A	0100 0001	1100 0001
B	0100 0010	1100 0010
C	0100 0011	1100 0011
D	0100 0100	1100 0100
E	0100 0101	1100 0101
F	0100 0110	1100 0110
G	0100 0111	1100 0111
a	0110 0001	1000 0001
b	0110 0010	1000 0010
c	0110 0011	1000 0011
d	0110 0100	1000 0100
e	0110 0101	1000 0101
f	0110 0110	1000 0110
g	0110 0111	1000 0111
!	0010 0001	0101 1010
#	0010 0011	0111 1011
$	0010 0100	0101 1011
+	0010 1011	0100 1110

Decimal Interchange Code (EBCDIC, pronounced "ebb-see-dik"), is used primarily on IBM and IBM-compatible mainframes. Figure 4-7 shows the ASCII and EBCDIC codes for a selected set of characters.

The 256-character capability of ASCII and EBCDIC is sufficient for English and Western European languages, but is much too small to handle the many different alphabets used throughout the rest of the world. The **Unicode** coding scheme is designed to solve this problem. Unicode uses two bytes (16 bits) to represent one character. This gives it the capability of representing $2^{16} = 65,536$ different characters—more than enough for all the world's languages. Unicode is downward-compatible with ASCII, meaning that Unicode recognizes ASCII characters. Most new operating systems and software packages include support for Unicode.

► THE SYSTEM UNIT

The **system unit** is the case that houses the electronic components of the computer system. The **motherboard,** the flat circuit board within the personal computer housing that holds the computer circuitry (Figure 4-8), is the main system unit component. The motherboard, also called the main circuit board, is a mass of chips and connections that organize the computer's activities. The central processing unit—the microprocessor—is the most important component of the motherboard. Most microcomputer system units also contain one or more storage devices, such as a hard drive, a floppy drive, and a CD-ROM or DVD-ROM drive. Some Apple Macintosh models include the system unit within the monitor housing.

Microprocessors

A miniaturized central processing unit can be etched on a chip, a tiny square of silicon. A central processing unit, or processor, on a chip is called a **microprocessor** (Figure 4-9). A microprocessor may be called a **logic chip** when it is used to control

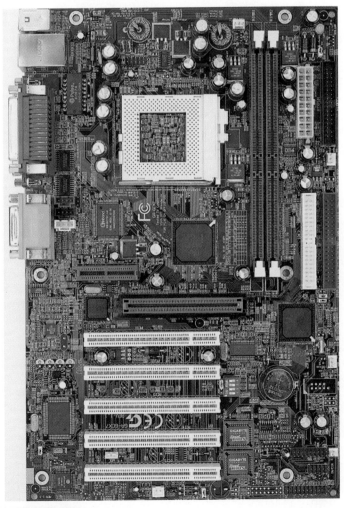

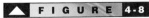 **FIGURE 4-8**

The Motherboard.

The motherboard is a flat circuit board that holds the computer circuitry, a mass of chips and connections that organize the computer's activities.

▲ **F I G U R E 4-9**

A Microprocessor.

A central processing unit, or processor, on a chip is called a microprocessor. Microprocessors contain millions of tiny transistors, electronic switches that may or may not allow current to pass through.

► M A K I N G C O N N E C T I O N S ◄

Let Your Idle Computer Earn You Money

The SETI (Search for Extraterrestrial Intelligence) project uses the Arecibo Radio Telescope in Puerto Rico to scan the universe for radio signals generated by intelligent aliens. The project gathers huge amounts of digital data, far more than the project's computers were able to handle. In 1995, project leaders came up with an idea to both gain significant processing power and generate interest in SETI among the public. Their idea was to harness the idle CPU cycles of personal computers by distributing packets of their gathered data and letting individual PCs process that data during idle time. They developed client software that PC users could download from the Internet and install like a screensaver. When the PC is idle, that software will download digital radio data and process it, sending the results back to SETI. The organizers released the software in mid-1999, hoping to get 100,000 people to participate. In

the first week, over 200,000 signed up, and the number exceeded 2,000,000 within a year, giving SETI the computing power of a supercomputer operating at over 12 trillion instructions per second!

How, you might ask, will this allow you to make money from your idle computer? After all, the SETI project is done on a strictly voluntary basis. Well, it didn't take long for entrepreneurs to realize the moneymaking potential of all this unused computing power. By mid-2000, several companies had begun registering users with the promise of payment for any work done on the users' computers. In turn, that computing power is then sold to businesses on an as-needed basis. If you are the altruistic sort, they will allow you to donate some or all of your computer's work efforts to nonprofit agencies. Unfortunately, you don't get a tax deduction.

specialized devices (such as the fuel system of a car). Microprocessors contain tiny **transistors,** electronic switches that may or may not allow current to pass through. If current passes through, the switch is on, representing a 1 bit. If current does not pass through, the switch is off, representing a 0 bit. Thus combinations of transistors can stand for combinations of bits, which, as we noted earlier, represent digits, letters, and special characters.

The transistor is the basic building block of the microprocessor. Today's microprocessors contain millions of transistors. Microprocessors usually include these key components: a control unit and an arithmetic/logic unit (the central processing unit), registers, and the system clock. Notably missing is memory, which usually comes on its own chips.

How much smaller can a processor be? How much cheaper? How much faster? Three decades of extraordinary advances in technology have packed increasingly greater power onto increasingly smaller chips. Engineers can now imprint as much circuitry on a single chip as filled room-size computers in the early days of computing. But are engineers approaching the limits of smallness? Current development efforts focus on a three-dimensional chip that is built in layers. Chip capacities in the future do seem almost limitless.

In addition to factors such as increased speed, microprocessors have historically increased their power by swallowing up functions that were previously accomplished by other hardware. For example, in the 1980s, chipmaker Intel incorporated a math coprocessor, a separate chip favored by engineers, into its microprocessor. Currently, Intel's **Pentium** chip includes multimedia instructions that boost a computer's ability to produce graphics, video, and sound. The more functions that are combined on a microprocessor, the faster the computer runs, the cheaper it is to make, and the more reliable it is.

Intel's Pentium® microprocessor is the current workhorse in the PC marketplace, with the PIII and P4 models in most of the PCs sold today. Intel also produces the Celeron™ for lower-cost PCs and the Xeon™ and Itanium™ for high-end workstations and network servers. Several companies, notably Cyrix and AMD, make Intel-compatible microprocessors. In the past, these companies have tended to follow Intel, but lately they have been pushing the technology envelope, sometimes beating Intel to market with faster speeds and more advanced capabilities.

There are two other microprocessors of note in the non-Intel world. The **PowerPC** family of chips was designed through the cooperative efforts of Apple, IBM, and Motorola and is currently manufactured by both IBM and Motorola. The PowerPC's primary use is in the Apple Macintosh family of personal computers, but it is also used in servers and embedded systems. The **Alpha** microprocessor, produced by Compaq, is used in high-end servers and workstations.

Memory Components

The first part of this chapter described the central processing unit and how it works with memory. Next is an examination of the memory components. Historically, memory components have evolved from primitive vacuum tubes to today's modern semiconductors.

SEMICONDUCTOR MEMORY   Most modern computers use **semiconductor memory** because it has several advantages: reliability, compactness, low cost, and lower power usage. Since semiconductor memory can be mass-produced economically, the cost of memory has been considerably reduced. Chip prices have fallen and risen and fallen again—all on the basis of a variety of economic and political factors—but they remain a bargain. Semiconductor memory is **volatile;** that is, it requires continuous electric current to represent data. If the current is interrupted, the data is lost.

Semiconductor memory is made up of thousands of very small circuits—pathways for electric currents—on a silicon chip. A chip is described as **monolithic** because all the circuits on a single chip together constitute an inseparable unit of storage. Each circuit etched on a chip can be in one of two states: either conducting an electric current or not—on or off. The two states can be used to represent the binary digits 1 and 0. As we noted earlier, these digits can be combined to represent characters, thus making the memory chip a storage bin for data and instructions.

One important type of semiconductor design is called **complementary metal oxide semiconductor (CMOS).** This design is noted for using relatively little electricity. In personal computers, one use for CMOS is CMOS RAM; a small amount of memory that, thanks to battery power, retains data when the computer is shut off. Thus CMOS RAM can be used to store information your computer needs when it boots up, such as time, date, and hardware configuration data. When the computer is running, CMOS RAM can be updated, and the new contents will remain until changed again.

RAM AND ROM   Memory keeps the instructions and data for whatever programs you happen to be using at the moment. Memory is referred to as **RAM—random-access memory**—in this discussion, both to emphasize its random function and to distinguish it from ROM. Data in memory can be accessed randomly, no matter where it is, in an easy and speedy manner. RAM is usually volatile; as we noted above, this means that its contents are lost once the power is shut off. RAM can be erased or written over at will by the computer software.

RAM can be of two types: static RAM **(SRAM)**—pronounced "ess-ram"—and dynamic RAM **(DRAM),** pronounced "dee-ram." DRAM must be constantly refreshed (recharged) by the central processing unit or it will lose its contents, hence the name dynamic. Static RAM will retain its contents without intervention from the CPU as long as power is maintained. Although SRAM is much faster, DRAM is used for most personal computer memory because of its size and cost advantages (Figure 4-10). Synchronous DRAM (**SDRAM,** pronounced "ess-dee-ram") is a faster type of DRAM used in most PCs today. An even newer technology, Rambus DRAM (**RDRAM,** pronounced "are-dee-ram"), is faster than SDRAM and will undoubtedly become popular once the cost declines. SRAM is used for special purposes that will be described shortly.

In recent years the amount of RAM storage in a personal computer has increased dramatically. An early personal computer, for example, was advertised with "a full 4K RAM." Now 128MB of RAM or even more is common. More memory has become a

▲ **F I G U R E 4-10**

DRAM.

Dynamic RAM (DRAM) must be constantly refreshed (recharged) by the CPU or it will lose its contents. DRAM is used for most personal computer memory because of its size and cost advantages.

F O C U S   O N   E T H I C S | **Are You Being Watched?**

A side effect of the explosive growth in personal computers and communications technology is the amount and detail of personally identifying information that is transmitted and recorded. Some examples:

- Cell phones will contain Global Positioning System (GPS) receivers that can transmit the user's location to within a few feet.

- Some Intel CPUs contain a unique identifying number that could be used to pinpoint the specific PC that sent an e-mail message or downloaded a Web page.

- Electronic toll-road transponders routinely record the time and speed of the user's vehicle at each tollbooth.

- Free bar code scanners distributed with catalogs for on-line browsing transmit a special code that could identify the user.

- Cable and DSL modems have a unique Media Access Controller (MAC) address that an ISP can use to track the specific services and sites used by each customer.

Each of these technologies has potential benefits to the consumer and the industry, but each could pose a threat to your privacy. Cite one or more of the examples above and list as many benefits and as many drawbacks as you can. What sort of policies could industry, government, or individuals adopt that would help to ensure that the benefits of the selected technology outweigh the costs?

---

necessity because sophisticated personal computer software requires significant amounts of memory. Also, many users have several programs active at the same time, each using its own portion of memory. You can augment your personal computer's RAM by buying extra memory modules to plug into your computer's motherboard. Memory normally is packaged on circuit boards called **single in-line memory modules (SIMMs)** or **dual in-line memory modules (DIMMs),** depending on whether the memory chips are installed on one side or both sides of the board. The motherboard design determines the maximum amount of memory that you can install in your computer.

Read-only memory (ROM) contains programs and data that are permanently recorded into this type of memory at the factory; they can be read and used, but they cannot be changed by the user. For example, the boot routine that is activated when you turn your computer on is stored in ROM. ROM is nonvolatile—its contents do not disappear when the power is turned off.

By using specialized tools called ROM burners, the instructions within some ROM chips can be changed. These chips are known as **PROM** chips, or **programmable read-only memory** chips. There are other variations on ROM chips, depending on the methods used to alter them. Programming and altering ROM chips are the province of the computer engineer.

The System Bus

As is so often the case, the computer term "bus" is borrowed from its common meaning—a mode of transportation. A **bus line** (or just **bus**) is a set of parallel electrical paths that transport electrical signals. The **system bus,** usually copper tracing on the surface of the motherboard, transports data between the CPU and memory. The number of bits of data that can be carried at one time is called the *bus width,* which indicates the number of electrical paths. The greater the width, the more data can be carried at a time. Just as a four-lane expressway can move traffic faster than a two-lane road, wider buses allow faster data transmission. The system bus width is dependent on the CPU design and is normally is the same as the CPU's word size. A larger bus size means that:

- The CPU can transfer more data at a time, making the computer faster.

- The CPU can reference larger memory address numbers, allowing more memory.

- The CPU can support a greater number and variety of instructions.

In general, the larger the word size or bus width, the more powerful the computer. Bus speed is another factor that affects system performance. As with processor speed, bus speed is measured in megahertz (MHz). The faster the bus speed, the faster data travels through the system.

Expansion Buses

In addition to the system bus, the motherboard also contains several expansion buses. Some of these buses connect to **expansion slots** on the motherboard. By plugging **expansion boards** (also called **interface cards** or **adapter cards)** into these slots, you can connect various peripheral devices to your computer (see Figure 4-11). Other buses provide external connectors, called **ports,** for you to plug in peripherals such as a printer, a mouse, and a keyboard. Ports come in two basic types: serial and parallel. **Serial ports** transmit data one bit at a time, similar to cars on a one-lane road, and are typically used for slow-speed devices such as the mouse and keyboard. **Parallel ports** transmit groups of bits together, similar to a group of cars traveling side-by-side down a multilane highway, and are used for faster devices such as printers and scanners (see Figure 4-12).

GETTING PRACTICAL | Should You Build Your Own Computer?

Building your own computer may seem like a fanciful idea indeed, especially if you have not even decided whether to buy a computer that comes prepackaged. However, the option of building a computer, once the territory of hard-core techies, is now a possibility for mainstream consumers. Some people like the idea of the adventure, and they also like getting exactly the components they want rather than what a PC manufacturer has decided to include.

What skills do you need? And what equipment? Surprisingly, very little of either. You will not need to do anything as dramatic as soldering. In truth, your task is really to acquire and then assemble the various components, screwing and snapping them into place, rather like an electronic Lego set.

Let us begin with the shopping list. You will need a motherboard, microprocessor, RAM, case with a power supply, diskette drive, hard drive, video card, monitor, keyboard, and mouse. You will likely also want a modem, a CD-ROM or DVD-ROM drive, a sound card, and speakers. Now the question becomes which ones. A visit to your local electronics store can be a high-tech reconnaissance mission in which you can gather information from both salespeople and fellow customers. Be sure to check the store's return policy; you should be able to return any component unconditionally

within a certain time frame. If reduced personal service is an acceptable trade-off for lower costs, you may prefer to buy from a mail-order house or an Internet site; check the advertising section of any major computer magazine. But do buy the major components from the same company to cut down on compatibility problems.

We do not have the space here to describe the components in detail, much less the assembly process. Detailed instructions, which you should read carefully, accompany each hardware item. You can get further advice from magazines, perhaps a local computer club, and the Internet.

Don't expect to save a lot of money. Profit margins are slim in the PC marketplace, and the PC manufacturers can buy components a lot cheaper than you can, so the total component cost will not be significantly less than what you would pay for a fully assembled computer. The real savings will come in the future when you are able to upgrade your computer on your own—adding more memory, a new microprocessor, a new hard drive, or whatever—rather than buying a new computer.

Building a computer can be a satisfying experience, but it is not for everyone. Generally speaking, if you have any doubts, don't do it.

◄ **F I G U R E 4-11**

An Interface Card.

By plugging expansion boards (also called interface cards or adapter cards) into expansion slots on the computer's motherboard, you can connect various peripheral devices to your computer.

The following are buses and ports that are commonly found on personal computers:

- **Industry Standard Architecture (ISA) bus.** The oldest expansion bus still in common use, the **Industry Standard Architecture (ISA) bus** is used for slow-speed devices such as the mouse and modem.

- **Peripheral Component Interconnect (PCI) bus.** The **Peripheral Component Interconnect (PCI) bus** is a high-speed bus used to connect devices such as hard disks and network cards.

- **Accelerated Graphics Port (AGP).** The **Accelerated Graphics Port (AGP)** is a bus that is designed to provide a dedicated connection between memory and an AGP graphics card. The direct connection provides much faster video performance without interfering with other peripherals.

- **Universal Serial Bus (USB).** Access to the **Universal Serial Bus (USB)** is provided through a port on the back of the system unit. Devices with USB connectors can be daisy-chained (connected in a series) to each other and plugged into the USB port, eliminating the need for multiple expansion cards. USB devices are *hot-swappable,* meaning that you can connect and disconnect them without turning off the power to your computer.

- **IEEE 1394 bus.** Also referred to as FireWire, the **IEEE 1394 bus** is a high-speed bus that is normally used to connect video equipment to your computer. It is also accessed through a port on the back of the system unit.

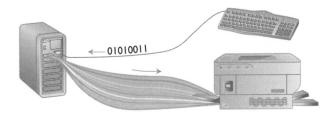

◄ **F I G U R E 4-12**

Serial and parallel transmission.

Serial ports, used for slower devices such as the keyboard, transmit bits one at a time. Parallel ports are used for higher-speed devices such as printers and transmit entire bytes at a time.

- **PC Card bus.** Access to **PC Card bus** is provided through a slot or slots in the computer case. The slot accepts credit card-sized PC Card devices and is normally found on laptops.

◀▶ SPEED AND POWER

The characteristic of speed is universally associated with computers. Power is a derivative of speed as well as of other factors such as memory size. What makes a computer fast? Or, more to the point, what makes one computer faster than another? Several factors are involved, including microprocessor speed, bus line size, and the availability of cache. A user who is concerned about speed will want to address all of these. More sophisticated approaches to speed include flash memory, RISC computers, and parallel processing. A discussion of each of these factors follows.

Computer Processing Speeds

Although all computers are fast, there is a wide diversity of computer speeds. The execution of an instruction on a very slow (old) computer may be measured in less than a **millisecond,** which is one thousandth of a second, or perhaps in **microseconds,** each of which is one millionth of a second. Modern computers have reached the **nanosecond** range—one billionth of a second. Still to be broken is the **picosecond** barrier—one trillionth of a second (see Figure 4-13).

One way of comparing the performance of personal computers is by comparing their microprocessor speeds. Microprocessor speeds are determined by their clock speed and are usually expressed in **megahertz (MHz),** millions of machine cycles per second. Thus a personal computer that is listed at 500MHz has a processor capable of handling 500 million machine cycles per second. A top-speed personal computer can be much faster, with newer ones reaching **gigahertz (GHz**—billions of machine cycles per second) speeds. Direct comparison of clock speeds is meaningful only between identical microprocessors. Thus, while it is accurate to say that a Pentium III running at 800MHz is approximately one third faster than a Pentium III running at 600MHz, it is not at all correct to say that a 600MHz Pentium III is faster than a 400MHz PowerPC. This is due to the internal designs of the microprocessors—each accomplishes a different amount of work during each of its clock ticks.

Another measure of computer speed is **MIPS,** which stands for one million instructions per second. For example, a computer with speed of 0.5MIPS can execute 500,000 instructions per second. High-speed personal computers can perform at 100MIPS and higher. MIPS is often a more accurate measure than clock speed, because some computers can use each tick of the clock more efficiently than others.

Term	Abbreviation	Fraction of a Second
millisecond	ms	1/1,000 second
microsecond	μ	1/1,000,000 second
nanosecond	ns	1/1,000,000,000 second
picosecond	psec	1/1,000,000,000,000 second

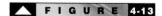

▲ **F I G U R E 4-13**

Fractions of a second.

Note that each fraction is 1/1,000th of the fraction above it in the table.

A third measure of speed is the **megaflop,** which stands for one million floating-point operations per second. It measures the ability of the computer to perform complex mathematical operations.

Cache

In computer terminology **cache** (pronounced "cash") is a temporary storage area designed to speed up data transfer within the computer. In this section we will discuss memory cache. Disk cache will be covered in Chapter 6. **Memory cache** is a relatively small block of very fast memory designed for the specific purpose of speeding up the internal transfer of data and software instructions (see Figure 4-14). Think of cache as a selective memory: The data and instructions stored in cache are those that are most recently or most frequently used. When the processor first requests data or instructions, these must be retrieved from main memory, which delivers at a pace that is relatively slow in comparison with the speed of the microprocessor. As they are retrieved, those same data or instructions are stored in cache. The next time the microprocessor needs data or instructions, it looks first in cache; if the needed items can be found there, they can be transferred at a rate that far exceeds a trip from main memory. Of course, cache is not big enough to hold everything, so the wanted data or instructions might not be there. But there is a good chance that frequently used items will be in cache. Since the most frequently used data and instructions are kept in a handy place, the net result is an improvement in processing speed.

Caching is such a vital technique that microprocessors now offer **internal cache** built right into the processor. This is referred to as **Level 1 (L1)** cache and is the fastest sort, since it is right there for the microprocessor to access. However, cache memory takes up precious space and increases the cost of the microprocessor, so a processor would probably have no more than 128KB of L1 cache. Most computers also include **external, or Level 2 (L2), cache** on separate chips, probably 256KB or 512KB. L2 cache uses SRAM technology and is cheaper and slower than L1 cache but still much faster (and more expensive) than memory. L2 cache beyond 512KB has been shown to give little additional improvement in system performance.

Flash Memory

We have stated that memory is volatile—that it disappears when the power is turned off—hence the need for secondary storage to keep data on a more permanent basis. A long-standing speed problem has been the slow rate at which data is accessed from a secondary storage device such as a disk, a rate that is significantly slower than internal computer speeds. It seemed unimaginable that data might someday be stored on nonvolatile memory chips—nonvolatile RAM—close at hand. A breakthrough has emerged in the form of nonvolatile **flash memory.** Flash chips are currently being used in cellular phones, digital cameras, and digital music recorders, and they are replacing disks in some handheld computers.

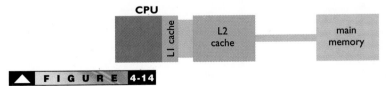

▲ **F I G U R E 4-14**

Memory Cache.

Memory cache is a temporary storage area designed to speed up transfer of data instructions between memory and the CPU. Level 1 (L1) cache is built into the CPU, while Level 2 (L2) cache is on separate chips.

Flash memory chips are being produced in credit card–like packages, which are smaller than a disk drive and require only half the power; that is why they are being used in notebook computers and the handheld personal digital assistants.

RISC Technology: Less Is More

It flies in the face of computer tradition: Instead of reaching for more variety, more power, more everything-for-everyone, proponents of **RISC—reduced instruction set computing**—suggest that we could get by with a little less. In fact, RISC-based microprocessors offer only a small subset of instructions; the absence of bells and whistles increases speed. So there is a back-to-basics movement in computer design.

RISC supporters say that in conventional microprocessors, which are based on **complex instruction set computing (CISC),** many of the most complex instructions in the instruction set are rarely used. Those underused instructions, they note, are an impediment to speedy performance, often taking several clock cycles to execute. RISC computers, with their stripped-down instruction sets, zip through programs like racing cars—at speeds 4 to 10 times those of CISC computers. They do slow down, however, when they run into program operations that are normally handled by the complex instructions that were deleted from their instruction set. These operations have to be broken down into smaller steps and handled by a sequence of simple instructions, slowing execution speed. For programs with few operations requiring complex instructions, typically those in graphics and engineering areas, RISC computers have a significant performance advantage. Of the processors discussed earlier, the PowerPCs and Alphas use RISC designs, while Intel's Pentium family follows the CISC approach.

Parallel Processing

The ultimate speed solution is **parallel processing,** a method of using multiple processors at the same time. Consider the description of computer processing you have seen so far in this chapter: The processor gets an instruction from memory, acts on it, returns processed data to memory, and then repeats the process. This is conventional **serial processing,** the execution of one instruction at a time. A variation on this approach is **pipelining,** in which an instruction's actions—fetch, decode, execute, store—need not be complete before the next instruction is begun. For example, once fetch is complete for an instruction and it moves to decode, fetch is begun for the next instruction (Figure 4-15).

▶ **F I G U R E 4-15**

Pipelining.

Pipelining is a processing technique that feeds a new instruction into the CPU at every step of the processing cycle so that four or more instructions are worked on simultaneously.

Machine cycle (without pipelining)

fetch	decode	execute	store
			instruction 1

Machine cycle (with pipelining)

fetch	decode	execute	store
			instruction 1
		instruction 2	
	instruction 3		
instruction 4			

The problem with the conventional computer is that the single electronic pathway, the bus line, acts like a bottleneck. The computer has a one-track mind because it is restricted to handling one piece of data at a time. For many applications, such as simulating the airflow around an entire airplane in flight, this is an exceedingly inefficient procedure. A better solution? Many processors, each with its own memory unit, working at the same time: parallel processing. Some computers using parallel processors are capable of operating in terms of **teraflops**—that is, trillions of floating-point instructions per second. Recall, for comparison, that a megaflop is a mere one million floating-point operations per second.

A number of computers containing parallel processors are being built and sold commercially. Some have a small number of processors, typically 4 to 16, and are used as network servers. Others use hundreds or even thousands of processors and fall within the realm of supercomputing.

▲

The future holds some exciting possibilities for computer chips. One day we may see computers that operate by using light (photonics) rather than electricity (electronics) to control their operation. Light travels faster and is less likely to be disrupted by electrical interference. And would you believe that someday computers might actually be grown as biological cultures? So-called biochips may replace today's silicon chip. As research continues, so will the surprises.

Whatever the design and processing strategy of a computer, its goal is the same: to turn raw input into useful output. Input and output are the topics of the next chapter.

CHAPTER REVIEW

► Summary and Key Terms

- The **central processing unit (CPU)** is a complex set of electronic circuitry that executes program instructions; it consists of a control unit and an arithmetic/logic unit.

- The central processing unit interacts closely with primary storage, or memory. Memory provides temporary storage of data while the computer is executing the program. Secondary storage holds the data that is permanent or semipermanent.

- The **control unit** of the central processing unit coordinates execution of the program instructions by communicating with the arithmetic/logic unit and memory—the parts of the system that actually execute the program.

- The **arithmetic/logic unit (ALU)** contains circuitry that executes the arithmetic and logical operations. The unit can perform four **arithmetic operations:** addition, subtraction, multiplication, and division. Its **logical operations** usually involve making comparisons that test for three conditions: the **equal-to condition,** the **less-than condition,** and the **greater-than condition.** The computer can test for more than one condition at once, so it can discern three other conditions as well: less-than-or-equal-to, greater-than-or-equal-to, and less-than-or-greater-than **(not-equal-to).**

- Symbols called **relational operators** (=, <, >) can define the comparison to perform.

- **Registers** are special-purpose, high-speed areas for temporary data storage.

- **Memory** is the part of the computer that temporarily holds data and instructions before and after they are processed by the arithmetic/logic unit. Memory is also known as **primary storage, primary memory, main storage, internal storage,** and **main memory.** Manufacturers often use the term **RAM,** which stands for *random-access memory.*

- The central processing unit follows four main steps when executing an instruction: It (1) fetches—gets—the instruction from memory, (2) decodes the instruction and determines the memory location of the data required, (3) moves the data from memory to ALU registers and directs the ALU to perform the actual operation on the data, and (4) directs the ALU to store the result of the operation in memory or a register. The first two steps are called **I-time** (instruction time), and the last two steps are called **E-time** (execution time).

- A **machine cycle** is the combination of I-time and E-time. The internal **system clock** of the central processing unit produces pulses at a fixed rate to synchronize computer operations. Each central processing unit has a set of commands that it can understand called the **instruction set.**

- The location in memory for each instruction and each piece of data is identified by an address. Address numbers remain the same, but the contents of the locations change. A meaningful name given to a memory address is called a **symbolic address.**

- Since a computer can recognize only whether electricity is on or off, data is represented by an on/off **binary system,** represented by the digits 1 and 0.

- Each 0 or 1 in the binary system is called a **bit** (binary digit). A group of bits (usually 8 bits) is called a **byte,** which usually represents one character of text data, such as a letter, digit, or special character. Memory capacity was once expressed in **kilobytes (KB or K).** One kilobyte equals 1024 bytes. A **megabyte (MB),** about one million bytes, is used today to express memory size. A **gigabyte (GB)** equals about one billion bytes. A **terabyte (TB)** is about one trillion bytes.

- A computer **word** is the number of bits that make up a unit of data, as defined by the CPU design.

- A **coding scheme** (or **code**) assigns each possible combination of 1s and 0s in a byte to a specific character. Two common coding schemes for representing characters in an 8-bit byte are **ASCII** (American Standard Code for Information Interchange), used on most personal computers, and **EBCDIC** (Extended Binary Coded Decimal Interchange Code). Each of these can represent 256 different characters. The **Unicode** coding scheme uses two bytes (16 bits) to represent a character and can represent 65,536 different characters.

- The **system unit** is the case that contains the **motherboard,** the flat board within the personal computer housing that holds the chips and circuitry that organize the computer's activities. The system unit may also house various storage devices.

- A central processing unit, or processor, on a chip is a **microprocessor.** A microprocessor may be called a **logic chip** when it is used to control specialized devices. Microprocessors contain tiny **transistors,** electronic switches that may or may not allow current to pass through, representing a 1 or 0 bit, respectively.

- The more functions that are combined on a microprocessor, the faster the computer runs, the cheaper it is to make, and the more reliable it is.

- Common personal computer microprocessors are the Intel **Pentium,** used in IBM-compatible PCs; the **PowerPC,** used in the Apple Macintosh; and the **Alpha,** used in high-end workstations and servers.

- **Semiconductor memory,** thousands of very small circuits on a silicon chip, is **volatile;** that is, it requires continuous electrical current to maintain its contents. A chip is described as **monolithic** because the circuits on a single chip constitute an inseparable unit of storage.

- An important type of semiconductor design is called **complementary metal oxide semiconductor (CMOS);** it is noted for using little electricity, making it especially useful for computers requiring low power consumption, such as portable computers.

- **Random-access memory (RAM)** keeps the instructions and data for whatever programs you happen to be using at the moment.

- RAM is often divided into two types: static RAM **(SRAM),** which is faster, and dynamic RAM **(DRAM),** which is slower and much less expensive. **SDRAM** and **RDRAM** are faster and more expensive types of DRAM.

- RAM is normally mounted on either **single in-line memory modules (SIMMs)** or **dual in-line memory modules** (DIMMs), boards that plug into the motherboard.

- **Read-only memory (ROM)** contains programs and data that are permanently recorded into this type of memory at the factory; they can be read and used but cannot be changed by the user. ROM is nonvolatile. The instructions within some ROM chips can be changed by using ROM burners; these chips are known as **PROM** chips, or **programmable read-only memory** chips.

- The motherboard contains several **bus lines,** or **buses,** sets of parallel electrical paths that transport electrical signals. The **system bus** transfers data between the CPU and memory. Bus width and speed affect system performance.

- Some expansion buses connect to **expansion slots** on the motherboard and can receive **expansion boards** (also called **interface cards** or **adapter cards**) that allow you to connect various peripheral devices to the computer. Other expansion buses provide external connectors, called **ports.** A **serial port** allows data transmission one bit at a time, while a **parallel port** transmits a group of bits at a time. Some ports and buses found on a typical personal computer are the **Industry Standard Architecture (ISA) bus,** the **Peripheral Component Interconnect (PCI) bus**, the **Accelerated Graphics Port (AGP),** the **Universal Serial Bus (USB),** the **IEEE 1394 bus,** and the **PC Card bus.**

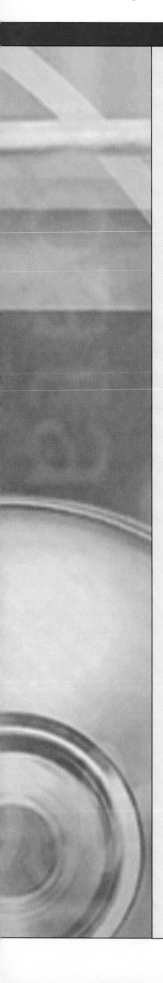

- Computer instruction speeds fall into various ranges, from a **millisecond,** which is one thousandth of a second; to a **microsecond,** one millionth of a second (for old computers); to a **nanosecond,** one billionth of a second. Still to be achieved is the **picosecond** range—one trillionth of a second.

- Microprocessor speeds are usually expressed in **megahertz (MHz),** millions of machine cycles per second or **gigahertz (GHz),** billions of cycles per second. Another measure of computer speed is **MIPS,** which stands for one million instructions per second. A third measure is the **megaflop,** which stands for one million floating-point operations per second.

- A **cache** is a relatively small amount of very fast memory that stores data and instructions that are used frequently, resulting in an improved processing speed. **Internal,** or **Level 1 (L1), cache,** the fastest kind, refers to cache built right into the processor's design. Most computers also include **external,** or **Level 2 (L2), cache** on separate chips.

- **Flash memory** is nonvolatile and is used to store programming in devices such as cellular phones and data in digital cameras and digital music recorders.

- **RISC—reduced instruction set computing**—microprocessors are fast because they use only a small subset of instructions. Conventional microprocessors using **complex instruction set computing (CISC)** include many instructions that are rarely used.

- Conventional **serial processing** uses a single processor and can handle just one instruction at a time. **Pipelining** means that an instruction's actions—fetch, decode, execute, store—need not be complete before the next instruction is begun. **Parallel processing** uses multiple processors in the same computer at the same time. Some parallel processors are capable of operating in terms of **teraflops**— that is, trillions of floating-point instructions per second.

► Critical Thinking Questions

1. Why is writing instructions for a computer more difficult than writing instructions for a person?

2. Do you think there is a continuing need to increase computer speed? Can you think of examples in which more speed would be desirable?

3. It will soon be possible to have microchips implanted in our bodies to monitor or improve our physical conditions. Do you think this is a good idea or a bad idea?

4. A common misconception is that the prefix *mega* means one million. Actually, if someone has one megabyte of memory, instead of having 1,000,000 bytes of memory they really have 1,048,576 bytes. Explain why it appears that there are an extra 48,576 bytes of memory.

5. There are two fundamental types of computer memory—RAM and ROM. Define what these letters represent, and explain the functional differences between these two types of memory.

6. Although processor speeds are frequently specified in *hertz* (machine cycles per second), explain why a 600MHz processor may not be twice as fast as a 300MHz processor.

7. The most popular method of transferring images from a digital camera to your computer is through a cable connection. Explain which type of computer port you would want to connect your digital camera to and why.

► **STUDENT STUDY GUIDE**

Multiple Choice

1. The electrical circuitry that executes program instructions is the
   a. register
   b. operator
   c. central processing unit
   d. bus line

2. The entire computer system is coordinated by
   a. the ALU
   b. the control unit
   c. registers
   d. arithmetic operators

3. A bus line consists of
   a. registers
   b. parallel data paths
   c. megabytes
   d. machine cycles

4. Equal-to, less-than, and greater-than are examples of
   a. logical operations
   b. subtraction
   c. locations
   d. arithmetic operations

5. The primary storage unit is also known as
   a. a register
   b. mass storage
   c. secondary storage
   d. memory

6. Data and instructions are put into primary storage by
   a. memory
   b. secondary storage
   c. the control unit
   d. the ALU

7. During E-time the ALU
   a. examines the instruction
   b. executes the instruction
   c. enters the instruction
   d. elicits the instruction

8. Computer operations are synchronized by
   a. the CPU clock
   b. the binary system
   c. megabytes
   d. E-time

9. Which is not a type of memory?
   a. SRAM
   b. ROM
   c. DRAM
   d. QRAM

10. Another name for a logic chip is
    a. PROM
    b. microprocessor
    c. memory
    d. ROM

11. Data is represented on a computer by a two-state on/off system called
    a. a word
    b. a byte
    c. the binary system
    d. RAM

12. A letter, digit, or special character is represented by a
    a. bit
    b. byte
    c. kilobyte
    d. megabyte

13. Memory capacity may be expressed in
    a. microseconds
    b. MHz
    c. megabytes
    d. cycles

14. _____ cache is built into the CPU chip.
    a. L1
    b. L2
    c. external
    d. disk

15. A design technique that allows the CPU to begin processing one instruction before the previous instruction is finished is called
    a. pipelining
    b. RISC
    c. parallel processing
    d. serial processing

16. The main circuit board in a personal computer is called the
    a. fatherboard
    b. motherboard

c. ram/bus board
d. ASCII board

17. The Intel processor that is used on IBM compatible computers is the
    a. Quantium
    b. Pentium
    c. PowerPC
    d. none of the above

18. The new FireWire bus is also known as the
    a. IEEE 1394 bus
    b. IEEE 2294 bus
    c. Universal serial bus
    d. PC card bus

19. The processor speed for top-end personal computers is measured in
    a. kilohertz (KHz)
    b. megahertz (MHz)
    c. gigahertz (GHz)
    d. terahertz (THz)

20. Which of the following is/are **not** part of the CPU?
    a. Control Unit
    b. ALU
    c. Registers
    d. Primary storage

True/False

T F 1. The control unit consists of the CPU and the ALU.

T F 2. Secondary storage holds data only temporarily.

T F 3. The control unit directs the entire computer system.

T F 4. MIPS is an abbreviation for megaflop.

T F 5. The electronic circuitry that controls all arithmetic and logical operations is contained in the ALU.

T F 6. The three basic logical operations may be combined to form a total of nine commonly used operations.

T F 7. Memory allows fast access to instructions in secondary storage.

T F 8. Registers are temporary storage areas located in memory.

T F 9. Memory is usually volatile.

T F 10. RISC computers use fewer instructions than traditional computers.

T F 11. All computers except personal computers can execute more than one instruction at a time.

T F 12. The machine cycle consists of four steps, from the first step of fetching the instruction to the last step of storing the result in memory.

T F 13. The internal clock of the CPU produces pulses at a fixed rate to synchronize all computer operations.

T F 14. A cache is a small amount of secondary storage.

T F 15. Computers represent data using the two-state binary system.

T F 16. A bit is commonly made up of 8 bytes.

T F 17. A kilobyte (KB) is 1024 bytes.

T F 18. Unicode is a coding scheme that uses two bytes to represent 65,536 different characters.

T F 19. The Pentium is the microprocessor used on most Apple Macintosh computers.

T F 20. SIMMs and DIMMs are boards containing memory chips that are plugged into the motherboard.

Fill-In

1. A millionth of a second is called a(n) _____.

2. The _____ consists of both the control unit and the arithmetic/logic unit.

3. Processing instructions one at a time is called _____.

4. When the control unit decodes an instruction, is the machine cycle in I-time or E-time? _____

5. MHz is an abbreviation for _____.

6. _____ is nonvolatile memory used in cellular phones and digital cameras.

7. The combination of I-time and E-time is called a(n) _____.

8. The symbols =; <, and > are called _____.

9. Each memory location is identified by a(n) _____.

10. A 0 or 1 in the binary system is called a(n) _____.

11. MIPS stands for _____.

12. _____ is a high-speed temporary storage location for data moving between memory and the CPU.

13. The _____ consists of all the commands a CPU is capable of executing.

14. The _____ is the main circuit board found inside the system unit.

15. A(n) _____ is a connector on the back of the system unit that allows you to connect slow-speed devices that transmit data one bit at a time.

16. Special-purpose, high-speed areas for the temporary storage of data is called _____.

17. _____ uses multiple processors in the same computer at the same time.

18. The four steps in a machine cycle are _____, _____, _____, and _____.

19. The ability of a computer to overlap the steps in a machine cycle is known as _____.

20. The primary storage unit is a bit. Actually, BIT is an acronym and it means _____.

21. The _____ transfers data between the CPU and memory.

► ANSWERS

Multiple Choice

1. c	6. c	11. c	16. b
2. b	7. b	12. b	17. b
3. b	8. a	13. c	18. a
4. a	9. d	14. a	19. c
5. d	10. b	15. a	20. d

True/False

1. F	6. F	11. F	16. F
2. F	7. F	12. T	17. T
3. T	8. F	13. T	18. T
4. F	9. T	14. F	19. F
5. T	10. T	15. T	20. T

Fill-In

1. microsecond
2. central processing unit
3. serial processing
4. I-time
5. megahertz
6. flash memory
7. machine cycle
8. relational operators
9. address
10. bit
11. one million instructions per second
12. cache
13. instruction set
14. motherboard
15. serial port
16. registers
17. parallel processing
18. fetch, decode, execute, and store
19. pipelining
20. **BI**nary digi**T** or **B**inary dig**IT**
21. system bus

Planet Internet

Computers Helping Computers

What better place to get help for your PC problems than on the Web?

Of course if there's no light on the monitor or your PC won't boot, you might have to use a friend's computer to actually surf the Web for help. But if your computer is running but just not quite working right, or if you could really use that upgrade or replacement, there are Web sites designed to help.

Building PCs is a step-by-step guide to building your own PC, with easy-to-understand instructions and pictures. Beginning with selection of the CPU, it provides basic information about available add-on's and options, links to sites for further detail, and links to sites to compare prices. Hardware Masters, by contrast, is aimed at more experienced computer users. It provides reviews of new products, articles, current computer news, links to related information, and other features on its site.

PC Mechanic features step-by-step guides to building a PC and upgrading your computer and reviews of and editorials on new products and companies. You can buy e-book versions of some of their publications, including one on how to set up a network. The site also has a troubleshooting FAQ,

addressing such questions as "My sound card doesn't make any sound and I show no conflicts" and "My drive crashed. How can I get to my data?" You can submit your own question, but they provide some general troubleshooting tips to try before asking your question, beginning by suggesting that you "think like a computer."

For example, suppose you use a modem to reach the Internet. There was a nasty storm last night, with thunder and lightning galore, and you can't surf today. Everything worked fine before the storm. It might be the modem, or it might be the phone line. You had your computer plugged into a surge protector outlet, but it turns out that doesn't protect your modem (higher-end models do provide that protection). Thinking like a computer leads to step-by-step processes such as the following:

1. If your modem has its own diagnostic software, run that. However, be aware that it won't necessarily detect that your modem won't talk to the phone line anymore.

2. Plug a phone into the line; if that works, the line is OK. If the line is OK, it's probably time to buy a new modem.

The Computer Care Association page includes recommendations for preventative maintenance for your PC and a variety of products to keep your PC in good working order and virus resistant. They also provide on-site PC care. Finally, don't forget to check TechTV's Call for Help show notes to see whether they have answered your question.

Internet Exercises:

1. **Structured exercise.** Begin with the URL http://www.prenhall.com/capron and link to the Computer Care Association page. Read the information about preventive maintenance for your computer. Answer the following questions if you own a computer, or interview someone you know who does own a computer.

   - Do you do everything on the list about as often as recommended? If not, why not?
   - Have you ever experienced a problem with your computer that could have been avoided if you had followed their preventive maintenance recommendations? What should you have done?

   - In your opinion, what are the three most important items on the list?

2. **Free-form exercise.** Write down the features you would need in a computer, including the applications you want, your budget, and so on. Consider how you plan to use the Internet. Then go to a Web site that helps you build and design your computer. If you already have a computer, do this exercise for a friend or family member who is thinking about buying a computer.

3. **Advanced exercise.** Practice troubleshooting a PC problem. Pick a question from the PC Mechanic site or a question that you have heard from someone else. Using an approach similar to that recommended on the PC Mechanic site, explain your troubleshooting process, step by step. Double-check your approach by seeing the answer on the Web page, by having a knowledgeable friend critique your approach, or by implementing your approach to solve a problem.

Making Microchips

Computer power in the hands of the people—we take it for granted now, but not so long ago computers existed only in enormous rooms behind locked doors. The revolution that changed all that was ignited by chips of silicon smaller than your fingernail: microchips.

Silicon is one of the most common elements on Earth, but there is nothing commonplace about designing, manufacturing, testing, and packaging the microprocessors that are made from silicon. In this gallery we will explore the key elements in the process by which those marvels of miniaturization—microchips—are made.

The Idea Behind the Microchip

Microchips form the lightning-quick "brain" of a computer. These devices, though complex, work on a very simple principle: They "know" when electric current is on and when it is off. They can process information because it is coded as a series of on-off electric signals. Before the invention of microchips, these signals were controlled by thousands of separate devices laboriously wired together to form a single circuit. However, thousands of circuits can be embedded on a single microchip; a microchip is often called an integrated circuit.

Silicon is a semiconductor–it conducts electricity only 'semi' well. This does not sound like such an admirable trait, but the beauty of silicon is that it can be doped, or treated, with different materials to make it conduct electricity well or not at all. By doping various areas of a silicon chip differently, designers can set up pathways for electricity to follow.

The pathways consist of grooves etched into layers placed over a silicon substrate. The silicon is doped so that the pathways conduct electricity. The surrounding areas do not conduct electricity at all.

1. This simplified illustration shows the layers and grooves within a transistor, one of thousands of circuit components on a single chip. Pathway C controls the flow of electricity through the circuit. (a) When no electric charge is added to pathway C, electricity cannot flow along the circuit pathway from area A to area B. Thus the transistor is "off." (b) A charge added to pathway C temporarily allows electricity to travel from area A to area B. Now the transistor is "on," and electricity can continue to other components in the circuit. The control of electricity here and elsewhere in the chip makes it possible for the computer to process information coded as "on-off" electric signals.

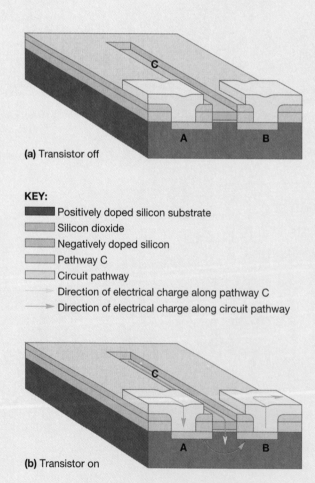

(a) Transistor off

KEY:

■ Positively doped silicon substrate
□ Silicon dioxide
□ Negatively doped silicon
□ Pathway C
□ Circuit pathway
→ Direction of electrical charge along pathway C
→ Direction of electrical charge along circuit pathway

(b) Transistor on

1. How a transistor conducts electricity.

Preparing the Design

Each microprocessor is constructed like a multistory building, with multiple layers of material combining to create a single complex unit. Try to imagine figuring out a way to place thousands of circuit components next to one another so that electricity flows through the whole integrated circuit the way it is supposed to. That is the job of chip designers. Essentially, they are trying to put together a gigantic multilayered jigsaw puzzle. The circuit design of a typical chip requires over a year's work by a team of designers. Computers assist in the complex task of mapping out the most efficient pathways for each circuit layer.

2. Microchip designers execute their plans using the computer.

2. A designer can arrange and modify circuit patterns and display them on a screen. Superimposing the color-coded circuit layers allows the designer to evaluate the relationships between them. The computer allows the designer to electronically store and retrieve previously designed circuit patterns.

3. Here the designer has used computer graphics software to display a screen image of the circuit design.

4. The computer system can also provide a printed version of any or all parts of the design. This large-scale printout allows the design team to discuss and modify the entire chip design.

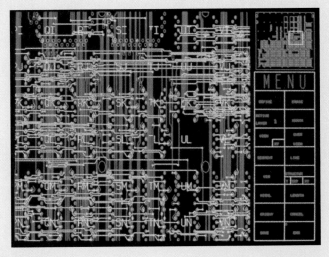

3. Close-up of what a chip designer sees on the screen.

4. A chip designer team works with an enlarged printout of the design.

Manufacturing the Chip

The silicon used to make computer chips is extracted from common rocks and sand. It is melted down into a form that is 99.9 percent pure silicon, and then doped with chemicals to make it either electrically positive or electrically negative.

6. A silicon wafer.

5. A cylinder of silicon that will be sliced into wafers.

7. Analogy of silicon being cooked.

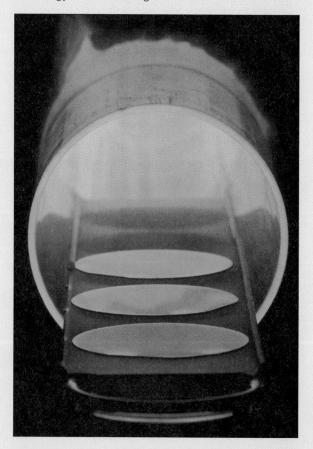

5. The molten silicon is then "grown" into cylindrical ingots in a process similar to candle dipping.

6. A diamond saw slices each ingot into circular wafers four or six or eight inches in diameter and four-thousandths of an inch thick. The wafers are sterilized and polished to a perfectly smooth, mirror-like finish. Each wafer will eventually contain hundreds of identical chips. One silicon wafer can produce more than 100 microprocessors.

Since a single speck of dust can ruin a chip, chips are manufactured in special laboratories called clean rooms. The air in clean rooms is filtered, and workers dress in "bunny suits" to lessen the chance of chip contamination. A chip-manufacturing lab is 100 times cleaner than a hospital operating room.

7. Chip-manufacturing processes vary, but one step is common: Electrically positive silicon wafers are placed in an open glass tube and inserted into a 1200° Celsius oxidation furnace. Oxygen reacts with the silicon, covering each wafer with a thin layer of silicone dioxide, which does not conduct electricity well. Each wafer is then coated with a gelatin-like substance called photoresist, which hardens. The final design of each circuit layer must be reduced to the size of the chip. A stencil called a mask, representing the schematic design of the circuit, is placed over the wafer. Ultraviolet light is shined through the mask, softening the exposed–nonmasked–photoresist on the wafer.

8. The wafer is then taken to a washing station in a specifically lit "yellow room," where the wafer is washed in solvent to remove the soft photoresist. This leaves ridges of material–hardened photoresist in the pattern of the mask–on the wafer. Next the silicon dioxide revealed by the washing is etched away by hot gases. The silicon underneath, which forms the circuit pathway, is then doped to make it electrically negative. In this way, the circuit pathway is distinguishable from the rest of the silicon. In the final step, aluminum is deposited to connect the circuit components and form the bonding pads to which wires will later be connected.

9. The result: one wafer with many chips.

10. Computerized coloration enhances this close-up view of a wafer with chips.

11. This image shows circuit paths on a microprocessor chip magnified 3000 times.

8. Wafer washing room.

9. Close-up of chips on a wafer.

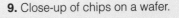

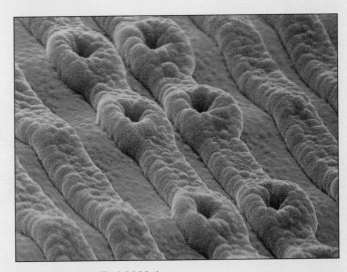

10. Chips still on the wafer.

11. A chip magnified 3000 times.

Testing the Chip

Microprocessor manufacturers devote extraordinary efforts to testing their chips. The chips are tested all along the way, from design to manufacturing to packaging. A microprocessor is so complex that it is impossible to literally check every possible state it could be in; the number of elements—millions of transistors—and the number of different combinations is simply too great. However, months of continuous, specialized, and extremely expensive testing will yield a working, reliable product. Even after a chip reaches production, testing continues. Each new chip is tested while still on the wafer and after it is packaged.

Although chips on a particular wafer may look identical, they do not perform identically.

12. A probe machine must perform millions of tests on each chip, to determine whether it conducts electricity in the precise way it was designed to. The needle-like probes contact the bonding pads, apply electricity, measure the results, and mark ink spots on defective chips.

12. Needle-like probes test each chip.

13. A defect review performed by a computer finds and classifies defects in order to eliminate them from the wafer.

14. After initial testing, a diamond saw cuts each chip from the wafer, and defective chips are discarded.

13. Classifying defects and eliminating bad chips.

14. Cutting chips from the wafer

Packaging the Chip

Each acceptable chip is mounted on a protective package.

15. An automated wire-bonding device wires the bonding pads of the chip to the electrical leads on the package, using aluminum or gold wire thinner than a human hair. A variety of packages are in use today.

16. Dual in-line packages have two rows of legs that are inserted into holes in a circuit board.

17. Square pin-grid array packages, which are used for chips requiring many electrical leads, look like a bed of nails. The pins are inserted into the holes in a circuit board. In this photo the protective cap has been cut away, revealing the ultrafine wires connecting the chip to the package.

15. Wiring the chip

16. Square pin-grid chip package

17. Chip mounted on surface so that legs can be inserted into holes on the circuit board

From Chip to Computer

At a factory that manufactures circuit boards, **18.** a robot makes a circuit board and **19.** another robot inserts a pin-grid package into holes in a circuit board. Several surface mount packages have already been placed on the board.

20. Dual in-line packages of various sizes have been attached to this circuit board.

21. This circuit board is being installed in a Compaq computer.

18. A factory robot makes a circuit board.

19. A factory robot lines up the pins on the chip package with holes on the receiving circuit board.

21. Installing the circuit board.

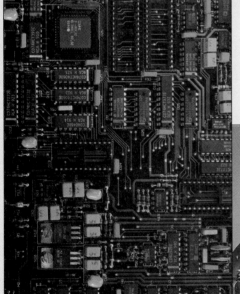

20. A finished circuit board.

Input and Output:
The User Connection

Input and Output:
The User Connection

C H A P T E R **5**

LEARNING OBJECTIVES

Describe the user relationship with computer input and output

Explain how data is input into a computer system and differentiate among various input equipment

Describe how a monitor works and the characteristics that determine quality

List and describe the different methods of computer output

Differentiate among different kinds of printers

Explain the function of a computer terminal and describe the types of terminals

cKenna University long ago abandoned the practice of having students stand in line to register for classes. Now almost everything is handled by phoning a computer. Since these procedures save time and trouble, they suit Rose Sierra just fine. Rose did begin with a manual procedure when she first applied to the university. Her application, the source document, was prepared by her and, after she was accepted, scanned into the university's computer. From that point forward, Rose has communicated directly with the computer.

Rose can phone the computer and supply it with her data, using her Touch-Tone phone as a sort of miniature keyboard. Once the computer responds to the number she dials, she enters her Social Security number, followed by the unique personal identification number (PIN) assigned to her by the university. She can then follow the procedure to register for classes, entering class item numbers from the college's class schedule. Various options are available, such as taking a class for credit or audit, by entering a number from her telephone keypad. The computer delivers voice output, telling her she has—or has not—been accepted in a class. Once she has entered all classes, Rose can push other buttons for other options, such as hearing her class schedule, dropping a class, hearing the tuition amount owed, and paying by credit card.

Once Rose is registered, the computer will print her student identification card, complete with bar code, which she can pick up in the library.

The ID card is used for checking books out of the library and for making use of computer and science labs. The computer produces a lot of other output, such as class rosters for instructors and registration summaries, that are only indirectly related to Rose.

Rose is not particularly familiar with computer-related input/output terms such as source document, scan, keyboard, voice output, and bar code, nor does she need to be to register. But understanding these terms, and other terms related to input and output, will help users to navigate all sorts of computer systems.

HARDWARE.

Prentice Hall
EXPLORE Generation **it**

► HOW USERS SEE INPUT AND OUTPUT

The central processing unit is the unseen part of a computer system; users are only dimly aware of it. But users are very much aware of the input and output associated with the computer. They submit input data to the computer to get processed information, the output.

Sometimes the output is an instant reaction to the input. Consider these examples:

- Zebra-striped bar codes on supermarket items provide input that permits instant retrieval of outputs—price and item name—right at the checkout counter.

- A forklift operator speaks directly to a computer through a microphone. Words such as *left, right,* and *lift* are the actual input data. The output is the computer's instant response, which causes the forklift to operate as requested.

- A sales representative uses an instrument that looks like a pen to enter an order on a special pad. The handwritten characters are displayed as "typed" text and are stored in the pad, which is actually a small computer.

- Factory workers input data by punching in on a time clock as they go from task to task. The time clock is connected to a computer. The outputs are their weekly paychecks and reports for management that summarize hours per project on a quarterly basis.

Input and output may be separated by time, distance, or both. Here are some examples:

- Data on checks is used as input to the bank computer, which eventually processes the data to prepare a bank statement once a month.

- Charge-card transactions in a retail store provide input data that is processed monthly to produce customer bills.

- Water sample data is collected at lake and river sites, keyed in at the environmental agency office, and used to produce reports that show patterns of water quality.

The examples in this section show the diversity of computer applications, but in all cases the process is the same: input–processing–output. This chapter examines input and output methods in detail.

► INPUT: GETTING DATA FROM THE USER TO THE COMPUTER

Some input data can go directly to the computer for processing. Input in this category includes bar codes, speech that enters the computer through a microphone, and data entered by means of a device that converts motions to on-screen action. Some

Perhaps you can send e-mail, and you may even have learned how to include a photograph. But can you talk face-to-face with someone using a computer connection? You can if you buy one of the video kits that have made the process easy and affordable. A typical kit includes a camera and software, both of which are easy to install. Shown here is Intel's *Create & Share Camera Pack;* note the camera atop the monitor. Of course, this works only if the party at the other end

of your communication has a video setup too.

The technology for video telephones has been around for a long time, but it never caught on with the general public. Perhaps people didn't want to be seen with their hair in curlers or in their bathrobes. But computer video telephony is attractive, partly because it is inexpensive even over long distances and partly because it is still sufficiently novel that it is planned in advance—no curlers.

---

input data, however, go through a good deal of intermediate handling, such as when it is copied from a **source document** (jargon for the original written data) and translated to a medium that a machine can read, such as a magnetic disk. In either case the task is to gather data to be processed by the computer—sometimes called *raw data*—and convert it into an electronic form that the computer can understand. Conventional input devices include the keyboard, mouse, trackball, touchpad, and joystick, which are explained in the following sections.

Keyboard

A **keyboard,** which usually is similar to a typewriter keyboard, may be part of a personal computer or part of a terminal that is connected to a computer somewhere else (Figure 5-1a). Not all keyboards are traditional, however. A fast-food franchise such as McDonald's, for example, uses keyboards whose keys represent items such as large fries or a Big Mac. Even less traditional is the keyboard shown in Figure 5-1b, which is used to enter Chinese characters. Figure 5-2 shows the complete layout of a traditional keyboard.

Pointing Devices

A **pointing device** is used to position a **pointer** on the screen. The pointer can have a number of shapes but is most often an arrow. A pointing device usually has one or more buttons or other mechanisms to indicate the action to take once the pointer has been positioned in the desired location. To modify text in an application such as word processing, you move the pointer to the desired place in the screen text, then click the button to set the **insertion point,** or **cursor.** (The insertion point can also be moved by pressing various keyboard keys.) The next text that is typed will begin at the insertion point. In graphics-based applications, you use the pointing device to control various drawing instruments, such as a paintbrush, pen, or eraser.

You can also use the pointing device to communicate commands to the operating system or an application program by clicking a button. In particular, a button is often used to click on an icon, a pictorial symbol on a screen; the **icon** represents a computer activity—a command to the computer—so clicking the icon invokes the command. The command may be to launch an application, such as word processing or a game, or to activate a feature within an application, such as underlining. The environment that permits communication with the computer by clicking on icons is referred to as a **graphical user interface (GUI).**

(a)

(b)

▲ **FIGURE 5-1**

Keyboards.

(a) A traditional computer keyboard. (b) Chinese characters are significantly more complicated than the letters and digits found on a standard keyboard. To enter Chinese characters into the computer system, one uses a special keyboard. Each letter key shows the characters that a user can type by holding down other keys while pressing that letter (as you would hold down a Shift key to make capital letters).

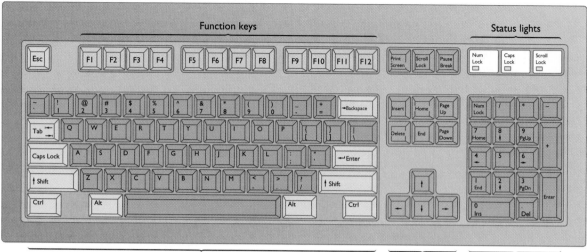

Function keys

Status lights

Main keyboard

Additional keys

Numeric keys

FIGURE 5·2

Finding your way around a keyboard.

Most personal computer keyboards have at least three main parts: function keys, the main keyboard in the center, and the numeric keys and status lights. Extended keyboards, such as the one shown here, have additional keys between the main keyboard and the numeric keys. **Function keys:** The function keys (highlighted in tan on the diagram) are an easy way to give certain commands to the computer. What each function key does is defined by the particular software you are using. Some keyboards have the function keys on the left instead of across the top. **Main keyboard:** The main keyboard includes the familiar keys found on a typewriter keyboard (dark blue), as well as some special command keys (light blue). The command keys have different uses that depend on the software being used. **Numeric keys:** The numeric keys (purple), serve one of two purposes, depending on the status of the Num Lock light. When the Num Lock light is on, these keys can be used to enter numeric data and mathematical symbols. When the Num Lock light is off, the numeric keys are used to move the cursor and perform other functions, as shown on the bottom of each key cap. The Num Lock key is used to toggle the Num Lock light on and off. **Additional keys:** Extended keyboards include additional keys (green) that duplicate the cursor movement functions of the numeric keys. Users who enter a lot of numeric data can leave their keyboards in the Num Lock mode and use these keys to control the cursor.

A number of different pointing devices are available for use on a computer. Your choice of device will depend both on personal preference and on the types of applications you use. Some of the most common pointing devices are described below.

MOUSE   The mouse is by far the most common pointing device for personal computers. A **mouse** is a palm-sized device that is moved around on a flat surface to cause a corresponding movement of the pointer on the screen. A **mechanical mouse** has a small ball on its underside that rolls as the mouse is moved. Sensors inside the mouse determine the direction and distance of movement and signal the computer to move the pointer on the screen accordingly. An **optical mouse** uses a light beam to monitor mouse movement. Older models require a special mouse pad that has gridlines on its surface, but newer optical mice will work on almost any non-reflective surface. Most mice connect via cable to a port on the computer. A **wireless mouse,** by contrast, communicates through an infrared beam and so must have a clear path between the mouse and the infrared port on the PC. As mice have evolved, new features and new buttons have been added. Mice such as Microsoft's IntelliMouse offers an extra wheel, positioned between the two mouse buttons, that can be clicked like a button or rolled to affect the cursor (Figure 5-3). With software designed to be used with this mouse, it can move through a document line-by-line or page-by-page, zoom in on a special spreadsheet cell, or flip backwards through Web pages you have already seen. Some mice have up to five programmable buttons.

TRACKBALL   The **trackball** is a variation on the mechanical mouse. You may have used a trackball to play a video game. The trackball is like an upside-down mechanical mouse—you roll the ball directly with your hand. Buttons are mounted along-side or below the ball. The popularity of the trackball surged with the advent of laptop computers, when traveling users found themselves without a flat surface on which to roll the traditional mouse. Trackballs are often built into portable computers, but they can also be used as separate input devices with any computer. (Figure 5-4).

TOUCHPAD   A **touchpad** is a rectangular pressure-sensitive pad. Just slide your finger across the touchpad's surface, and corresponding pointer movements will be made on the screen. Buttons at the bottom of the unit serve the same functions as mouse buttons, but most touchpads also recognize a finger tap as a click. Stand-alone touchpads are available to use with any computer, but most are built into laptops.

POINTING STICK   A **pointing stick** is a small pressure-sensitive post mounted in the center of the keyboard between the *G* and *H* keys (Figure 5-5). Pushing the post in one direction causes the pointer to move in that direction. The pointer stops moving when pressure is released. Buttons are located below the keyboard.

JOYSTICK   A **joystick** is a short lever with a handgrip that resembles the floor-mounted gearshift in a sports car (Figure 5-6). The distance and speed of movement control the screen pointer's position. Pressing *triggers*, buttons on the lever, causes various actions to take place, depending on the software in use. Although the joystick is most often used with games such as flight simulators, it can be used as a mouse replacement.

GRAPHICS TABLET   A **graphics tablet,** also called a **digitizing tablet,** is a rectangular board that contains an invisible grid of electronic dots (Figure 5-7). As the user moves a pen-like **stylus** or a mouse-like **puck** with crosshairs around the board, the dot locations that are passed over are sent to the computer. Architects and engineers use these tablets to trace or create precise drawings.

TOUCH SCREENS   One way of getting input directly from the source is to have a human simply point to a selection. The edges of some **touch screens** emit horizon-

▲ **F I G U R E 5-3**

Mouse.

As the mouse is moved over a smooth surface, the pointer on the computer screen makes a corresponding movement.

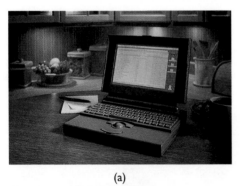

(a)

(b)

▲ **F I G U R E 5-4**

Trackball.

The rotation of the ball causes a corresponding movement of the pointer on the screen. (a) Trackballs are often used with laptop computers because, especially on an airplane, there may be no handy surface on which to roll a mouse. Notice that the ball is placed in the center, both for compactness and to accommodate both right- and left-handed users. (b) This trackball, which looks rather like an oversized egg, is called EasyBall because it can be grasped and manipulated by a child's small hand.

Pointing stick.

The keyboard uses a pointing stick embedded in its center to move the pointer on the screen.

Joystick.

The joystick is most commonly used for playing action games.

Graphics tablet.

Architects and engineers often use graphics tablets to enter and make changes to technical drawings.

tal and vertical beams of light that crisscross the screen. When a finger touches the screen, the interrupted light beams can pinpoint the location selected on the screen. Another type of touch screen senses finger pressure to determine the location. A variation of this concept has the user use a **light pen** for pointing. Light pens allow a greater level of precision in pinpointing screen locations. Some light pens require a special monitor; others will work with any monitor.

Kiosks—self-contained self-help stations often found in public places such as malls and supermarkets—offer a variety of services. A kiosk's touch screen is so easy to use that it attracts patrons (Figure 5-8). Wal-Mart, for example, uses kiosks to let customers find items such as auto parts. Many delicatessens use kiosks to let you point to salami on rye, among other selections. But the most widespread use of kiosks is in government offices. They are becoming sufficiently commonplace that people are no longer startled when a pleasant female voice from the kiosk screen says, "If you want to file for divorce, touch here." In fact, kiosks in California, Arizona, and Utah handle uncontested divorces, probates, evictions, small claims, and other legal matters.

PEN-BASED COMPUTING   Small handheld computing devices often use an electronic pen, or stylus, to input data. The pen can be used as a pointer on the device's screen or to input data in handwritten form. Software translates the handwriting into characters that the computer can work with (Figure 5-9).

Source Data Automation: Collecting Data Where It Starts

Efficient data input means reducing the number of intermediate steps required between the origination of data and its processing. This is best accomplished by **source data automation**—the use of special equipment to collect data at the source, as a by-product of the activity that generates the data, and send it directly to the computer. Recall, for example, the supermarket bar code, which can be used to send data about the product directly to the computer. Source data automation eliminates keying, thereby reducing costs and opportunities for human-introduced mistakes. Since data about a transaction is collected when and where the transaction takes place, source data automation also improves the speed of the input operation and is much less expensive than other methods.

For convenience this discussion is divided into the primary areas related to source data automation: magnetic-ink character recognition, scanners and other optical recognition devices, and even your own voice, finger, or eye.

Magnetic-Ink Character Recognition

Magnetic-ink character recognition, or **MICR** (pronounced "mike-er"), involves using a machine to read characters made of magnetized particles. The banking

◄ **F I G U R E 5-8**

A Kiosk.

Kiosks use touch screens to provide information and services to the public. Kiosks are found in public places like malls, supermarkets, and banks.

industry is the predominant user of MICR equipment. Banks use the numbers encoded across the bottom of your personal check to route your check from the bank cashing the check to the bank where you have your account. Figure 5-10 shows what some of these numbers and symbols represent.

Most magnetic-ink characters are preprinted on your check. If you compare a check that you wrote that has been cashed and cleared by the bank with one that is still unused in your checkbook, you will note that the amount of the cashed check has been reproduced in magnetic characters in the lower-right corner. These characters were added by a person at the bank where the check was deposited by using a **MICR inscriber.**

Scanner

There was a time when the only way to transfer an existing document into the computer was to retype it. Now, however, an **optical scanner,** usually referred to as just a **scanner,** can convert text or even a drawing or picture into computer-recognizable data by using a form of optical recognition. **Optical recognition** systems use a light beam to scan input data and convert it into electrical signals, which are sent to the computer for processing. Optical recognition is by far the most common type of source input; just think of all those supermarket scanners.

Electronic Pen.

Small hand-held computers often use an electronic pen, or stylus, to input data. The pen can be used as a pointer on the device's screen or to input data in handwritten form.

The symbols on your check.

Magnetic-ink numbers and symbols run along the bottom of a check. The symbols on the left are preprinted. The MICR characters in the lower-right corner of a cashed check are entered by the bank that receives it; these numbers should correspond to the amount of the check.

Preprinted on check

Virtual Ads

If you've ever watched a baseball game on television, chances are you've seen a virtual ad—an ad that doesn't exist at the ballpark.

Prior to the event, an operator selects which advertisements to insert and chooses where in the stadium they will appear. During the broadcast, the system then automatically inserts the advertisement into position, correctly adjusted for the position of the television camera. The inserted images appear as if they actually exist in the stadium, even to the extent that players pass in front of—obscure—the inserted image.

Unlike the usual 30-second television commercial, this ad may loom in front of a viewer for much of the game. Furthermore, advertisers can target local audiences, showing an ad for hot soup in Juneau while, in the same spot, showing an ad for cold soda in San Diego.

Now consider all those drawers filled with receipts, warranties, and old checks. If you would let the computer take care of them, you could save space and, even better, be able to find an item when you wanted it. Large businesses often use a process called **document imaging,** in which a scanner converts all incoming paper documents (invoices, order forms, etc.) to an electronic version, which can then be stored on disk, routed to the proper people, and retrieved when needed. But most consumers use a scanner to turn snapshots into images that can be printed, incorporated into a craft project, e-mailed, or posted on their Web site. Another popular use is converting printed documents, perhaps a letter or magazine article, into text that can be edited—changed or revised—by word processing software.

Business people also find imaging useful, since they can view an exact computer-produced replica of the original document at any time. Processed by related software, the words and numbers of the document can be manipulated by word processing and other software. The Internal Revenue Service uses imaging to process 17,000 tax returns per hour, a significant improvement over hand processing.

Optical scanners fall into three categories. A **flatbed scanner** typically scans one sheet at a time, though some offer an attachment for scanning multiple sheets. Flatbed scanners are space hogs, taking up about as much room as a tabletop copy machine (Figure 5-11a). The advantage of a flatbed scanner is that it can be used to scan bound documents, such as pages from books and other bulky items. In a **sheetfed scanner,** motorized rollers feed the sheet across the scanning head. A key attraction of sheetfed scanners is that they are usually designed to fit neatly between the keyboard and the monitor (Figure 5-11b). However, sheetfed scanners are less versatile than flatbed scanners and are more prone to errors. A **handheld scanner,** the least expensive and least accurate of the three, is a handy portable option. It is often difficult to get a good scan with a handheld scanner because the user must move the scanner in a straight line at a fixed rate. If the document being scanned is wider than the scanner, several passes must be made, and software must "stitch" the images together, a tedious and error-prone process.

Many users like scanners because they can use them to scan photographs directly into the computer. However, if you want to scan text and then be able to edit it using word processing, another step is involved. Since the result of a scan is simply a picture of the document being scanned, special software—usually called **OCR** software, for **optical character recognition**—must analyze the picture and convert it into characters. Most scanners come accompanied by OCR software.

 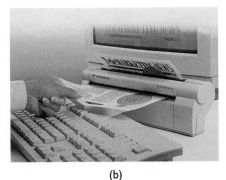

(a)   (b)

▲ **FIGURE 5-11**

Scanners.

Once an image has been scanned into the computer, it can be stored and used again, perhaps in a document that combines text with photos. (a) With a flatbed scanner, the image to be scanned is laid face down on the scanner, which looks something like a small copy machine. (b) Paper can be fed to the motorized rollers of a sheetfed scanner, which has the added advantage of fitting nicely between keyboard and monitor.

More Optical Recognition Methods

In addition to text and images, optical recognition can process data appearing in a variety of forms: optical marks, optical characters, bar codes, and even handwritten characters.

OPTICAL MARK RECOGNITION   **Optical mark recognition (OMR)** is sometimes called **mark sensing** because a machine senses marks on a piece of paper. As a student, you may immediately recognize this approach as the technique used to score certain tests. Using a pencil, you make a mark in a specified box, circle, or space that corresponds to what you think is the answer. The answer sheet is then graded by an optical device that recognizes the locations of the marks and converts them to computer-recognizable electrical signals.

OPTICAL CHARACTER RECOGNITION   **Optical character recognition (OCR)** devices also use a light source to read special characters and convert them into electrical signals to be sent to the central processing unit. The characters—letters, numbers, and special symbols—can be read by both humans and machines. They are often found on sales tags on store merchandise. A standard typeface for optical characters, called **OCR-A,** has been established by the American National Standards Institute (Figure 5-12).The handheld **wand reader** is a popular input device for reading OCR-A. Wands are being used more and more in libraries, hospitals, and factories, as well as in retail stores.

BAR CODES   Each product on the store shelf has its own unique number, which is part of the **Universal Product Code (UPC).** This code number is represented on the product label by a pattern of vertical marks, or bars, called **bar codes.** (UPC, by the way, is an agreed-on standard within the supermarket industry; many other kinds of bar codes exist. You need only look as far as the back cover of this book to see an example of another kind of bar code.) These stripes can be sensed and read by a **bar-code reader,** a photoelectric device that reads the code by means of reflected light. When you buy, say, a can of corn at the supermarket, the checker moves it past the bar-code reader (Figure 5-13a). The bar code merely identifies the product to the store's computer; the code does not contain the price, which may vary. The price is stored in a file that can be accessed by the computer. (Obviously, it is easier to change the price in the computer than it is to restamp the price on each can of corn.)

```
A B C D E F G
H I J K L M N
O P Q R S T U
V W X Y Z ⌐ .
⇋ / * Ñ ⅃ 1 2 3
4 5 6 7 8 9 0
```

▲ **FIGURE 5-12**

The OCR-A typeface.

This is a common typeface for optical character recognition.

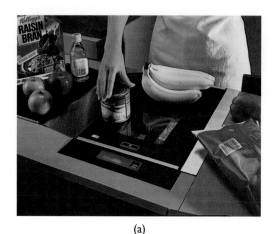
(a)

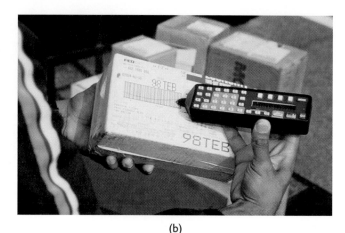
(b)

▲ FIGURE 5-13

Bar codes.

(a) This photoelectric bar code scanner, often seen at supermarket checkout counters, reads the product's zebra-striped bar code. The bar code identifies the product for the store's computer, which retrieves price and description information. The price is then automatically rung up on the point-of-sale terminal. (b) FedEx uses a bar code system to identify and track packages in transit.

The computer returns the price; then a printer prints the item description and price on a paper tape for the customer. Some supermarkets are moving to do-it-yourself scanning, putting the bar-code reader—as well as the bagging—in the customer's hands.

Although bar codes were once found primarily in supermarkets, there are a variety of other interesting applications. Bar coding has been described as an inexpensive and remarkably reliable way to get data into a computer. It is no wonder that virtually every industry has found a niche for bar codes. Federal Express, for example, attributes a large part of the corporation's success to the bar-coding system it uses to track packages (Figure 5-13b). Each package is uniquely identified by a 10-digit bar code, which is input to the computer at each point as the package travels through the system. An employee can use a computer terminal to query the location of a given shipment at any time; the sender can request a status report on a package or track the package on the FedEx Web site.

HANDWRITTEN CHARACTERS   Machines that can read handwritten characters are yet another means of reducing the number of intermediate steps between capturing data and processing it. In many instances it is preferable to write the data and imme-

▶ FIGURE 5-14

Handwritten characters.

Legibility is important in making handwritten characters readable by optical recognition systems.

	Good	Bad
1. Make your letters big	EWING	EWING
2. Use simple shapes	57320	57320
3. Use block printing	KENT	Kent
4. Connect lines	5B E4	5B E4
5. Close loops	9068	9068
6. Do not link characters	LOOP	LOOP

◄ **F I G U R E** 5-15

How voice input works.

The user speaks into a microphone or telephone. A chip on a board inside the computer analyzes the waveform of the word and changes it to binary numbers that the computer can understand. These digits are compared with the numbers in a stored vocabulary list; if a match is found, the corresponding word is displayed on the screen.

diately have it usable for processing rather than having data entry operators key it in later. However, not just any scrawl will do; the rules governing the size, completeness, and legibility of the handwriting are fairly rigid (Figure 5-14).

Voice Input

Speaking to a computer, known as **voice input** or **speech recognition,** is another form of source input. **Speech recognition devices** accept the spoken word through a microphone and convert it into binary code (0s and 1s) that can be understood by the computer (Figure 5-15). Typical users are the disabled, those with "busy hands" or hands too dirty for the keyboard, and those with no access to a keyboard. Uses for speech recognition include changing radio frequencies in airplane cockpits, placing a call on a car phone, asking for stock-market quotations over the phone, inspecting items moving along an assembly line, and allowing physically disabled users to issue commands (Figure 5-16).

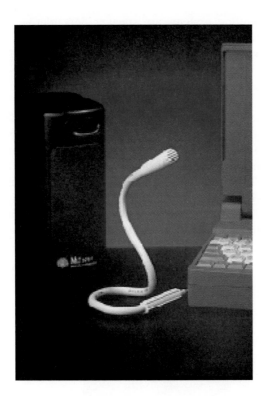

◄ **F I G U R E** 5-16

Microphone.

This twistable—and inexpensive—microphone is an input device for speech recognition.

GETTING PRACTICAL | **Digital Darkroom**

Never mind the traditional darkroom, where a photo buff squints in dim red light while sloshing photos through smelly development chemicals. And, frankly, the results of all that sloshing, especially enlargements, probably would not be confused with professional work. But now that has changed. With the right computer equipment, you can be a professional—or close enough. You can make prints and enlargements that could not be differentiated from professional work without the aid of a magnifying glass.

First, let us consider the source of your pictures. How does one get the photos into the computer in the first place? There are several possibilities. A straightforward approach is to use a digital camera, storing the pictures in some computer-readable form—chip or card or disk—and transferring the images directly to the computer. If your photos were recorded on the camera's embedded chip, they can be transferred by means of a cable hooked up to your computer's serial port or USB port, a plug-like input in the back. Another choice is to scan photos into the computer; a good-quality scanner will maintain the quality of the photos.

Another possible photo source is the Internet, which offers free images, some as part of clip-art collections. Keep in mind, however, that professional photos on Internet sites are probably fee-based. Therefore if your interest goes beyond casual snapshots, you can pay for and download images from professional services on the Internet. Whatever method you choose to input photos, the net result is that you then can edit and reproduce those photos.

Once you have the photos in digital form, you will probably want to use some photo-imaging software to manipulate them. Such software is an option rather than a necessity, but many people find that they like to improve or change their pictures in some way. However, despite a bit of photo manipulation by software, the printed photo image you hope for can be only as good as the image the program is given to work with.

Processing photographs at home is a trend in progress. People love to take pictures. People also love enlargements. Yet, mostly because of the high cost, only a tiny percentage of photos are enlarged. Home computer photography systems offer a new level of flexibility and creativity, enabling users to make professional-looking prints, reprints, and enlargements of photos that can be incorporated into personalized greeting cards, calendars, and postcards.

Most speech recognition systems are speaker-dependent—that is, they must be separately trained for each individual user. The speech recognition system "learns" the voice of the user, who speaks isolated words repeatedly. The voiced words the system "knows" are then recognizable in the future. Speaker-independent speech recognition systems are designed to recognize anyone's voice, but have a much more limited vocabulary.

Speech recognition systems that are limited to isolated words are called **discrete word systems,** and users must pause between words. These systems are very accurate and are often used to allow users to issue brief commands to the computer. However, they are very tedious and awkward to use for inputting large amounts of text, as in dictation. The technology for **continuous word systems,** which can interpret sustained speech so that users can speak almost normally, has improved dramatically in the last few years. A key advantage of delivering input to a computer in a normal speaking pattern is ease of use. It is faster and easier for most people to dic-

▶ **FIGURE 5-17**

Digital camera.

Digital cameras do not use film. They store images internally and then send them via cable or disk to your computer.

tate a letter than to key it in. Soon, most new personal computers will be equipped with speech recognition.

Although speech recognition has made great strides, the computer still has extreme difficulty in understanding the meaning of the words that are recognized. Teaching the computer to understand normal human speech is one of the major challenges facing computer scientists.

Digital Cameras

Point, shoot, edit, print; the steps that are noticeably missing are loading film and, later, trips to the photo-processing lab. A **digital camera** takes photos that it stores internally on a chip; there is no film (Figure 5-17). The photos can then be sent by cable directly to your computer; some cameras place the image on a removable card that can be added to an adapter and inserted into the computer's disk drive. Some cameras record images directly onto a diskette. Once in the computer, the photos can be edited with the software that accompanied the camera. When you are satisfied with a photo, you can print it. Photos printed on your everyday printer will not rival film-based images, but you may buy a special printer designed for photos that uses heavyweight coated paper and produces good results.

A particular advantage of digital cameras is their little LCD windows that let you see the photo you just took. If you do not like it, simply delete it and try again.

▶ OUTPUT: INFORMATION FOR THE USER

As we noted earlier, computer output usually takes the form of screen or printer output. Other forms of output include voice, sound, and various forms of graphics output. Devices have even been designed to produce odors as computer output.

A computer system may be designed to produce several kinds of output. An example is a travel agency's computer system. If a customer asks about airline connections to, say, Toronto, Calgary, and Vancouver, the travel agent will probably make a few queries to the system and receive on-screen output indicating availability and pricing for the various flights. After the reservations have been confirmed, the agent can ask for printed output that includes the tickets, the traveler's itinerary, and the invoice. In addition, the agency's management may periodically receive printed reports and charts, such as monthly summaries of sales figures or pie charts of regional costs.

Computer Screen Technology

A user's first interaction with a computer screen may be to view the screen response to that user's input. When data is entered, it appears on the screen. The computer response to that data—the output—also appears on the screen. The screen is part of the computer's **monitor,** which also includes the housing for its electrical components. Monitors usually include a stand that can be tilted or swiveled to allow the monitor to be easily adjusted to suit the user.

Screen output is known in the computer industry as **soft copy** because it is intangible and temporary, unlike **hard copy,** which is produced by a printer on paper, is tangible, and can be permanent.

Computer screens come in many varieties (Figure 5-18), but the most common kind is the **cathode ray tube (CRT).** CRT monitors that display text and graphics are in common use today. Although most CRTs are color, some are **monochrome,** meaning that only one color, usually green or amber, appears on a contrasting background. Monochrome screens, which are less expensive than those with color, are used in business applications such as customer inquiry or order entry, which have no need for color.

Most CRT screens use a technology called **raster scanning,** a process of sweeping electron beams across the back of the screen. The backing of the screen display has a phosphorous coating that glows whenever it is hit by a beam of electrons. But the phosphorus does not glow for very long, so the image must be **refreshed** often. If the screen is not refreshed often enough, the fading screen image appears to flicker. A **scan rate**—the number of times the electron beam refreshes the screen—of 80 to 100 times per second is usually adequate to retain a clear screen image. This is essentially the same process used to produce television images.

A CRT display has hundreds of horizontal lines, which are scanned from left to right and from top to bottom. On inexpensive monitors the screen is sometimes scanned in **interlaced** fashion: the odd-numbered lines on one pass of the electron beam and then the even-numbered lines on the next pass. This allows for a lower refresh rate without producing flicker. With text and fixed graphics displays, this scheme can work well. However, with animated graphics—especially images that move or change form rapidly—interlacing can produce an irritating flutter effect. Thus most screens today are advertised as **noninterlaced (NI),** that is, all lines are scanned on each pass.

A computer display screen that can be used for graphics is divided into dots that are called **addressable** because they can be addressed individually by the graphics software. Each dot can be illuminated individually on the screen. Each dot is referred to as a *pic*ture *ele*ment, or **pixel.** The resolution of the screen—its clarity—is directly related to the number of pixels on the screen: The more pixels, the higher the resolution. Another factor of importance is **dot pitch,** the amount of space between the dots. The smaller the dot pitch, the better the quality of the screen image.

The electrical output signals that the control unit sends to the monitor have to be converted into the signals that control the monitor. This can be accomplished by

A variety of screens.

(a) Laptop computers, once limited to monochrome screens, now usually have color screens. (b) This high-resolution brilliance is available only on a color graphics display.

(a)   (b)

chips permanently affixed to the motherboard, but most computers have a **graphics card,** or **graphics adapter board,** plugged into an expansion slot. This approach allows the user to upgrade the graphics capability if desired. The graphics card and the monitor must be compatible to produce a high-quality image.

Graphic standards were established in the early years of the personal computer. The intention of standards is to agree on resolutions, colors, and so forth, to make it easier for the manufacturers of personal computers, monitors, graphics boards, and software to ensure that their products work together.

The standards in most common use today are SVGA and XGA. There are several varieties of **SVGA (Super Video Graphics Adapter),** each providing a different resolution: 800 (horizontal) × 600 (vertical) pixels, 1024 × 768, 1280 × 1024, and 1600 × 1200. All SVGA standards support a palette of 16 million colors, but the number of colors that can be displayed simultaneously is limited by the amount of video memory installed in a system. One SVGA system might display only 256 simultaneous colors while another displays the entire palette of 16 million colors.

XGA (extended graphics array) is a high-resolution graphics standard designed to replace older standards. It provides the same resolutions but supports more simultaneous colors. In addition, XGA allows monitors to be noninterlaced.

Is bigger really better? Screen sizes are measured diagonally. However, unlike television screens, computer screen size is not regulated. Manufacturers sometimes fudge a bit. When making comparisons, a user would do well to bring a ruler. A typical office worker who handles light word processing and spreadsheet duties will probably find a 15- or 17-inch screen adequate. A user who is involved with high-powered graphics will probably want a 19-inch screen. At the high end, screens can be purchased that are as large as television sets, 21 inches and up.

To answer the question, yes, bigger is usually better, but it is also more expensive and takes up more space on your desk. For your own personal computer, once you try a larger screen you will not want to go back. In addition to the reduced strain on the eyes, it is particularly useful for Web pages, page layout, graphics, and large photos and illustrations.

Flat-Panel Screens

Another type of screen technology is the **liquid crystal display (LCD),** a flat-panel display often seen on watches and calculators. LCD screens are commonly used on laptop computers. But flat-panel screens are getting bigger and are making their way to desktop computers (Figure 5-19). Although traditional CRT monitors get deeper as they get wider, flat-panel monitors maintain their depth—a superskinny few inches—regardless of screen size. LCD monitors can use one of two basic technologies—**active-matrix,** based on **TFT** (thin-film transistor technology), and **passive-matrix.** Passive-matrix technology uses fewer transistors and therefore is cheaper and uses less power, but TFT displays produce a brighter image and can be viewed from wider angles.

Flat-panel screens are wonderful to look at, with crisp, brilliant images. They are also easy on the eyes; they do not flicker but just brightly shine on. The full dimension of a flat-panel screen is usable, so a 15-inch flat-panel monitor has a viewing area nearly as large as that of a 17-inch CRT monitor. Although prices of flat-panel screens are coming down, they are still quite a bit higher than prices for equivalent-sized CRT monitors.

Printers

A **printer** is a device that produces information on paper output. Some older printers produce only letters and numbers, but most printers used with personal computers today can also produce information in graphic form. Most printers have two **orientation** settings: portrait and landscape mode. The default setting is **portrait mode,** in

► F I G U R E 5-19

Flat panel desktop monitor.

Flat panel screens are slim and present bright images.

Disappearing Act
It looks just like a copy machine. But unlike a copier, it does not add to the glut of paper in the office. In fact, it subtracts. The Decopier removes text and other detritus from the sheets of used paper that are fed to it.

The machine applies a nontoxic chemical at low heat to a sheet of printed paper to loosen up the toner and ink, then sweeps away the flakes. The paper emerges at the other end spanking new—or, at least, recycled.

which output, such as a memo, is printed in a vertical alignment, that is, with the longest dimension up and down. **Landscape mode** prints output "sideways," or horizontally, with the longest dimension across the width of the paper; this is especially useful for spreadsheets that have a lot of data across the sheet. Graphics images may be more suited for printing in one mode over another.

There are two ways of printing an image on paper: the impact method and the nonimpact method. An **impact printer** uses some sort of physical contact with the paper to produce an image, physically striking paper, ribbon, and print hammer together. Mainframe users who are more concerned about high volume than high quality usually use **line printers**—impact printers that print an entire line at a time. These users are likely to print lengthy reports, perhaps relating to payroll or costs, for internal use. Impact printers are needed when multiple copies of a report are printed; the impact carries the output through to the lower copies. Personal computer users who need to print multi-part forms can use **dot-matrix printers,** which have a print head consisting of one or more columns of pins. These pins form characters and images as a pattern of dots produced by the pins striking the ribbon against the paper as the print head moves back and forth across the paper. Dot-matrix printers used to be the primary type of printer found on microcomputer systems, but they have largely been replaced by ink-jet and laser printers.

A **nonimpact printer** places an image on a page without physically touching the page. The major technologies competing in the nonimpact market are laser and ink-jet, the two kinds of printers that you will find in your local computer store. **Laser printers** use a light beam to help transfer images to paper (Figure 5-20). Today's laser printers print 600 or 1200 **dots per inch (dpi),** producing extremely high-quality results. Laser printers print a page at a time at impressive speeds, using technology similar to that of a photocopier. Printing speeds of personal laser printers are generally around 8 to 10 **pages per minute (ppm),** while network laser printers are capable of between 35 and 50 ppm. Large organizations such as banks and insurance companies use expensive, high-volume laser printers that can produce reports at up to 1000 ppm. Low-end black-and-white laser printers for use with personal computers can now be purchased for a few hundred dollars. Color laser printers are more expensive.

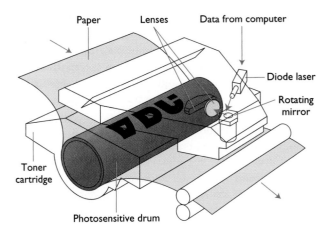

Paper   Lenses   Data from computer

Diode laser

Rotating mirror

Toner cartridge

Photosensitive drum

◄ **F I G U R E** 5-20

Laser printers.

A laser printer works like a photocopy machine. Using patterns of small dots, a laser beam conveys information from the computer to a positively charged drum inside the laser printer. Wherever an image is to be printed, the laser beam is turned on, causing the drum to become neutralized. As the drum passes by a toner cartridge, toner sticks to the neutral spots on the drum. The toner is then transferred from the drum to a piece of paper. In the final printing step, heat and pressure fuse the toner to the paper. The drum is then cleaned for the next pass.

Ink-jet printers, which spray ink from multiple jet nozzles, can print in both black and white and several different colors of ink to produce excellent graphics (Figure 5-21). However, the print quality of an ink-jet printer, though more than adequate, usually will not match that of a laser printer. Nor will the printing be as speedy. Furthermore, ink-jet printers need a fairly high quality of paper so that the ink does not smear or bleed. Nevertheless, low-end ink-jet printers, which cost a little more than a hundred dollars, are a bargain for users who want color output capability.

If you choose a color printer, whether ink-jet or laser, you will find that its colors are not perfect. The color you see on your computer screen is not necessarily the exact color you will see on the printed output. Nor is it likely to be the color you would see on a professional four-color offset printing press.

Choosing between a laser printer and an ink-jet printer comes down to a few factors. If printing speed is important to you or if the quality of the printed text is a top priority, you probably want a black-and-white laser printer. If you cannot resist the prospect of color and are not overly concerned about text quality or speed, an ink-jet may be your best choice. If you want it all, color laser printers are available, but in a higher price range.

Voice Output

We have already examined voice input in some detail. As you will see in this section, computers are frequently like people in the sense that they find it easier to talk than to listen. **Speech synthesis**—the process of enabling machines to talk to people—is much easier than speech recognition. "The key is in the ignition," your car says to you as you open the car door to get out. Machine voices are the product of **voice synthesizers** (also called **voice-output devices** or **audio-response units**), which convert data in main storage to vocalized sounds understandable to humans.

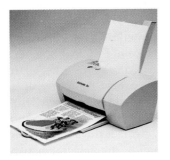

◄ **F I G U R E** 5-21

Ink-jet printers.

A color ink-jet printer is an affordable and popular addition to many computer systems.

The Eyes Have It

The computer can be a godsend for many people who have physical limitations. Various input devices have been developed to assist people with varying degrees of limitations. But what about the totally paralyzed, who lack the ability to do almost anything other than move their eyes? A system called the Eye Science Gaze Tracker allows users to perform mouse functions with their eyes. Two low-powered infrared LEDs mounted on the monitor illuminate the user's eye. The reflections from the eye are detected by a digital camera, which is also mounted on the monitor. By analyzing the image from the camera, software can determine where on the screen the user is looking and move the screen pointer accordingly. Mouse clicks can be simulated by slow eye blinks or by allowing the gaze to linger for a time on one location. No hardware has to be attached to the user, a big advantage over previous systems that required affixing electrodes to the eye muscles. The Gaze Tracker will even work with eyeglasses, though contact lenses can confuse it.

There are two basic approaches to getting a computer to talk. The first is **synthesis by analysis,** in which the device analyzes the input of an actual human voice speaking words, stores and processes the spoken sounds, and reproduces them as needed. The second approach to synthesizing speech is **synthesis by rule,** in which the device applies a complex set of linguistic rules to create artificial speech. Synthesis based on the human voice has the advantage of sounding more natural, but it is limited to the number of words stored in the computer.

Voice output has become common in such places as airline and bus terminals, banks, brokerage houses, and even some automobiles. It is typically used when an inquiry is followed by a short reply, such as a bank balance or flight time. Many businesses have found other creative uses for voice output over the telephone. Automatic telephone voices take surveys, inform customers that catalog orders are ready to be picked up, and perhaps remind consumers that they have not paid their bills.

Music Output and Other Sounds

In the past personal computer users occasionally sent primitive musical messages, feeble tones that wheezed from the computer's tiny internal speaker. Today's personal computers can be equipped with speakers placed on either side of the computer or, in some cases, mounted on the sides of the monitor or buried in the computer housing. Users want good-quality sound from certain kinds of software, especially the sophisticated offerings called *multimedia,* which include multiple sight and sound effects. Even the zap-and-crash sounds of action games deserve to be heard. To enhance the listening experience further, manufacturers are now producing sound cards containing sophisticated audio chips that, by varying the frequencies and timing of the sound waves as they reach the human ear, can fool the brain into thinking that it is hearing three-dimensional sound from two speakers.

MIDI (Musical Instrument Digital Interface), pronounced "mid-ee," is a set of rules designed for connecting devices that produce and process digital music signals. Devices that conform to the MIDI standard can communicate with each other and with a computer containing a MIDI interface. In much the same way that two computers communicate via modems, two musical devices can communicate via MIDI. The information exchanged between two MIDI devices is musical in nature. MIDI information tells a synthesizer, in its most basic mode, when to start and stop playing a specific note. Other information that is shared may include the volume and modulation of the note. A number of software programs are available for composing and editing music that conforms to the MIDI standard. They offer a variety of functions: For instance, when you play a tune on a keyboard connected to a computer, a music program can translate what you play into a written score. MIDI is supported by many makes of personal computer sound cards.

► TERMINALS: COMBINING INPUT AND OUTPUT

A **terminal** is a device (or combination of devices) that combines both input and output capabilities. The simplest type of terminal, known as a **dumb terminal** because it has no processing capability, consists of a keyboard for input and a monitor for output and connects directly to a host computer. Everything that is typed into the keyboard is sent to the host for processing, which sends results back to the terminal screen to be displayed. An **intelligent terminal** combines a keyboard and monitor with memory and a processor, giving it the ability to perform limited processing functions. For example, an intelligent terminal could display an input form on the screen, accept user input through the keyboard, perform editing and error-checking functions on the data (requesting reentry if necessary) and then send the entire set of data to the host computer for processing. When the results are sent back, the terminal could format and display those results on the screen.

A **point-of-sale (POS) terminal** is a combination of input and output devices designed to capture retail sales data at the point where the transaction takes place. The most familiar POS terminal is the supermarket checkout station. The primary input device is the bar code reader built into the counter. For items with no bar code, such as loose produce, the cashier can use a keyboard to enter the data. Checkout stations may also include a digital scale to weigh items sold by weight and a magnetic stripe reader to read credit card information. For output the station includes both a small screen display and a printer that prints the customer receipt. Another common POS terminal in retail stores uses a wand reader to read the merchandise code from the product tag and transmits it to the computer, which retrieves a description (and possibly the price, if it is not on the tag) of the item. A small printer produces a customer receipt that shows the item description and price. The computer calculates the subtotal, the sales tax (if any), and the total. This information is displayed on the screen and printed on the receipt.

The raw purchase data captured by the POS terminal becomes valuable information when it is summarized by the computer system. This information can be used by the accounting department to keep track of how much money is taken in each day, by buyers to determine what merchandise should be reordered, and by the marketing department to analyze the effectiveness of its ad campaigns.

► COMPUTER GRAPHICS

Now for everyone's favorite: computer graphics. You have probably seen the lines and charts of business graphics (Figure 5-22). Just about everyone has seen TV commercials or movies that use computer-produced animated graphics. Computer graphics can also be useful in education, science, sports, computer art, and more. But their most prevalent use today is still in business.

Business Graphics

Graphics can be a powerful way to impart information. Colorful graphics, maps, and charts can help managers compare data more easily, spot trends, and make decisions more quickly. Also, the use of color helps people get the picture—literally. Although color graphs and charts have been used in business for years, usually to make presentations to upper management or outside clients, the computer allows them to be rendered quickly, before information becomes outdated. Also, as the underlying data changes, the graphs and charts can be updated instantaneously. One user refers to business graphics as "computer-assisted insight." Business graphics will be discussed in more detail in Chapter 13.

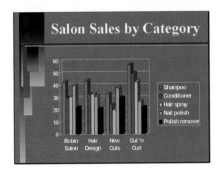

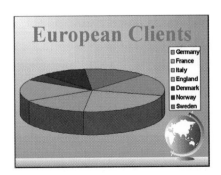

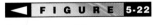
FIGURE 5-22

Business graphics.

These charts were made with powerful but easy-to-use graphics software.

Video Graphics

Video graphics can be as creative as an animated cartoon. Although they operate on the same principle as a moving picture or cartoon—one frame at a time in quick succession—**video graphics** are produced by computers. Video graphics have made their biggest splash on television, but many people do not realize that they are watching a computer at work. The next time you watch television, skip the trip to the kitchen and pay special attention to the commercials. If there is no live human in the advertisement (and perhaps even if there is), the moving objects you see, such as floating cars and bobbing electric razors, are doubtlessly computer output. Another fertile ground for video graphics is a television network's logo and theme. Accompanied by music and swooshing sounds, the network symbol spins and cavorts and turns itself inside out, all with the finesse that only a computer could supply.

Video graphics are well known to people who like to play arcade games; their input device is the joystick, which allows fingertip control of figures on the screen.

Computer-Aided Design/Computer-Aided Manufacturing

Computer graphics have become part and parcel of a field known by the abbreviation **CAD/CAM,** short for **computer-aided design/computer-aided manufacturing.** On the CAD side, computer software is used to create two- and three-dimensional designs of everything from hand tools to tractors to highway designs. Once the design is complete, additional software can perform various engineering tests, such as stress tests and performance analyses. The design data can then be passed to CAM systems, which use computers to control production equipment.

CAD/CAM provides a bridge between design (planning what a product will be) and manufacturing (actually making the planned product). As a manager at DaimlerChrysler said, "Many companies have design data and manufacturing data, and the two are never the same. At Chrysler, we have only one set of data that everyone dips into." Keeping data in one place, of course, makes changes easier and encourages consistency.

Computer-integrated manufacturing (CIM) integrates CAD/CAM and the entire manufacturing process. Production planning, scheduling, materials management, and production control are automated under computer control, providing a balanced, efficient production process.

► ETHICS AND DATA

Few people pause to ponder the relationship between ethics and data, but it is an important one. Once the data is in the computer, there are many ways in which it can be used, sold, or even altered. Data can also be input and stored in a great variety of ways. Consider these data ethics issues, all of which are at least debatable and most of which could be defensible in some situations:

- Is it ethically acceptable to use a computer to alter photographs? Is it ethical to substitute one person for another in a photograph? Should we be able to change pictures of ourselves? Of group photos from school or work? Is it ethical to use a computer to add a celebrity to a photo? Does it matter whether the celebrity is alive or dead?

- Suppose you perceive that the contents of certain e-mail messages may be of interest to a plaintiff who is suing your company. Is it ethical to erase the messages?

• A friend who has worked on a political campaign has a disk file of donors. Is it ethical to use that same list to solicit for your candidate?

Note that not all of these scenarios inherently require a computer. But the computer makes it that much easier.

▲

New forms of computer input and output are announced regularly, often with promises of multiple benefits and new ease of use. Part of the excitement of the computer world is that these promises are usually kept, and users reap the benefits directly. Input and output just keep getting better.

CHAPTER REVIEW

▶ **Summary and Key Terms**

- A **source document** is the original written data to be input into the computer.

- A **keyboard** is a common input device that may be part of a personal computer or a terminal connected to a remote computer.

- A **pointing device** is used to position a **pointer** on the screen. The pointer can have a number of shapes but is most often an arrow. You move the pointer and then click the button to place the **insertion point,** or **cursor,** at the pointer location. An **icon,** a pictorial symbol on a screen, can be clicked to invoke a command to the computer, an environment called a **graphical user interface (GUI).**

- A **mouse** is an input device whose movement on a flat surface causes a corresponding movement of the pointer on the screen. A **mechanical mouse** has a ball on its underside that rolls as the mouse is moved. An **optical mouse** uses a light beam to monitor mouse movement. A **wireless mouse** uses an infrared beam rather than a cord to send signals to the computer. A **trackball** is like an upside-down mechanical mouse—the ball is rolled with the hand. A **touchpad** uses finger movement on its surface to control the pointer. A **pointing stick** is a small pressure-sensitive post mounted in the center of the keyboard that uses pressure to indicate the direction of pointer movement. A **joystick** is a short lever with a hand-grip that is moved in one direction or another to move the pointer.

- A **graphics tablet,** also called a **digitizing tablet,** is a rectangular board that contains an invisible grid of electronic dots. As the user moves a pen-like **stylus** or a mouse-like **puck** with crosshairs around the board, the dot locations passed over are sent to the computer.

- **Touch screens** allow the user to input information by pointing to locations on the screen with a finger. Some screens use a **light pen** as the input device, allowing more precise pointing.

- **Source data automation** involves the use of special equipment to collect data at its origin and send it directly to the computer.

- **Magnetic-ink character recognition (MICR)** allows a machine to read characters made of magnetized particles, such as the preprinted characters on a personal check. Some characters are preprinted, but others, such as the amount of a check, are added by a person using a **MICR inscriber.**

- An **optical scanner,** or just **scanner,** can convert text or even a drawing or photograph into computer-recognizable form by using **optical recognition,** a system that uses a light beam to scan input data and convert it into electrical signals that are sent to the computer for processing. In a process called **document imaging,** a scanner converts those papers to an electronic version, which can then be stored on disk and retrieved when needed.

- A **flatbed scanner,** a tabletop machine, typically scans a sheet at a time, although some offer an attachment for scanning multiple sheets. A **sheetfed scanner,** usually designed to fit neatly between the keyboard and the monitor, uses motorized rollers to feed the sheet across the scanning head. A **handheld scanner,** the least expensive and least reliable of the three, is handy for portability. **Optical character recognition (OCR)** software can convert the digital picture produced by the scanner in text for processing.

- **Optical mark recognition (OMR**—also called **mark sensing)** devices recognize marks on paper. **Optical character recognition (OCR)** devices read special characters, such as those on price tags. These characters are often in a standard typeface called **OCR-A.** A commonly used OCR device is the handheld **wand reader.** A **bar-code reader** is a photoelectric scanner used to input a **bar code,** a pattern of vertical marks; one standard represents the **Universal Product Code**

(UPC) that identifies a product. Some optical scanners can read precise handwritten characters.

- **Voice input,** or **speech recognition,** is the process of presenting input data to the computer through the spoken word. **Speech recognition devices** convert spoken words into a digital code that a computer can understand. The two main types of devices are **discrete word systems,** which require speakers to pause between words, and **continuous word systems,** which allow a normal rate of speaking.

- A **digital camera** takes photos that are stored internally on a chip or card, then sent directly to your computer, where they can be edited and printed.

- The **monitor** features the computer's screen, includes the housing for its electrical components, and often sits on a stand that tilts and swivels. Screen output is known in the computer industry as **soft copy** because it is intangible and temporary, unlike **hard copy,** produced by a printer on paper, which is tangible and can be permanent.

- The most common kind of computer screen is the **cathode ray tube (CRT).** Some computer screens are **monochrome**—the characters appear in one color, usually green or amber, on a contrasting background. Most CRT screens use a technology called **raster scanning,** in which the backing of the screen display has a phosphorous coating, which will glow whenever it is hit by a beam of electrons. The screen image must be **refreshed** often to avoid flicker. The **scan rate** is the number of times the screen is refreshed per second. **Interlaced** screens refresh one half the lines in each pass; **non-interlaced (NI)** screens refresh all lines on each pass, producing a better image.

- A computer display screen that can be used for graphics is divided into dots that are called **addressable** because they can be addressed individually by the graphics software. Each screen dot is called a **pixel.** The more pixels, the higher the **screen resolution,** or clarity. **Dot pitch** is the amount of space between the dots on a screen. If a computer does not come with built-in graphics capability, you will have to add a **graphics card** or **graphics adapter board.**

- Common graphics standards are **SVGA (Super VGA),** providing various high resolutions and potentially supporting a palette of 16 million colors, and **XGA (extended graphics array),** a high-resolution graphics standard that provides the same resolutions but supports more simultaneous colors and can be non-interlaced.

- A **liquid crystal display (LCD)** is a type of flat-panel screen found on laptop computers and on some desktop computers. **Active-matrix** displays, also known as **TFT** displays, produce a better image but use more power and are more expensive than **passive-matrix** displays. These screens are noted for their slimness and bright, flicker-free images, but they are more expensive than CRTs.

- **Printers** produce printed paper output. The default printer **orientation** setting is **portrait mode,** in which output is printed with the longest dimension up and down; **landscape mode** prints output "sideways" on the paper. Printers can be classified as either **impact printers,** which form characters by physically striking the paper, or **nonimpact printers,** which use a noncontact printing method. **Line printers** are impact printers used on mainframe systems that print an entire line at a time. **Dot-matrix printers** use a print head containing one or more columns of pins to produce images as a pattern of dots. **Laser printers** and **ink-jet printers** are nonimpact printers. Today's laser printers print 600 or 1200 **dots per inch (dpi),** producing extremely high-quality results. Laser printers print an entire page at a time, and their speed is rated in **pages per minute (ppm).**

- Computer **speech synthesis** has been accomplished through **voice synthesizers** (also called **voice-output devices** or **audio-response units**). One approach to speech synthesis is **synthesis by analysis,** in which the computer analyzes stored tapes of spoken words. In the other approach, called **synthesis by rule,** the computer applies linguistic rules to create artificial speech.

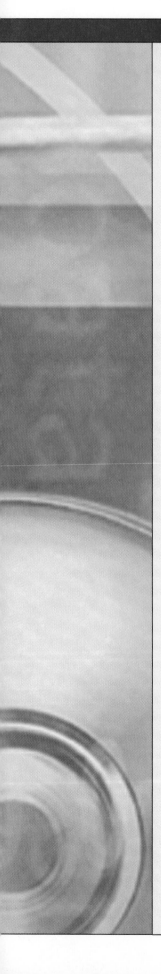

- **MIDI (Musical Instrument Digital Interface),** pronounced "mid-ee," is a set of rules designed for recording and playing back music on digital synthesizers.

- A **terminal** is a device (or combination of devices) that combines both input and output capabilities. A **dumb terminal** consists of a screen and keyboard and has no processing power of its own. An **intelligent terminal** combines a keyboard and monitor with memory and a processor, giving it the ability to perform limited processing functions.

- A **point-of-sale (POS) terminal** is a combination of input and output devices designed to capture retail sales data at the point where the transaction takes place.

- **Video graphics** are a series of computer-produced pictures. Video-graphic arcade games are played with a joystick, which allows fingertip control of figures on the screen.

- In **computer-aided design/computer-aided manufacturing (CAD/CAM),** computers are used to design and manufacture products. **Computer-integrated manufacturing (CIM)** integrates CAD/CAM and the entire manufacturing process.

► Critical Thinking Questions

1. For this question, either use your knowledge from reading or experience or imagine the possibilities. What kind of input device might be convenient for these types of jobs or situations?

   a. A supermarket stock clerk who takes inventory by surveying items that are currently on the shelf

   b. A medical assistant who must input existing printed documents to the computer

   c. An airport automated luggage-tracking system

   d. A telephone worker who takes orders over the phone

   e. A restaurant in which customers place their own orders from the table

   f. An inspector at the U.S. Bureau of Engraving who monitors and gives a go/no-go response on printed money passing by on an assembly line

   g. A retailer who wants to move customers quickly through the checkout lines

   h. A psychologist who wants to give a new client a standard test

   i. An environmental engineer who hikes through woods and streams to inspect and report on the effects of pollutants

   j. A small-business owner who wants to keep track of employee work hours

2. Do you think that voice input is practical for your own use?

3. If price were not a consideration, what kind of printers would you buy for your home or business personal computers?

► STUDENT STUDY GUIDE

Multiple Choice

1. The distance between the pixels on a screen is called
   a. OCR
   b. LCD
   c. dot pitch
   d. refresh rate

2. A pictorial screen symbol that represents a computer activity is called a(n)
   a. pointer
   b. icon
   c. touch screen
   d. MICR

3. Using computers to design and manufacture products is called
   a. inscribing
   b. CAD/CAM
   c. detailing
   d. imaging

4. Soft copy refers to
   a. printed output
   b. music sounds
   c. screen output
   d. digitizing

5. The type of scanner that fits between the keyboard and the monitor is the
   a. sheetfed scanner
   b. handheld scanner
   c. flatbed scanner
   d. video scanner

6. An ink-jet printer is an example of a(n)
   a. laser printer
   b. impact printer
   c. LCD printer
   d. nonimpact printer

7. Entering data as a by-product of the activity that generates the data is known as
   a. source data automation
   b. a discrete word system
   c. CAD/CAM
   d. MICR entry

8. The rate of screen refreshment is called
   a. pixel speed
   b. bit-map speed
   c. raster rate
   d. scan rate

9. Magnetic characters representing the check amount are entered onto your bank checks by
   a. bar-code readers
   b. mice
   c. MICR inscribers
   d. OCR

10. "Mark sensing" is another term for
    a. MICR
    b. POS
    c. OMR
    d. XGA

11. A(n) _____ is a device that is used for optical character recognition.
    a. wand reader
    b. cursor
    c. stylus
    d. MICR reader

12. OCR-A is a
    a. portrait
    b. standard typeface
    c. wand reader
    d. bar code

13. Some POS terminals are similar to
    a. calculators
    b. Touch-Tone telephones
    c. UPCs
    d. cash registers

14. A(n) _____ monitor shows single-color characters on a contrasting background.
    a. monochrome
    b. blank
    c. addressable
    d. liquid crystal display

15. Voice input devices convert voice input to
    a. digital codes
    b. bar codes
    c. OCR-A
    d. optical marks

16. Document imaging uses what device to input data?
    a. scanner
    b. bar-code reader
    c. icon
    d. tablet

17. The pointer can be moved by rolling this device on a flat surface:
    a. mouse
    b. UPC
    c. wand reader
    d. interactive tablet

18. Which input device is often attached to laptop computers?
    a. trackball
    b. graphic display
    c. inscriber
    d. wand reader

19. A(n) _____ is a screen that is lighter and slimmer than a CRT.
    a. OCR
    b. graphics card
    c. flat-panel
    d. terminal

20. Computer animation is a form of
    a. LCD
    b. CAD/CAM
    c. video graphics
    d. color printer output

True/False

T   F   1. The greater the number of pixels, the poorer the screen clarity.

T   F   2. Printers produce hard copy.

T   F   3. Discrete word systems allow a normal rate of speaking.

T   F   4. Data is scanned into the computer by using a mouse.

T   F   5. "CRT" stands for "computer remote terminal."

T   F   6. Optical recognition technology is based on magnetized data.

T   F   7. OMR senses marks on paper.

T   F   8. A wand reader can read OCR characters.

T   F   9. A "sideways" printer orientation is called portrait mode.

T   F   10. LCD is a type of flat screen found on laptop computers.

T   F   11. The personal computer screen standard with the highest resolution is VGA.

T   F   12. A mouse can be clicked to invoke a command.

T   F   13. The MICR process is used primarily in retail stores.

T   F   14. The cursor indicates the location of the next interaction on the screen.

T   F   15. Dot pitch refers to the number of pixels on a screen.

T   F   16. The best way to scan a page from a book is with a flatbed scanner.

T   F   17. Non-interlaced screens are best for animated graphics.

T   F   18. A touchpad is used by moving it across a hard surface.

T   F   19. MIDI is the accepted standard for LCD screens.

T   F   20. To avoid flicker, a CRT screen needs to be refreshed often.

T   F   21. The most common use for a joystick is CAD/CAM applications.

T   F   22. Flat screens can be found on desktop computers as well as laptop computers.

T   F   23. A laser printer uses impact technology to produce characters.

T   F   24. A digital camera uses an embedded chip to focus the picture but records the picture on regular film.

T   F   25. The type of scanner that produces the highest quality image is the handheld scanner.

Fill-In

1. The written document that contains data to be keyed into the computer is called the _____.

2. LCD stands for _____.

3. The standard typeface read by OCR devices is known as _____.

4. A(n) _____ captures data where a retail sale takes place.

5. A(n) _____ is a pictorial screen symbol that represents a command or action.

6. MICR is most commonly used in the _____ industry.

7. TFT flat-panel displays are also known as _____ displays.

8. The phrase that is used to describe collecting computer data at the point at which it is created is _____.

9. The UPC is a(n) _____ used to identify grocery items.

10. A(n) _____ is a pointing device with which the user moves the pointer by rolling a ball with the fingers.

11. A(n) _____ is a single dot on the screen that can be addressed by software.

12. The method that uses a light beam to sense marks on machine-readable test forms is called _____.

13. The tabletop scanner that can handle a book page is the _____ scanner.

14. Which technology is more challenging: voice input or voice output? _____.

15. A(n) _____ printer uses a print head to create characters as a pattern of dots.

16. In synthesis by _____, speech is created by replaying stored spoken sounds.

17. _____ provides an interface that allows two digital musical devices to exchange musical data.

18. A(n) _____ terminal consists of a monitor and keyboard and has no processing capability.

19. _____ integrates CAD/CAM with the entire manufacturing process.

20. A screen that accepts input from a pointing finger is called a(n) _____.

▶ **ANSWERS**

Multiple Choice

1. c	6. d	11. a	16. a
2. b	7. a	12. b	17. a
3. b	8. d	13. d	18. a
4. c	9. c	14. a	19. c
5. a	10. c	15. a	20. c

True/False

1. F	8. T	15. F	22. T
2. T	9. F	16. T	23. F
3. F	10. T	17. T	24. F
4. F	11. F	18. F	25. F
5. F	12. T	19. F	
6. F	13. F	20. T	
7. T	14. T	21. F	

Fill-In

1. source document
2. liquid crystal display
3. OCR-A
4. point-of-sale terminal
5. icon
6. banking
7. active-matrix
8. source data automation
9. bar code
10. trackball
11. pixel
12. OMR (or optical mark reading or mark sensing)
13. flatbed
14. voice input
15. dot-matrix
16. analysis
17. MIDI
18. dumb
19. CIM or computer-integrated manufacturing
20. touch screen

Planet Internet

FAQS and Help

When people begin to learn something new, they usually have many questions. In fact, people who are being introduced to the same new subject often have exactly the same questions. Rather than answer each question individually, it makes sense to keep the most frequently asked questions—FAQs—in a handy place that anyone can access. FAQs are a long-standing tradition on the Internet.

Where are the FAQs on the Internet?

The use of FAQs is so widespread that you are likely to come across them on many sites. However, some sites specialize in comprehensive Internet-related FAQs—and answers—for beginners, notably the long-standing Web Browser Open FAQs. Another good place to start is Beginner's Central. Several sites, such as the Net Lingo site, offer lists of Internet-related definitions. You can also pose questions to the Surf Guru.

Where can I get some general information about the Internet?

Some sites include a history of the Internet as one of many offerings. Others, such as the History of the Internet, Net History, Hobbes Internet Timeline, and World Wide Web: Origins and Beyond sites, offer a long and detailed history, with names, organizations, and timelines. You can get demographic information about the Internet—official and unofficial statistics—from sites such as Internet Statistics.

Where can I get some help on making a home page?

Advice abounds, usually with titles such as the Getting Started site. Most users who have an interest in making a Web page start with information about HTML. A good place to start would be the Beginner's Guide to HTML; actually, there are several sites with that exact name. There are dozens of useful HTML sites, such as Webmonkeys. If you find one HTML site, it probably will have a list of links to others.

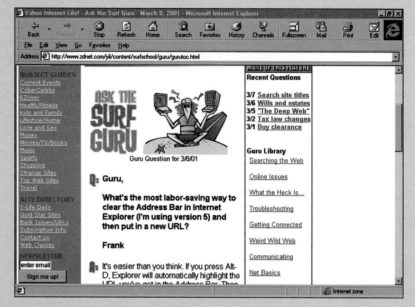

Anything else for making a page?

There are many sites that offer design advice and free clip art images. Getting Started is a popular home page advice site. David Seigel's Casbah site is highly regarded for its excellent page design advice.

Where else can I get help?

There are several possibilities besides teaching yourself. Many colleges include home page creation as part of an Internet course. This may be via HTML or one of several authoring programs, such as FrontPage. Private firms advertise courses to teach you the basics in a few hours. Serious users, usually businesses that want a Web presence, may engage the services of consultants who can create a sophisticated Web site.

Internet Exercises:

1. **Structured exercise.** Begin with the URL http://www.prenhall.com/capron and link to the Web Browser Open FAQs. Provide the answer in your own words, in writing or orally, to three questions that you found most helpful or to three questions that help a friend or family member who is curious about the subject.

2. **Free-form exercise.** Go to the Beginner's Guide to HTML and click on some of the links listed there. Explain in writing or orally the three most useful pieces of information you found for friends of family members who are thinking about setting up their own home page. Be sure to consider the reason your friends or family members want to have their own page.

3. **Advanced exercise.** Select a topic from one of the chapters in this book and write a short FAQ of at least five questions. Provide URLs from Web sites you've found that support the answers to these questions and provide additional information about the topic.

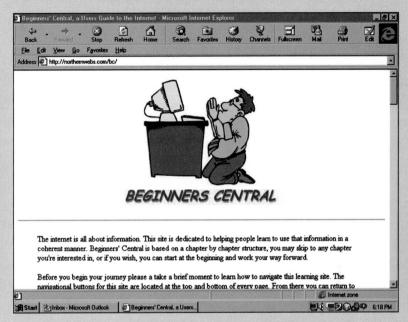

Storage and Multimedia:
The Facts and More

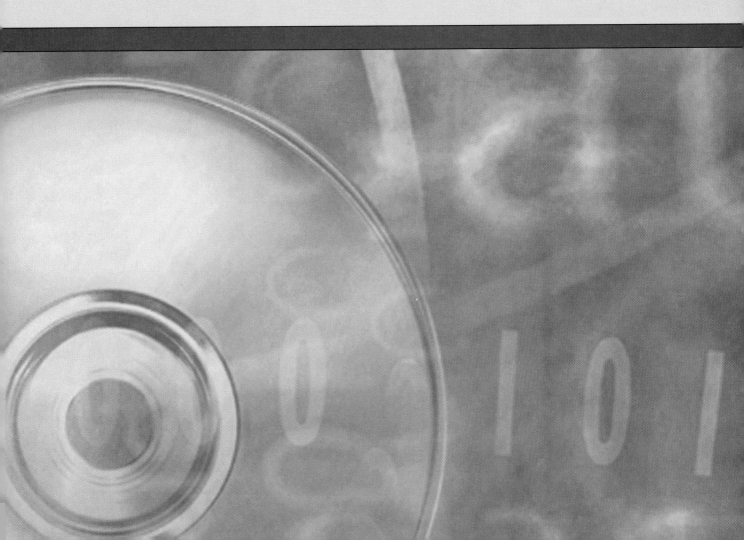

Storage and Multimedia:
The Facts and More

CHAPTER 6

LEARNING OBJECTIVES

List the benefits of secondary storage

Identify and describe storage media that are available for personal computers

Differentiate among the principal types of secondary storage

Describe how data is stored on a disk

Discuss the benefits of multimedia

Explain how data is organized, accessed, and processed

heri Urquhart, Tate Kirschner, and Taylor Russell met in college, where they were studying to become architects. They did both undergraduate and graduate work together and then went their separate ways into the work force. But they remained in the same metropolitan area and kept in touch.

Seven years later, at a professional conference, their casual conversation over dinner turned serious, and they began to consider forming their own architectural firm. The details of accomplishing this were complex and involved many months of planning. Our concern here is what they decided to do about computers, particularly computer storage.

Architectural drawings are made with special software; the software alone takes up many millions of bytes of storage. In addition, the architectural drawings themselves are storage hogs. The three architects did not hesitate to include hard disks with many gigabytes of storage.

Another issue was the need to be able to produce computer-generated "walk-through" movies, simulated tours to show their clients the planned structure. For this they chose DVD-ROM, a type of high-capacity storage disk that can hold a full-length movie with room to spare.

Each of the architects already had a computer at home. They thought that they should upgrade the storage capacity of their individual computers so that they could bring work home. They also wanted some sort of transfer storage device so that they could carry drawings on disk between home and office; they settled on the Zip drive, which holds a high-capacity diskette.

The situation just described is more complicated than the ones most people face. However, it is true that disk storage is an ongoing issue for most users—we can never seem to get enough. A rule of thumb among computer professionals is to estimate disk needs generously and then double that amount. But estimating future needs is rarely easy.

HARDWARE

Prentice Hall
EXPLORE Generation **it**

► THE BENEFITS OF SECONDARY STORAGE

Picture, if you can, how many filing cabinet drawers would be required to hold the millions of files of, say, tax records kept by the Internal Revenue Service or archives of employee records kept by General Motors. The record storage rooms would have to be enormous. Computers, by contrast, permit storage on tape or disk in extremely compressed form. Storage capacity is unquestionably one of the most valuable assets of the computer.

Secondary storage, sometimes called **auxiliary storage,** is storage that is separate from the computer itself, where software and data can be stored on a semipermanent basis. Since memory, or primary storage, loses its contents when power is turned off, secondary storage is needed to save both data and programs for later use.

The benefits of secondary storage can be summarized as follows:

- **Space.** Organizations may store the equivalent of a roomful of data on sets of disks that take up less space than a breadbox. A simple diskette for a personal computer can hold the equivalent of 500 printed pages, or one book. An optical disk can hold the equivalent of approximately 500 books.

- **Reliability.** Data in secondary storage is basically safe, since secondary storage is physically reliable. (We should note, however, that disks sometimes fail.) Also, it is more difficult for untrained people to tamper with data on disk than with data stored on paper in a file cabinet.

- **Convenience.** With the help of a computer, authorized users can locate and access data quickly.

- **Economy.** Together, the three previous benefits indicate significant savings in storage costs. It is less expensive to store data on disk or tape (the principal means of secondary storage) than to buy and house filing cabinets. Data that is reliable and safe is less expensive to maintain than is data that is subject to errors. But the greatest savings can be found in the speed and convenience of filing and retrieving data.

These benefits apply to all the various secondary storage devices, but, as you will see, some devices are better than others. The discussion begins with a look at the various storage media, including those used for personal computers, and then moves to what it takes to get data organized and processed.

► MAGNETIC DISK STORAGE

Diskettes and hard disks are magnetic media; that is, they are based on a technology of representing data as magnetized spots on the surface of a spinning disk—with a magnetized spot representing a 1 bit and the absence of such a spot representing a

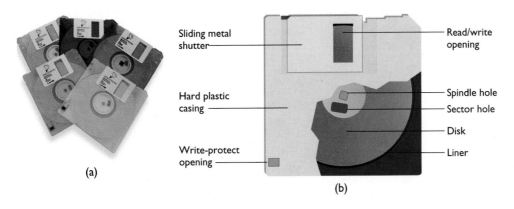

(a)

Sliding metal shutter

Hard plastic casing

Write-protect opening

Read/write opening

Spindle hole

Sector hole

Disk

Liner

(b)

◄ **F I G U R E 6-1**

Diskette.

(a) These 3½-inch diskettes are protected by a rigid plastic exterior cover. (b) A cutaway view of a 3½-inch diskette.

0 bit. Reading data from the disk means converting the magnetized data to electrical impulses that can be sent to the processor. Writing data to disk is the opposite; it involves sending electrical impulses from the processor to be converted to magnetized spots on the disk.

Diskettes

A **diskette** is made of flexible Mylar and coated with iron oxide, a substance that can be magnetized. A diskette can record data as magnetized spots on tracks on its surface. Diskettes became popular along with the personal computer. Most computers use the 3½-inch diskette, whose capacity is 1.44 megabytes of data (Figure 6-1). The diskette has the protection of a hard plastic jacket and fits conveniently in a shirt pocket or purse. The key advantage of diskettes is portability. Diskettes easily transport data from one computer to another. Workers, for example, carry their files from office computer to home computer and back on a diskette instead of carrying a stack of papers in a briefcase. Students use the campus computers but keep their files on their own diskettes. Diskettes are also a convenient vehicle for backup: It is easy to place an extra copy of a hard disk file on a diskette.

However, the venerable 3½-inch diskette, a standard for a decade, is being challenged. Two new high-capacity drives are challenging the standard floppy disk. One can store 120 megabytes per disk, while the other can store 200 megabytes. Although each uses its own high-capacity disk, they both can read and write to standard diskettes. However, the technology with a head start is Iomega's Zip drive, already installed by over 20 million users. The Zip drive holds 250-megabyte disks, 175 times the capacity of traditional diskettes (Figure 6-2). The disadvantage of the Zip drive is that it is not compatible with 3½-inch diskettes.

Even a high-capacity diskette can be problematic if, for example, you want to take a large file back and forth between your office and home computers. One possibility is **data compression,** the process of squeezing a big file into a small place. Compression can be as simple as removing all extra space characters, inserting a single repeat character to indicate a string of repeated characters, and substituting smaller data strings for frequently occurring characters. This kind of compression can reduce a text file to 50 percent of its original size. Compression is performed by a program that uses a formula to determine how to compress or decompress data. To be used again, the file must, of course, be uncompressed. Compression is also useful to speed up the transfer of files from one computer to another via data communications.

Hard Disks

A **hard disk** is a rigid platter coated with magnetic oxide that can be magnetized to represent data. Hard disks come in a variety of sizes. Several platters can be assembled into a **disk pack.** There are different types of disk packs, the number of platters varying by model. Each disk in the pack has top and bottom surfaces on which to

▼ **F I G U R E 6-2**

The Iomega Zip disk drive.

Shown here is a separate drive unit, but many users have their Zip drive installed in a bay in the computer's housing.

G E T T I N G   P R A C T I C A L | **Diskette and CD Care**

Although diskettes and CDs are fairly rugged, you should take precautions to protect them from damage.

General Guidelines

- CDs and diskettes will provide the best service if they are stored vertically. Don't stack them on top of each other or place heavy weight on them.
- Avoid extremes of temperature. The inside of a car on a hot, sunny day can be deadly.
- Insert and remove diskettes and CDs carefully—never force them into a drive. If you encounter difficulty in insertion, remove the item and try again, gently. If you still have problems, get help from a service technician.
- Keep diskettes and CDs away from food, drink, and smoke.

Diskette Care

- Keep diskettes away from magnets or anything that could generate a magnetic field. This includes stereo speakers and telephones.

- Don't touch the recording surface behind the metal slide.
- Be careful with disk labels. Loose labels or labels in several layers could become stuck inside the drive.

CD Care

- Store in a protective case—a jewel box or paper sleeve.
- Handle the CD by its edge. Avoid touching either surface.
- Don't write on the label side—you could destroy data.
- If necessary, clean the bottom (shiny) side with warm water and a soft cloth. Do not clean the label surface.

With proper care, both CDs and diskettes should have a long, trouble-free life. However, in the case of diskettes and writable CDs, be sure to back up any data you can't afford to lose.

---

record data, although some drives do not record data on the top of the top platter or on the bottom of the bottom platter.

A **disk drive** is a device that allows data to be read from a disk or written to a disk. A disk pack is mounted on a disk drive that is a separate unit connected to the computer. Large computers have dozens or even hundreds of external disk drives; in contrast, the hard disk for a personal computer is contained within the computer housing. In a disk pack, all disks rotate at the same time, though only one disk is being read from or written to at any one time. The mechanism for reading or writing data to a disk is an **access arm;** it moves a read/write head into position over a particular location (Figure 6-3a). The **read/write head** on the end of the access arm hovers a few millionths of an inch above the platter but does not actually touch the surface. When a read/write head does accidentally touch the disk surface, it is called a **head crash,** and data will be destroyed. Data can also be destroyed if a read/write head encounters even minuscule foreign matter on the disk surface (Figure 6-3b). A disk pack has a set of access arms that slip in between the disks in the pack (Figure 6-3c). Two read/write heads are on each arm, one facing up to access the surface above it and one facing down to access the surface below it. All the arms move together as a unit; however, only one read/write head can operate at any one time.

Most disk packs combine the platters, access arms, and read/write heads in an airtight, sealed module. These disk packs are assembled in clean rooms so that even microscopic dust particles do not get on the disk surface.

Most hard disks for personal computers are sealed modules that mount in a 3½-inch bay within the computer's case (Figure 6-4). Hard disk capacity for personal computers has soared in recent years; older hard disks have capacities of hundreds of megabytes, but new ones offer tens of gigabytes of storage. Terabyte capacity is on the horizon.

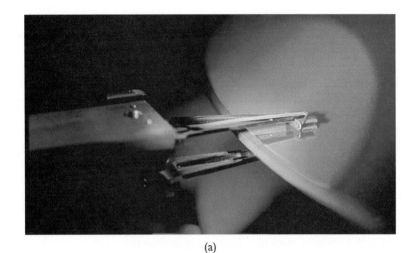

(a)

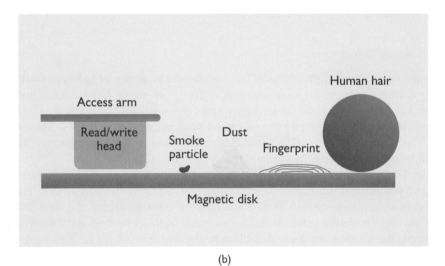

(b)

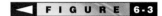

◄ **F I G U R E 6-3**

Read/write heads and access arms.

(a) This photo shows a read/write head on the end of an access arm poised over a hard disk. (b) When in operation, the read/write head comes very close to the surface of the disk. On a disk, particles as small as smoke, dust, a fingerprint, and a hair loom large. If the read/write head encounters one of these, a head crash occurs, destroying data and damaging the disk. (c) Note that there are two read/write heads on each access arm. Each arm slips between two disks in the disk pack. The access arms move simultaneously, but only one read/write head operates at any one time.

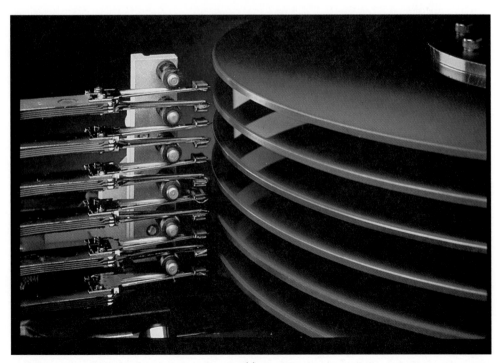

(c)

Although an individual probably cannot imagine generating enough output—letters, budgets, reports, pictures, and so forth—to fill a hard disk, software packages take up a lot of space and can make a dent rather quickly. Furthermore, graphics images and audio and video files require large amounts of disk space. Perhaps more important than capacity, however, is the speed advantage. Personal computer users find that accessing files on a hard disk is many times faster and much more convenient than accessing files on a diskette.

Removable hard disk systems are available for PCs. These systems consist of a drive that is installed either within the computer's case or in a separate case connected to the computer via a cable. The disk itself is contained in a cartridge that can be removed from the drive. Although the capacity of the removable cartridges is much greater than that of the high-capacity diskettes described above (up to 2-GB), they are not as spacious as the built-in hard disk systems on most PCs. Removable hard disk cartridges combine the portability advantages of diskettes with access speed close to that of the built-in systems. Their biggest disadvantage for home users is the expense of the cartridge—over $100. The Iomega Jaz drive is one of the more popular removable hard drive systems (Figure 6-4b).

Hard Disks in Groups

No storage system is completely safe, but a **redundant array of independent disks (RAID)** comes close. RAID storage uses a group of small hard disks that work together as a unit. The most basic RAID system—RAID level 1—simply duplicates data on separate disk drives, a concept called **disk mirroring** (Figure 6-5b). Thus no data is lost if one drive fails. This process is reliable but expensive. However, expense may not be an issue when the value of the data is considered.

Higher levels of RAID take a different approach called **data striping** (Figure 6-5c), which involves spreading the data across several disks in the array, with one disk used solely as a check disk to keep track of what data is where. If a disk fails, the check disk can reconstitute the data. Higher levels of RAID process data more quickly than simple data mirroring does. RAID is now the dominant form of storage for mainframe computer systems.

How Data Is Organized on a Disk

Several characteristics determine how data is physically organized on a disk. The characteristics that we consider here are tracks, sectors, clusters, and cylinders. Unless specifically noted, these concepts apply equally to diskettes and hard drives.

TRACK   A **track** is the circular portion of the disk surface that passes under the read/write head as the disk rotates (Figure 6-6). The number of tracks on a particular disk's surface depends on how precisely the arm can position the read/write head. While the standard 1.44-MB floppy has 80 tracks on each of its two surfaces, a hard disk may have 1000 or more tracks on each surface of several platters.

SECTOR   Each track on a disk is divided into **sectors** that hold a fixed number of bytes, typically 512 (Figure 6-7a). Data on the track is accessed by referring to the surface number, track number, and sector number where the data is stored.

The fact that a disk is circular presents a problem: The distance around the tracks on the outside of the disk is greater than that around the tracks on the inside. A given amount of data that takes up one inch of a track on the inside of a disk might be spread over several inches on a track near the outside of a disk. This means that the tracks on the outside are not storing data as efficiently.

Zone recording takes maximum advantage of the storage available by dividing a disk into zones and assigning more sectors to tracks in outer zones than to those in inner zones (Figure 6-7b). Since each sector on the disk holds the same amount of

(a)

(b)

▲ **F I G U R E 6·4**

Hard disk for a personal computer.

(a) The innards of a 3½-inch hard disk with the access arm visible. (b) The Iomega Jaz hard disk drive with removable cartridge.

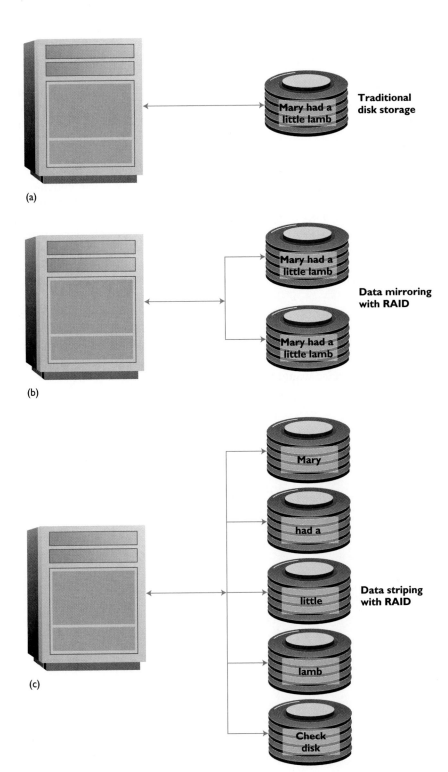

(a)

(b)

(c)

◄ **F I G U R E** **6-5**

RAID storage.

(a) Data is stored on disk in traditional fashion. (b) Disk mirroring with RAID stores a duplicate copy of the data on a second disk. (c) In a system called data striping with RAID, data is scattered among several disks, with a check disk that keeps track of what data is where so that data lost on a bad disk can be re-created.

Traditional disk storage

Data mirroring with RAID

Data striping with RAID

FIGURE 6·6

Tracks.

Each unique position of the read/write head results in a track on the disk surface. Each track contains the magnet representation of the binary ones and zeros.

data, more sectors mean more data storage than there would be if all tracks had the same number of sectors.

CLUSTERS A **cluster** is a fixed number of adjacent sectors that are treated as a unit of storage by the operating system. Clusters typically contain from two to eight sectors, depending on the operating system. Each file is stored in an integral number of clusters; even if a file is only a few bytes in length, it will be allocated an entire cluster.

CYLINDER On a hard disk that has multiple platters, a **cylinder** consists of the track on each surface that is beneath the read/write head at a given position of the read/write arms (Figure 6-8). When a file is larger than the capacity of a single track, the operating system will store it in tracks within the same cylinder, rather than spreading it across tracks on the same platter. The purpose is to reduce the time it takes to move the access arms of a disk pack into position. Once the access arms are in position, they don't have to be moved to access additional tracks within the same cylinder.

To appreciate this, suppose you had an empty disk pack on which you wished to store a large file. You might be tempted to record the data horizontally—to start with the first surface and fill track 000, track 001, track 002, and so on and then move to the second surface and again fill tracks 000, 001, 002, and so forth. However, each new track and new surface would require movement of the access arms, a relatively slow mechanical process.

FIGURE 6·7

Sectors and zone recording.

(a) When data is organized by sector, the address is the surface, track, and sector where the data is stored. (b) If a disk is divided into traditional sectors, as shown here on the left, each track has the same number of sectors. Sectors near the outside of the disk are wider, but they hold the same amount of data as sectors near the inside. If the disk is divided into recording zones, as shown on the right, the tracks near the outside have more sectors than the tracks near the inside. Each sector holds the same amount of data, but since the outer zones have more sectors, the disk as a whole holds more data than the disk on the left.

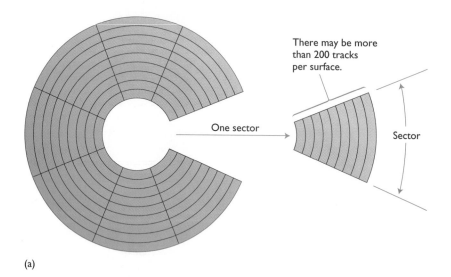

(a)

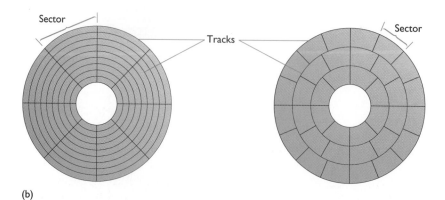

(b)

Recording the data vertically, on the other hand, substantially reduces access arm movement. The data is recorded on the tracks that can be accessed by one positioning of the access arms—that is, on one cylinder. Instead of moving the access arm to the next track each time a track is filled, the arm needs to be moved only after all the tracks in a cylinder are filled. To visualize cylinder organization, pretend that a cylindrically shaped item, such as a tin can, is dropped straight down through all the disks in the disk pack. All the tracks thus encountered, in the same position on each disk surface, make up a cylinder.

Disk Access Speed

Three primary factors determine **access time,** the time needed to access data directly on disk:

- **Seek time. Seek time** is the time it takes the access arm to get into position over a particular track. Keep in mind that all the access arms move as a unit, so they are simultaneously in position over a set of tracks that make up a cylinder.

- **Head switching.** The access arms on the access mechanism do not move separately; they move together, all at the same time. However, only one read/write head can operate at any one time. **Head switching** is the activation of a particular read/write head over a particular track on a particular surface. Since head switching takes place at electronic speed, the time it takes is negligible.

- **Rotational delay.** Once the access arm and read/write head are in position and ready to read or write data, the read/write head must wait for a short period until the desired data on the track rotates under it. On the average, this **rotational delay** is equal to one-half the time for a complete revolution of the disk.

Once the data has been found, the next step is **data transfer,** the process of transferring data between memory and the place on the disk track—from memory to the track if the computer is writing, from the track to memory if the computer is reading. One measure for the performance of disk drives is the average access time, which is usually measured in milliseconds (ms). On current hard disk drives, access time is under 10 ms. Another measure is the **data transfer rate,** which tells how fast data can be transferred once it has been found. This will usually be stated in terms of megabytes of data per second.

Disk caching can be used to improve the effective access time. When the disk drive reads data from disk, it will also read adjacent data and store it in an area of memory called the **disk cache.** When the next read instruction is issued, the drive will first check to see whether the desired data is in the disk cache. If it is, no physical read is necessary, greatly reducing access time. This is the same principle used in memory caching, which was discussed in Chapter 4.

▶ OPTICAL DISK STORAGE

The explosive growth in storage needs has driven the computer industry to provide inexpensive and compact storage with greater capacity. This demanding shopping list is a description of the **optical disk** (Figure 6-9a). The technology works like this: A laser hits a layer of metallic material spread over the surface of a disk. When data is being entered, heat from the laser produces tiny spots, or pits, on the disk surface. To read the data, the laser scans the disk, and a lens picks up light reflections from the spots. Optical storage technology is categorized according to its read/write capability. **Read-only media** are disks that are recorded by the manufacturer and can be read from but not written to by the user. Such a disk cannot, obviously, be used for your files, but manufacturers can use it to supply software. An applications software package could include a dozen diskettes or more; all these can fit on one optical disk

▲ **FIGURE 6-8**

Cylinder data organization.

To visualize a cylinder on disk, imagine dropping a cylinder such as a tin can straight down through all the disks in a disk pack. Within cylinder 150, the track surfaces are vertically aligned and are numbered from top to bottom.

with room to spare. Furthermore, software can be more easily installed from a single optical disk than from a pile of diskettes.

Write-once, read-many media, also called **WORM media,** may be written to once. Once filled, a WORM disk becomes a read-only medium. A WORM disk is non-erasable. For applications that demand secure storage of original versions of valuable documents or data, such as legal records, the primary advantage of nonerasability is clear: Once they are recorded, no one can erase or modify them.

A hybrid type of disk, called **magneto-optical (MO),** combines the best features of magnetic and optical disk technologies. A magneto-optical disk has the high-volume capacity of an optical disk but can be written over like a magnetic disk. The disk surface is coated with plastic and embedded with magnetically sensitive metallic crystals. To write data, a laser beam melts a microscopic spot on the plastic surface, and a magnet aligns the crystals before the plastic cools. The crystals are aligned so that some reflect light and others do not. When the data is later read by a laser beam, only the crystals that reflect light are picked up.

(a)

(b)

FIGURE 6-9

Optical disks.

(a) Optical disks store data using laser beam technology. (b) Many laptop computers include a CD-ROM drive. Laptop users can use CD-ROM applications to make on-the-road presentations or can pop in a CD-ROM encyclopedia to find some needed information.

► COMPACT DISKS

Compact disk (CD) technology is an optical technology that uses the same media used for audio CDs. In fact, with the proper software, computer CD drives can play audio CDs. There are several types of CD drives, categorized according to their ability to read and write CDs.

CD-ROM The **CD-ROM (compact disk read-only memory) drive** is capable only of reading data from CDs—it cannot record anything. CD-ROM has a major advantage over other optical disk designs: The disk format is identical to that of audio compact disks, so the same dust-free manufacturing plants that are now stamping out digital versions of Wynton Marsalis or the Backstreet Boys can easily convert to producing

---

► MAKING CONNECTIONS ◄ **Internet Disk Drives**

If you have ever used a PC on a local area network at school or work, you are probably familiar with the concept of network drives. A network drive is disk storage space located on a network server that is available for you to store data just as if it were on your own PC. Network drives enable you to back up data, share files with others on the network, and, in a school lab environment, access your files no matter which PC you use.

Several companies are making the ultimate network drive available even to users who aren't connected to a local area network, as long as they have an Internet connection. Companies such as X:drive, and Driveway will provide you with disk space on their Internet servers that you can use as an extension of your hard drive. You can place your data on your Internet drive and get to it from anywhere you can get Internet access—work, school, or even the public library.

You can also allow others access to some or all of the data on your virtual drive, providing an easy method of sharing files that are too large to transport via floppy.

Another use of your Internet drive is for off-site backup. Storing an extra copy of valuable data files, such as your financial records, your Ph.D. thesis, or that Great American Novel you've been working on for years is great protection against a fire or flood that might destroy your PC and the backup copies stored on the shelf next to it. Most of these companies provide some space for free (25-MB is typical) and allow you to pay a monthly or yearly fee for additional space. One not-so-obvious limitation is the speed of your Internet connection—uploading and downloading multi-megabyte files can take quite a while with a 56-kbps modem.

anything from software to a digitized encyclopedia. Furthermore, CD-ROM storage is substantial—up to 700 megabytes per disk, the equivalent of more than 450 standard 3½-inch diskettes. As the size of software applications has increased, CD-ROM has become the primary medium for software distribution.

CD-R   Although CD-ROMs are read-only, a different technology called **CD-R (compact disc-recordable)** permits writing on optical disks—but just once; mistakes cannot be undone. CD-R technology requires a CD-R drive, special CD-R disks that look just like regular CDs except that they are marked "CD-R," and the accompanying CD-R software. Once a CD-R disk is written on, it can be read not only by the CD-R drive but also by any CD-ROM drive.

CD-RW   Another variation, **CD-RW (compact disk-rewritable),** is more flexible, allowing you to erase and record over data multiple times. CD-RW technology requires a CD-RW drive, special CD-RW disks, and the CD-RW software. Some compatibility problems may be encountered in reading CD-RW disks on standard CD-ROM drives.

► DVD-ROM

The new storage technology that outpaces all others is called **DVD-ROM,** for **digital versatile disk** (originally digital *video* disk). Think of a DVD, as it is called for short, as an overachieving CD-ROM. Although the two look the same, a DVD has up to 4.7-gigabyte capacity, almost seven times more than that of the highest-capacity CD-ROM. And that is just the plain variety. DVDs have two layers of information— one clear and one opaque—on a single side; this so-called double-layered DVD surface can hold about 8.5-GB. Furthermore, DVDs can be written on both sides, bumping the capacity to 17-GB. And a DVD-ROM drive can also read CD-ROMs. It is not surprising that DVD-ROM technology is being seen as a replacement for CD-ROMs over the next few years.

Operating very much like CD-ROM technology, DVD uses a laser beam to read microscopic spots that represent data. But DVD uses a laser with a shorter wavelength, permitting it to read more densely packed spots, thus increasing the disk capacity. The benefits of this storage capacity are many, including exquisite sound and the ability to hold full-length movies. Audio quality on DVD is comparable to that of current audio compact disks. DVDs will eventually hold high-volume business data. It is just a matter of time until all new personal computers will come with a DVD drive as standard equipment. The writable version of DVD is **DVD-RAM.** Under current standards, DVD-RAM stores 5.2-MB on a double-sided disk that is readable only by DVD-RAM drives.

If you have a CD-ROM or a DVD-ROM drive, you are on your way to one of the computer industry's great adventures: multimedia.

► MULTIMEDIA

Multimedia stirs the imagination. For example, have you ever thought that you could see a film clip from *Gone with the Wind* on your computer screen? One could argue that such treats are already available on videocassette, but the computer version provides an added dimension for this and other movies: reviews by critics, photographs of movie stars, lists of Academy Awards, the possibility of user input, and much more. Software described as **multimedia** typically presents information with text, illustrations, photos, narration, music, animation, and film clips. Until the advent of the optical disk, placing this much data on a disk was impractical.

Stamps from Your Computer
That's right—no more trips to the post office, no standing in line. Several sites on the Internet, including PostagePlus, shown here, let you pay for postage and store it right on your hard disk. When you need a stamp, you just print it on the envelope. Well, it does not look much like a real stamp, but the post office accepts it just the same.

Here is how it works. From your personal computer, you access a site that sells postage. You pay for postage, usually with a credit card. The postage company grants you permission to print a certain amount of postage, sending that amount and the stamp image to your "vault"—a file—on your hard disk. (Alternatively, some companies keep your account on their own files.) Then, just print and mail.

The convenience is remarkable, but there are downsides: signup and monthly fees in addition to the postage—and fewer colorful stamps in circulation.

FOCUS ON ETHICS	Not So Fast

When preparing a multimedia presentation, take a moment to reflect before adding music, images, or video clips. Have you obtained permission from the copyright owner to use the item? Even featuring statuary you have photographed in front of a civic structure might not be a simple matter. The artist who created the work of art could still own the copyright even if the statues themselves have been sold. In general, unless you created a work of art, you must consider ownership issues.

Locate examples of this sort of violation on the Internet. What justification do you think those who use copyrighted material without permission would give? Do you think their arguments are valid?

However, the large capacity of optical disks means that the kinds of data that take up huge amounts of storage space—photographs, music, and film clips—can now be readily accommodated.

Multimedia Requirements

To use multimedia software, you must have the proper hardware. In addition to the aforementioned CD-ROM or DVD-ROM drive, you also need a sound card or sound chip (installed internally) and speakers, which may be internal, that is, built into the computer housing or external, connected to the computer via cables. Special software accompanies the drive and sound card. In particular, if full-motion video is important to you, be sure that your computer is equipped to handle **MPEG (Motion Picture Experts Group),** a set of widely accepted video standards. Another video-related issue is the speed of the drive: The faster the better. The higher the drive speed, the faster the transfer of data and the smoother the video showing on the screen.

Should your next computer be a multimedia personal computer? Absolutely. There is no doubt that multimedia is the medium of choice for all kinds of software.

Multimedia Applications

If you take a moment to peruse the racks of multimedia software in your local store, you can see that most of the current offerings come under the categories of entertainment or education—or possibly both. You can study *and hear* works by Stravinsky or Schubert. You can explore the planets or the ocean bottom through film clips and narrations by experts. You can be "elected" to Congress, after which you tour the Capitol, decorate your office, hire staff, and vote on issues. You can study the battle of Gettysburg—and even change the outcome. You can study the Japanese language, seeing the symbols and hearing the intonation. You can buy multimedia versions of reference books, magazines, children's books, and entire novels.

But this is just the beginning. Businesses are already moving to this high-capacity environment for street atlases, national phone directories, and sales catalogs. Coming offerings will include every kind of standard business application, all tricked out with fancy animation, photos, and sound. Educators will be able to draw on the new sight and sound capabilities for everything from human anatomy to time travel. And just imagine the library of the future, consisting not only of the printed word but also of photos, film, animation, and sound recordings—all flowing from the computer.

► MAGNETIC TAPE STORAGE

We saved magnetic tape storage for last because it has now taken a subordinate role in storage technology. **Magnetic tape** looks like the tape used in music cassettes—plastic tape with a magnetic coating. As in other magnetic media, data is stored as

Magnetic tape units.

Tapes are always protected by glass from outside dust and dirt. These modern tape drives, called "stackers", accept several cassette tapes, each with its own supply and take-up reel.

extremely small magnetic spots. Tapes come in a number of forms, including ½-inch-wide tape wound on a reel, ¼-inch-wide tape in data cartridges and cassettes, and tapes that look like ordinary music cassettes but are designed to store data instead of music. Tape capacity is expressed in terms of **density**, which is the number of **characters per inch (cpi)** or **bytes per inch (bpi)** that can be stored on the tape.

Figure 6-10 shows a **magnetic tape unit** that might be used with a mainframe. The tape unit reads and writes data using a **read/write head.** When the computer is writing on the tape, the **erase head** first erases any data that was previously recorded on the tape.

Tape now has a limited role because disks have proved to be the superior storage medium. Disk data is quite reliable, especially within a sealed module. Furthermore, as we will show, disk data can be accessed directly, in contrast to sequential data on tape, which can be accessed only by passing by all the data ahead of it on the tape. Consequently, the primary role of tape today is as an inexpensive backup medium.

► BACKUP SYSTEMS

Although a hard disk is an extremely reliable device, it is subject to electromechanical failures that cause loss of data, as well as physical damage from fire and natural disasters. Furthermore, data files, particularly those accessed by several users, are subject to errors introduced by users. There is also the possibility of errors introduced by software. With any method of data storage, a **backup system**—a way of storing data in more than one place to protect it from damage and errors—is vital. As we have already noted, magnetic tape is used primarily for backup purposes. For personal computer users, an easy and inexpensive way to back up a hard disk file is simply to copy it to a diskette or Zip disk whenever it is updated. But this is not practical for a system with many files or many users.

Personal computer users have the option of purchasing their own tape backup system, to be used on a regular basis for copying all data from hard disk to a high-capacity tape. Data thus saved can be restored to the hard disk later if needed. A key advantage of a tape backup system is that it can copy the entire hard disk to a single tape in minutes; also, with the availability of gigabytes of hard disk space, it is not really feasible to swap diskettes into and out of the machine. Furthermore, tape

backup can be scheduled to take place when you are not going to be using the computer. CD-R and CD-RW media can also be used for backup, but they are limited to storing less than 1GB of data, while tape cartridges with more than 10GB of storage capacity are available at reasonable cost.

► ORGANIZING AND ACCESSING STORED DATA

As users of computer systems, we offer data as we are instructed to do, such as punching in our identification code at an automated teller machine or perhaps filling out a form with our name and address. But data cannot be dumped helter-skelter into a computer. Some computer professional—probably a programmer or systems analyst—has to have planned how data from users will be received, organized, and stored and in what manner data will be processed by the computer.

This kind of storage goes beyond what you may have done to store a memo created in word processing. Organizations that store data usually need a lot of data on many subjects. For example, a charitable organization would probably need detailed information about donors, names and schedules of volunteers, and perhaps a schedule of fund-raising events. A factory would need to keep track of inventory (name, identification number, location, quantity, and so forth), the scheduled path of the product through the assembly line, records of quality-control checkpoints, and much more. All this data must be organized and stored according to a plan. First consider how data is organized.

Data: Getting Organized

To be processed by the computer, raw data is organized into characters, fields, records, files, and databases. First is the smallest element: the character.

- A **character** is a letter, digit, or special character (such as $, ?, or *).

- A **field** contains a set of related characters. For example, suppose that a health club is making address labels for a mailing. For each person it might have a member number field, a name field, a street address field, a city field, a state field, a zip code field, and a phone number field.

- A **record** is a collection of related fields. On the health club mailing list, one person's member number, name, address, city, state, zip code, and phone number constitute a record.

- A **file** is a collection of related records. All the member records for the health club compose a file. Figure 6-11 shows how data for a health club member might look.

- A **database** is a collection of interrelated files stored together with minimum redundancy. Specific data items can be retrieved for various applications. For instance, if the health club is opening a new outlet, it can pull out the names of people with zip codes near the new club and send them an announcement. Database concepts will be discussed in more detail in Chapter 14.

A field of particular interest is the **key,** a unique identifier for a record. It might seem at first that a name—of a person, say, or a product—would be a good key; however, since some names may be the same, a name field is not a good choice for a key. When a file is first computerized, existing description fields are seldom used as keys. Although a file describing people might use a Social Security number as the key, it is more likely that a new field will be developed that can be assigned unique values, such as customer number or product number.

In addition to organizing the expected data, a plan must be made to access the data on files.

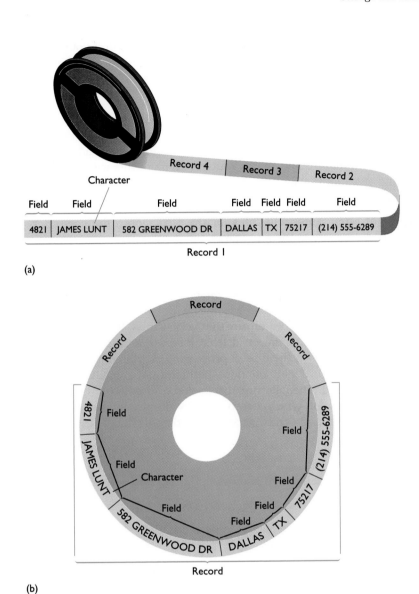

◄ **F I G U R E** **6-11**

How data is organized.

Whether stored on tape or on disk, data is organized into characters, fields, records, and files. A file is a collection of related records. These diagrams represent (a) magnetic tape and (b) magnetic disk.

The File Plan: An Overview

Now that you have a general idea of how data is organized, you are ready to look at the process used to decide how to place data on a storage medium. Consider this chain: (1) It is the application—payroll, airline reservations, inventory control, whatever—that determines how the data must be accessed by users. (2) Once an access method has been determined, it follows that there are certain ways in which the data must be organized so that the needed access is workable. (3) The organization method, in turn, limits the choice of storage medium. The discussion begins with an appreciation of application demands, then moves to a detailed look at organization and access.

The following application examples illustrate how an access decision might be made:

- A department store offers its customers charge accounts. When a customer makes a purchase, a sales clerk needs to be able to check the validity of the customer's account while the customer is waiting. The clerk needs immediate access to the individual customer record in the account file.

- A major oil company supplies its charge customers with credit cards, which it considers sufficient proof for purchase. The charge slips collected by gas stations are

forwarded to the oil company, which processes them in order of account number. Unlike the retail example just given, the company does not need access to any one record at a specific time but merely needs access to all customer charge records when it is time to prepare bills.

- A city power and light company employee accepts reports of burned-out streetlights from residents over the phone. Using a key made up of unique address components, the clerk immediately finds the record for the offending streetlight and prints out a one-page report that is routed to repair units within 24 hours. To produce such quick service for an individual streetlight, the employee needs immediate access to the individual streetlight record.

- Airline flight attendants' schedules for the next month are computer-produced monthly and delivered to the attendants' home-base mailboxes. The schedules are put together from information based on flight records, and the entire file can be accessed monthly at the convenience of the airline and the computer-use plan.

As you can see, the question of access seems to come down to whether a particular record is needed right away, as it was in the first and third examples. This immediate need for a particular record means that access must be *direct.* It follows that the organization must also be direct, or at least *indexed,* and that the storage medium must be disk. Furthermore, the type of processing, a related topic, must be *transaction processing.* The critical distinction is whether or not immediate access to an individual record is needed. The following discussion examines all these topics in detail. Although the organization type is determined by the type of access required, the file must be organized before it can be accessed, so organization is the first topic.

File Organization: Three Methods

There are three major methods of organizing data files in secondary storage:

- Sequential file organization, in which records are stored in order by key

- Direct file organization, in which records are not physically stored in any special order

- Indexed file organization, in which records are stored sequentially but indexes are built into the file to allow a record to be accessed either sequentially or directly

SEQUENTIAL FILE ORGANIZATION **Sequential file organization** means that records are stored in order according to a key field. As we noted earlier, a file containing information on people will be in order by a key that uniquely identifies each person, such as Social Security number or customer number. If a particular record in a sequential file is wanted, all the prior records in the file must be read before the desired record is reached. Tape storage is limited to sequential file organization. Disk storage may be sequential, but records on disk can also be accessed directly.

DIRECT FILE ORGANIZATION **Direct file organization** (also called **random file organization**) allows **direct (random) access,** the ability to go directly to the desired record by using a record key; the computer does not have to read all preceding records in the file as it does if the records are arranged sequentially. Direct processing requires disk storage; in fact, a disk device is called a **direct-access storage device (DASD)** because the computer can go directly to the desired record on the disk. It is this ability to access any given record instantly that has made computer systems so convenient for people in service industries—for catalog order-takers determining whether a particular sweater is in stock, for example, or bank tellers checking individual bank balances. An added benefit of direct-access organization is the ability to read, change, and return a record to its same place on the disk; this is called **updating in place.**

◀ F I G U R E 6-12

A hashing scheme.

Dividing the key number 1269 by the prime number 17 yields a remainder of 11, which can be used to indicate the address on a disk.

Obviously, if we have a completely blank area on the disk and can put records anywhere, there must be some predictable system for placing a record at a disk address and then retrieving the record at a subsequent time. In other words, once the record has been placed on a disk, it must be possible to find it again. This is done by choosing a certain formula to apply to the record key, thereby deriving a number to use as the disk address. The **hashing,** or **randomizing, algorithm** is the mathematical operation that is applied to a key to yield a number that represents the address. Even though the record keys are unique, it is possible for a hashing algorithm to produce the same disk address, called a **synonym,** for two different records; such an occurrence is called a **collision.** There are various ways to recover from a collision; one way is simply to use the next available record slot on the disk.

There are many different hashing schemes; although the example in Figure 6-12 is far too simple to be realistic, it can give you a general idea of how the process works. An example of how direct processing works is provided in Figure 6-13.

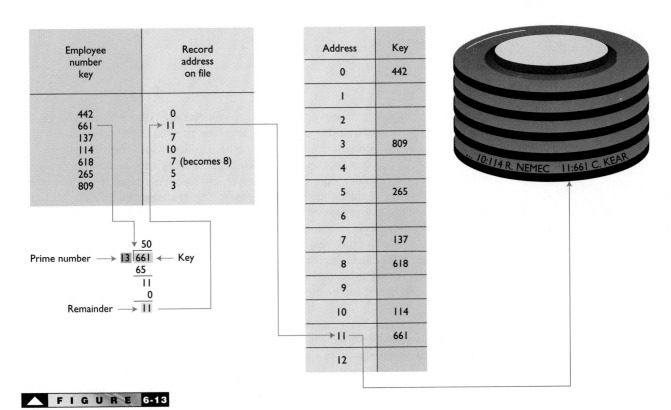

▲ F I G U R E 6-13

An example of direct access.

Assume that there are 13 addresses (0 through 12) available in the file. Dividing the key number 661, which is C. Kear's employee number, by the prime number 13 yields a remainder of 11. Thus, 11 is the address for key 661. However, for the key 618, dividing by 13 yields a remainder of 7, a synonym, since this address has already been used by the key 137, which also has a remainder of 7. Hence the address becomes the next location—that is, 8. Note, incidentally, that keys (and therefore records) need not appear in any particular order. (The 13 record locations available are, of course, too few to hold a normal file; a small number was used to keep the example simple.)

INDEXED FILE ORGANIZATION **Indexed file organization** is a third method of file organization, and it represents a compromise between the sequential and direct methods. It is useful in applications in which a file needs to be processed sequentially but, in addition, access to individual records is needed.

An indexed file works as follows: Records are stored in the file in sequential order, but the file also contains an index. The index contains entries consisting of the key to each record stored on the file and the corresponding disk address for that record. The index is like a directory, with the keys to all records listed in order. For a record to be accessed directly, the record key must be located in the index; the address associated with the key is then used to access the record on the disk. Accessing the entire file of records sequentially is simply a matter of beginning with the first record and proceeding one at a time through the rest of the records.

► PROCESSING STORED DATA

Once there is a plan for accessing the files, they can be processed. Most business file processing involves processing transactions to update a master file. A **transaction** is a business event that requires the business's records to be updated. A retail sale, the receipt of ordered goods, and the issuance of a paycheck are examples of transactions. A **master file** contains data that must be updated as transactions occur. Examples of master files are an inventory file, an employee file, and a customer file. There are several methods of processing data files in a computer system. The two main methods are batch processing (processing transaction data in groups at a more convenient later time) and transaction processing (processing transactions immediately, as they occur).

Batch Processing

Batch processing is a technique in which transactions are collected into groups, or batches, to be processed at a time when the computer may have few online users and thus be more accessible, often during the night. Unlike transaction processing, a topic that we will discuss momentarily, batch processing involves no direct user interaction. Let us consider updating the health club address-label file, a list of all members of the health club and their addresses. The **transaction file** contains all changes to be made to the master file: additions (transactions to create new master records for new members), deletions (transactions with instructions to delete master records of members who have resigned from the health club), and revisions (transactions to change items such as street addresses or phone numbers in fields in the master records). Periodically, perhaps monthly or weekly, the master file is **updated** with the changes called for in the transaction file. The result is a new, up-to-date master file (Figure 6-14).

In batch processing, before a transaction file is matched against a master file, the transaction file must be sorted (usually by computer) so that all the transactions are in sequential order according to a key field. In updating the health club address-label file, the key is the member number assigned by the health club. The records on the master file are already in order by key. Once the changes in the transaction file are sorted by key, the two files can be matched and the master file updated.

During processing, the computer matches the keys from the master and transaction files, carrying out the appropriate action to add, revise, or delete. At the end of processing, a newly updated master file is created; in addition, an error report is usually printed. The error report shows actions such as an attempt to update or delete a nonexistent record or an attempt to add a record that already exists.

The biggest advantage of batch processing is its efficiency. The biggest disadvantage is that the master file is current only immediately after processing.

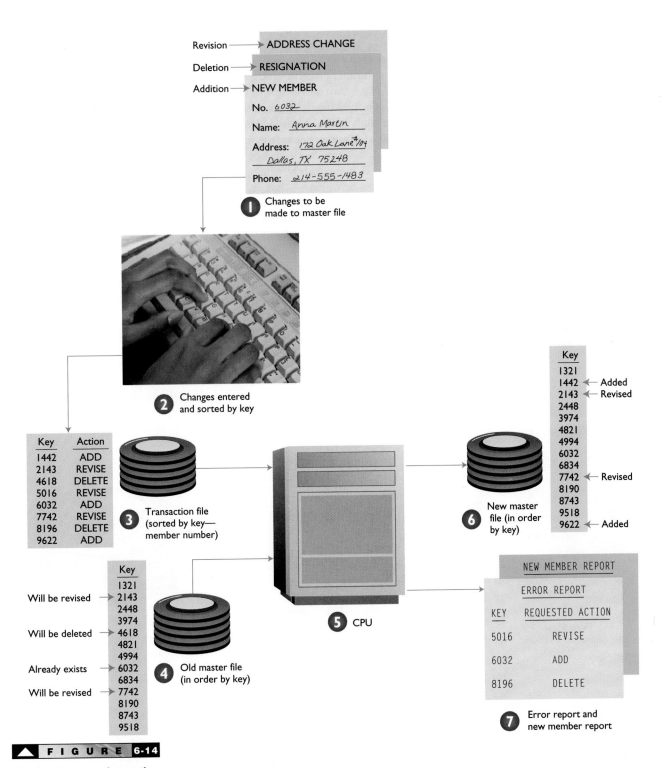

Revision ——▶ ADDRESS CHANGE

Deletion ——▶ RESIGNATION

Addition ——▶ NEW MEMBER

No. *6032*

Name: *Anna Martin*

Address: *172 Oak Lane #104*
Dallas, TX 75248

Phone: *214-555-1483*

1 Changes to be made to master file

2 Changes entered and sorted by key

Key	Action
1442	ADD
2143	REVISE
4618	DELETE
5016	REVISE
6032	ADD
7742	REVISE
8196	DELETE
9622	ADD

3 Transaction file (sorted by key— member number)

Key
1321
2143	Will be revised
2448
3974
4618	Will be deleted
4821
4994
6032	Already exists
6834
7742	Will be revised
8190
8743
9518

4 Old master file (in order by key)

5 CPU

6 New master file (in order by key)

Key	
1321	
1442	◀— Added
2143	◀— Revised
2448	
3974	
4821	
4994	
6032	
6834	
7742	◀— Revised
8190	
8743	
9518	
9622	◀— Added

NEW MEMBER REPORT

ERROR REPORT

KEY	REQUESTED ACTION
5016	REVISE
6032	ADD
8196	DELETE

7 Error report and new member report

▲ **F I G U R E 6-14**

How batch processing works.

The purpose of this system is to update the health club's master address-label file. The updating will be done sequentially. (1) Changes to be made (additions, deletions, and revisions) are input with (2) a keyboard, sorted, and sent to a disk, where they are stored in (3) the transaction file. The transaction file contains records in sequential order, according to member number, from lowest to highest. The field used to identify the record is called the key; in this instance the key is the member number. (4) The master file is also organized by member number. (5) The computer matches transaction file data and master file data by member number to produce (6) a new master file and (7) an error report and a new member report. Note that since this was a sequential update, the new master file is a completely new file, not just the old file updated in place. The error report lists member numbers in the transaction file that were not in the master file and member numbers that were included in the transaction file as additions that were already in the master file.

Transaction Processing

Transaction processing is a technique of processing transactions—a bank withdrawal, an address change, a credit charge—in random order, that is, in any order in which they occur. Note that although batch processing also uses transactions, in that case they are grouped together for processing; the phrase *transaction processing* means that each transaction is handled immediately. Transaction processing is real-time processing. **Real-time processing** means that a transaction is processed fast enough for the result to come back and be acted on right away. For example, a teller at a bank can find out immediately what your bank balance is. For processing to be real-time, it must also be **online**—that is, the terminals must be connected directly to the computer. Transaction processing systems use disk storage because disks allow direct access to the desired record.

Advantages of transaction processing are immediate access to stored data (and thus immediate customer service) and immediate updating of the stored data. For example, a sales clerk could access the computer via a terminal to verify the customer's credit and also record the sale via the computer (Figure 6-15). Later, by the way, those updated records can be batch-processed to bill all customers.

Batch and Transaction Processing: The Best of Both Worlds

Numerous computer systems combine the best features of both methods of processing. Generally speaking, transaction processing is used for activities related to the current needs of people—especially workers and customers—as they go about their

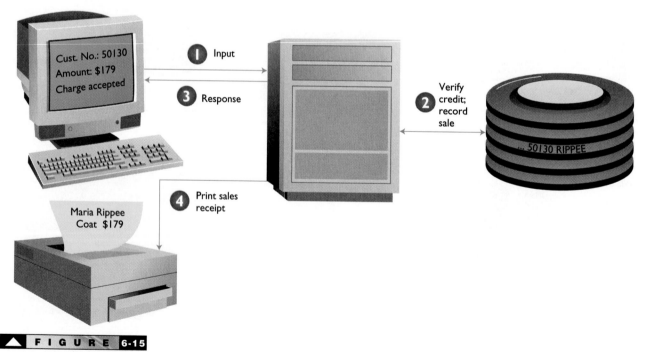

▲ **FIGURE 6-15**

How transaction processing works.

The purposes of this retail sales system are to verify that a customer's credit is good, record the credit sale on the customer's record, and produce a sales receipt. Since customers may have the same name, the file is organized by customer account number rather than by name. Here Maria Rippee, account number 50130, wishes to purchase a coat for $179. (1) The sales clerk uses the terminal to input Maria's account number and the sale. (2) When the computer receives the data from the clerk, it uses the account number to find Maria's record on the disk file, verify her credit, and record the sale so that she will later be billed for it. (3) The computer returns an acceptance to the clerk's terminal. (4) The computer sends sales receipt information to the clerk's printer. All this is done within seconds while the customer is waiting. This example is necessarily simplified, but it shows a system that is real-time (immediate response) and online (directly connected to the computer).

daily lives. Batch processing, by comparison, can be done at any time, even in the middle of the night, without worrying about the convenience of the people who are ultimately affected by the processing.

A bank, for instance, may use transaction processing to check your balance and individually record your cash withdrawal transaction during the day at the teller window. However, the deposit that you leave in an envelope in an "instant" deposit drop may be recorded during the night by means of batch processing. Printing your bank statement is also a batch process. Most store systems also combine both methods: A point-of-sale terminal finds the individual item price as a sale is made and immediately updates inventory, while batch processing is used to produce daily and weekly sales reports.

Police license-plate checks for stolen cars work in the same way. As cars are sold throughout the state, the license numbers, owners' names, and so on, are updated in the motor vehicle department's master file, usually via batch processing on a nightly basis. But when police officers see a car that they suspect may be stolen, they can radio headquarters, where an operator with a terminal uses transaction processing to check the master file immediately to find out whether the car has been reported missing. Some officers have a laptop computer right in the car and can check the information themselves.

Auto junkyards, which often are computerized big businesses, can make an individual inquiry for a record of a specific part needed by a customer who is waiting on the phone or in person. As parts are sold, sales records are kept to update the files nightly using batch processing.

As you can see from these examples, both workers and customers eventually see the results of transaction processing in the reports output by batch processing. Managers will see further batch processing output in the form of information gathered and summarized about the processed transactions. Finally, new transaction processing is possible based on the results of previous batch processing.

▲

What is the future of storage? Perhaps holographic storage, which would be able to store thousands of pages on a device the size of a quarter and would be much faster than even the fastest hard drives. Whatever the technology, it seems likely that there will be greater storage capabilities in the future to hold the huge data files for law, medicine, science, education, business, and, of course, the government.

To have access to all that data from any location, we need data communications, the subject of the next chapter.

CHAPTER REVIEW

► Summary and Key Terms

- **Secondary storage,** sometimes called auxiliary storage, is storage that is separate from the computer itself, where software and data can be stored on a semipermanent basis. Secondary storage is necessary because memory, or primary storage, can be used only temporarily.

- The benefits of secondary storage are space, reliability, convenience, and economy.

- Diskettes and hard disks are magnetic media, based on a technology of representing data as magnetized spots on the disk.

- **Diskettes** are made of flexible Mylar. Advantages of diskettes, compared with hard disks, are portability and backup. The 3½-inch diskette standard may be challenged by new, higher-capacity disks whose drives can handle both the new disks and the traditional 3½-inch disk or perhaps by Iomega's Zip drive, whose disk has a high capacity but is not compatible with 3½-inch diskettes.

- **Data compression** makes a large file smaller by temporarily removing nonessential characters.

- A **hard disk** is a rigid platter coated with magnetic oxide that can be magnetized to represent data. Several platters can be assembled into a **disk pack.**

- A **disk drive** is a device that allows data to be read from a disk or written to a disk. A disk pack is mounted on a disk drive that is a separate unit connected to the computer. The disk **access arm** moves a **read/write head** into position over a particular track, where the read/write head hovers above the track. A **head crash** occurs when a read/write head touches the disk surface and causes data to be destroyed.

- A **redundant array of independent disks,** or simply **RAID,** uses a group of small hard disks that work together as a unit. RAID level 1, **disk mirroring,** duplicates data on separate disk drives. Higher levels of RAID use **data striping,** spreading the data across several disks in the array, with one disk used solely as a check disk to keep track of what data is where.

- A **track** is the circular portion of the disk surface that passes under the read/write head as the disk rotates.

- Each track is divided into **sectors** that hold a fixed number of bytes. Data on the track is accessed by referring to the surface number, track number, and sector number where the data is stored. **Zone recording** involves dividing a disk into zones to take maximum advantage of the storage available by assigning more sectors to tracks in outer zones than to those in inner zones.

- A **cluster** is a fixed number of adjacent sectors that are treated as a unit of storage by the operating system; it consists of two to eight sectors, depending on the operating system.

- On a hard disk that has multiple platters, a **cylinder** consists of the track on each surface that is beneath the read/write head at a given position of the read/write arms.

- Three factors determine **access time,** the time needed to access data directly on disk: **seek time,** the time it takes to get the access arm into position over a particular track; **head switching,** the activation of a particular read/write head over a particular track on a particular surface; and **rotational delay,** the brief wait until the desired data on the track rotates under the read/write head. Once data has been found, **data transfer,** the transfer of data between memory and the place on the disk track, occurs.

- Access time is usually measured in milliseconds (ms). The **data transfer rate,** which tells how fast data can be transferred once it has been found, is usually stated in terms of megabytes of data per second.

- Disk caching uses an area of memory called **disk cache** to temporarily store data from disk that the program might need soon. If desired data is found in the disk cache, time is saved because no actual read is necessary.

- **Optical disk** technology uses a laser beam to enter data as spots on the disk surface. To read the data, the laser scans the disk, and a lens picks up different light reflections from the various spots. **Read-only media** are recorded on by the manufacturer and can be read from but not written to by the user. **Write-once, read-many media,** also called **WORM media,** may be written to once. A hybrid type of disk, called **magneto-optical (MO),** has the large capacity of an optical disk but can be written over like a magnetic disk. **CD-ROM,** for **compact disk read-only memory drive,** which has a disk format identical to that of audio compact disks, can hold up to 700 megabytes per disk. **CD-R (compact disc-recordable)** technology permits writing on optical disks. **CD-RW (compact disk-rewritable)** technology is more flexible, allowing you to erase and record over data multiple times.

- **DVD-ROM,** for **digital versatile disk,** has astonishing storage capacity, up to 17-GB if both layers and both sides are used. The writable version of DVD is **DVD-RAM.**

- **Multimedia** software typically presents information with text, illustrations, photos, narration, music, animation, and film clips—possible because of the large capacity of optical disks. **MPEG (Motion Picture Experts Group)** is a set of widely accepted video standards.

- **Magnetic tape** stores data as extremely small magnetic spots on tape similar to that used in music cassettes. Tape capacity is expressed in terms of **density,** which is the number of **characters per inch (cpi)** or **bytes per inch (bpi)** that can be stored on the tape.

- A **magnetic tape unit** reads and writes data using a **read/write head;** when the computer is writing on the tape, the **erase head** first erases any data that was previously recorded.

- A **backup system** is a way of storing data in more than one place to protect it from damage and loss. Most backup systems use tape, but CD-R or CD-RW media can also be used.

- A **character** is a letter, digit, or special character (such as $, ?, or *). A **field** contains a set of related characters. A **record** is a collection of related fields. A **file** is a collection of related records. A **database** is a collection of interrelated files stored together with minimum redundancy; specific data items can be retrieved for various applications. A **key** field uniquely identifies each record.

- **Sequential file organization** means that records are in order according to the key field. If a particular record in a sequential file is wanted, then all the prior records in the file must be read before the desired record is reached. Tape storage is limited to sequential file organization.

- **Direct file organization** (also called **random file organization**), allows **direct (random) access,** the ability to go directly to the desired record by using a record key. Direct processing requires disk storage; a disk device is called a **direct-access storage device (DASD).** Besides instant access to any record, an added benefit of direct-access organization is the ability to read, change, and return a record to its same place on the disk; this is called **updating in place.** The **hashing,** or **randomizing, algorithm** is the mathematical operation that is applied to a key to yield a number that represents the address. A hashing algorithm may produce the same disk address, called a **synonym,** for two different records; such an occurrence is called a **collision.**

- **Indexed file organization** stores records in the file in sequential order, but the file also contains an index of keys; the address associated with the key can be used to locate the record on the disk.

- A **transaction** is a business event that requires the business's records to be updated. A **master file** contains data that must be updated as transactions occur.

- **Batch processing** is a technique in which transactions are collected into groups, or batches, to be processed at a time when the computer has few online users and therefore is more accessible. A **transaction file,** sorted by key, contains all changes to be made to the master file: additions, deletions, and revisions. The master file is **updated** with the changes that are called for in the transaction file.

- **Transaction processing** is a technique of processing transactions in any order, as they occur. **Real-time processing** means that a transaction is processed fast enough for the result to come back and be acted upon right away. **Online** processing means that the terminals must be connected directly to the computer.

▶ Critical Thinking Questions

1. If you were buying a personal computer today, what would you expect to find as standard secondary storage? What storage might you choose as an option?

2. Can you imagine new multimedia applications that take advantage of sound, photos, art, and perhaps video?

3. Provide your own example to illustrate how characters of data are organized into fields, records, files, and (perhaps) databases. If you wish, you may choose one of the following examples: department store, airline reservations, or Internal Revenue Service data.

4. Provide your own examples of systems that combine both batch and transaction processing.

▶ STUDENT STUDY GUIDE

Multiple Choice

1. The density of data stored on magnetic tape is expressed as
   a. units per inch
   b. tracks per inch
   c. packs per inch
   d. bytes per inch

2. Another name for secondary storage is
   a. cylinder storage
   b. density
   c. auxiliary storage
   d. memory

3. A magnetized spot on disk or tape represents
   a. cpi
   b. a zone
   c. MB
   d. 1 bit

4. A field contains one or more
   a. characters
   b. databases
   c. records
   d. files

5. Processing transactions in groups is called
   a. data transfer
   b. transaction processing
   c. head switching
   d. batch processing

6. A hard disk can be backed up efficiently by using
   a. zoning
   b. a tape system
   c. a transaction file
   d. WORM

7. Data that must be updated as a result of business activity is contained in
   a. a field
   b. memory
   c. a transaction file
   d. a master file

8. DASD is another name for
   a. disk storage
   b. tape storage
   c. fields
   d. sorting

9. Optical disk technology uses
   a. helical scanning
   b. DAT
   c. a laser beam
   d. RAID

10. Higher levels of RAID spread data across several disks, a method called
    a. mirroring
    b. hashing
    c. data striping
    d. duplication

11. The time required to position the access arm over a particular track is known as
    a. rotational delay
    b. seek time
    c. data transfer
    d. head switching

12. A way of organizing data on a disk pack to minimize seek time uses
    a. sequential files
    b. cylinders
    c. sequential order
    d. hashing

13. The speed with which a disk can find data being sought is called
    a. access time
    b. direct time
    c. data transfer time
    d. cylinder time

14. The disk storage that uses both a magnet and a laser beam is called
    a. hashing
    b. CD-ROM
    c. magneto-optical
    d. WORM

15. The RAID method of duplicating data is called
    a. zoning
    b. the sector method
    c. data mirroring
    d. data striping

16. Before a sequential file can be updated, the transactions must first be
    a. numbered
    b. sorted
    c. labeled
    d. updated

17. A hashing algorithm uses a _____ as input to produce a disk address.
    a. key
    b. file
    c. record
    d. character

18. Several small disk packs that work together as a unit are called
    a. CD-ROM
    b. WORM
    c. RAID
    d. MO

19. Assigning more sectors to outer disk tracks is called
    a. zone recording
    b. data transfer
    c. randomizing
    d. sectoring

20. The ability to write a changed disk record back to its original location is called
    a. magneto-optical
    b. multimedia
    c. rotational delay
    d. updating in place

True/False

T   F   1. Real-time processing means that a transaction is processed fast enough for the result to come back and be acted upon right away.

T   F   2. CD-R technology permits writing on CD-ROMs.

T   F   3. A field is a set of related records.

T   F   4. A magnetic tape unit records data on tape but cannot retrieve it.

T   F   5. A transaction file contains records to update the master file.

T   F   6. WORM media can be written once; then it becomes read-only.

T　F　7. A collision occurs when the hashing algorithm produces the same disk address for two different record keys.

T　F　8. Density is the number of characters per inch stored on magnetic tape.

T　F　9. The most common backup medium is CD-ROM.

T　F　10. Another name for randomizing is zoning.

T　F　11. Transaction processing systems are online systems.

T　F　12. Multimedia software can include film clips.

T　F　13. Hard disks have platters, access arms, and read/write heads in a sealed module.

T　F　14. Magneto-optical refers to a special type of tape that records data diagonally.

T　F　15. A magnetic disk records data on concentric circular tracks.

Fill-In

1. Adding more sectors to the outer tracks of a disk is called _____.

2. Processing transactions in a group is called _____.

3. The primary advantage of optical disk technology lies in its _____.

4. The type of software that can offer photos, narration, music, and more is called _____.

5. DASD stands for _____.

6. The type of access that a file requires is determined by _____.

7. The two methods of file access are
   a. _____.
   b. _____.

8. If a read/write head touches a hard disk surface, this is called a _____.

9. What does CD-ROM stand for? _____.

10. A(n) _____ is a group of disk sectors treated as a unit of storage.

11. The concept of using a group of small disk drives as a storage unit is called ___.

12. A(n) _____ is a unique identifier for a record.

13. The smallest unit of raw data is the _____.

14. A(n) _____ consists of the group of tracks beneath the read/write heads at one time.

15. Another name for a hashing algorithm is _____.

16. Four benefits of secondary storage are
    a. _____
    b. _____
    c. _____
    d. _____

17. The three kinds of components in a sealed data module are
    a. _____
    b. _____
    c. _____

18. The three primary factors that determine access time for disk data are
    a. _____
    b. _____
    c. _____

19. Three major methods of file organization are
    a. _____
    b. _____
    c. _____
20. Transactions must be _____ before being used to update a sequential file.

▶ **ANSWERS**

Multiple Choice

1. d	6. b	11. b	16. b
2. c	7. d	12. b	17. a
3. d	8. a	13. a	18. c
4. a	9. c	14. c	19. a
5. d	10. c	15. c	20. d

True/False

1. T	5. T	9. F	13. T
2. F	6. T	10. F	14. F
3. F	7. T	11. T	15. T
4. F	8. T	12. T	

Fill-In

1. zone recording
2. batch processing
3. capacity
4. multimedia
5. direct-access storage device
6. the application
7. a. sequential
   b. direct (random)
8. head crash
9. compact disk read-only memory
10. cluster
11. redundant array of independent disks (RAID)
12. key
13. character
14. cylinder
15. randomizing algorithm
16. a. space
    b. reliability
    c. convenience
    d. economy
17. a. disks
    b. access arms
    c. read/write heads
18. a. seek time
    b. head switching
    c. rotational delay
19. a. sequential
    b. direct
    c. indexed sequential
20. sorted

Planet Internet

FREE OR NOT FREE

Many people, especially those associated with schools and government organizations, have free access to the Internet. But is the information available on Internet sites also free? Often, the answer is yes. But remember that almost anything you find on the Internet is copyrighted and you must follow copyright law, unless the site specifically grants you exemption from the provisions of the copyright law.

What information is free and what isn't?

There are no uniform rules to guide you. Although some information providers make a blanket "help yourself" statement, much information is unaccompanied by a proprietary statement.

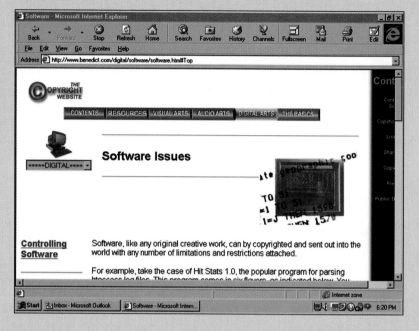

Other information best fits in an "almost free" category. The Copyright Web site discusses six categories of software availability. *Copyhoarding* involves creating software only for your own use and not distributing it to anyone else. *Licensing* is the standard "pay for use" deal, whereby you pay for the use of software under conditions specified by the owner. Generally, you are allowed to make a backup copy for personal use, but your rights to modify, share, or rearrange to code typically end there. *Shareware* is made available free for a trial period, generally on the honor system. If you like the software and want to use it after the trial period, you should send the specified payment to the software owner. *Freeware* is free. Both shareware and freeware software developers generally retain copyright and may place restrictions on use of the code. *Copylefting*, developed by the GNU Project with the Free Software Foundation, allows users to have free access to the source code of the software. Modifications may be made to the software. If a user makes improvements and modifications to the code, they must be made available to subsequent users.

The last category is public domain, where all creative works will eventually end up. Users will then be free to modify at will; however, there is no provision that useful modifications will be easily available to other users, as with the Copylefting approach.

What quality differences exist among the six types of software discussed above?

Is licensed software consistently superior to the other categories? It depends on how the software was developed, tested, and maintained. Some shareware, freeware, and copylefted software is of excellent quality, even superior to newly licensed software, which is often far from bug-free. Some shareware programs, such as WinZip (originally known as PKZip), have been in use for many years and are extremely reliable. However, some shareware software has not been well tested and might or might not always work correctly. Part of the goal of copylefted or Open Source software is to ensure robustness; it is widely agreed that Linux software is as robust as widely available licensed software.

Can I download a copy of a computer image I found on the Web for my own use?

It depends on how you want to use the image and what additional uses the copyright owner might allow. Generally, you can save an image to use as the background on your computer, but you cannot add the image to your advertising brochure or club newsletter without permission. Many artists sell their works over the Internet and watermark their images to protect their copyright. A watermarked image will make it difficult, if not impossible, to remove identifying information about the owner of the artwork. Other Web sites deal with this issue by blocking downloading of images using JavaScript or transparent overlays.

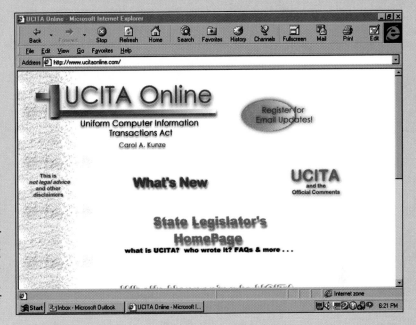

1. **Structured exercise.** Read a Microsoft software license. Is it posted on the company's Web site and easily available for study before buying the product? What rights do you have as a user? What limitations does the license place on your use of the software? Can you sell it to someone else or install it on your mother's new computer? What will the company do if you have problems with the software; in particular, how does it handle bugs in its software?

2. **Free-form exercise.** Find a site that offers freeware or shareware. What is the licensing agreement? Is it posted on the Web site and easily available for study before downloading the product? What rights do you have as a user?

What limitations does the license place on your use of the software? Can you sell it to someone else or install it on your mother's new computer? What will the company do if you have problems with the software; in particular, how does it handle bugs in its software?

3. **Advanced exercise.** Locate a copy of the Uniform Computer Information Transaction Act (UCITA) and read it carefully. The provisions discussed might well change your options for use of computer software in the future. What is its current status? How many states have passed it? Is your state considering a similar law? Be sure to check information from at least one site expressing concern about the impact of the proposed legislation as well as a site that strongly supports the proposed legislation. For example, check out UCITA Online and Kaner's Badsoftware site.

Planet Internet

Networking:
Computer Connections

Networking:
Computer Connections

CHAPTER 7

iguel Santora owns a small but growing wholesale office supplies business in the Miami area. From the very beginning 10 years ago, Miguel's business has used computers, but only as stand-alone desktop tools. His two salespeople use word processing to prepare customer proposals and a database program to keep track of customer information. The office manager uses a simple accounting package to prepare payroll checks and maintain the general ledger. Miguel himself uses a spreadsheet program to keep track of inventory and a database program to store supplier information.

Two years ago, Miguel signed up with an Internet service and had modems installed in the salespeople's computers to allow them to communicate with their customers via e-mail. Shortly thereafter, he decided to get a modem for his own computer so that he could more easily keep track of bid requests posted on the Internet by the various local governments that were a major part of his customer base. He had to add two more telephone lines as he and the salespeople began to spend more time online. He briefly considered installing a network to connect the company's computers, but dismissed the idea as too expensive and complicated.

Last month, Miguel's son Carlos graduated from college with a degree in business, with a minor in information systems. Carlos immediately saw the need for a network and used his knowledge of LAN technology to

design and install a simple peer-to-peer LAN that allowed everyone in the office to communicate electronically with each other and to access the Internet at the same time without tying up the telephone lines.

You will not get enough detailed information from this chapter to design your own LAN, as Carlos did, but you will gain an understanding of basic communications principals.

◼▶ DATA COMMUNICATIONS

Mail, telephone, TV and radio, books, newspapers, and periodicals—these are the traditional ways in which users send and receive information. However, **data communications systems**—computer systems that transmit data over communications lines such as telephone lines or cables—have been evolving since the mid-1960s. Let us take a look at how they came about.

In the early days of computing, **centralized data processing** placed everything— all processing, hardware, and software—in one central location. But centralization proved inconvenient and inefficient. All input data had to be physically transported to the computer, and all processed material had to be picked up and delivered to the users. Insisting on centralized data processing was like insisting that all conversations between people occur face-to-face in one designated room.

In the late 1960s businesses began to use computers that were often at a distance from the central computer. These systems were clearly decentralized because the smaller computers could do some processing on their own, yet some also had access to the central computer. This new setup was labeled **distributed data processing,** which accommodates both remote access and remote processing. A typical application of a distributed data processing system is a business or organization with many locations—perhaps branch offices or retail outlets.

The whole picture of distributed data processing has changed dramatically with the advent of networks of personal computers. A **network** is a computer system that uses communications equipment to connect two or more computers and their resources. Distributed data processing systems are networks. Of particular interest in today's business world are local area networks (LANs), which are designed to share data and resources among several individual computer users in an office or building. Networking will be examined in more detail in later sections of this chapter.

The next section previews the components of a communications system, to give you an overview of how these components work together.

◼▶ PUTTING TOGETHER A NETWORK: A FIRST LOOK

Even though the components needed to transmit data from one computer to another seem quite basic, the business of putting together a network can be extremely complex. This discussion begins with the initial components and then moves to the list of factors that a network designer needs to consider.

Getting Started

The basic configuration—how the components are put together—is rather straightforward, but there is a great variety of components to choose from, and the technology is ever changing. Assume that you have some data—a message—to transmit from one place to another. The basic components of a data communications system that are used to transmit that message are (1) a sending device, (2) a communications link, and (3) a receiving device. Suppose, for example, that you work at a sporting goods store. You might want to send a message to the warehouse to inquire about a Wilson tennis racket, an item that you need for a customer. In this case the sending device is your computer terminal at the store, the communications link is the phone line, and the receiving device is the computer at the warehouse. However, as you will see later, there are many other possibilities.

There is another often-needed component that must be mentioned in this basic configuration, as you can see in Figure 7-1. This component is a modem, which is usually needed to convert computer data to signals that can be carried by the communications channel and vice versa. Modems will be discussed in detail shortly. (And, by the way, most modems now are internal, that is, plugged into an expansion slot within the computer's housing. We use the external variety in the illustration just to make a point.)

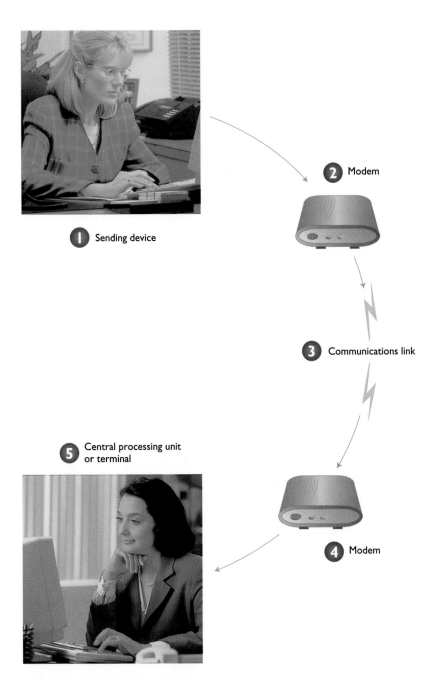

◄ FIGURE 7-1

Communications system components.

Data originating from (1) a sending device is (2) converted by a modem to data that can be carried over (3) a communications link and (4) reconverted by a modem at the receiving end before (5) being received by the destination computer.

2 Modem

1 Sending device

3 Communications link

5 Central processing unit or terminal

4 Modem

Network Design Considerations

The task of network design is a complex one, usually requiring the services of a professional specifically trained in that capacity. Although you cannot learn how to design a network in this brief chapter, you can ask some questions that can help you to appreciate what the designer must contemplate. Here is a list of questions that might occur to a customer who was considering installing a network; these questions also provide hints of what is to come in the chapter.

Question: I've heard that different kinds of modems and cables send data at different speeds. Does that matter?

Answer: Yes. The faster the better. Generally, faster means lower transmission costs too.

Question: Am I limited to communicating via the telephone system?

Answer: Not at all. There are all kinds of communications media, with varying degrees of speed, reliability, and cost. There are trade-offs. A lot depends on distance, too—you wouldn't choose a satellite, for example, to send a message to the office next door.

Question: So the geographical area of the network is a factor?

Answer: Definitely. In fact, network types are described by how far-flung they are: A *wide area network* might span the nation or even the globe, but a *local area network* would probably be campuswide or cover an office.

Question: Can I just cable the computers together and start sending data?

Answer: Not quite. You must decide on some sort of plan. There are various standard ways, called *topologies,* to physically lay out the computers and other elements of a network. Also available are standard software packages, which provide a set of rules, called a *protocol,* that defines how computers communicate.

Question: I know one of the advantages of networking is sharing disk files. Where are the files kept? And can any user get any file?

Answer: The files are usually kept on a particular computer, one that is more powerful than the other computers on the network. Access depends on the network setup. In some arrangements, for example, a user might be sent a whole file, but in others the user would be sent only the particular records needed to fulfill a request. The latter is called *client/server,* a popular alternative.

Question: This is getting complicated.

Answer: Yes.

These and other related considerations will be presented first, followed by an example of a complex network—or rather a set of networks. You need not understand all the details, but you will have an appreciation for the effort that is required to put together a network. Let us see how the components of a communications system work together, beginning with how data is transmitted.

► DATA TRANSMISSION

A terminal or computer produces digital signals, which are simply the presence or absence of an electric pulse. The state of being on or off represents the binary number 1 or 0, respectively. Some communications lines accept digital transmission directly, and the trend in the communications industry is toward digital signals. However, most telephone lines through which these digital signals are sent were originally built for voice transmission, and voice transmission requires analog signals.

The next section describes these two types of transmission and then modems, which translate between them.

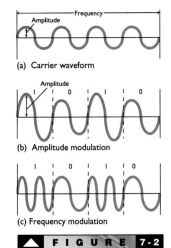

(a) Carrier waveform

(b) Amplitude modulation

(c) Frequency modulation

Digital and Analog Transmission

Digital transmission sends data as distinct pulses, either on or off, in much the same way that data travels through the computer. However, some communications media are not digital. Communications media such as telephone lines, coaxial cables, and microwave circuits are already in place for voice (analog) transmission. The easiest choice for most users is to piggyback on one of these. Therefore the most common communications devices all use **analog transmission,** a continuous electrical signal in the form of a wave.

To be sent over analog lines, a digital signal must first be converted to an analog form. It is converted by altering an analog signal, called a **carrier wave,** which has alterable characteristics (Figure 7-2a). One such characteristic is the **amplitude,** or height, of the wave, which can be increased to represent the binary number 1 (Figure 7-2b). Another characteristic that can be altered is the **frequency,** or number of times a wave repeats during a specific time interval; frequency can be increased to represent a 1 (Figure 7-2c).

Conversion from digital to analog signals is called **modulation,** and the reverse process—reconstructing the original digital message at the other end of the transmission—is called **demodulation.** An extra device is needed to make the conversions: a modem.

▲ **FIGURE 7-2**

Analog signals.

(a) An analog carrier wave moves up and down in a continuous cycle. (b) The analog waveform can be converted to digital form through amplitude modulation. As is shown, the wave height is increased to represent a 1 or left the same to represent a 0. (c) In frequency modulation the amplitude of the wave stays the same but the frequency increases to indicate a 1 or stays the same to indicate a 0.

Modems

A **modem** is a device that converts a digital signal to an analog signal and vice versa (Figure 7-3). Modem is short for *mo*dulator/*dem*odulator.

TYPES OF MODEMS   Modems vary in the way they connect to the telephone line. Most modems today are directly connected to the phone system by a cable that runs from the modem to the wall jack. A **direct-connect modem** is directly connected to the telephone line by means of a telephone jack. An **external modem** is separate from the computer. Its main advantage is that it can be used with a variety of computers. To have a modem that is literally out of sight, an **internal modem** board can be inserted into the computer; in fact, most personal computers today come with an internal modem as standard equipment.

Notebook and laptop computers without internal modems can use modems that come in the form of **PC cards,** originally known as PCMCIA cards, named for the Personal Computer Memory Card International Association. The credit card–sized PC

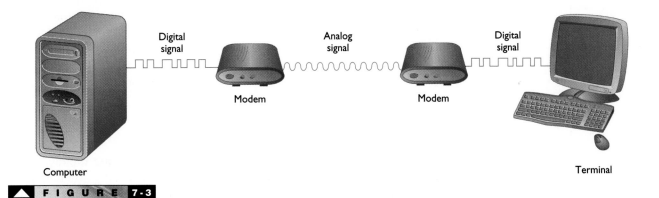

Computer · Digital signal · Modem · Analog signal · Modem · Digital signal · Terminal

▲ **FIGURE 7-3**

Modems.

Modems convert—modulate—digital data signals to analog signals for sending over communications links, then reverse the process—demodulate—at the other end.

▲ FIGURE 7-4

A PC card modem.

This PC card modem, although only the size of a credit card, packs a lot of power: data reception at 56,000 bytes per second. The card, shown here resting against a laptop keyboard, is slipped into a slot on the side of the laptop. Look closely at the right end of the modem and you can see the pop-out jack. So it goes in this order: Slide in the card, pop out the jack, and snap in the phone cord.

card slides into a slot in the computer (Figure 7-4). A cable runs from the PC card to the phone jack in the wall. PC cards and internal modems have given portable computers full connectivity capability outside the constraints of an office.

MODEM DATA SPEEDS The World Wide Web has given users an insatiable appetite for fast communications. This, as well as costs based on time use of services, provides strong incentives to transmit as quickly as possible. The old—some very old— standard modem speeds of 9600, 14,400, 28,800, and 33,600 **bits per second (bps)** have now been superseded by modems rated at 56,000 bps. Note, however, that because of FCC restrictions on power output, 56K modem receiving speeds are limited to 53 Kbps while transmission speeds top out at 31.2 Kbps. Line conditions and other variables often result in even lower speeds.

ISDN

As we noted earlier, communication via phone lines requires a modem to convert between the computer's digital signals and the analog signals used by phone lines. But what if another type of line could be used directly for digital transmission? One technology is called **Integrated Services Digital Network,** usually known by its acronym, **ISDN.** The attraction is that an ISDN adapter can move data at 128,000 bps, a vast speed improvement over any modem. Another advantage is that an ISDN circuit includes two phone lines, so a user can use one line to connect to the Internet and the other to talk on the phone at the same time. Still, ISDN is not a panacea. Although prices are coming down, initial costs are not inexpensive. You need both the adapter and phone service and possibly even a new phone line, depending on your current service. Also, monthly fees may be significant. Furthermore, ISDN is unavailable in some geographic areas.

Digital Subscriber Line

Digital subscriber line (DSL) service uses advanced electronics to send data over conventional copper telephone wires. Like traditional analog modems, DSL modems translate digital computer messages to analog signals to send over the lines and then convert the message back to digital signals at the destination. However, DSL spreads the analog signals over a large range of frequencies, acting as though dozens of modems were sending signals at the same time. xDSL is a catchall term for the varieties of DSL: ADSL, RADSL, and others. Since DSL lacks industry standards, various manufacturers are proposing their own variations. Currently, DSL service has a wide range of costs and speeds, depending on the variety and provider, but even the slowest speeds are many times faster than standard 56-K modems. Some providers offer a range of speeds, with pricing for the higher speeds aimed at the business market. DSL service can also share the line—you can use your telephone at the same time that you are surfing the Web. This saves the cost of an extra telephone line for Web access. Although prices vary, and special equipment is needed, the cost of basic DSL service is not much more than the cost of your current Internet service plus the cost of an extra line. However, to get DSL, you must be located within about three miles of your telephone company's switching office, and the DSL provider must have equipment installed in that office.

Cable Modems

Another approach, now available in limited markets but expanding rapidly, is the **cable modem,** a speedster that uses the coaxial television cables that are already in place without interrupting normal cable TV reception. Cable modems can be stunningly fast, receiving data at up to 10 million bps. Furthermore, a cable modem is always "on," like a TV channel, and does not require dialing or placing a call to get started. However, all users on a cable segment share its capacity; as more households in a neighborhood use the service, everyone's speed decreases. One other problem is security. With relatively inexpensive equipment, anyone on a cable segment can view all the data traveling on that segment.

Cellular Modems

Cellular modems can be used to transmit data over the cellular telephone system. While this can be very useful for people on the move, the transmission speed is generally less than half what it would be on the regular telephone system. The use of cellular modems to connect to the Internet will be discussed in more detail in the next chapter.

Asynchronous and Synchronous Transmission

Sending data off to a far destination works only if the receiving device is ready to accept it. But *ready* means more than just available; the receiving device must be able to keep in step with the sending device. Two techniques that are commonly used to keep the sending and receiving units dancing to the same tune are asynchronous and synchronous transmission.

When **asynchronous transmission** (also called **start/stop transmission**) is used, a special start signal is transmitted at the beginning of each group of message bits—a group is usually just a single character. Likewise, a stop signal is sent at the end of the group of message bits (Figure 7-5a). When the receiving device gets the start signal, it sets up a timing mechanism to accept the group of message bits. This type of transmission is typically used for low-speed communications.

Synchronous transmission is a little trickier because a large block of characters is transmitted together in a continuous stream (Figure 7-5b). There are no call-to-action signals for each character. Instead, the sending and receiving devices are synchronized by having their internal clocks put in time with each other via a bit pattern transmitted at the beginning of the message. Furthermore, error-check bits are transmitted at the end of each message to make sure all characters were received properly. Synchronous transmission equipment is more complex and more expensive, but without all the start/stop bits, transmission is much faster.

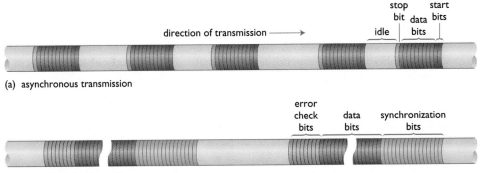

(a) asynchronous transmission

(b) synchronous transmission

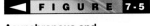

◄ FIGURE 7-5

Asynchronous and synchronous transmission.

(a) Asynchronous transmission uses start/stop signals surrounding each character. (b) Page-width constraints preclude showing the true amount of continuous data that can be transmitted synchronously between start and stop characters. Unlike asynchronous transmission, which has one start/stop set per character, synchronous transmission can send many characters, even many messages, between one start/stop set. Note that synchronous transmission requires a set of error-check bits to make sure all characters were received properly.

Simplex, Half-Duplex, and Full-Duplex Transmission

Data transmission can be characterized as simplex, half-duplex, or full-duplex, depending on permissible directions of traffic flow. **Simplex transmission** sends data in one direction only; everyday examples are television broadcasting and arrival/departure screens at airports. **Half-duplex transmission** allows transmission in either direction but only one way at a time. An analogy is talk on a CB radio. In a bank a teller using half-duplex transmission can send the data about a deposit, and after it is received, the computer can send a confirmation reply. **Full-duplex transmission** allows transmission in both directions at once. An analogy is a telephone conversation in which, good manners aside, both parties can talk at the same time.

► COMMUNICATIONS MEDIA

The cost for linking widely scattered computers is substantial, so it is worthwhile to examine the communications options. Telephone lines are the most convenient communications channel because an extensive system is already in place, but there are many other options. A **communications medium** is the physical means of data transmission. The range of frequencies that a medium can carry is known as its bandwidth; **bandwidth** is a measure of the capacity of the link.

Types of Communications Media

There are several types of communications media. Some may be familiar to you already.

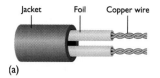

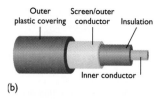

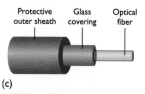

WIRE PAIRS   One of the most common communications media is the **wire pair,** also known as the **twisted pair.** Transmission of an electrical signal requires two conductors. In twisted pair wire, the two conductors are twisted around each other to reduce electrical interference and then sheathed in plastic. Multiple twisted pairs can be combined into a single cable (Figure 7-6a). Wire pairs are inexpensive. Furthermore, they are often used because they have already been installed in a building for other purposes or because they are already in use in telephone systems. However, they are susceptible to electrical interference, or noise. **Noise** is anything that causes distortion in the signal when it is received. High-voltage equipment, lightning, and even the sun can be sources of noise. Shielded twisted pair wiring has a metallic protective sheath, which reduces noise and increases the transmission speed capability.

COAXIAL CABLES   Known for sending a strong signal, a **coaxial cable** consists of a center conductor wire surrounded by a layer of insulation, which in turn is surrounded by a braided outer conductor. The whole cable is then encased in a protective sheath (Figure 7-6b). Coaxial cable has much higher bandwidth and much less susceptibility to noise than does twisted pair wire. The cable that connects your TV to the cable TV system is the most common type of coaxial cable.

FIBER OPTICS   Traditionally, most phone lines transmitted data electrically over wires made of metal, usually copper. These metal wires had to be protected from water and other corrosive substances. **Fiber-optic** technology eliminates this requirement (Figure 7-6c). Instead of using electricity to send data, fiber optics uses light. The cables are made of glass or plastic fibers, each thinner than a human hair, that can guide light beams for miles. Fiber-optic cable has much higher bandwidth than coaxial cable, yet the materials are substantially lighter and less expensive. Since it uses light rather than electricity, fiber-optic cable is immune to electrical noise and much more secure—any attempt at intercepting a signal would be easily noticed.

▲ **FIGURE 7-6**

Communications links.

(a) Twisted-pair cable consists of pairs of wires twisted together, then grouped to form a cable, which is then insulated. (b) A coaxial cable is a single conductor wire surrounded by insulation. (c) Fiber optics consists of hairlike glass fibers that carry voice, television, and data signals.

MICROWAVE TRANSMISSION   Another popular medium is **microwave transmission,** which uses what is called line-of-sight transmission of data signals through the atmosphere (Figure 7-7a). Since these signals cannot bend to follow the curvature of the earth, relay stations—often antennas in high places such as the tops of mountains and buildings—are positioned at points approximately 30 miles apart to continue the transmission. Microwave transmission offers high speed, cost-effectiveness, and ease of implementation. One problem is susceptibility to interference by weather conditions.

SATELLITE TRANSMISSION   **Satellite transmission** is a form of microwave transmission in which a satellite acts as the relay station. Its basic components are **earth stations,** which send and receive signals, and a satellite component called a transponder (Figure 7-7b). The **transponder** receives the transmission from an earth station (the **uplink**), amplifies the signal, changes the frequency, and retransmits the data to a receiving earth station (the **downlink**). (The frequency is changed so that the weaker incoming signals will not be impaired by the stronger outgoing signals.) This entire process takes only a fraction of a second.

If a signal must travel thousands of miles, satellites are often part of the link. A message being sent around the world probably travels by cable or some other physical link only as far as the nearest earth-satellite transmission station (Figure 7-8). From there it is beamed to a satellite, which sends it back to another transmission station near the data destination. Communications satellites are launched into space, where they are suspended about 22,300 miles above the earth. Why 22,300 miles? That is where satellites reach geosynchronous orbit—the orbit that allows them to remain positioned over the same spot on the earth. However, not all satellites are in geosynchronous orbit; some are much closer to the earth.

MIXING AND MATCHING   A network system is not limited to one kind of link and, in fact, often works in various combinations, especially over long distances. An office worker who needs data from a company computer on the opposite coast will most likely use wire pairs in the phone lines, followed by microwave and satellite transmission (Figure 7-9). Astonishingly, the trip across the country and back, with a brief stop to pick up the data, may take only a second or two.

Protocols

A **protocol** is a set of rules for the exchange of data between a terminal and a computer or between two computers. Think of a protocol as a sort of precommunication agreement about the form in which a message or data is to be sent and receipt is to be acknowledged. Protocols are handled by hardware and software related to the network, so users need worry only about their own data.

PROTOCOL COMMUNICATIONS   Two devices must be able to ask each other questions (Are you ready to receive a message? Did you get my last message? Is there trouble at your end?) and to keep each other informed (I am sending data now.). Of course, we are referring here to binary codes, not actual words. In addition, the two devices must agree on how data is to be transferred, including data transmission speed and duplex setting. But this must be done in a formal way. When communication is desired among computers from different vendors (or even different models from the same vendor), the software development can be a nightmare because different vendors use different protocols. Standards help.

SETTING STANDARDS   Standards are important in the computer industry; it saves money if users can all coordinate effectively. Communications standards exist and are constantly evolving and being updated for new communications forms. Perhaps the most important protocol is the one that makes Internet universality possible. Called **Transmission Control Protocol/Internet Protocol (TCP/IP),** this protocol

Surf and Sleep

When you travel, what do you look for as the most important feature of a hotel room? A comfortable bed? A quiet room? Cable TV? Is a high-speed Internet connection on your list? If you travel on business a lot and have to maintain contact with your customers, your office, or your colleagues, it probably is.

By the time you read this, both the Hyatt International and Holiday Inn hotel chains say, every room in their hotels will be provided with an Ethernet socket. All you have to do is plug your laptop's network card in to get a broadband Internet connection. If you run into any problems, both chains will have around-the-clock tech support available. These two chains are not the only ones planning to provide this service. One market research firm estimates that 80% of hotel rooms will be wired by 2002.

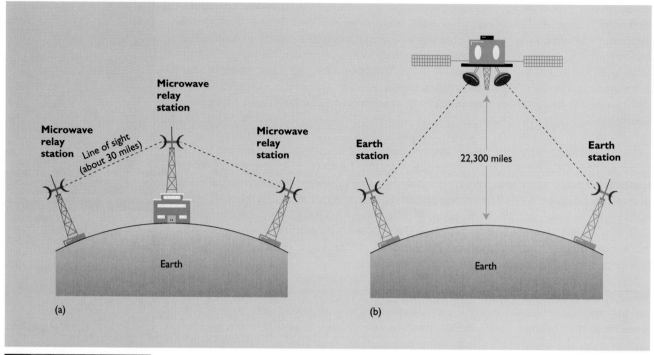

▲ **FIGURE 7-7**

Microwave and satellite transmission.

(a) To relay microwave signals, dish-shaped antennas such as these are often located atop buildings, towers, and mountains. Microwave signals can follow a line-of-sight path only, so stations must relay this signal at regular intervals to avoid interference from the curvature of the earth. (b) In satellite transmission a satellite acts as a relay station and can transmit data signals from one earth station to another. A signal is sent from an earth station to the relay satellite, which changes the signal frequency before transmitting it to the next earth station.

▶ **FIGURE 7-8**

A satellite dish.

A satellite dish is not usually the prettiest sight on the horizon, but a photographer has taken this shot of a dish with an exaggerating "fish-eye" lens, emphasizing the relationship between the dish and the signals that come from the satellite in space.

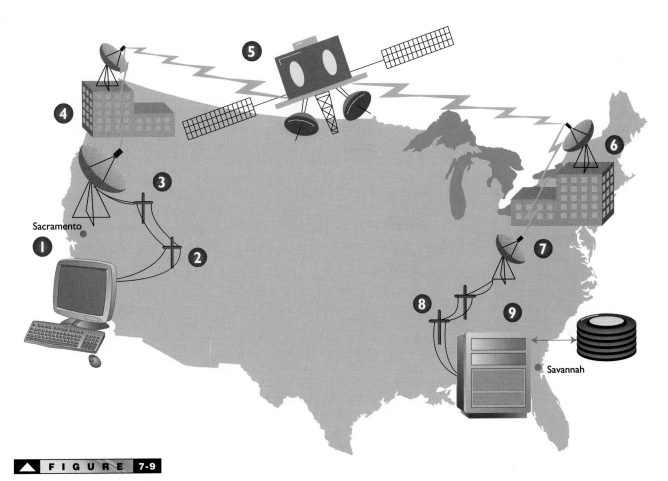

▲ FIGURE 7-9

A variety of communications links.

Say that an accountant working in the Sacramento office needs certain tax records from the headquarters computer files in Savannah. One possibility for the route of the user request and the response is as follows: (1) The accountant makes the request for the records, which (2) goes out over the local phone system to (3) a nearby microwave station, which transmits the request to (4) the nearest earth-satellite transmission station, where (5) it is relayed to a satellite in space, which relays it back to earth (6) to an earth-satellite station near Savannah, where it is sent to (7) a microwave station and then (8) via the phone lines to (9) the headquarters computer. Once the tax records are retrieved from the Savannah computer files, the whole process is reversed as the requested records are sent back to Sacramento.

permits any computer at all to communicate with the Internet. This is rather like everyone in the world speaking one language.

▶ NETWORK TOPOLOGIES

BUILDING A NETWORK

Prentice Hall
EXPLORE Generation **it**

The physical layout of a network is called a **topology.** There are three common topologies: star, ring, and bus networks. In a network topology a component is called a **node,** which is usually a computer on a network. (The term "node" is also used to refer to any device that is connected to a network, including the server, computers, and peripheral devices such as printers.)

A **star network** has a central (hub) computer that is responsible for managing the network (Figure 7-10a). All messages are routed through the hub computer, which acts as a traffic cop to prevent collisions. Any connection failure between a node and the hub will not affect the overall system. However, if the hub computer fails, the network fails.

▶ F I G U R E 7-10

Topologies.

(a) The star network topology has a central computer that runs the network. (b) The ring network topology connects computers in a circular fashion. (c) The bus network topology connects all nodes in a line and can preserve the network if one computer fails.

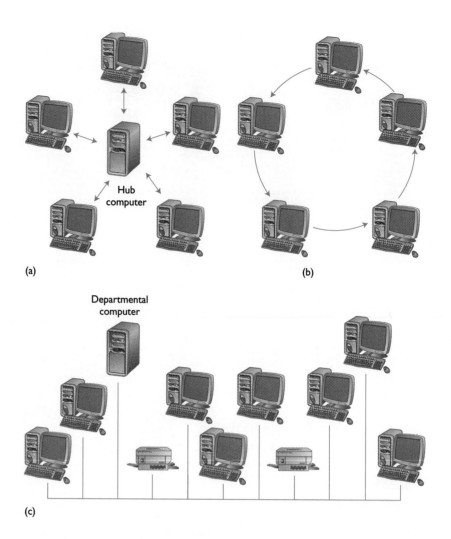

(a)

(b)

(c)

A **ring network** links all nodes together in a circular chain (Figure 7-10b). Data messages travel in only one direction around the ring. Each node examines any data that passes by to see whether that node is the addressee; if not, the data is passed on to the next node in the ring. Since data travels in only one direction, there is no danger of data collision. However, if one node fails, the ring is broken and the entire network fails.

A **bus network** has a single line (the bus) to which all the network nodes are attached (Figure 7-10c). Computers on the network transmit data in the hope that it will not collide with data transmitted by other nodes; if this happens, the sending node simply tries again. Nodes can be attached to or detached from the network without affecting the network. Furthermore, if one node fails, it does not affect the rest of the network.

▶ WIDE AREA NETWORKS

Networks can be classified by the geographical area they cover. The largest in scope is the **wide area network (WAN)**, which can span the world or just link computers in adjacent cities.

Communication Services

A WAN typically uses communication services provided by **common carriers,** companies that are licensed by the Federal Communications Commission (FCC) to pro-

► MAKING CONNECTIONS ◀   Bluetooth

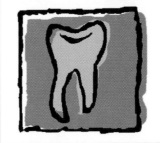

Notebook computers, cellular phones, and personal digital assistants have certainly been a boon for travelers, especially business professionals. No matter what your job is, or where it takes you, there is a device you can carry that will make connectivity easier. There is just one problem: For every device you add to your mobile computing arsenal, you must have another wire, cradle, or adapter of some sort to connect that device to your personal computer, as well as software to make the two devices talk to each other. But how much more can your briefcase take before it explodes in a mass of tangled wires?

Short-Range Radio Technology

Instead, you could do away with the wires and insert small chips—radio chips. Suppose now that those devices in your briefcase can communicate with each other—wirelessly. The ability to have wireless connectivity around the globe is a powerful concept, but getting connected across a room is equally important. That is the premise behind Bluetooth, the code name for a low-cost, wireless communications solution based on short-range radio technology.

Scenarios

What could you actually do with Bluetooth? Here are some possibilities:

● Imagine that you are in a meeting with your notebook computer open in front of you. Suddenly, the cursor begins to blink, and a new e-mail message is displayed on the screen. Your computer is not plugged into anything, and your cellular phone is in your briefcase under the table, but you are receiving e-mail over the wireless network. This is possible because your notebook is communicating with your cell phone, which in turn is communicating with the wireless network via the Bluetooth technology radio chip.

● You could walk into your office, put your briefcase down, and have the notebook computer inside it automatically

sense that it is in range of your desktop and initiate the exchange of data to update both systems.

● You could walk into a meeting and automatically send copies of your presentation to the computers of everyone in the room.

You could get off a plane with a cell phone in hand and a notebook computer in your carry-on luggage and transfer all the notebook's incoming and outgoing e-mail by simply pressing a couple of buttons on the phone. Data would be transferred between the notebook and the phone using Bluetooth; the phone would then transmit the notebook's data over the cellular phone network. You would not even need to remove the notebook from your carry-on bag.

How It Will Work

Bluetooth technology will use integrated radio transceivers built on tiny microchips about a half-inch square. Bluetooth chips will be embedded into both computer and communication devices. Thus begins the long-anticipated convergence of computing and communications. Bluetooth technology will use—bear with us for a minute—the 2.45-GHz ISM (Industrial Scientific Medical) frequency band of the radio spectrum, which is free and is not licensed by the Federal Communications Commission (FCC). This means that you will not have to get permission from the FCC to use the band and that Bluetooth devices can be used globally. Equipped with the radio chip, Bluetooth devices will be able to talk to one another—exchanging voice and data information—at data speeds up to 1MB per second, within a range of about 30 feet. Unlike existing infrared networking, the radio-based technology of Bluetooth will work when line of sight is not available; the connecting devices need not even be in the same room. Each device will have a unique 48-bit address. Built-in encryption and verification will be provided.

---

vide these services to the public. These services fall into two general categories: switched and dedicated. A **switched,** or **dial-up, service** establishes a temporary connection between two points when a call is placed. The connection remains in place for the duration of the call. When the call is ended, the connection is broken. The public telephone system, sometimes referred to as **plain old telephone service (POTS),** is the most common dial-up system. A **dedicated service** provides a permanent connection between two or more locations. Companies may build their own dedicated circuits using one or more of the media (cable, microwave, fiber optics, or satellite) described earlier, or they may lease dedicated circuits from a common carrier, in which case the circuits are referred to as **leased lines.** A company may lease standard telephone lines, ISDN or DSL lines, or larger-capacity digital lines. The two most common high-capacity digital lines are the T1 and T3 lines. The T1 line has a capacity of 1.54 Mbps, enough to carry 24 simultaneous voice connections. The T3 line combines the capacity of 28 T1 lines, or 43 Mbps. These lines are quite expensive

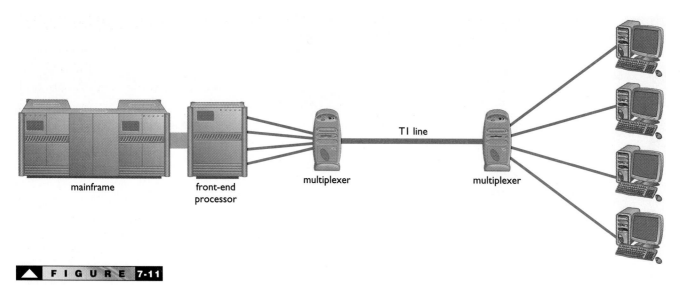

T1 line

mainframe front-end multiplexer multiplexer
processor

▲ **F I G U R E** **7-11**

Multiplexer.

A multiplexer (MUX) combines the data from several slow-speed devices for transmission over a high-speed circuit.

and are justified only for high-volume continuous traffic. Choosing among all these service options is a very complex task, one performed by network design experts.

WAN Hardware and Software

WANs are normally controlled by one or more mainframe computers, called **host computers.** These host computers typically connect to the WAN through a **front-end processor (FEP),** which is actually a computer in itself. Its purpose is to relieve the host computer of some of the communications tasks and thus free it for processing applications programs. In addition, a front-end processor usually performs error detection and recovery functions. The multiplexer is another device that is often found in WANs. A **multiplexer** combines the data streams from a number of slow-speed devices, such as PCs or terminals, into a single data stream for transmission over a high-speed circuit, such as a T1 line (Figure 7-11.) A multiplexer on the other end of the transmission would be necessary to break the high-speed stream into its component parts for processing.

In business a personal computer sending data over a WAN is probably sending it to a mainframe computer. Since these larger computers are designed to be accessed by terminals, a personal computer can communicate with a mainframe only if the personal computer emulates, or imitates, a terminal. This is accomplished by using **terminal emulation software** on the personal computer. The larger computer then considers the personal computer or workstation as just another user input/output communications device—a terminal.

When smaller computers are connected to larger computers, the result is sometimes referred to as a **micro-to-mainframe** link. If a personal computer is being used as a terminal, **file transfer software** permits users to download data files from the host or upload data files to the host. To **download** a file means to retrieve it from another computer. To **upload,** a user sends a file to another computer.

► LOCAL AREA NETWORKS

A **local area network (LAN)** is a collection of computers, usually personal computers, that share hardware, software, and data. In simple terms, LANs hook personal computers together through communications media so that each personal computer can share the resources of the others. As the name implies, LANs cover short distances, such as within a campus, building, or office.

Local Area Network Components

LANs do not use the telephone network. Networks that are LANs are made up of a standard set of components:

- All networks need some system for interconnection. In some LANs the nodes are connected by a shared **network cable.** Low-cost LANs are connected with twisted wire pairs, but many LANs use coaxial cable or fiber optic cable, which may be more expensive but are faster. Some local area networks, however, are **wireless,** using infrared or low-power radio wave transmissions instead of cables. Wireless networks are easy to set up and reconfigure, since there are no cables to connect or disconnect, but they have slower transmission rates and limit the distance between nodes.

- A **network interface card,** sometimes called a **NIC,** connects each computer to the wiring in the network. A NIC is a circuit board that fits in one of the computer's internal expansion slots. The card contains circuitry that handles sending, receiving, and error checking of transmitted data.

- Similar networks can be connected by a **bridge,** a hardware/software combination that recognizes the messages on a network and passes on those addressed to nodes in other networks. For example, a fabric designer whose computer is part of a department LAN for a textile manufacturer could send cost data, via a bridge, to someone in the accounting department whose computer is part of another company LAN, one used for financial matters. It makes sense for each department, design and finance, to maintain separate networks because their interdepartmental communication is only occasional. A **router** is a special computer that directs communications traffic when several networks are connected together. If traffic is clogged on one path, the router can determine an alternative path. More recently, now that many networks have adopted the Internet protocol (IP), routers are being replaced with **IP switches,** which are less expensive and, since no protocol translation is needed, faster than routers.

- A **gateway** is a collection of hardware and software resources that lets a node communicate with a computer on another dissimilar network. One of the main tasks of a gateway is protocol conversion. For example, a gateway could connect an attorney on a local area network to a legal service offered through a wide area network.

Now let us move on to the types of local area networks. Two ways to organize the resources of a LAN are client/server and peer-to-peer.

Client/Server Networks

A **client/server** arrangement involves a **server,** the computer that controls the network. In particular, a server has hard disks holding shared files and often has the highest-quality printer, another resource to be shared (Figure 7-12). The clients are all the other computers on the network. Under the client/server arrangement, the clients sent requests for service to the server. The server fulfills the request and sends any results back to the client. A computer that has no disk storage ability and is used basically to send input to the server for processing and then receive the output is called a **thin client.** Sometimes the server and the client computer share processing. For example, a server, on request from the client, could search a database of cars in the state of Maryland and come up with a list of all Jeep Cherokees. This data could be passed on to the client computer, which could process the data further, perhaps looking for certain equipment or license plate letters. In this example the server is providing database service. This method can be contrasted with a **file server** rela-

The Networked Home

Networks aren't just for businesses anymore. As more and more families become multiple-PC households, the need for home networking grows.

Two possible approaches to home networking are borrowed from the office environment. You can connect all your computers with cables and set up a miniature Ethernet or you can set up a wireless network using low-power, high-frequency radio transceivers on each PC. However, if you find stringing a mess of cables all over the house unappealing and the wireless approach is too pricey, consider two other alternatives that use existing home wiring. One approach uses the phone lines in your house to transmit data between computers without interfering with normal telephone use. If you don't have telephone jacks near all your computers, you can use your home's electrical wiring to connect your computers. Special adapters plug into the computer's parallel port, then into any wall outlet.

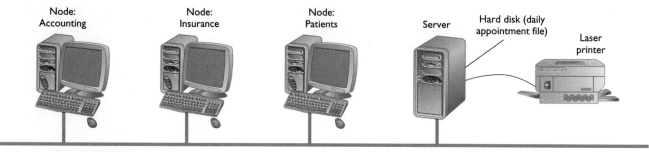

▲ **F I G U R E** 7-12

Server and peripheral hardware.

In this network for a clinic with seven doctors, the daily appointment records for patients are kept on the hard disk associated with the server. Workers who, using their own computers, deal with accounting, insurance, and patient records can access the daily appointment file to update their own files.

tionship, in which the server transmits the entire file to the client, which does all its own processing. In the Jeep example, the entire car file would be sent to the client, instead of just the extracted Jeep Cherokee records (Figure 7-13). Other types of services that a server might provide to clients include print services and file storage services. In large LANs, separate servers might provide each of these services.

Client/server has attracted a lot of attention because a well-designed system reduces the volume of data traffic on the network and allows faster response for each client computer. Also, since the server does most of the heavy work, less-expensive computers can be used as nodes.

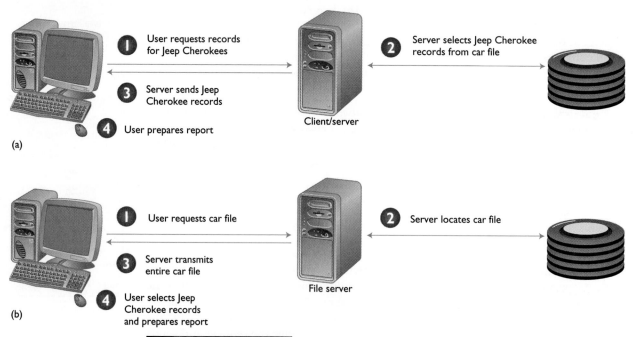

▲ **F I G U R E** 7-13

Client/server contrasted with file server.

(a) In a client/server relationship, (1) a user makes a request to the server to select only Jeep Cherokee records from a state car file; (2) the server does so and (3) sends the records back to the user, who (4) uses those specific records to prepare a report. (b) In a file server relationship, (1) a user asks for the entire state car file, which (2) the server locates and then (3) transmits to the user, who then (4) selects the Jeep Cherokee records and prepares a report. The client/server setup places most of the processing burden on the more powerful server and also significantly reduces the amount of data being transferred between server and user.

Peer-to-Peer Networks

All computers in a **peer-to-peer** arrangement have equal status; no one computer is in control. With files and peripheral devices distributed across several computers, users share one another's data and devices as needed. Peer-to-peer networks are common in small offices with perhaps a dozen personal computers. The main disadvantage is lack of speed—peer-to-peer networks slow down under heavy use. Many networks are hybrids, containing elements of both client/server and peer-to-peer arrangements.

Local Area Network Protocols

As we have already noted, networks must have a set of rules—protocols—that are used to access the network and send data. Recall that a protocol is embedded in the network software. The two most common network protocols for LANs are Ethernet and the Token Ring network.

Ethernet, the network protocol that dominates the industry, uses a high-speed network cable. Ethernet uses a bus topology and is inexpensive and relatively simple to set up. Since all the computers in a LAN use the same cable to transmit and receive data, they must follow a set of rules about when to communicate; otherwise, two or more computers could transmit at the same time, causing garbled or lost messages. Operating much like a party line, a computer "listens" to determine whether the cable is in use before transmitting data. If the cable is in use, the computer must wait. When the cable is free from other transmissions, the computer can begin transmitting immediately. This transmission method is called by the fancy name **carrier sense multiple access with collision detection,** or **CSMA/CD.**

If by chance two computers transmit data at the same time, the messages collide. When a **collision** occurs, the data is destroyed and the resulting electrical noise is sensed by the transmitting computers. Each computer waits a random period of time (a small fraction of a second) and then transmits again. Since the wait period for each computer is random, it is unlikely that they will begin transmitting again at the same time. However, either may have a collision with another transmitting computer. When too many computers are attempting to transmit too many messages, many collisions occur and performance is degraded.

A **Token Ring network,** which is closely associated with IBM, works on the concept of a ring network topology, using a token—a kind of electronic signal. The method of controlling access to the shared network cable is called **token passing.** The idea is similar to the New York City subway: If you want to ride—transmit data— you must have a token. However, unlike the subway, only one token is available. The token circulates from computer to computer along the ring-shaped LAN.

When a computer on the network wishes to transmit, it waits for an empty token, then attaches its message to the token and transmits. The receiving computer strips the token from the message and sends the token back onto the network. Since only one token is circulating around the network, only one device is able to access the network at a time. Some larger networks allow for multiple tokens, permitting more than one message at a time to be transmitted.

▶ THE WORK OF NETWORKING

The use of automation in the office is as varied as the offices themselves. As a general definition, however, **office automation** is the use of technology to help people do their jobs better and faster. Much automated office innovation is based on communications technology. This section begins with several important office technology topics: electronic mail, facsimile technology, groupware, teleconferencing, and electronic data interchange.

Electronic Mail

Electronic mail, or **e-mail,** is the process of sending a message directly from one computer to another, where it is stored until the recipient chooses to receive it. A user can send data to a colleague downstairs, a message across town to that person who is never available for phone calls, a query to the headquarters office in Switzerland, and even memos simultaneously to regional sales managers in Chicago, Raleigh, and San Antonio. Electronic mail users shower it with praise. It can reach many people with the same message, it reduces the paper flood, and it does not interrupt meetings the way a ringing phone does. Since e-mail does not require both participants to be present at the time of transmission, it is a boon to people who work on the same project but live in different time zones.

Facsimile Technology

Operating something like a copy machine connected to a telephone, **facsimile technology** uses computer technology and communications links to send graphics, charts, text, and even signatures almost anywhere in the world. The drawing—or whatever—is placed in the facsimile machine at one end, where it is digitized. A built-in modem converts the digital signal to analog form and transmits it through the telephone system, where it is received and reassembled at the other end to form a nearly identical version of the original picture. All this takes only minutes—or less. Facsimile is not only faster than overnight delivery services, it is less expensive. Facsimile is abbreviated **fax,** as in "I sent a fax to the Chicago office." The word "fax" is also used as a verb, as in "I faxed her the contract."

Personal computer users can send and receive faxes directly by means of a **fax modem,** which also performs the usual modem functions. Virtually all modems sold today have fax capability. A user can send computer-generated text and graphics as a fax. When a fax comes in, it can be reviewed on the computer screen and printed out only if necessary. Be aware that a fax transmission is basically a "picture" of the original. For the recipient of a faxed document to process it with word processing software, the document must first be converted into text using optical character recognition (OCR) software.

Groupware

Groupware is any kind of software that lets a group of people share things or track things together. The data that the workers share is in a database on disk. But the key to their being able to share that data is their access to it via communications lines. We mention groupware to emphasize the role of communications systems in letting people, who may be in far-flung locations, work together.

Teleconferencing

An office automation development with cost-saving potential is **teleconferencing,** a method of using technology to bring people and ideas together despite geographic barriers. There are several varieties of teleconferencing, but most common today is **videoconferencing,** whose components usually include a large screen, video cameras that can send live pictures, and an online computer system to record communication among participants (Figure 7-14). Although this setup is expensive to rent and even more expensive to own, the costs seem trivial when compared with travel expenses—airfare, lodging, meals—for in-person meetings.

Videoconferencing has some drawbacks. Some people are uncomfortable about their appearance on camera. A more serious fear is that the loss of personal contact will detract from some business functions, especially those related to sales or negotiations.

GETTING PRACTICAL

Everything You Always Wanted to Know About E-Mail

● **I know generally what hardware and software need to be in place for e-mail, but how do I get in on the action?** You must first sign up with an online service, Internet service provider, or e-mail service, probably giving a credit card number for monthly payments and then being prompted to make up your own e-mail address and password. Thus established, you will probably click a screen icon to invoke your e-mail service whenever you want it.

● **I don't know how I actually send e-mail.** Your e-mail service or e-mail software will provide menus of choices, one of which is to write e-mail. The look of the screen may vary, but generally, all e-mail write systems have the same elements—a place for the e-mail address of the recipient, a place to put the message title, and a place for you to type your message. You can see these three elements on the America Online (AOL) screen shown here.

● **That's it?** Well, some e-mail software will let you get a bit fancier if you wish. For example, as you can see here, AOL offers buttons for changing fonts, checking spelling, adding a photo, and so on.

● **How does my message get to the recipient?** First, you click a Send button—in this case, Send Now if you are online (connected to AOL) or Send Later if you are offline. AOL, or whatever service you are using, will take care of delivery.

● **How do I know someone's e-mail address?** Just ask. You will have a collection of your friends' and colleagues'

addresses in no time. And since you are not expected to memorize them, just keep them in the clickable address book. There are also several Internet e-mail directories where you can look up people's e-mail addresses.

● **How do I get my own e-mail?** It varies by the service, of course, but generally, when you go online, you will be informed that you have mail; AOL intones the famous "You've got mail!" In offices where users are online to their company servers all day, a quiet chiming sound may indicate that new mail has arrived. Other systems simply display a small window on the screen, with a message that mail has arrived. You click the list of mail and click each item to read it. You may also, of course, choose to ignore it.

● **Can I just stay online for hours writing e-mail?** Theoretically, yes, but it is not a good idea. You would be tying up a connection unnecessarily. You can write your e-mail offline and then, once the mail is ready, go online and send it. Most people write—and read—their e-mail offline.

● **Can I get free e-mail?** Probably. You may be able to hook up to your college system. You will likely have e-mail at your place of work, although your employer may limit personal messages. You can get free e-mail on your personal computer from several sources, notably Juno, which will set you up on its own server in return for supplying some personal information used for marketing.

◄ **FIGURE 7-14**

A videoconferencing system.

Geographically distant groups can hold a meeting with the help of videoconferencing. A camera transmits images of local participants for the benefit of distant viewers.

Electronic Data Interchange

Businesses use a great deal of paper in transmitting orders. One method that has been devised to cut down on paperwork is **electronic data interchange (EDI).** EDI is a series of standard formats that allow businesses to transmit invoices, purchase orders, and the like electronically. In addition to eliminating paper-based ordering forms, EDI can help to eliminate errors in transmitting orders that result from transcription mistakes made by people. Since EDI orders go directly from one computer to another, the tedious process of filling out a form at one end and then keying it into the computer at the other end is eliminated. Many firms use EDI to reduce paperwork and personnel costs. Some large firms, especially discounters such as Wal-Mart, require their suppliers to adopt EDI and, in fact, have direct computer hookups with their suppliers.

Electronic Fund Transfers: Instant Banking

Using **electronic fund transfer (EFT),** people can pay for goods and services by having funds transferred from various accounts electronically, using computer technology. One of the most visible manifestations of EFT is the **ATM—the automated teller machine** that people use to obtain cash quickly. A high-volume EFT application is the disbursement of millions of Social Security payments by the government directly into the recipients' checking accounts.

Computer Commuting

A logical outcome of computer networks is **telecommuting,** the substitution of communications and computers for the commute to work (Figure 7-15). That is, a telecommuter works at home on a personal computer and probably uses the computer to communicate with office colleagues or customers. In fact, some telecommuters are able to link directly to the company's network. Many telecommuters stay home two or three days a week and come in to the office the other days. Time in the office permits the needed face-to-face communication with fellow workers and also provides a sense of participation and continuity. Approximately 20 million people are classified as telecommuters.

The Internet

The Internet, as we indicated earlier in this book, is not just another online activity. The other topics discussed in this section pale in comparison. The Internet is considered by many to be the defining technology of the beginning of the twenty-first cen-

► **FIGURE 7-15**

Telecommuting.
Using CAD/CAM software, this architect works at home four days a week. He goes in to the office one day a week for meetings and conferences.

What's in a Name?

Internet domain names such as www.prenhall.com are valuable commodities. Businesses want short, memorable names that Web surfers will clearly connect to their company name or their products. Suppose you were appointed to the Internet Committee on Assigned Names and Numbers(ICANN) and were asked to decide who should get to control various domain names. How would you decide the following cases? Why?

1. Two long-established organizations have competing claims to a domain name that contains their initials. For example, the World Wrestling Federation and the World Wildlife Fund might both want wwf.com.

2. Someone has registered a domain name identical to that of a well-established company, except that the new name takes advantage of a common typo. For instance, imagine that a company wants to register www.pren hall.com to collect "hits" from readers of this text who make typographical errors.

3. A group of disgruntled customers of MegaMerger Corporation want to register www.megamergercorp stinks.com. MegaMerger says this should be stopped.

4. MegaMerger Corporation wants to buy 150 domain names (www.megamergerisevil.com, www.megamerg-eristoobig.com, etc.) to prevent unhappy customers, disgruntled employees or Internet troublemakers from using them.

tury, and it may well hold that status for several years. Since we are devoting separate chapters and features exclusively to the Internet, we mention it here only to make the list complete.

► THE COMPLEXITY OF NETWORKS

Networks can be designed in an amazing variety of ways, from a simple in-office group of three personal computers connected to a shared printer to a global spread including thousands of personal computers, servers, and mainframes. The latter, of course, would not be a single network but, instead, a collection of connected networks. You have already glimpsed the complexity of networks. Now let us consider a set of networks for a toy manufacturer (Figure 7-16).

The toy company has a bus LAN for the marketing department, consisting of six personal computers, a modem used by outside field representatives to call in for price data, and a server with a shared laser printer and shared marketing program and data files. The LAN for the design department, also a bus network, consists of three personal computers and a server with shared printer and shared files. Both LANs use the Ethernet protocol and have client/server relationships. The design department sometimes sends its in-progress work to the marketing representatives for their evaluation; similarly, the marketing department sends new ideas from the field to the design department. The two departments communicate, one LAN to another, via a bridge. It makes sense to have two separate LANs, rather than one big LAN, because the two departments need to communicate with each other only occasionally.

In addition to communicating with each other, users on each LAN, both marketing and design, occasionally need to communicate with the mainframe computer, which can be accessed through a gateway. All communications for the mainframe are handled by the front-end processor. Users in the purchasing, administrative, and personnel departments have terminals that are connected directly to the mainframe computer. The mainframe also has T1 connection to the Internet, which it uses to communicate with the mainframe computer at corporate headquarters in another state.

Network factors that add to complexity but are not specifically addressed in Figure 7-16 include the electronic data interchange setups between the toy manufacturer's purchasing department and seven of its major customers and the availability of electronic mail throughout the networks.

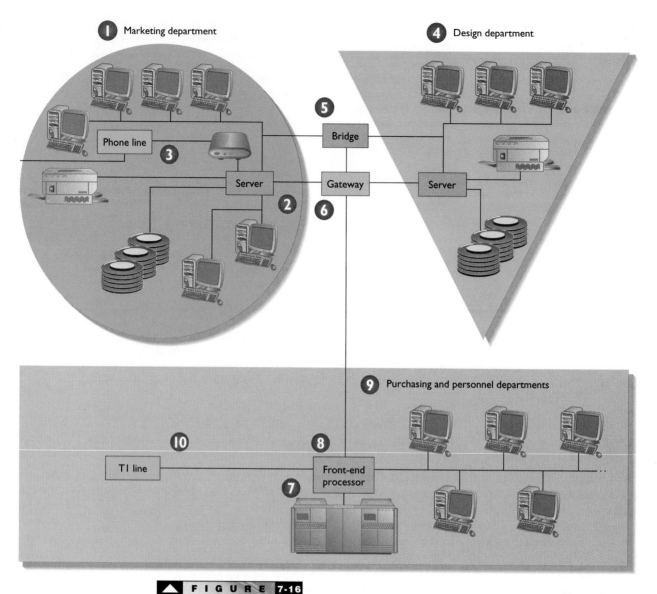

▲ **F I G U R E 7-16**

Example of a network.

In this set of networks for a toy manufacturer, (1) the marketing department has a bus LAN whose six
personal computers use a shared printer. Both program and data files are stored with the (2) server.
Note (3) the modem that accepts outside inquiries from field representatives. (4) The design department, with just three personal computers, has a similar LAN. The two LANs can communicate via (5) a
bridge. Either LAN, via (6) a gateway, can access (7) the mainframe computer, which uses (8) a front-
end processor to handle communications. Users in (9) the purchasing and personnel departments have
terminals attached directly to the mainframe computer. The mainframe computer also has (10) a T1 connection to the mainframe at the headquarters office in another state.

▲

The near future in data communications is not difficult to see. The demand for
services is just beginning to swell. Electronic mail already pervades the office and the
campus and is growing rapidly in the home. Expect instant access to all manner of
information from a variety of convenient locations. Prepare to become blasé about
communications services available in your own home and everywhere you go.

CHAPTER REVIEW

► Summary and Key Terms

- **Data communications systems** are computer systems that transmit data over communications lines, such as telephone lines or cables.

- **Centralized data processing** places all processing, hardware, and software in one central location.

- Businesses with many locations or offices often use **distributed data processing,** which allows both remote access and remote processing. Processing can be done by the central computer and the other computers that are hooked up to it.

- A **network** is a computer system that uses communications equipment to connect two or more computers and their resources.

- The basic components of a data communications system are a sending device, a communications link, and a receiving device.

- **Digital transmission** sends data as distinct on or off pulses. **Analog transmission** uses a continuous electric signal in a **carrier wave** having a particular **amplitude** and **frequency.**

- Digital signals are converted to analog signals by **modulation** (change) of a characteristic, such as the amplitude of the carrier wave. **Demodulation** is the reverse process; both processes are performed by a device called a **modem.**

- A **direct-connect modem** is connected directly to the telephone line by means of a telephone jack. An **external modem** is not built into the computer and can therefore be used with a variety of computers. An **internal modem** is on a board that fits inside a personal computer. Notebook and laptop computers often use a **PC card** modem that slides into a slot in the computer.

- Modem speeds are usually measured in **bits per second (bps).**

- An ISDN adapter, based on **Integrated Services Digital Network (ISDN),** can move data at 128,000 bps, a vast improvement over any modem.

- **Digital subscriber line (DSL)** service uses advanced electronics to send data over conventional copper telephone wires many times faster than a conventional modem.

- **Cable modems** use the cable TV system to transmit data at very high speeds. The actual speed depends on the number of subscribers in a neighborhood using the service.

- **Cellular modems** can be used to transmit data over the cellular telephone system.

- Two common methods of coordinating the sending and receiving units are **asynchronous transmission** and **synchronous transmission.** The asynchronous, or **start/stop,** method keeps the units in step by including special signals at the beginning and end of each group of message bits—a group is usually a character. In synchronous transmission the internal clocks of the units are put in time with each other at the beginning of the transmission, and the characters are transmitted in a continuous stream.

- **Simplex transmission** allows data to move in only one direction (either sending or receiving). **Half-duplex transmission** allows data to move in either direction but only one way at a time. With **full-duplex transmission,** data can be sent and received at the same time.

- A **communications medium** is the physical means of data transmission. **Bandwidth** refers to the range of frequencies that a medium can carry and is a measure of the capacity of the link. Common communications media include **wire pairs** (or **twisted pairs**), **coaxial cables, fiber optics, microwave transmis-**

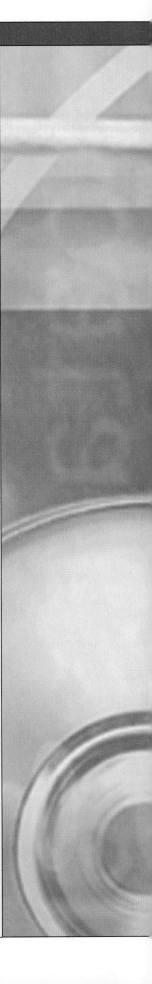

sion, and **satellite transmission.** In satellite transmission, which uses **earth stations** to send and receive signals, a **transponder** ensures that the stronger outgoing signals (the **downlink**) do not interfere with the weaker incoming **(uplink)** ones. **Noise** is anything that causes distortion in the received signal.

- A **protocol** is a set of rules for exchanging data between a terminal and a computer or between two computers. The protocol that makes Internet universality possible is **Transmission Control Protocol/Internet Protocol (TCP/IP),** which permits any computer at all to communicate with the Internet.

- The physical layout of a local area network is called a **topology.** A **node** usually refers to a computer on a network. (The term "node" is also used to refer to any device that is connected to a network, including the server, computers, and peripheral devices such as printers.) A **star network** has a central computer, the hub, that is responsible for managing the network. A **ring network** links all nodes together in a circular manner. A **bus network** has a single line, to which all the network nodes and peripheral devices are attached.

- Computers that are connected so that they can communicate among themselves are said to form a network. A **wide area network (WAN)** is a network of geographically distant computers and terminals. WANs typically use communication services provided by **common carriers.** These services fall into two general categories: **switched,** or **dial-up,** and **dedicated.** The public telephone system, sometimes referred to as **plain old telephone service (POTS),** is the most common dial-up system. Common carriers provide dedicated service over **leased lines.**

- WANs are normally controlled by one or more mainframe computers, called **host computers.** These host computers typically connect to the WAN through a **front-end processor (FEP)** that handles communications tasks. A **multiplexer** combines the data streams from a number of slow-speed devices into a single data stream for transmission over a high-speed circuit.

- To communicate with a mainframe, a personal computer must employ **terminal emulation software.** When smaller computers are connected to larger computers, the result is sometimes referred to as a **micro-to-mainframe** link. In a situation in which a personal computer or workstation is being used as a network terminal, **file transfer software** enables a user to **download** files (retrieve them from another computer and store them) and **upload** files (send files to another computer).

- A **local area network (LAN)** is usually a network of personal computers that share hardware, software, and data. The nodes on some LANs are connected by a shared **network cable** or by **wireless** transmission. A **network interface card (NIC)** may be inserted into a slot inside the computer to handle sending, receiving, and error checking of transmitted data.

- If two LANs are similar, they may send messages among their nodes by using a **bridge.** A **router** is a special computer that directs communications traffic when several networks are connected together. Since many networks have adopted the Internet protocol (IP), some use **IP switches,** which are less expensive and faster than routers. A **gateway** is a collection of hardware and software resources that connects two dissimilar networks, including protocol conversion.

- A **client/server** arrangement involves a **server,** a computer that controls the network. The server has hard disks holding shared files and often has the highest-quality printer. Processing is usually done by the server, and only the results are sent to the node. A computer that has no disk storage capability and is used basically for input/output is called a **thin client.** A **file server** transmits the entire file to the node, which does all its own processing.

- All computers in a **peer-to-peer** arrangement have equal status; no one computer is in control. With all files and peripheral devices distributed across several computers, users share each other's data and devices as needed.

- **Ethernet** is a type of network protocol that accesses the network by first "listening" to determine whether the cable is free; this method is called **carrier sense multiple access with collision detection,** or **CSMA/CD.** If two nodes transmit data at the same time, a **collision** occurs. A **Token Ring network** controls access to the shared network cable by **token passing.**

- **Office automation** is the use of technology to help people do their jobs better and faster. **Electronic mail (e-mail)** allows workers to transmit messages to other people's computers. **Facsimile technology (fax)** can transmit text, graphics, charts, and signatures. **Fax modems** for personal computers can send or receive faxes, as well as handle the usual modem functions.

- **Groupware** is any kind of software that lets a group of people share things or track things together, often using data communications to access the data.

- **Teleconferencing** is usually **videoconferencing,** in which computers are combined with cameras and large screens. **Electronic data interchange (EDI)** allows businesses to send common business forms electronically.

- In **electronic fund transfer (EFT),** people pay for goods and services by having funds transferred from various checking and savings accounts electronically, using computer technology. The **ATM—the automated teller machine**—is a type of EFT.

- In **telecommuting,** a worker works at home on a personal computer and probably uses the computer to communicate with office colleagues or customers.

▶ Critical Thinking Questions

1. Suppose you ran a business out of your home. Pick your own business or choose one of the following: catering, motorcycle repair, financial services, a law practice, roofing, or photo research. Now, assuming that your personal computer is suitably equipped, determine the purposes for which you might use one or more—or all—of the following: e-mail, fax modem, the Internet, electronic fund transfers, and electronic data interchange.

2. Discuss the advantages and disadvantages of telecommuting versus working in the office.

3. Do you expect to have a computer on your desk on your first full-time job? Do you expect it to be connected to a network?

▶ STUDENT STUDY GUIDE

Multiple Choice

1. _____ is the protocol that governs communications on the Internet.
   a. EFT
   b. TCP/IP
   c. MAN
   d. EDI

2. A computer that has no hard disk storage but sends input to a server and receives output from it is called a
   a. thin client
   b. host
   c. MAN
   d. transponder

3. Devices that send and receive satellite signals are called
   a. modems
   b. earth stations
   c. tokens
   d. servers

4. Housing all hardware, software, storage, and processing in one site location is called
   a. time-sharing
   b. a distributed system
   c. centralized processing
   d. a host computer

5. Transmission permitting data to move both directions but only one way at a time is called
   a. half-duplex
   b. full-duplex
   c. simplex
   d. start/stop

6. The process of converting from analog to digital is called
   a. modulation
   b. telecommuting
   c. line switching
   d. demodulation

7. The device used with satellite transmission that ensures that strong outgoing signals do not interfere with weak incoming signals is the
   a. microwave
   b. cable
   c. transponder
   d. modem

8. _____ is the medium that is least susceptible to noise.
   a. twisted pair
   b. fiber optics
   c. microwave
   d. cellular phone

9. The Token Ring network controls access to the network using
   a. contention
   b. ISDN
   c. a bus
   d. token passing

10. The arrangement in which most of the processing is done by the server is known as
    a. simplex transmission
    b. a file server
    c. electronic data interchange
    d. a client/server relationship

11. Distortion in a signal is called
    a. phase
    b. IP switch
    c. noise
    d. amplitude

12. Two or more computers connected to a hub computer is a
    a. ring network
    b. CSMA
    c. node
    d. star network

13. A _____ provides a connection between similar networks.
    a. router
    b. bridge

    c. gateway
    d. fax

14. The physical layout of a LAN is called the
    a. topology
    b. link
    c. contention
    d. switch

15. The network type in which all computers have equal status is called
    a. a communications link
    b. WAN
    c. peer-to-peer
    d. a gateway

16. The type of modulation that changes the strength of the carrier wave is
    a. frequency
    b. amplitude
    c. phase
    d. prephase

17. A network that connects all nodes with a single cable is
    a. star
    b. switched
    c. ring
    d. bus

18. Signals produced by a computer to be sent over standard phone lines must be converted to
    a. modems
    b. digital signals
    c. analog signals
    d. microwaves

19. The device that is used between LANs that use the Internet protocol is a(n)
    a. bus
    b. gateway
    c. IP switch
    d. token

20. Microwave transmission, coaxial cables, and fiber optics are examples of
    a. modems
    b. routers
    c. communication media
    d. ring networks

21. A network of geographically distant computers and terminals is called a(n)
    a. bus
    b. ATM
    c. WAN
    d. LAN

22. Two dissimilar networks can be connected by a
    a. gateway
    b. bus
    c. node
    d. server

23. Graphics and other paperwork can be transmitted directly by using
    a. CSMA/CD
    b. facsimile
    c. token passing
    d. transponder

24. _____ refers to the range of frequencies that can be carried on a transmission medium.
    a. WAN
    b. bandwidth
    c. EFT
    d. EDI

25. Software that is used to make a personal computer act like a terminal is
    a. fax
    b. bridge
    c. videoconferencing
    d. emulation

True/False

T F 1. DSL modems use the cable TV network for data transmission.

T F 2. Local area networks are designed to share data and resources among several computers in the same geographical location.

T F 3. A WAN is usually limited to one office building.

T F 4. A front-end processor is a computer.

T F 5. A thin client has no disk storage.

T F 6. An internal modem can be easily used with a variety of computers.

T F 7. A modem can be used for both modulation and demodulation.

T F 8. Synchronous transmission sends many characters in a single block.

T F 9. A transponder ensures that the stronger incoming signals do not interfere with the weaker outgoing ones.

T F 10. Full-duplex transmission allows transmission in both directions at once.

T F 11. A multiplexer combines several slow-speed transmissions into a single high-speed stream.

T F 12. A standard modem can transmit data faster than ISDN can.

T F 13. Another name for file server is peer-to-peer.

T F 14. A digital signal can be altered by frequency modulation.

T F 15. Synchronous transmission is also called start/stop transmission.

T F 16. Interactions among networked computers must use a protocol.

T F 17. The term "node" may refer to any device that is connected to a network.

T F 18. Ethernet and Token Ring are identical protocols.

T F 19. A ring network has no central host computer.

T F 20. A file server usually transmits the entire requested file to the user.

T F 21. A gateway connects two similar computers.

T F 22. A bus network uses a central computer as the server

T F 23. Fax boards can be inserted inside computers.

T F 24. Ethernet systems "listen" to determine whether the network is free before transmitting data.

T F 25. Telecommuting is a type of information utility.

Fill-In

1. _____ are computer systems that transmit data across telephone lines or cables.

2. TCP/IP stands for _____.

3. The kind of signal that most telephone lines require is _____.

4. What device converts a digital signal to an analog signal and vice versa? _____

5. _____ technology allows you to send a copy of an image across telephone lines, where it can be printed out at the other end.

6. Distortion in the received signal is called _____.

7. The ranges of frequencies that can be transmitted on a medium at one time is referred to as _____.

8. What is the general term for the use of technology in the office? _____

9. A(n) _____ is a company that is licensed by the FCC to provide communications services to the public.

10. A(n) _____ network links distant computers and terminals.

11. The physical layout of a network is called the _____.

12. _____ software allows a PC to communicate with a main frame as if it were a terminal.

13. _____ lines are dedicated lines provided by a common carrier.

14. POTS stands for _____.

15. NIC stands for _____.

▶ ANSWERS

Multiple Choice

1. b	8. b	15. c	22. a
2. a	9. d	16. b	23. b
3. b	10. d	17. d	24. b
4. c	11. c	18. c	25. d
5. a	12. d	19. c	
6. d	13. b	20. c	
7. c	14. a	21. c	

True/False

1. F	8. T	15. F	22. F
2. T	9. F	16. T	23. T
3. F	10. T	17. T	24. T
4. T	11. T	18. F	25. F
5. T	12. F	19. T	
6. F	13. F	20. T	
7. T	14. F	21. F	

Fill-In

1. data communications systems
2. Transmission Control Protocol/Internet Protocol
3. analog
4. a modem
5. facsimile (fax)
6. noise
7. bandwidth
8. office automation
9. common carrier
10. wide area network (WAN)
11. topology
12. terminal emulation
13. leased
14. plain old telephone service
15. network interface card

Online Privacy

"Privacy is dead. Get over it." It's certainly not the first controversial statement from Sun Microsystems CEO Scott McNealy. After all, a guy who plays in pickup ice hockey games with his employees is unlikely to take a purely conventional stand on much of anything. Still, McNealy's comments on privacy symbolize the face-off between governments, corporations, privacy advocates, and individuals over how information should be collected and shared over the Web.

Who's collecting information about my Web-browsing?
The short answer is "Almost everyone." Web site operators, e-commerce businesses, ISPs, Internet "information merchants," and even government agencies all may have recorded information about your browsing habits.

Web site operators want to collect information about who is using their pages so as to attract more advertisers. E-commerce sites are very interested in your browsing and purchasing habits, with the aim of better targeting advertising and promotions. Some Internet businesses specialize in collecting and reselling information about your Web browsing and shopping habits. Some "information merchants" have even used surreptitious measures such as secret backdoors in popular shareware packages and tracking programs hidden in HTML. Thirteen government sites recently acknowledged that they use browser cookies for tracking users who browse on their sites.

Your e-mail or Web page views may even have been tracked by the FBI's Carnivore system, even if you are not guilty of a crime or if you have sent e-mail to, or received e-mail from, someone who is being monitored.

Why should I be concerned if some company knows what pages I went to? They don't know who I am anyway.
Information merchants can and do know who you are. The problem is not so much the knowledge that a single Web site or e-commerce site has about you. Surely they have to know whose credit card is being used, and it may be a real benefit to have an e-commerce site "remember" your typical purchases and offer related specials from time to time. The problem

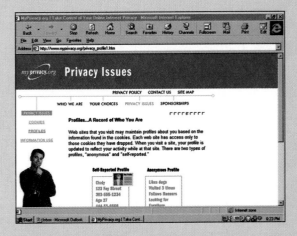

lies more in the sharing of information between enterprises and the personally identifying and revealing patterns that emerge when information from multiple sites is combined into a single database.

For example, your might believe that you are browsing health care sites anonymously, but the lack of clear guidelines, and the availability of tracking information in the form of browser cookies means that your health-related inquiries on HIV risk, for instance, could be made available to potential insurers. Your records of day-trading stocks and subsequent Internet searches for "debt restructuring OR bankruptcy" are probably not information that you would care to see in the hands of potential employers, either.

Most consumers would rightly be concerned about the distribution of the very kinds of personal information that we work so hard to protect in other contexts if they were aware of the information collection facilities that exist now.

The government protects my online privacy, right?
Not yet. Although concern is clearly evident in government, little concrete action has emerged as yet. The Federal Trade Commission has said that it is studying privacy issues on the Web, some congressional action has been proposed, and a few states have enacted legislation, little of which is yet in force. As in so many other contexts, our technological advances have outstripped the pace of legislation and consumer awareness.

What is the situation in other countries?

Policies about the protection of personal information on the Internet vary widely from one country to another. However a notable example of privacy policies that are significantly stronger and clearer than those in the United States are the guidelines produced by the European Union. These guidelines state five basic principles that must be satisfied not only among member nations, but also by global trading partners such as the United States. They include limitations on the transfer and reuse of collected data, standards for data accuracy and fairness, requirements that the purpose of collection and the identity of the collector be revealed, guarantees that the information collected is held securely, and procedures for challenges and corrections to the data. Delays in adopting these policies by the United States for commerce with the European Union have been the subject of much negotiation and concern.

What can I do to protect my on-line privacy?

Short-term solutions include the following:

- Become more aware of the privacy policies (or the lack of privacy) at the e-commerce sites you use.

- Disable the unquestioning acceptance of "cookies" by your browser.

- Use programs to find and remove cookies from your computer.

- Turn off "one-click" ordering on e-commerce sites, where available.

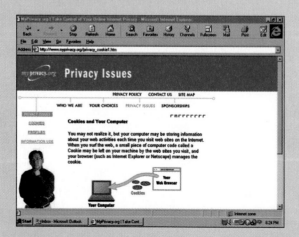

- Consider using strong encryption for e-mail or other transactions that you wish to remain private.

- Learn about the available anonymous browsing tools on the Internet.

- Scan software reviews to find out whether shareware or freeware you have downloaded is known to secretly upload information about your browsing or downloads to third parties.

Longer-term solutions include the following:

- Contact e-commerce sites where you shop and ask them to beef up their information privacy policies and to limit information sales to third parties as a condition of your continued business.

- Write or e-mail the Federal Trade Commission and your local senators or members of Congress to express your concern about Internet privacy.

Internet Exercises:

1. **Structured exercise.** Using this text's Web site as a starting point, examine the privacy policies of one or more e-commerce sites you select. Evaluate the e-merchant's privacy policy in light of the guidelines from the European Union mentioned above. More detailed explanations of the European Union's guidelines are also available from URLs listed at http://www.prenhall.com/capron.

2. **Free-form exercise.** Compare the number of privacy-related Internet articles this year compared to last. You might use a search engine to form a query for "privacy and policy" with appropriate date ranges or use the search feature built into various Internet news pages such as CNN or MSNBC. Do interest and controversy over privacy seem to be decreasing or increasing? Try to categorize the privacy-related postings. How many concern theft of information, how many concern governmental monitoring, how many concern disbursement of medical or other personal information?

3. **Advanced exercise.** Use a tool such as Cookie Pal to examine the cookies on your own or the school's computer. Links to these tools are available at http://www.prenhall.com/capron. How many cookies did you find? Which Web sites did you recognize? Evaluate how the information from some of the Web sites identified from these cookies could be used to profile the user.

Planet Internet

The Internet:
A Resource for All of Us

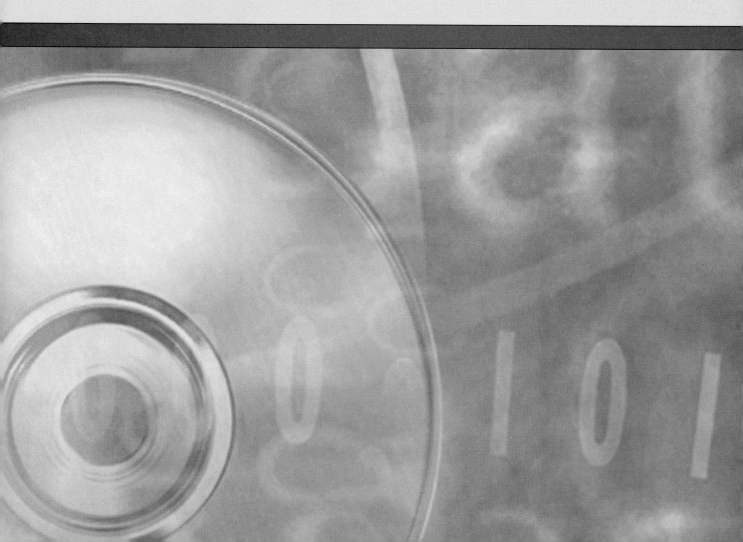

The Internet:

A Resource for All of Us

CHAPTER 8

hitney Bonilla had heard about the Internet, although she did not know quite what it was. She thought it had something to do with connecting to other people in other places. She also thought that it somehow contained a lot of information, information that might be handy for research for her college papers. She was right on both counts.

During her first week on campus, Whitney set out to hunt down the Internet. She discovered that there were several computer labs on campus and that one specialized in helping students get started on the Internet. But Whitney needed a lab pass to gain entry. A lab pass, for a fee, entitled a student to a certain number of hours on the Internet. The lab passes went first to students enrolled in computer classes and then to other students on a first-come, first-served basis. Unfortunately, Whitney was not among the first and was not able to get a pass at all.

All was not lost, however. Whitney found Internet access at the main library on campus. A librarian (who liked to call herself a "cybrarian") offered an hour-long beginners' class, repeated every day at noon and available to any student. Although subsequent computer access was limited to 30 minutes per session and no more than twice a week, Whitney found this sufficient to get her feet wet. She learned to get on the Internet, to move from site to site, and to find what she wanted.

She registered at the earliest possible date for the following quarter and included a beginning Internet course in her class schedule. She also got a lab pass.

Army or Education? Both!

The U.S. Army's strongest competitors for recruits are institutions of higher learning. Rather than fighting them, the Army has decided to join them—in a big way! Its Army University Access Online project plans to provide all one million of its soldiers (and their spouses) with access to a comprehensive array of college and university online courses. In addition, each soldier would receive a laptop computer, a printer, and an ISP account, enabling soldiers to pursue their education wherever duty takes them. In addition to attracting recruits who might otherwise bypass military service, the Army hopes to have its forces better prepared for the battlefield of the future.

▶ THE INTERNET AS A PHENOMENON

The Internet exploded into the public consciousness in the mid-1990s. Because of its nature, it is impossible to determine exactly how many people are connected, but all estimates agree that the growth rate of Internet sites and Internet users can only be described as unprecedented. One reliable study stated that the number of host computers on the Internet grew from 43.2 million in 1999 to 72.4 million in 2000, a 68 percent increase in one year! Another study estimated the number of individuals using the Internet worldwide to be about 333 million. Consider that the telephone took 91 years to reach 100 million users and television took 54 years to reach the same level, while the Internet more than tripled that number of users in its first 10 years of public availability.

These are dramatic numbers, but the effect on people's lives is, and will be, even more dramatic. E-commerce is growing rapidly. Busy people can do much of their shopping online, even buying groceries for next-day delivery. Many workers telecommute via the Internet at least a few days a week. Internet-based startup companies have created thousands of new millionaires. By some estimates, information technology and Internet-based development have accounted for over half the economic growth in the United States in the past several years. This chapter and the next will look at the technologies involved in individual and business uses of the Internet and discuss some of the trends for its future.

▶ DON'T KNOW MUCH ABOUT HISTORY

The history of the Internet bears telling. It is mercifully short. The reason that there is little to say is that the Internet slumbered and stuttered for approximately 20 years before the general public even knew it existed. It was started by obscure military and university people as a vehicle for their own purposes. They never in their wildest dreams thought that it would become the international giant it is today. Let us look back briefly, to understand their point of view.

First Stirrings at the Department of Defense

Ever heard of a fallout shelter? In the cold war of the 1950s, people worried about a nuclear attack whose radiation aftereffects—fallout—would be devastating. Some people built underground shelters, usually under their own houses or in their backyards, to protect themselves. It was in this climate of fear that the U.S. Department of Defense became concerned that a single nuclear bomb could wipe out its computing capabilities. Working with the Rand Corporation, they decided to rely on not one but several computers, geographically dispersed, and networked together. No one computer would be in charge.

A message to be sent to another computer would be divided up into **packets,** each labeled with its destination address. Each packet would wind its way individually through the network, probably taking a different route from the other packets but each heading in the direction of its destination and eventually being reconstituted into the original message at the end of the journey. The idea was that even if one computer was knocked out, the others could still carry on by using alternative routes. A packet can travel a variety of paths; the chosen path does not matter as long as the packet reaches its destination. The software that took care of the packets was **Transmission Control Protocol/Internet Protocol (TCP/IP).** TCP does the packeting and reassembling of the message. The IP part of the protocol handles the addressing, seeing to it that packets are routed across multiple computers.

The new set of connections was called **ARPANet,** an acronym that stands for Advanced Research Projects Agency Network. The year was 1969. Before long, computers from research universities and defense contractors joined the network. But the network was limited to people who had some technical expertise—a major reason why it was not yet of particular interest to the general public.

Tim and Marc

Tim Berners-Lee is arguably the pivotal figure in the surging popularity of the Internet: He made it easy. In 1990 Dr. Berners-Lee, a physicist at a laboratory for particle physics in Geneva, Switzerland, perceived that his work would be easier if he and his far-flung colleagues could easily link to one another's computers (Figure 8-1). He saw the set of links from computer to computer to computer as a spider's web; hence the name **Web.** The **CERN site,** the particle physics laboratory where Dr. Berners-Lee worked, is considered the birthplace of the **World Wide Web.**

A **link** on a Web site is easy to see: It is either colored text called **hypertext** or an icon or image called a **hyperregion** (Figure 8-2). A mouse click on the link appears to transport the user to the site represented by the link, and in common parlance one speaks of moving or transferring to the new site; actually, data from the new site is transferred to the user's computer.

A **browser** is interface software that is used to explore the Internet. **Marc Andreessen** was a college student when, in 1993, he led a team that invented the first graphical browser (Figure 8-3). Until then, browsers such as Lynx were text-only. Andreessen's browser, named **Mosaic,** featured a graphical interface so that users could see and click on pictures as well as text. This made Web page multimedia possible. For the viewing public, the Internet now offered both easy movement with Dr. Berners-Lee's links and attractive images and a graphical interface provided by Mosaic. Today there are several competitive browsers, one of which is Netscape Communicator, produced by a company founded by Marc Andreessen and others. Netscape, Inc. was later purchased by America Online.

INTERNET AND THE WWW

Prentice Hall
EXPLORE Generation **it**

◄ **F I G U R E** **8-1**

Dr. Tim Berners-Lee.

Working at the CERN particle physics lab in Geneva, Switzerland, Dr. Berners-Lee invented a method of linking from site to site so that he could easily communicate with his colleagues worldwide. Thus was born the World Wide Web or, simply, the Web.

► **FIGURE 8-2**

Links.

On this screen showing Earthweb's home page, the underlined blue words are hypertext links and the rectangular images to the left of each hypertext link are hyperregion links.

► **FIGURE 8-3**

Marc Andreessen.

As a student, Marc Andreessen led a team of college students that developed the first graphical browser, called Mosaic. He later developed a commercial product, the Netscape Navigator browser (later Netscape Communicator), which was an instant success.

The Internet Surges Ahead

TCP/IP is software in the public domain. Since no one was really in charge of the network, there was no one to stop others from just barging in and linking up wherever they could. The network became steadily more valuable as it embraced more and more networks. Meanwhile, corporate networks, especially LANs of personal computers, were growing apace. Companies and organizations, noting an opportunity for greater communication and access to information, hooked their entire networks to the burgeoning network. A new name, taken from the name of the TCP/IP protocol, evolved: the Internet. The original ARPANet eventually disappeared altogether. Its users hardly noticed. Its functions continued and improved under the broader Internet.

In summary, the emergence of the Internet is due to four factors: (1) the universal TCP/IP standard, (2) the web-like ability to link from site to site, (3) the ease of use provided by the browser's graphical interface, and (4) the growth of personal computers and their local area networks that could be connected to the Internet.

Although statistics and projections vary, the growth of the Internet has been swift and unprecedented. No one thinks it is a fad. Almost everyone agrees that it is a true technological revolution. It continues to evolve.

► GETTING STARTED

History is interesting, but most people want to know how to use the Internet, or at least how to get started. We cannot be specific here because many factors—computers, servers, browsers, and more—vary from place to place and time to time. But we can talk about overall strategy and what the various services and software applications have to offer.

The Internet Service Provider and the Browser

An Internet user needs a computer with a modem (or possibly a network interface) and its related software, an Internet service provider, and a browser. An **Internet service provider (ISP)** provides the server computer and the software to connect to the Internet. If you are accessing the Internet from a school, an organization, or a workplace, it is likely that these elements are already in place. Your only task would be to activate the browser and know how to use it.

If you wish to access the Internet from your own personal computer, one possibility is to sign up for an **online service,** (also called an **information utility**) such as America Online, that includes Internet access. The Internet service provider and browser are included in the package, and thus Internet access is available to you as soon as you have signed up for the online service. The main difference between an ISP and an online service is that an ISP is a vehicle to access the Internet, but an online service offers, in addition, members-only services and information. Online services provide content on every conceivable topic, all in a colorful, clickable environment that even a child can use. Content includes news, weather, shopping, games, educational materials, electronic mail, forums, financial information, and software product support. You will probably prefer an online service over an ISP if you are new to the online experience, if most of your friends and colleagues use the same online service, if people of different skill levels will use your computer to go online, or if you want to control what your children see online.

Approximately two-thirds of Internet users connect via an online service; the other one-third use an ISP. People who prefer an ISP are usually less interested in the managed resources of an online service and more interested in a freewheeling Internet experience that they can control themselves. You probably want an ISP if you prefer a different browser, plan to use a special communications link such as DSL, or want to put up a complex Web site.

If you elect to go directly to an Internet service provider, you will first need to select one. Some people seek advice from friends; others begin with advertisements in their phone books or the business section of the newspaper. Note the Getting Practical feature called "Choosing an Internet Service Provider." Once you have arranged to pay the fees (possibly an installation fee and certainly a monthly fee), you will set up your ISP interaction according to your provider's directions. The ISP may provide a disk that, once inserted into your computer's disk drive, will automatically set up the software, dial up the ISP, and set up your account, all with minimal input from you.

The next step is to configure the browser software on your computer. If you bought your computer within the last few years, you probably already have a browser installed. If not, you can purchase a browser in your local software retail outlet or, if you have some other online access vehicle, possibly download it free from the browser vendor's Web site. As you are configuring the browser, you will be asked for information about your ISP, for which your ISP will have prepared you. (An ISP typically furnishes several pages of detailed instructions.) Once you are set up, you invoke the browser as you would any software on your computer, and it will begin by dialing the Internet service provider for you. You are on your way to the Internet experience.

The Browser in Action

As we mentioned earlier, a browser is software used to explore the Internet. When they first came on the scene, graphical browsers were a great leap forward in Internet friendliness. A number of browsers are available, some better organized and more useful than others. Two popular browsers are Netscape Communicator and Microsoft's Internet Explorer.

When you run your browser software, it will dial up the Internet service provider and, once successfully connected, display either the **home page**—initial page—of the Web site for the company that created your particular browser or some other site designated by your ISP. The browser shows three parts on the screen: two very obvious chunks and a third that is just a line at the bottom (Figure 8-4). The top part is the browser control panel, consisting of lines of menus and buttons, to be described momentarily. The lower part, by far the largest part of the screen, is the browser display window. At the very bottom of the screen is a status line, which indicates the progress of data being transferred as you move from site to site. The status line may also show other messages, depending on the browser. The browser control panel at the top stays the same—except for the changing address of the visited site—as you travel from site to site through the Web; the browser display window changes, showing, in turn, each new Internet site you visit. Note, by the way, that it is common to refer to "going to a site," but in actual fact you are going nowhere; the information from the site is coming to you. The data from the "visited" site is sent from its source computer across the Internet to your computer.

When you first start the browser, the Web site window generally shows material according to the browser vendor's wishes, usually useful information and possibly advertisements for their products. (However, most browsers allow you to change the first page you see when you sign on to one of your own preference.) Note that the site display is not limited to the size of your screen; your screen size merely determines how much of the site you can see at one time. The page can be **scrolled**—moved up and down—by using the **scroll bar** on the right; simply press your mouse button over a scroll bar arrow to see the page move. If the site display is wider than your screen a scroll bar at the bottom allows you to move the page right and left. As you move the page, note that the browser control panel stays in place; it is always available no matter what the browser display window shows.

Browser Functions and Features

Next, let us examine the functions of the browser control panel. You can follow along on Figure 8-4 as you read these descriptions. Again, this discussion is necessarily generic and may vary from browser to browser. First, note the browser's welcome banner, touting its own name and logo, across the top of the screen. Next, usually off to the right, is the browser logo shown in Figure 8-4. The logo is active—shimmering, changing colors, rotating, *something*—when it wants to let you know that it is in the process of moving you to a new site. Since this sometimes takes a while, it would be disconcerting to stare at a static screen and wonder whether anything is happening. Note also that the status line at the bottom of the page provides information about the progress in contacting and receiving data from the desired site. If the transfer to the new site takes too long, you can cancel the move by clicking the browser's Stop button.

MENUS AND BUTTONS   Using a mouse lets you issue commands through a set of **menus,** a series of choices normally laid out across the top of the screen. The menus

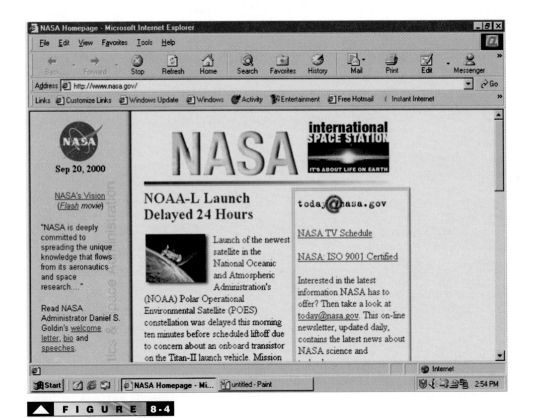

▲ **F I G U R E 8-4**

Browser control panel.

Most browsers offer pretty much the same functions; the example here is a popular browser called Internet Explorer. Just below the browser's welcome banner, showing the name of the Web site and browser display, is a set of pull-down menus; each such menu has several submenus. Just below the menus is a line of buttons. The buttons grouped to the left refer to the current Web site in the browser display window: Back (go to the previous site), Forward (go forward to the next site, assuming you already went back), Stop (stop an incoming site that is taking too long to load or that, after just a brief look, you wish to see no further), Refresh (redo the current site), and Home (return to browser's home page). The middle buttons are Search (find sites on the Web), Favorites (keep a list of sites to which one might return), History (lists of sites you visited, by week and by day), and Channels (a list of Web sites chosen to deliver content from the Internet to your computer). The buttons on the right are Fullscreen (let the browser display window take up the entire screen), Mail (get e-mail if you are set up on an account) and Print (print the content of the current site). Below the button line is the Address window, which contains the URL of the site in the browser display window.

GETTING PRACTICAL | Choosing an Internet Service Provider

If you have decided that you want to connect your computer to the Internet directly via an Internet service provider, you have to choose among many offerings. Many ISPs are national in scope; others are regional or local services. The best rates generally come from local ISPs. Local ISPs are usually what are called retail ISPs; that is, they deal primarily with individuals and small businesses.

You can begin by checking the Yellow Pages of your local phone directory, which probably has listings under "Internet." Also check out ISP advertisements in monthly computer magazines and, in urban areas, in your local newspaper. Many advertisements include a toll-free number that you can call for free software and a free trial subscription of a month or of a certain number of online hours.

An online resource called The List is by far the most comprehensive and useful list of ISPs (http://www.thelist.com). It is, of course, available only to people who are already able to get online, but you should be able to access it through your school or local library Internet connections. It features thousands of ISPs and is searchable by state, province (in Canada), and telephone area code.

If you are willing to put up with advertisements appearing on your screen as you surf, consider one of the free ISPs. A search on "free ISP" on any of the search engines should turn up a number of candidates. Check their Web pages to see if they have local access numbers in your area.

Here are some further tips:

● Look for an ISP whose access is only a local phone call away. Otherwise, long-distance charges will figure promi-

nently in your monthly phone bill. Even if a seemingly toll-free number is offered, the provider will recoup the cost in charges to you.

● If you plan on traveling with a laptop, consider one of the national ISPs that have local numbers all over the country.

● If you plan on using one of the faster access methods, such as ISDN, DSL, or cable modem, you need to find out whether the ISP offers that service.

● Ideally, find a provider with software that will automate the registration process. Configuring the right connections on your own is not a trivial task.

● Figure out how likely you are to want to get help. At the very least, ask for the phone numbers and hours of the help line. If help is available only via e-mail, take your business elsewhere.

● ISPs are volatile. Make sure your contract includes terms that let you opt out if your ISP wants to transfer your account to a different ISP or if your ISP is bought out. For that matter, make sure you can opt out for your own reasons.

Finally, don't fall for an unrealistic bargain. Like anything else, if it sounds too good to be true, it probably is. You will probably find that a "bargain" service is oversubscribed, underpowered, and prone to busy signals. Even worse, your call for technical help may garner only a "this number has been disconnected" message. Stability is worth something.

are called **pull-down menus** because each initial choice, when clicked with a mouse, reveals lower-level choices that pull down like a window shade from the initial selection at the top of the screen. You can also invoke commands using **buttons** for functions such as Print to print the current page, Home to return to the browser home page, and—perhaps the ones you will use the most—Back and Forward to help you retrace sites you have recently visited. If you rest the cursor over a button for just a few seconds, a small text message will reveal its function. Note that all functions are listed in the pull-down menus; the buttons are just convenient shortcuts for the most commonly used functions.

URL   The location slot, sometimes called the address window, will usually contain a **Uniform Resource Locator (URL),** a rather messy-looking string of letters and symbols, which is the unique address of a Web page or file on the Internet. An URL (pronounced "earl" or, alternatively, "U-R-L") has a particular format (Figure 8-5). A Web page URL begins with the protocol *http,* which stands for **HyperText Transfer Protocol.** This protocol is the means of communicating by using links, the clickable

Protocol   ISP address (domain)   Path, directory, file name

▲ **FIGURE 8-5**

A dissected URL.

The Uniform Resource Locator represents a unique address of an Internet site or file. Whenever you are looking at a Web site, you can see its URL near the top of the screen in the browser's control panel, in the location (address) slot. The example here shows a Web address for the Intel host, using a file called index.htm in the pressroom directory.

text or image that transports a user to the desired site. Next comes the **domain name,** which is the address of the Internet service provider or other host (ISPs, by the way, must register each domain name and pay an ongoing fee). The last part of the domain name, "com" in Figure 8-5, is called a **top-level domain** and represents the purpose of the organization or entity—in this case, "com" for "commercial." In some cases, the top-level domain name is a two-letter code that stands for the country of origin. Note the usage of top-level domain names in Figure 8-6. The last part of the URL, often the

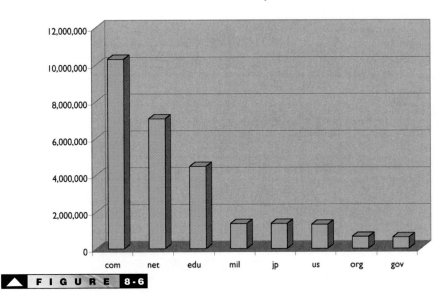

▲ **FIGURE 8-6**

Distribution of top-level domain names.

A glance at the chart shows that the majority of Web sites, worldwide, have the top-level domain "com"; that is, they are business sites. Sites using "net" are often business sites too. The other domains shown here are "edu" for education; "mil" for military; "jp" for Japan; "us" for United States, for those wishing to distinguish it from sites in other countries; "org" for nonprofit organizations; and "gov" for government. Country domains use two letters; typical examples are "fi" (Finland), "uk" (United Kingdom), "de" (Germany), "ca" (Canada), "au" (Australia), "nl" (Netherlands), and "se" (Sweden). In November 2000, seven new top-level domain names were approved for use beginning in early 2001, although legal challenges may delay their implementation. The new names are: ".biz" for business sites; ".pro" for professionals such as lawyers, doctors and accountants; ".name" for personal sites; ".aero"; ".coop"; ".info"; and "museum."

most complex, contains directories and file names that zero in on a very specific part of a site. Parts of the URL to the right of the domain, that is, the directory and file names, are case-sensitive; that is, you must type uppercase or lowercase characters exactly as indicated.

Most sites have a home page that acts as a directory by linking to what are often numerous pages of content. That home page is typically accessed by using a short URL that ends with the domain name. Also, many advertised URLs neglect to even mention the "*http://*" part of their address, partly because newer browser versions supply the "*http://*" for you.

No one likes to type URLs. There are several ways to avoid it. The easy way, of course, is simply to click links to move from one site to another. Another way is to click a pre-stored link on your browser's **hot list**—called Bookmarks, Favorites, or something similar—where you can store your favorite sites and their URLs.

FRAMES   Most browsers support a concept called **frames,** which allow a given page to be divided into rectangular sections, each of which can operate independently of the others (Figure 8-7). It is like having several small pages on the same screen; some may be static, and others may be scrolled up and down. The advantage is that a site can offer several different functions or areas of focus. A disadvantage of frames is that a small screen, notably a laptop screen, may look cluttered. A classic approach to frames is the three-frame look: a static title frame across the top and a left-side navigation frame that targets the main content frame to the right.

COMPETITION   Not just functional buttons, but buttons that illuminate when the cursor passes over them. Not just English, but French, German, and Italian. Not just

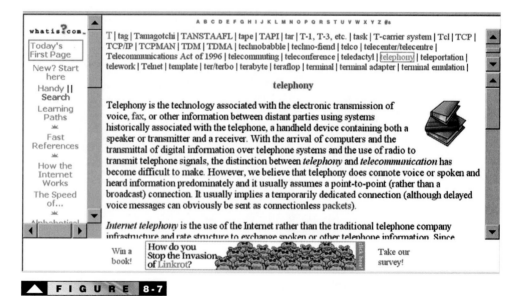

▲ **F I G U R E 8-7**

Frames.

This unusual site, WhatIs, has a total of five separate rectangular sections, called frames. The site is designed to offer computer-related definitions. The narrow frame across the top contains a row of clickable alphabet letters, which cause the frame just below to change; in this example the letter T has been clicked in the top frame, calling up the list of terms beginning with T. The list of terms is scrollable, up and down, as are the frames along the left side and also the center section. Note that each of these three frames has its own scroll bar. Once a term has been highlighted, its definition will appear in the large frame below; in this case the word "telephony" is defined. A fifth frame, across the bottom, holds a banner advertisement.

frames, but borderless frames. You begin to get the idea. As browsers compete to be the best, they get fancier. And we, the users, get more browser functionality. In fact, some browsers are considered a whole suite of programs, including rich software tools for communicating and sharing information and offering support for mail, security, collaboration, and Web page authoring.

PLUG-INS   In addition to the browsers themselves, various vendors offer **plug-ins,** software that enhances the value of a browser by increasing its functionality or features. Typical plug-ins can enhance a site's audio-video experience or improve image viewing. Most plug-ins can be downloaded from their own Web sites. Once the plug-in is downloaded and installed, usually a simple procedure, the browser can automatically handle the newly enabled features. An example of a plug-in is Adobe Acrobat Reader, which is used to display and print documents that have been created in Portable Document Format (PDF). Since everything from product descriptions to IRS forms is on the Web in PDF, it is important that a browser be equipped to handle the format. Perhaps the most popular plug-in is Shockwave, from a company named Macromedia. Shockwave permits viewing sites that include quality animation and other effects.

Java

In the early days of the Web, everything presented on a Web page was static, composed of material that had already been prepared. A user was basically accessing the electronic version of a printed page. Even though that access was certainly a convenience, the content of the Web page offered nothing innovative—until Java. It is Java that permits the dancing icons, sound clips, flashing messages, banners that scroll across the page—and much more. **Java** is a programming language, developed by Sun Microsystems, that is used to write software that can run on any machine, hence its appeal to the multifaceted Internet.

The programs that provide multimedia effects, the moving images and sound clips on a Web page, are called **applets,** a sort of abbreviation for "little applications" (Figure 8-8). Applets can make Web pages perform virtually any task—display animations, receive input, perform calculations, and so forth. Java also provides the possibility of dynamic interaction, in which the user can receive immediate feedback and the programs actually do things on their own.

Microsoft provides a feature called **ActiveX controls** that provides capabilities similar to Java applets. To benefit from Java applets or ActiveX controls, a user must have a browser that is capable of running either or both, as, indeed, the most popular browsers are. If you are thus equipped, you will doubtless see many applets and controls in action as you cruise the Web. One word of caution: Both Java applets and ActiveX controls present some security risks, so some users set their browsers to deactivate them.

►◄ F I G U R E   8-8

Applets.

Applets are extremely common on Web sites; you probably will see a great variety. In these simple applets the flag waves, the WOW bounces, and the cow's propeller spins.

Moving from Site to Site

There are several ways to leave your browser's home page and start moving to other sites. Most browsers provide a list of clickable categories, such as sports, weather, news, technology, and even comic strips. Also a button click away are lists of new sites, "cool" sites, and various comprehensive directories. All of these come under the category of—yes—browsing.

But suppose you have something more specific in mind. If you know the URL for a desired site, delete the current URL in the location box, then type in the new one—carefully—and press Enter on the keyboard. You will be moved to the site just as if you had clicked a link. Sometimes—too often—an URL does not work. That is, a message is returned saying "Unable to Locate Server" or, simply, "Not Found." The former may mean that you typed the URL incorrectly. The latter probably means that the specific site you want is no longer on that ISP. People and companies do move their sites around, from ISP to ISP, and they do not always provide a forwarding address.

Keep in mind that moving from site to site, whether by link or by URL, is not magic. Although the movement from site to site is relatively effortless for the user, all the concepts described here are in play. That is, link requests move from your computer to your server and across networks of computers, all using TCP/IP, until the destination site is reached. Then the process is reversed, carrying the requested information back to your computer.

Wireless Internet Access

In the last year there has been explosive growth in the number of people using mobile handheld devices to access the Internet. These devices include text pagers, personal digital assistants (PDAs), pocket computers, and even Web-enabled cellular phones. Some use a pen-based system to enter characters through the screen, while others are equipped with a miniature keyboard. All have a limited display area that makes it difficult to browse the Web as you would with your PC. However, they are adequate for sending and receiving e-mail, checking weather forecasts, making airline reservations, and many other functions that mobile professionals find useful. To access the Web with these devices, you must establish an account with a wireless access service provider and, if your device is not already so equipped, buy a cellular modem card or adapter. Many wireless access providers use the **Wireless Application Protocol (WAP)** to convert Web pages into a format that is more compatible with the limited capabilities of handheld devices. Access speeds are much slower than even a basic telephone modem connection, but since very few graphics are transmitted, most users find the speed adequate. Evolving wireless standards promise significant speed increases in the not-too-distant future.

► SEARCHING THE INTERNET

Although a browser, true to its name, lets a user browse by listing clickable categories of information—sports, business, kids, whatever—most users soon want to find something specific. A **search engine** is software, usually located at its own Web site, that lets a user specify search terms; the search engine then finds sites that fit those terms. A browser usually offers links to one or more search engines, or a user can simply link to the site of a favorite search engine.

A search engine does not actually go out to the Web and "look around" each time a search is requested. Instead, the search engine, over time, builds a database of searchable terms that can be matched to certain Web sites. To build this database, a search engine uses software called a **spider** (also called a robot, or just bot) to follow links across the Web, calling up pages and automatically indexing to a database some or all the words on the page. In addition, sites are submitted by their owners to the search engine, which indexes them.

As the result of a search request, the search engine will present a list of sites in some format, which varies by search engine. In fact, the nature of the search varies according to the search engine. Initially, users are astonished at the number of sites found by the search engine, often thousands and perhaps tens of thousands.

Hot Search Engines

The title of this section is somewhat facetious, since a new "hot" search engine can show up overnight. Furthermore, some early search engines, less than half-a-dozen years old, are considered hackneyed and dull. Nevertheless, of the dozens of search engines in existence, a list of a few useful search engines is appropriate. Note that the use of these search engines is free, although you will, of course, encounter some advertising. Table 8-1 offers a comparison chart.

TABLE 8-1	A selection of Internet search tools
Directories	
Yahoo!	Well-organized categories let the user switch from browsing to searching in a certain area; but finds only keywords, not any word on a site
NetGuide	Reviews entries before including, links to articles written for NetGuide
Search Engines	
AltaVista	Very fast; indexes every word on every page of every site; searches Usenet too; excellent for custom searches
Excite	Good returns for simple searches; provides related hints and an array of extra content. Also includes directory
Google	Results ranked by algorithm based on number of links from other pages
HotBot	Fast; unique search options let you restrict searches; very comprehensive; excels at finding current news
Infoseek	Searches not only the Web but also newsgroups, FAQs, and e-mail addresses; extras such as foreign language searching and searching by geographical region
Lycos	Numerous search options, a comprehensive directory, and good returns on simple searches
Northern Light	Powerful and well organized; groups results by subject, type, source, and language
Metasearch Sites	
MetaCrawler	Accepts search terms and submits to several popular search engines; eliminates duplicates and ranks by relevancy
Dogpile	Well-designed, easy-to-use interface; can search Usenet

Although it might seem that the same search query ought to produce the same list of sites no matter what the search engine, this is hardly the case. Search engines vary widely in size, content, and search methodology. Keeping this in mind, serious researchers sometimes put the same query to each of several search engines and expect to be given a somewhat different list of sites from each. The ultimate search method, called a **metasearch,** uses software that searches the search engines. That is, it runs your query on several different search engines, probably the top seven or eight, simultaneously. Table 8-1 also lists several of the metasearch engines.

Internet Directories

Yahoo, one of the most popular "search engines" on the Internet, really isn't a search engine at all, but rather a directory. A **directory** is the work of human researchers, who sift through sites and organize them by content categories, allowing you to quickly focus on a group of sites that interest you. Many smaller directories concentrate on specific content areas, such as art and artists, and even rate listed sites for quality. Of course, any rating is the subjective judgment of the people who compile the directory. Several directories are included in Table 8-1.

Narrowing the Search

A simple one-word search will yield many sites, most of which will be irrelevant to your purposes. Suppose, for example, you are considering a driving trip through Utah. If you submit the word *Utah* as your search criterion, you will retrieve everything from Utah Lake to the Utah Jazz basketball team. The trick is to customize your search criteria. In this case, adding the word *vacation* to the search criteria will produce a list that begins with various hotels and parks in Utah. You can refine and narrow your search repeatedly.

There are more sophisticated methods for narrowing your search and for getting it right the first time. Different search engines offer different methods. Take a look at the search site's page, and you will probably see a clickable phrase such as Custom Search, Advanced Search, or Options. Click the phrase to see how your request can be made to order. For example, the AltaVista search engine permits quotation marks. If you type *"World Trade Center"* as your search criterion, you will get results that focus on that institution. If, instead, you type *World, Trade,* and *Center* as just three words in a row, the search engine will find every instance of each of the three words, alone and in combination—possibly several thousand sites. Alas, even the quote method is imperfect. For example, a site on a completely different topic will show up if the phrase *World Trade Center* appears anywhere on the site.

Most search engines offer operators with special functions based on a mathematical system called **Boolean logic.** The operators that are most commonly used are AND, OR, and NOT. The words can be further qualified with parentheses. AND means both; OR means either or both. Used correctly, these simple words can reduce search output to a dozen relevant sites instead of thousands of unrelated ones. Consider these examples: You want information on the companies called Cirrus and Intel. Type in *Cirrus* OR *Intel* for output that gives any site that mentions either or both companies. Suppose you need the population of the country of Jordan. If you key *Jordan,* you will see many sites for Michael Jordan, among others. Instead, key *Jordan* AND NOT *Michael.* Most requests combine several terms and operators. For example, suppose you want to go to college in Illinois but want to live in a town smaller than Chicago, and you want to inquire about tuition. Try *Illinois* AND NOT *Chicago* AND (*college* OR *university*) AND *tuition* AND *admission.* This query is quite specific, and it will produce mostly desired sites.

Other ways of refining search results are to specify the language (e.g., English or Russian) of the site, its most recent update, and whether the page includes an image or audio or video.

Search Engine Limitations

Search engines are known for turning up too much information, hence the need for Boolean terms and other methods to fine-tune the results. It is perhaps counterintuitive, then, to realize that search engines examine only a fraction of the Web. The Web's vastness simply foils even the best search engines. The two search engines that have the broadest coverage, HotBot and AltaVista, search only about a third of all the pages on the Web. Some search engines cover less than 20 percent of available Web pages. That leaves page after page, floating out there somewhere, unreachable by anyone who lacks the specific Web address.

Furthermore, the problem is going to get worse. The Web has approximately 700 million pages, and millions of pages are added every year. It is probably impossible to index the entire Web. The futility of trying to build giant databases of Web pages will probably lead to a trend toward smaller, specialized search sites. For instance, HotBot now runs a special search engine called NewsBot that constantly patrols a special set of news-related sites. With a concentrated effort, such a site can be made smarter and more thorough in its own field. Some services avoid the issue entirely by providing only highlights of the Web. For now the best bet for users who are hunting down some elusive piece of information is to use a metasearch site or manually submit the request to multiple search engines. Using a half-dozen search engines approximately doubles the results obtained with the most prolific individual search engine.

▶ BRANCHING OUT

Although the World Wide Web is usually the focus of any Internet discussion, there are other parts of the Internet that deserve attention. All of them, in fact, predate the Web. One way to identify such sites is to observe the protocol. Instead of *http*, which you may be accustomed to seeing used for Web sites, you may see *news* or *ftp*.

Newsgroups

Usenet is an informal network of computers that allows the posting and reading of messages in newsgroups that focus on specific topics. A more informal name is simply **newsgroups.** Topics of newsgroup discussions cover almost any subject you could imagine. If you have a passion for herbal remedies, for Macintosh computers, or for Chinese politics, you can find not just one person but an entire group of people who share your interest and have something to say about it. Today there are more than 20,000 newsgroups offering conversation and, in some cases, files to download. Participating in newsgroups requires software called a **newsreader.** This software is included in most browsers, but some newsgroup participants prefer to use stand-alone newsreaders with lots of extra features.

Think of a Usenet as a series of bulletin boards, each devoted to a specific topic. If you happen along, you can read other people's postings. If you wish to respond to a message or just contribute your own original thought, you leave a message. The process is just about that simple. Once you find a newsgroup that interests you, a suggested rule is that you observe the newsgroup for a while, an activity called **lurking,** before you jump in. That is, just read messages without writing any. That way you will get the flavor of the group before you participate and learn what kind of discussion is customary and what is discouraged.

In many newsgroups anyone can post messages about anything, whether or not it relates to the topic of the newsgroup. Some people take perverse delight in posting messages attacking others, often in the crudest terms. This type of message, referred to as a **flame,** can provoke a **flame war,** back-and-forth exchanges of flames. To avoid problems with flames and inappropriate material, some newsgroups are moderated. In a **moderated newsgroup,** all postings are first sent to a **moderator,** who decides whether the message is appropriate for posting.

FTP: Downloading Files

You already know that you can access files that reside on remote computers through the Internet and view them on your own computer screen. That is, you are allowed to look at them. But what if you wanted to keep a file; that is, what if you wanted your own copy of a file on your own computer? It may be possible to download— get—the file from the distant computer and place it on the hard disk of the computer you are using.

Whether or not a file is available for downloading depends on two things: (1) whether you are allowed to download files to the hard disk of the computer you are using and (2) whether the file you want is available for copying. Whether or not you are permitted to download files to the computer you are using may depend on the availability of disk space, which is at a premium in some locations. Of course, if you are using your own personal computer, you may do whatever you like.

Many computer files are proprietary, and a user who wants them must have an account on that computer and a password. However, all kinds of files—programs, text, graphics images, even sounds—are available to be copied without restriction. The free files are public archives, often associated with an educational institution or government.

There are many reasons you might want someone else's file. Perhaps, for example, a colleague in another city has just written a 150-page grant proposal and wants to send it to you; it is not convenient to send large files via e-mail. Perhaps you want some NASA space photos or some game software. Perhaps you have nothing particular in mind but, knowing that free stuff is out there, you simply go to a popular FTP site and look around. You can also upload—send your own files to another computer—but most people do a lot more downloading than uploading.

Computers on the Internet have a standard way to transfer copies of files, a program called **FTP,** for **file transfer protocol.** The term has become so common that FTP is often used as a verb, as in "Jack FTP-ed that file this morning." Most downloading is done by a method called **anonymous FTP.** This means that instead of having to identify yourself with a proper account on the remote computer, you can simply call yourself Anonymous. Also, instead of a password, you just use your e-mail address. This is merely background information; your browser will do all this work for you when you indicate that you want to transfer to an FTP site to select a file and download it.

Telnet: Using Remote Computers

Many applications on large systems require users to access a host computer through a terminal. **Telnet** is a protocol that allows remote users to use their PC to log onto a host computer system over the Internet and use it as if they were sitting at one of that system's local terminals. Usually, the user has to have an account on the host system and enter an appropriate user ID and password. However, some systems are set up to allow *guest* logins, for which no prior account is necessary. Most Web browsers include Telnet capability.

► MAKING CONNECTIONS ◄   Free Internet E-Mail Accounts

You probably already have an e-mail account provided by your ISP, employer, or school. So why do you need another one? Consider the following:

● You graduate from college, change employers, or decide to find a better ISP. All three situations result in a change of e-mail address and the resulting bother and possible confusion in notifying all your correspondents.

● Your employer doesn't approve of employees using business e-mail accounts for personal communications. And remember, most employers keep e-mail messages in log files, even after you delete them.

● You would like the convenience of checking your e-mail no matter where you are—a friend's house, the library, home, or at work.

● You don't have your own Internet access or e-mail address, relying instead on friends' computers or those at the local library.

In all of these situations a free Internet e-mail account could be just the answer. A number of sites now provide these accounts. The granddaddy of all is Hotmail, now offered by MSN. Most Internet portals, such as Yahoo! and Excite, include free e-mail to encourage you to keep returning. And some other sites, such as Ziplip, exist for the sole purpose of providing free e-mail.

To establish your free account, visit the site and click on the link that says, "Register for free e-mail" or something similar. The resulting screen(s) will ask you to enter registration information, including your choices for a user name and

password. Unless it's a brand-new service, don't expect to find any neat names left—they're already spoken for. If you choose a user name that somebody else already has, you'll be asked to choose again, often with some alternatives offered. Once you settle on an available name and fill in the required registration information, you're all set. You can send and retrieve e-mail from any computer that is logged onto the Internet just by visiting your e-mail site and signing on with your user name and password.

The following are some things to look for in choosing a free e-mail provider:

● What is their privacy policy? What do they do with the personal data you provide when you register? Most use that data to provide targeted ads when you visit the site, but some may sell the data (including your e-mail address) to others. Some, such as Ziplip, require no personal data at all. There should be a link labeled "Privacy Policy" or something similar on the site. Read it!

● How easy is the service to use? Some are easy and intuitive; others require a lot more work to understand. All have a Help link, but not all Help is that helpful. The easiest way to evaluate ease of use is to sign up for an account and use it several times. After all, it's free. If you find it doesn't suit you, you can try another service.

● What features are supported? Some providers allow you to create a group address, so that a single message will be sent to everyone in the group. Providers also vary in the amount of storage provided for old e-mail. If you save everything, this could be important.

E-Mail

E-mail, already discussed in the chapter on networking, is the most-used feature of the Internet, used by even more people than the Web. Before the Internet, e-mail users were limited to communicating only with others on the same network. As a network of networks, the Internet has made it possible for any user connected to the Internet to send e-mail to anyone else on the Internet. This is similar to the telephone system. No matter what company provides your local telephone service, you can call anyone in the world, since all telephone companies are now connected to each other.

If you are connected to the Internet through your employer's or school's network, that network will provide a **mail server** that collects and stores your e-mail in a **mailbox** that you can access at your convenience. Some networks will send an audible alarm (usually a soft chime) or display a small message box on your screen for a

Online Travel Resources

Planning a trip? Most people are aware of the online reservation systems of the airlines, major hotel chains, and car rental agencies. But the Internet can aid your travel plans in many other ways. For instance, if the major hotels don't interest you, try the Bed & Breakfast Channel (*bbchannel.com*)—it lists over 19,000 bed-and-breakfast inns throughout the United States, most including photos. If your plans include overseas travel, check out the Centers for Disease Control Travel Advisory (*cdc.gov/travel*) for required inoculations and strategies to avoid any local health problems at your destination. You also might want to visit the Universal Currency Converter site (*xe.net/currency*) to find out the current rate of monetary exchange and Travlang (*travlang.com*) to pick up some useful foreign words and phrases. Travlang even supplies sound clips to help with the proper pronunciation.

brief period when new mail arrives. If you connect to the Internet through an ISP, the mail server resides on the ISP's computer, and you will have to check periodically for new mail. Your **e-mail address** consists of the user name assigned to you by your ISP or network administrator, followed by the @ symbol, then the domain name of your mail server.

E-mail client software on your PC allows you to retrieve, create, send, store, print, and delete your e-mail messages. Additional features include an address book, from which you can select addressees for new mail, and the ability to attach files containing graphics, audio, video, and computer programs to your e-mail. Be aware, however, that for security reasons, some networks will block some or all attachments from incoming messages. Basic e-mail client software is included with most browsers, but many people use separate e-mail software that include advanced features such as **filters** that can direct incoming e-mail to specific folders and even reject spam.

▶ NOT QUITE PERFECT YET

The Internet has been heaped with well-deserved praise. But still there are concerns. To begin with, no one really knows exactly who is out there on the Internet and what they are doing online. It's a little worrisome. On the other hand, many users find the freewheeling, no-controls aspect of the Internet appealing. Many fear government censorship attempts, such as the Communications Decency Act of 1996, which was declared unconstitutional by the Supreme Court, and the Child Online Protection Act of 1998, which a federal court has blocked from enforcement pending a Supreme Court ruling on constitutionality.

Behavior Problems

There really are some behavior problems on the Internet. But there are behavior problems in any aspect of society, from the playground to the boardroom. Those who abuse the Internet are, relatively speaking, small in number. Even so, solutions to the problems posed by abusers include a proposed ratings system and filtering software for parental control of the types of sites or newsgroups accessed by children.

Meanwhile, the community of Internet users has made serious efforts to monitor behavior on the Internet. One consistent effort is **netiquette,** which refers to appropriate behavior in network communications. For example, users are admonished not to type in caps (IT'S LIKE SHOUTING). Netiquette rules are published on several sites and in every book about the Internet.

Useless, Overburdened, and Misinformed

Some people consider some home pages useless. In fact, there is a site called Useless Pages that maintains a listing of pages the site manager deems useless. However, many people are willing to pay for the connection to a Web server to promote a home page they fancy, whatever anyone else may think. Others put out birth or wedding announcements, complete with photos. One useless page does nothing except count the number of times that page is accessed. At the other end of the spectrum are sites that apparently have so much value that their popularity renders them mostly inaccessible. Any list of "cool" sites, a favorite Web word, is likely to be crowded.

There are no guarantees. The Internet is full of misinformation. Just because something is on the Internet does not mean that it is true. If someone steps up to announce that the government uses black helicopters to spy on us or that tapes sound better if you soak them in water first, you need not accept such information as fact. It's not that people intend to be wrong, it's just that they sometimes are. If you are doing serious research on the Internet, be sure to back it up with other sources, especially non-Internet sources.

▲

The Internet is interesting and even fun. Perhaps the best aspect of the Internet is that even a novice computer user can learn how to move from site to site on the Internet with relative ease.

CHAPTER REVIEW

 Summary and Key Terms

- A message to be sent to another computer is divided up into **packets,** each labeled with its destination address; the packets are reassembled at the destination address. The software that takes care of the packets is **Transmission Control Protocol/Internet Protocol (TCP/IP)**. TCP does the packeting and reassembling of the message. The IP part of the protocol handles the addressing, seeing to it that packets are routed across multiple computers.

- In 1969 the Defense Department set up a connected group of geographically dispersed computers called **ARPANet,** for Advanced Research Projects Agency Network.

- In 1990 **Tim Berners-Lee** made getting around the Internet easier by designing a set of links for one computer to connect to another. He saw the set of links as a spider's web; hence the name **Web.** Berners-Lee's laboratory at the **CERN site** is considered the birthplace of the **World Wide Web.** A **link** on a Web site is easy to see: It is colored text called **hypertext** or an icon or image called a **hyperregion.** A mouse click on the link transports the user to the site represented by the link.

- A **browser** is interface software used to explore the Internet. As a student in 1993, **Marc Andreessen** led a team that invented **Mosaic,** the first graphical browser.

- An Internet user needs a computer with a modem and its related software, an Internet service provider, and a browser. An **Internet service provider (ISP)** provides the server computer and the software to connect to the Internet. An **online service** (also called an **information utility**) also provides an Internet connection but additionally includes extensive members-only content.

- When you invoke your browser software, it will dial up the Internet service provider and, once successfully connected, display the **home page** of the browser's Web site. The browser shows three parts on the screen: the *browser control panel*, consisting of lines of menus and buttons; the *browser display window* to show the current site; and a *status line* at the bottom. The page can be **scrolled**—moved up and down—by using the **scroll bar** on the right.

- Using a mouse permits commands to be issued through a series of **menus,** a series of choices that are normally laid out across the top of the screen. The menus are called **pull-down menus** because each initial choice, when clicked with a mouse, reveals lower-level choices. **Buttons** can also invoke commands.

- The **Uniform Resource Locator (URL)** is a string of letters and symbols that is the unique address of a Web page or file on the Internet. A Web page URL begins with the protocol *http*, which stands for **HyperText Transfer Protocol,** the means of communicating using links. Next comes the **domain name,** which is the address of the Internet service provider or other host. The last part of the domain name is called a **top-level domain** and represents the purpose of the organization or entity.

- A **hot list**—called Bookmarks, Favorites, or something similar—stores favorite sites and their URLs.

- In browsers, **frames** allow a given page to be divided into rectangular sections, each of which can operate independently of the other.

- A **plug-in** is software that enhances the functionality of a browser.

- **Java,** a programming language developed by Sun Microsystems, can be used to write software that can be used on any machine. Java **applets** are small programs that provide multimedia effects and other capabilities on Web pages. Microsoft's **ActiveX controls** provide similar functionality.

- The **Wireless Application Protocol (WAP)** is used by wireless access providers to format Web pages for viewing on mobile handheld devices.

- A **search engine** is software that lets a user specify search terms; the search engine then finds sites that fit those terms. A **spider** program follows links throughout the Web, indexing the pages it finds in the search engine's database. A **metasearch** uses software that automatically runs your query on several search engines. An Internet **directory** employs human researchers to organize and categorize Internet sites. A way to narrow a search is to use a mathematical system called **Boolean logic,** which uses the operators AND, OR, and NOT.

- **Usenet,** or **newsgroups,** is an informal network of computers that allow the posting and reading of messages in newsgroups that focus on specific topics. **Newsreader** software, included in most browsers, is used to participate in newsgroups. Reading messages in a newsgroup without writing any is called **lurking.** An abusive message attacking someone is called a **flame.** A **flame war** is an exchange of flames. **Moderated newsgroups** are controlled by a **moderator,** who determines what messages are posted.

- Computers on the Internet have a standard way to transfer copies of files, a set of rules called **FTP,** for **file transfer protocol.** Most downloading is done by a method called **anonymous FTP,** meaning that a user can be named Anonymous and the password can be simply the user's e-mail address.

- **Telnet** is a protocol that allows remote users to use their PC to log onto a host computer system over the Internet and use it as if they were sitting at a local terminal of that system.

- **E-mail** is the most-used feature of the Internet. E-mail is provided through a **mail server** maintained by your network or ISP that provides you with an **e-mail address,** consisting of your user name and the mail server's domain name, and a **mailbox** to store your messages. **E-mail client software** on your PC allows you to retrieve, create, send, store, print, and delete your e-mail messages. E-mail **filters** can direct incoming e-mail to specific folders and even reject spam.

- **Netiquette** refers to appropriate behavior in network communications.

▶ Critical Thinking Questions

1. After he left school, Marc Andreessen, in his own words, wanted to make a "Mosaic killer." He felt that he had not been given sufficient credit for his college efforts and set out to make his fortune commercially with Netscape Navigator, the forerunner of Netscape Communicator. He did. Dr. Tim Berners-Lee, however, rejected numerous commercial offers. He felt that if he cashed in on his invention, it would compromise the Web, which he wanted to be available to everyone. Are both these positions defensible? Comment.

2. How reliable are search engines? Why might one search engine give a different set of results than another?

3. In addition to sending text messages in the body of an e-mail message, many e-mail client software applications allow users to attach files in native formats—.doc, .xls, .jpg, etc. Have you ever sent or received an e-mail attachment? Which file type(s) have you sent or received?

Was the recipient able to open and view the attachments?

4. Explain the difference between an Internet search engine and an Internet directory. Name one example of each. Which type do you use most often when seeking Internet information?

5. Have you ever used the ftp protocol to upload or download files? If you have, which FTP software application did you use? Was it easy to use? How did you acquire this software application?

 Online Activity

Internet domain names are like vehicle vanity plates, and you cannot acquire one if it has already been purchased. When trying to get a vanity plate, you are competing with residents of a single state. However, when you are trying to get a domain name, you are competing with residents of the entire planet! Consequently, many domain names are already taken. We are going to see if you can successfully create your own personal domain name.

a. Design a domain name based on your name, initials, interests, etc., and explain why it is special to you.
b. Visit http://www.register.com/ to see if that domain name has been registered.
c. If the name has been registered:
    i. Who owns it?
    ii. Visit the Web site and describe the content/purpose of the site.
    iii. While some individuals or businesses purchase domain names for personal or professional use, others purchase domain names as an investment, and they are willing to sell their domain names. Some are actively available for auction, and for those domain names that are not, an unsolicited purchase offer can be sent to the owner. Visit http://www.afternic.com/ for buying, selling, or appraising domain names, and see if your domain name is available for purchase.
    iv. Try a variation on your original design and repeat step b until you have successfully created a unique domain name.
d. What is the purchase price for a domain name, and how long does it remain registered to the owner?

▶ **STUDENT STUDY GUIDE**

Multiple Choice

1. The creator of the Web was
   a. Rand Corporation
   b. ARPANet
   c. Tim Berners-Lee
   d. Marc Andreessen

2. Which is *not* a Boolean operator?
   a. OR
   b. IN
   c. AND
   d. NOT

3. The protocol for downloading files over the Internet carries the abbreviation
   a. HTTP
   b. FTP
   c. ISP
   d. URL

4. The action of moving a page up or down on the screen is called
   a. scrolling
   b. linking
   c. lurking
   d. framing

5. The software on a user's computer that provides a graphical interface to access the Internet is called a(n)
   a. URL
   b. FTP
   c. ISP
   d. browser

6. Which factor was *not* a major contributor to the emergence of the Internet?
   a. links
   b. browsers
   c. frames
   d. TCP/IP

7. The first graphical browser was called
   a. Internet Explorer
   b. FTP
   c. ARPANet
   d. Mosaic

8. The birth of the World Wide Web took place at
   a. Rand Corporation
   b. CERN
   c. ARPA
   d. Microsoft

9. Giving this element would *not* help to narrow a search:
   a. language
   b. applet
   c. Boolean operator
   d. date

10. A message to be sent to another computer over the Internet is divided into
    a. URLs
    b. hyperregions
    c. packets
    d. frames

11. ISP stands for
    a. Internet Serial Port
    b. Internet Switching Protocol
    c. Internet Service Provider
    d. none of the above

12. A Web site's initial page is called a(n)
    a. home page
    b. mother page
    c. primary page
    d. entry page

13. The first major computer network was
    a. World Wide Web
    b. BIGnet
    c. EarthNet
    d. ARPANet

14. America Online is the largest
    a. Wide Area Network (WAN)
    b. online service
    c. phone company
    d. manufacturer of modems

15. The most used top-level domain is
    a. .net
    b. .edu
    c. .com
    d. .gov

16. Adobe Acrobat files are stored in what format?
    a. Portable Document Format (PDF)
    b. Adobe Acrobat File (AAF)
    c. Document (DOC)
    d. Text (TXT)

17. Microsoft adds functionality to Web pages by using which of the following?
    a. Java
    b. Helper Apps
    c. JavaScript
    d. ActiveX controls

18. HotFoot is a
    a. directory
    b. search engine
    c. metasearch site
    d. none of the above

19. A newsreader is
    a. a person who reads a newspaper
    b. a software that is used for Usenet
    c. a device used by the visually impaired
    d. none of the above

20. IRC stands for
    a. Internet Renewable Charges
    b. Internet Ready Communication
    c. Internet Relay Chat
    d. Internet Resource Check

True/False

T   F   1. Browser software is kept on the server computer.

T   F   2. In an URL, the domain name is the address of the ISP.

T   F   3. The inventor of the graphical browser is Marc Andreessen.

T   F   4. TCP/IP is the standard Internet protocol.

T   F   5. An Internet search engine employs human researchers to categorize sites.

T   F   6. FTP allows you to remotely access a host computer via the Internet.

T   F   7. The first ISP was Mosaic.

T   F   8. Plug-ins increase the functionality of browsers.

T   F   9. "com" is an example of a top-level domain.

T   F   10. A link on a Web site is usually colored text or an image or icon.

T   F   11. Dogpile is a metasearch engine.

T   F   12. Spamming means sending a message that attacks others.

T   F   13. JavaScript applets are used to add functionality to Web pages.

T   F   14. Marc Andreessen is credited with developing Internet Explorer.

T   F   15. Plug-ins enhance the functionality of a browser.

T   F   16. Search engines cover more than 75 percent of the existing Web sites.

T   F   17. The anonymous Telnet protocol is used to upload and download files.

T   F   18. E-mail is the most used feature of the Internet.

T   F   19. The newer browser versions no longer require users to enter http://

T   F   20. Java is the name of the newest Internet browser.

Fill-In

1. _____ is the protocol that uses links to move from one site to another on the Internet.

2. Java _____ are small programs that can be included in Web pages to provide animation effects.

3. _____ is a protocol that formats Web pages for viewing on handheld devices.

4. A(n) _____ runs your search request on several search engines simultaneously.

5. _____ is an informal network of computers that allows the posting and reading of messages that focus on specific topics.

6. Appropriate behavior in network communications is referred to as _____.

7. A(n) _____ newsgroup is controlled by an individual who determines which messages get posted.

8. Search engines use a _____ program that follows links through the Web to index sites for the search engine's database.

9. The _____ is a string of letters and symbols that is the unique address of a Web page or file on the Internet.

10. E-mail _____ can direct incoming e-mail to specific folders and even reject spam.

11. A URL consists of three main components: _____, _____, and _____.

12. A hot list is also known as _____ or _____.

13. _____ allow a Web page to be divided into rectangular regions.

14. _____ is a protocol that allows remote users to use their PC to log onto a host computer system over the Internet and use it as if they were sitting at a local terminal of that system.

15. Netscape was recently purchased by _____.

16. _____ was the first graphical browser.

17. The last part of the domain name is called a _____ and represents the purpose of the organization or entity.

18. _____ is one of the most popular plug-ins and is used for viewing quality animation.

19. On a Web site, a link appears in colored text called _____ or an icon or image called a(n) _____.

20. A message to be sent to another computer is divided up into _____, each labeled with its destination address.

▶ **ANSWERS**

Multiple Choice

1. c	6. c	11. c	16. a
2. b	7. d	12. a	17. d
3. b	8. b	13. d	18. d
4. a	9. b	14. b	19. b
5. d	10. c	15. c	20. c

True/False

1. F	6. F	11. T	16. F
2. T	7. F	12. F	17. T
3. T	8. T	13. F	18. T
4. T	9. T	14. F	19. T
5. F	10. T	15. F	20. F

Fill-In

1. HyperText Transfer Protocol, or http
2. applets
3. Wireless Access Protocol, or WAP
4. metasearch
5. Usenet, or newsgroups
6. netiquette
7. moderated
8. spider
9. Uniform Resource Locator, or URL
10. filters
11. protocol, domain, and path/directory/file name
12. bookmarks or favorites
13. frames
14. Telnet
15. America Online
16. Mosaic
17. top-level domain
18. Macromedia Shockwave
19. hypertext; hyperregion
20. packets

Planet Internet

Let's Chat

Want to send text messages to a distant friend in real-time? Want to participate in discussions on one of over 12,000 topics while chatting on the equivalent of the old-time "party line" telephone? Want to enter the world of nicks, ops, IRC cops, and bots? Then Internet Relay Chat (IRC) is for you.

What is IRC?

IRC is an old medium by Internet standards. Originally developed in 1988, IRC messages were already whizzing around the Net well before the invention of the graphical Web browser. IRC is organized into channels, each of which is transmitted worldwide by one or more servers.

How do I get started?

To get started on IRC, you need to download a client. This is a program that lets you connect to an IRC server and exchange messages. Two of the most popular clients are mIRC and pirch.

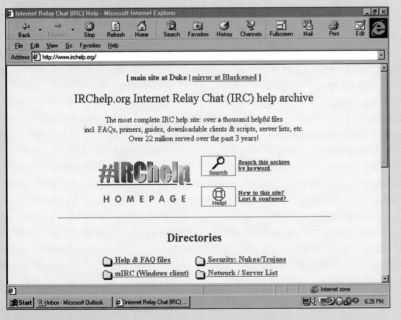

Once you install the client, you choose a "nick," or nickname, that identifies you online. Then you can choose from a list of servers to which you can connect. Some servers are part of networks, host computers that all carry the same channels. The channel #chat on one Efnet network server will be the same #chat as on another Efnet server. Larger servers may have over 30,000 simultaneous users spread over the channels they carry.

What's next?

To find a channel of interest, type/list. You will be shown a list of channels you can enter, the number of users currently in that channel, and their nominal topic. You will quickly note that the channel names (preceded by #) will not necessarily have anything to do with their current content. Channels don't always have to stick to a specific topic; you might find people in #windows talking about football teams, for instance.

Planet Internet

Caution.

Keep in mind that the content of some channels is not appropriate for all audiences, and parents should be particularly careful not to allow young children unsupervised access. Anonymity is one of the key features of IRC, so take advantage of it by never revealing personally identifying information such as your street address or credit information.

Mean robots.

Once you enter a channel, you'll see a list of other IRC users who are currently in the channel. Some users might have an @ before their nick. That means that the person is a channel operator, or Op for short. These users are in charge of the channel and can kick off offending users, change the topic of the channel, and alter other settings. Sometimes the Op is really a bot (short for robot). Bots are programs created in a language such as C or Perl, usually for keeping control of a channel, providing help, responding to otherwise unanswered queries, or even asking trivia questions. Like the robots of science fiction, not all bots are good, and a few may do malicious things such as taking control of the channel or harassing other channel users.

Ain't Misbehavin'.

If you behave irresponsibly on an IRC channel, you might be kicked from the channel by an Op. This means that you will have to reconnect to the channel to continue. If someone is repeatedly kicked for irresponsible or inappropriate behavior, that person might find himself or herself banned from the server

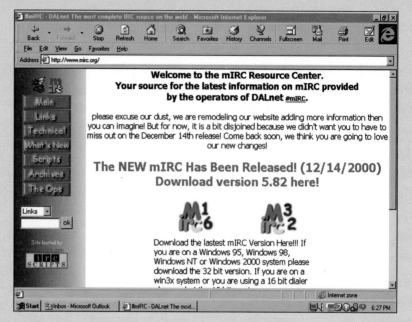

carrying the channel by an administrator or "IRC Cop." Banning might go beyond a single offender. More than a few students have found that their entire school's network is banned from some server because of the problems the server administration had with previous users from the same addresses. Even AOL has been banned from at least one IRC network because of offenses by its users.

Internet Exercises:

1. **Structured exercise.** Browse to one of the introductory IRC pages linked from http://www.prenhall.com/capron. Answer the following questions:

- How would you "wave" to someone on IRC?

- How do you change your "nick" on IRC?

- What IRC client program would be required for you own, or your school's computer?

2. **Free-form exercise.** Find the code of conduct, chat rules, or etiquette guidelines for an IRC chat server or channel. For what specific behaviors, over and above those that are clearly illegal in your country, can a user be kicked or banned from the server?

3. **Advanced exercise.** Using an IRC client program, or one of the browser-based chat programs, enter a channel of your choice and note the following:

- Which channel did you choose? Why?

- Did the majority of participants stick to the nominal topic of the channel?

- How many users were in the channel when you were there?

- What conduct, if any, did you see that seemed to violate the server rules?

- How helpful, educational, or entertaining would you rate your experience?

The Internet in Business:
Corporations, Businesses, and Entrepreneurs

The Internet in Business:
Corporations, Businesses, and Entrepreneurs

C H A P T E R

LEARNING OBJECTIVES

Discuss the pervasiveness and inevitability of business on the Internet

Explain how money factors, especially advertising, affect the Web

Describe the likely success factors for Web entrepreneurs

Differentiate between business-to-consumer and business-to-business sites

Explain the importance of Internet transmission speed for business sites

Differentiate between intranets, extranets, and virtual private networks

er friends, only half-teasing, tell everyone that Kathleen Cameron is "browsing for housing." Although Kathleen and her husband, John, are mildly amused, they actually see their approach as practical. They are buying a house on the Internet.

The adventure began in San Francisco, where Kathleen and John were living when he took a new job with a venture capital firm in Atlanta. Kathleen, a photo researcher, had plenty of experience searching the Internet and figured that was a good place to get a head start on house hunting.

When real estate professionals dream of the ideal customer, they may have someone like the tech-savvy Kathleen in mind. She is the harbinger of the future: a user of the houses-on-computers system that has taken many dollars to put in place. Both national and local real estate Web sites are racing to attract customers.

The National Real Estate Association estimates that there are approximately 100,000 real estate and related Web sites. Many sites offer an amazing amount of information, including maps of cities and neighborhoods, listings showing the outside of the house, and even a virtual tour through the inside of the house. Kathleen is particularly interested in the search feature that allows her to narrow her focus by zip code, price, number of bedrooms, view, schools, and more. Most sites also offer help with planning home financing.

Before Kathleen and John made the cross-country trip to go house hunting in person, they already knew what neighborhood they wanted to live in and had preselected seven possible houses. They enlisted the aid of a local real estate agent, chose one of the preselected houses, and closed the deal—all within three days.

Real estate sales are, in fact, a local activity requiring in-person encounters, so perhaps to say that you can "buy a house on the Internet" is a bit of an exaggeration. But this is about as close as one can get. Home buying is just one of many business activities on the Internet.

► E-COMMERCE: RETAIL SITES

The world of **electronic commerce,** or, more commonly, **e-commerce,** buying and selling over the Internet, represents nothing less than a new economic order. Even the word "retail" is evolving to "etail," short for "electronic retail." With a few clicks of your mouse, you can buy a suit in Thailand, an out-of-print biography, a particular used car, or a bargain airline ticket. Or, considering more mundane items, you can buy music CDs, videos, clothes, computers, baby equipment, jewelry, sporting goods, office supplies, cosmetics, flowers, gifts, and your weekly groceries—still with just a few clicks (Figure 9-1). You can make those clicks from the comfort of your home, in the middle of the night, and with your hair in curlers, if you wish.

Retail businesses understand the attractions of online shopping for consumers and are scrambling to capture their share of sales. They also understand that Internet sales mean cost savings, including the costs of a physical store building and employing salespeople. Finally, they understand that consumers are in a unique position to comparison shop; in fact, there are sites devoted exclusively to helping consumers compare prices. So the bottom line is that cost savings will probably translate to more competitive prices. But first they must attract potential customers to their sites. In the late 1990s, many dot-com retail start-ups planned on losing money for several years while they built a large customer base. Items were frequently sold below cost and included free shipping. Companies spent huge amounts of money on advertising, often more than their sales income. In 2000, the bubble burst, and many etailers failed to survive the year.

Adding Content

Retail Web sites have begun adding **content** to attract visitors and boost sales. That is, rather than just the usual lists and views of products and prices, the site includes something of more general interest to attract visitors and keep them coming back, even if they don't intend to buy anything. As markets get more crowded, strong content can be a differentiator. Updating content is important. If visitors see the same content each time they return, they won't be back very often.

Interestingly, content-rich sites that were not originally retail sites are adding products and pitching sales. Thus the difference between content and commerce sites is becoming narrower.

Only Flirting with the Internet

Some companies would love to embrace the Internet but must settle for half measures. Although manufacturers know that the Internet could be an effective sales

Not.com

The intense hype and self-promotion by the huge number of Internet *dot-coms*, companies that exist only in cyberspace, is creating a backlash among a small number of Internet-based companies. Anxious to disassociate themselves from what they see as the fly-by-night impression given by some of the bizarre dot-com advertising appearing in the media, these companies are trying to present a more substantial image to consumers.

Lucy.com, an etailer of exercise wear, has decided to skip advertising and mail out hundreds of thousands of printed catalogs. Sue Levin, CEO, says that Lucy.com is trying to look and feel more like a "real" company. A number of other companies, including eToys, aren't willing to go quite that far, but have deleted the .com suffix from their advertising.

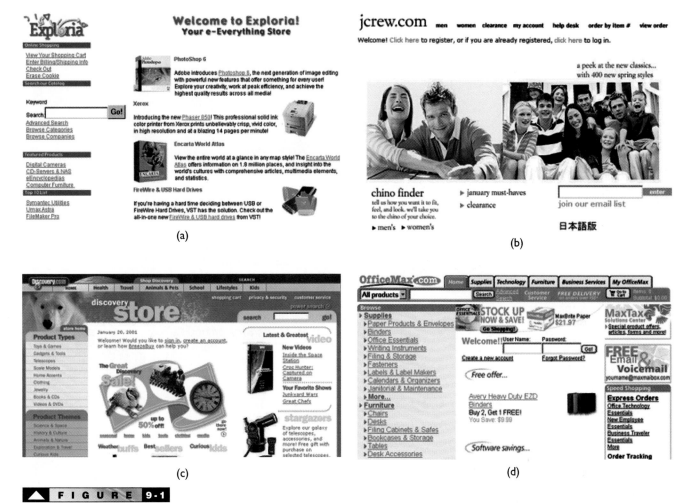

▲ FIGURE 9-1

Retail Web sites.

All these businesses have physical "bricks and mortar" stores, but they also sell their goods directly from their Web sites. Just click an item into your "shopping cart" and, when done, "check out" by supplying your credit card and a shipping address. Shown here are (a) Exploria, (b) J. Crew, (c) Discovery Store, and (d) OfficeMax.

tool, they fear that selling a product from their own site will alienate the sales representatives and stores with which they have established relationships. In fact, online commerce is seen as a menace to the men and women who do in-person selling or distribution and who still control a high percentage of most companies' order flow. As a result, jittery corporate strategists are trying to capitalize on the Internet's potential without sabotaging traditional sales channels.

There are a variety of solutions, none of which is completely satisfactory. Some companies keep prices on their Web sites high, so that the flesh-and-blood salesperson can offer an obvious discount. Others placate dealers and sales-people with a cut of each transaction, whether or not they played a part in generating it. For the moment, the most popular approach may be site marketing up to the point of actual sale, then recommending a local store to complete the transaction.

Looking at it from a different point of view, sometimes a successful Web site can alienate others who are only indirect business associates. Take Dave Smith Motors, in Kellogg, Idaho, seller of Chrysler cars and trucks. Dave put up his own Web site, and it attracted so much attention that customers came to Dave's from miles around. Other dealers boycotted Chrysler because it allocated more cars to Dave's successful lot. The Federal Trade Commission declared the boycott anticompetitive and illegal,

E-COMMERCE

Prentice Hall
EXPLORE Generation **it**

inside chrysler　　　　locate a dealer　　　worldwide　　　assistance

Saturday, January 20, 2001

PROWLER

□□□□□□□□□■□

SELECT A VEHICLE

READY TO BUY?

SHOPPING...
HOME
PROWLER
MODELS
INTERIOR
EXTERIOR
PERFORMANCE
TECHNOLOGY
SPECIFICATIONS
VEHICLE REVIEWS
AVAILABLE INCENTIVES
GET A BROCHURE
VEHICLE ACCESSORIES
BUILD YOUR OWN
GET CONNECTED TO A
FIVE STAR DEALER

American Icon

At Chrysler, we believe **hot rods are representative of the national character**... icons of a collective, restless impatience with the way things are - and of the will and the talent to try and make things better. That's what embodies the American hot rod, and that's why we build the Prowler.

ASSEMBLY PLANT

Learn more about the Conner Avenue Assembly Plant where the Prowler is built.

CHRYSLER MERCHANDISE

▲ **FIGURE 9-2**

Dealers and manufacturers.

Chrysler established a site that could be used by all Chrysler dealers, letting customers configure cars and find a dealer.

but Chrysler came to the rescue by making a generic Web site that all its dealers can use (Figure 9-2). Chrysler's site lets customers configure a vehicle, pick a dealer, and request a price quote.

Once a retail site exists, it must make its presence known. There are various ways to promote a site; one of the most effective ways is to advertise on a portal.

► PORTALS AND ADVERTISING

You know how network television earns money: Although broadcasts are free to viewers, the networks collect revenues from advertisers. Furthermore, the amount of money the networks charge advertisers is directly related to how popular the show is, that is, how many viewers are on hand to see the advertising. Now apply this technique to Web sites. Web sites that carry advertisements can charge for them at rates that are directly related to the number of visitors to the site: The more visitors, the higher the advertising rates.

Thus it is that a Web site wants to be your **portal** to the Internet—your everyday first stop, your neighborhood, your hangout. The site owners want you to come early and often. But, most of all, they want to persuade you to use them as your guide to the rest of the Internet.

Getting Personal

To be a good guide, the portal site begins by presenting content and links on a wide variety of topics, from health to movies to shopping. But to be a good guide to you personally, the portal site needs some information from you that it can use to personalize your use of the site. You will see a link on the portal site saying something like "My _____" (fill in the site name), or perhaps "Personalize" or "Customize." On the basis of the personal data you supply, the site can present local weather conditions, local news and sports scores, and even a portfolio of stocks you own. The more the portal offers you, the greater the likelihood that you will drop by often. Some portals go further, offering instructions on how to make the portal site the "home page" that appears each time you activate your browser to begin surfing the Internet.

Another Source of Money

Referral fees provide an even more significant revenue stream for portal Web sites. The portal Web site offers the news, sports, shops, and so forth from sources called **affiliates,** which the portal chooses. The affiliates—based on deals made with the portal—pay for the privilege. They may pay only for being listed on the portal site or—more likely—pay a percentage of a sale to any visitor who has clicked there from the portal site. For example, if a visitor at the Yahoo! site clicks on Clifford's Flowers, and then sends balloons from Clifford's to her sister across the country, Yahoo! will get a percent of the profit from that sale, simply because it made the referral.

Just who are these portal sites? Most are familiar names to Web surfers. Many started out as search engines and then expanded their content and retail connections. A well-known portal is Yahoo!, which was begun as a search site by two college students (Figure 9-3). (By the way, they named it Yahoo! as an acronym for "Yet

Auctions

Messenger

Check Email

YAHOO!

What's New

Personalize

Help

NEW! Play free
Survivor Pick'em Game

Answer Five Trivia Questions **Business** .com
WIN AN ACURA MDX™ [Go!]

NEW! Play free
Fantasy Golf

[   ] **Search** advanced search

Y! Shopping - Apparel, Books, Computers, DVD/Video, Luxury, Electronics, Music, Sports **and** more

Auctions · Classifieds · PayDirect · Shopping · **Travel** · Yellow Pgs · Maps **Media** **Finance/Quotes** · News · Sports · Weather
nnect Chat · **Clubs** · Experts · GeoCities · Greetings · Invites · **Mail** · Members · Messenger · Mobile · Personals · People Search
rsonal Addr Book · Briefcase · Calendar · **My Yahoo!** · Photos **Fun** Games · Kids · **Movies** · Music · Radio · **TV** **more...**

Yahoo! Auctions - Bid, buy, or sell anything!				In the News
Categories		**Items**		· Bush becomes 43rd U.S. president
· Antiques	· Computers	· PlayStation 2	· Palm Pilots	· Clinton grants pardons, bids farewell
· Autos	· Electronics	· MP3 Players	· Lincoln Pennies	· Oil spill threatens Galapagos
· Coins	· Sports Cards	· Hello Kitty	· Cameras	· College hoops, Figure skating
· Comic Books	· Stamps	· Kate Spade	· Longaberger	more...
Charity Auctions - Super Bowl Tix, 'Family Law' Walk-On Role				

Marketplace
· Yahoo! PayDirect - **send and receive money online**
· Get your own Web domain
· Y! Travel - **buy tickets, check arrival times**

Arts & Humanities
Literature, Photography...

News & Media
Full Coverage, Newspapers, TV...

Business & Economy
B2B, Finance, Shopping, Jobs...

Recreation & Sports
Sports, Travel, Autos, Outdoors...

▲ **FIGURE 9-3**

A portal.
Portal sites hope to be your main site, the place where you jump off to the rest of the Web. Yahoo!, shown here, is a popular portal site.

Another Hierarchical Officious Oracle," although no one bothers with that windy title anymore.) Yahoo!'s advertising campaign has been so successful that it is familiar even to people who have never used the Internet. Other content-rich portals are MSN, Snap!, Excite, Netscape, Go Network, and America Online. The America Online site is indeed the first site seen by AOL customers jumping from AOL-specific content to the Internet, but it is also a portal site in its own right that often is accessed by people who are not members of AOL.

Portals continue to grow in number and in content. The ultimate goal of each portal is to make its site your one-stop site on the Internet. Surfers would never settle for one site, of course, but it seems likely that they will settle on one site as their personalized—and often-visited—home page. Home sweet home page.

(a)

(b)

▲ **F I G U R E 9-4**

Banner ads.

Major traffic sites carry banner advertisements that are strategically placed to match the subject matter. (a) The Lycos site, which is a search engine as well as a portal, opens with an extensive list of categories. If you click Computers, you might see the screen shown here, which includes three computer-related ads (only one of them in the actual shape of a banner). (b) Starting with the HotBot search engine/portal, click Travel to see the screen shown here, which has three travel-related ads.

More Advertising

We have lived with advertising all our lives. It can be intrusive and annoying, but often it is informative, interesting, or even funny. For the most part, however, it is just in the background. For the user, the main advantage of advertising is that it pays all or most of the costs of the message on radio and television, in magazines and newspapers, and on the Internet.

Most advertisements on Web sites are in the form of **banner ads,** which were originally in the shape of a long rectangle (Figure 9-4). Advertisers pay the host site for the privilege of showing their ad on the site; it is their hope, of course, that users will be sufficiently attracted to the ad that they will click on the banner and thus be transported to the site of the advertiser. Many small ads are, in fact, in a variety of shapes. Some of them are little applets, showing some sort of motion to get our attention.

Banners do not work as well as advertisers would like because users are often reluctant to **click through,** that is, leave the current site, in which they are presumably interested, and go to the advertised site. One solution to this problem is the **live banner,** which lets a user get more information about a product—a pitch—without leaving the current site. This approach has proved popular but is not without drawbacks: The live banners work slowly, especially with slower modems, and are expensive to develop.

The most effective Web advertisements are **context-sensitive;** that is, the ad is related to the subject matter on the screen. As the advertisers put it, there is greater "click through and conversion," meaning that the ad is more likely to be clicked and, once at the advertised site, the user is more likely to buy something. Notice, for example, in Figure 9-5, that choosing the topic Computers elicits ads about software, whereas choosing the topic Travel summons ads for cars and planes. Since the user is in control of the path through the Web, it is reasonable to assume that he or she is receptive to ads on his or her chosen topic.

Web site ads have disadvantages for users. One is that they often have graphics and perhaps even applets, both of which take time to load. Another disadvantage is that as the page is loading on the screen, the ads load first, or at least early, so that you will not see the entire page until the ads are in place. That is, the site manager wants to make sure that you see the advertisements before you go clicking off somewhere else.

FOCUS ON ETHICS	**High Speed Pump and Dump?**

The speed with which information can be communicated via the Internet has led to new twists on old scams. One teenager grossed $800,000 in an investment scheme known as "pump and dump." After buying large blocks of low-priced stocks, the teen then talked up the prospects for the stock on financial message boards and in chat rooms. When the stock price rose, he was able to sell the stock at a very significant profit.

After an investigation by the Securities and Exchange Commission (SEC) this individual was fined $285,000 dollars, which left him with a profit of about $500,000. He received no further punishment, and he bought his parents expensive cars with the profits.

Answer the following questions:
1. Was the behavior ethical? Why or why not?
2. If this behavior was unethical, how would you distinguish "pump and dump" from regular stock trading?
3. The teen made frequent use of multiple screen-names to make it appear that his "buy" recommendations were coming from more than one person. Does this affect your evaluation of the ethical situation in this case?
4. What lessons would you draw for online investing from this case?

▶ PAYMENTS AND TAXES

You have seen the ads and perused the site, and now you want to make a purchase. How will you pay for it? And must you pay taxes on your purchase? These simple questions have rather complex answers that have kept the industry's attention since the beginning of online sales.

E-Commerce Payments

Some retail sites give you the option of phoning or faxing your order. Others allow you to place the order online, then call with your credit card number. They do this because they know that some people are leery of submitting their credit-card numbers over the network to an online retail site. These people fear that the card number may be intercepted in transit and then used illicitly to run up charges on the card. Although this is theoretically possible, it is highly unlikely. To begin with, the messages between the buyer and reputable online retailers are encrypted—encoded—so that they are not readable to the casual observer. It would take a skilled programmer to undo the encryption; frankly, there are more fruitful places to attack. The de facto standard for online transaction payments is the **Secure Sockets Layer (SSL)** protocol. However, most sites simply refer to it as "our secure server," and many customers have become comfortable using it. Unfortunately, some retail sites aren't as careful with your credit card information once they've received it. As recent media reports have highlighted, hackers have penetrated the security of several sites and stolen thousands of credit card numbers.

E-Commerce Taxes

One of the little thrills of catalog shopping is that you might not have to pay local sales taxes on articles purchased. Under U.S. federal law, if a mail-order company from which you order is located out of state, it has to collect sales taxes for your state only if the company has some sort of physical *presence* (sometimes called a *nexus*) in your state, such as a branch store or a warehouse. Now try to apply that to Internet commerce, whose sellers are likely to be far away and whose "presence" any place is debatable. But that is just the beginning of the long-running debate on taxing the Internet. Some folks want to tax even using the Internet.

There are approximately 30,000 taxing entities—states, counties, cities—in the United States. If all of them were to be turned loose to get their slice of the pie, the Internet would be seriously burdened and perhaps irreparably harmed. The compromise, passed into law in October 1998, is called the **Internet Tax Freedom Act.** The act has four basic components:

1. It prohibits state and local governments from imposing taxes on Internet access charges, such as those billed by America Online or an Internet service provider.

2. It prohibits taxes from being imposed on out-of-state businesses through strained interpretations of "presence."

3. It creates a temporary commission to study taxation of Internet commerce and report back to Congress on whether the Internet ought to be taxed.

4. It calls on the executive branch to demand that foreign governments keep the Internet free of taxes and tariffs.

In summary, the act provides that the Internet be free of new taxes for three years while a committee determines whether taxes should be imposed and, if so, how to do so in a uniform way. Further, notice that nothing has changed in regard to imposing sales taxes. The act refers only to *new* taxes or to trying to interpret "presence" in some new way. State and local governments are allowed to impose sales taxes on Internet sales, provided that the tax is the same as that which would be imposed on the transactions if they were conducted in a more traditional manner, such as over the phone or through mail order. Although the act was set to expire in 2001, the **Internet Non-Discrimination Act,** passed in 2000, extends these provisions through 2005.

► ENTREPRENEURS

Starting your own business on the Internet is a game anyone can play. And we do mean anyone, from those involved in agriculture to real estate to finance. Even the smallest entrepreneur can get in on the act. Individuals can gain access to people and markets—including global markets—that are not readily affordable or even available elsewhere. For a minimal investment, far less than that needed for a physical store or office, you can have a server link and a smashing home page that exactly expresses the nature of your business. You can even alter the page as your business grows and changes.

The statements that we have just made are true—but a bit rosy in color. Even though "anyone can play," the Internet is not a level playing field. Firms with multi-million-dollar marketing budgets and customer bases in the hundreds of thousands are more likely to be able to draw large numbers of people to their Web sites than is the most creative garage-based entrepreneur. Does this mean that the little guys do not have a chance? They have a chance, but not a level playing field.

Success Factors

Nothing guarantees success, defined as making a profit from your Internet business. It can be done, and most certainly is being done, but business on the Internet is not a panacea. Just as in a regular store, the key success factor for any commercial Web site is repeat business. How do you keep customers coming back? Some primary success factors are content, uniqueness, self-help, and community.

The body of your site, what you have to say and offer, is the *content.* The site must offer something—preferably several somethings—to keep interest up. What will it be? Observe the variety of content as you examine business sites. You will find news about their products, scores, contests, searches, and much more. The site cannot be static. If it is exactly the same as it was on a previous visit, most users will not bother returning.

One site that is loaded with daily-changing content is The Motley Fool (Figure 9-5). The name is inspired by Shakespeare's *As You Like It*: "I met a fool i' the forest, a motley fool." Despite their trademark jester costumes, no one would take brothers David and Tom Gardner for fools. The Motley Fool is the name of their online forum, which lets investors ask questions and share knowledge. Hundreds of thousands of visitors, frustrated by lack of investing knowledge from traditional sources, visit the site each month.

Can you be *unique?* One recommendation for success is to have a specialty, something that is not offered elsewhere. Twins Jason and Matthew Olim, jazz fans who had trouble finding a good selection of recordings in their local stores, decided to set up a Web site that they called CDnow, offering every jazz album made in the United States and thousands of imports. The beauty of the scheme was that there was no initial outlay for a store or even for inventory. A shopper places an order with CDnow, which in turn contacts distributors. The disk is usually delivered within 24 hours. CDnow eventually added other kinds of music and also movies. Another successful

Introducing the new standard in online brokerage...

American Express Brokerage

Click Here

| HOME | DISCUSSION BOARDS | QUOTES & DATA | STOCK RESEARCH | SHOP FOOLMART | MY PORTFOLIO | MY FOOL | LOGIN |

NEWS | SPECIAL FEATURES | INVESTING STRATEGIES | RETIREMENT | PERSONAL FINANCE | FOOL'S SCHOOL | HELP

CHOOSE A BROKER | Search: [____] Go | Quotes: [____] Go | BECOME A FOOL

Stocks to Avoid

Learn to spot which stocks and strategies spell T-R-O-U-B-L-E.

Giving Too Much to IRS?
Start early and we can help you save time, money, and sanity.

Win a Cruise
Make your Super Bowl predictions and take a cruise on us.

Play Fooball & Win! FOOLBALL

The Motley Fool. Fool.com. away.com

What's Here

Become a Fool
Member Benefits

Start Here (Read This First)
What's The Motley Fool?, 13 Steps to Investing, Beginning Investing Seminar, Tour, My Finance Guide

Our Investing Strategies
Rule Breaker, Rule Maker, FOOL 50,

Today's Headlines

Saturday, January 20, 10:31 p.m. ET

Nine Ways to Cut Your Debt
Check out our nine possible solutions for your debt problems.

Why Own Just One Biotech?
A decent basket of

Hello, Fool!

Start Here

Whether you're brand new or an old hand, The Motley Fool is dedicated to making you a better investor.

Begin >

"Humorous and savvy"
- *Wall Street Journal*

▲ **FIGURE 9-5**

A successful entrepreneur site.

One of the hallmarks of the Motley Fool Web site is that it has ever-changing content, which brings investors to the site again and again, many of them daily or even hourly.

---

specialty site is Hot-Hot-Hot!, which offers an enormous variety of hot sauces from around the world. Note that in each of these two examples, the site not only offers something unique but also appeals to an audience that will be repeat customers.

Customers like to take care of themselves as much as possible, so some *self-help* features are both useful and a winning strategy. If your site is, or becomes, large, you should include a search component so that users can find what they want easily. Again, depending on the complexity of the site, customers want to be able to do research, configure and order products, troubleshoot problems, check on the status of an order, or track a delivery.

A key to the success of a commercial site is a sense of *community*. An outstanding example of this is the Amazon.com site. Amazon features notes from authors about their own books and lets any customer write a review about a book. Customers perusing book offerings can just click an icon to read the reviews for a certain book. People who love books return again and again to this site. Customers who agree to register by filling out an on-screen form are eligible for book prizes. The prizes are attractive, and the registration data—name, e-mail address, and possibly book interests—provides Amazon with future marketing information.

My Mother, the Conglomerate

Mom-and-pop businesses have learned on the Web, anybody can look like a conglomerate. The same is true for teenagers, college students, stay-at-homes, and anyone else who is operating a business from a den or garage. Visitors at the College Depot site, which sells college oriented merchandise, may be surprised to learn that the business is based in the Gleeson family home in Trumbull, Connecticut. The site offers 50,000 different products, has secure online ordering, and gives the impression of a large retail operation. The Gleesons want to convey the image that they are a substantial company because they think it helps to build trust.

As we noted, anyone can do this—in theory. We do not want to convey the impression that success is automatic. Many small businesses, even those on the Internet, do not succeed. But, still, success is a possibility—and the initial investment need not be daunting.

► THE WORLD OF E-COMMERCE

The type of business activity that we have discussed so far takes place between businesses and individuals. In Internet jargon, this retail activity is referred to as **business-to-consumer (B2C)** e-commerce. B2C e-commerce has gotten all the media attention: outlandishly expensive Superbowl commercials, .com addresses at the bottom of almost every newspaper ad and TV commercial, and numerous news stories concerning the successes and, more recently, notable among the major players. Although there have been some spectacular failures (Toysmart.com, Petstore.com, Boo.com) among Internet retailers, analysts agree that B2C e-commerce will continue to grow rapidly. Some reliable estimates have it growing from $38 billion in 1998 to over $800 billion by 2005. In case you thought e-commerce was a U.S. phenomenon, these same sources estimate that more than half of all online sales will take place outside the United States by 2004.

Business-to-business (B2B) e-commerce involves one business providing another business with the materials and supplies it needs to conduct its operations. You don't read much about this type of e-commerce because, as one writer put it, "A story about companies bidding against one another for contracts to supply nuts and bolts to create agricultural machinery is not hot copy." However, the numbers show that B2B e-commerce has a much greater impact on the economy than the B2C variety: B2B e-commerce is expected to grow from $92 billion in 1998 to $2.0 trillion in 2004.

Although much B2B e-commerce currently takes place directly between a business and its suppliers, B2B Internet exchanges are being developed to provide electronic marketplaces for buyers and sellers in a number of industries. For example, the big three U.S. automakers (GM, Ford, and Chrysler) are backing an exchange for auto industry suppliers. On a smaller scale, an exchange based in Orlando, Florida, provides a site for suppliers of fresh cut flowers to market their wares to florists (Figure 9-6). Advantages for buyers include reduced costs of procurement and the ability to consider a larger number of suppliers. Possible problems include security—a hacker attack on a major B2B exchange could bring an entire industry to its knees—and antitrust concerns that the exchanges could lead to price fixing within an industry.

► TRAFFIC JAMS

The Internet was not planned for its current users. The original Internet was a low-speed, text-based network designed to send messages among a few government sites and the research and defense contracting communities. No one then envisioned today's millions of users, some surfing for hours at a time and downloading high-

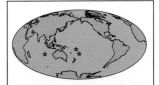

What's in a Name?
All the good names are taken! The .com domain names, that is. Everyone starting an e-business wants a .com domain name—that's where all the e-commerce action is. Sparked by a demand for good, easy-to-remember names, cybersquatters have been snapping up .com names for several years, hoping to sell them for a big profit. If you can come up with a snappy name that nobody has registered, you could become rich. After all, somebody sold business.com for $7.5 million in November 1999. America.com is up for sale at $10 million, and celebrity.com for only $2 million—with no takers for either, as yet.

If those prices are too rich for you and you can't think of a useful name that's not already taken (over 98 percent of the words in Webster's dictionary are registered), try a name that uses the two-character country top-level domain names.

HOME   INFORMATION   COMMUNITY   MARKETPLACE   SUPPORT   SIGNUP

MY ACCOUNT   LOGIN   WELCOME | WELKOM | BIENVENUE | WILKOMMEN | BIENVENIDO

Marketplace

Overview
Tradelink
FPN
SPN
Floramall
Florashops

Seminars
Consulting
Group Lessons
Keynote Speaker

In a marketplace revolutionized by the Internet, many believe business-to-business e-commerce will be the centerpiece of future company models. World Commerce Online, owner of Floraplex, is banking on it. It's the first company to market a global "b to b" network to the floral industry.

▶ Account Summary

Floraplex™ members who utilize the Marketplace can receive all their invoices, orders awaiting their attention, sales history, purchase history, and more by using our one-stop Account Summary Page.

[Account Summary]

The Flower Purchase Network FPN allows buyers to negotiate directly with the growers, the FPN system provides growers an opportunity to expand their markets and increase profits quickly and efficiently. Users will buy from Holland, Africa and Israel with service through the Dutch Auctions and from South and North America with service through self-provided logistics providers. Current Tradelink users Click Here

The Supply Purchase Network SPN is an e-commerce trading exchange within the Floraplex marketplace where manufacturers and suppliers of nonperishable products can sell to customers worldwide.

▲ F I G U R E 9·6

B2B Web site.
Floraplex is a B2B exchange that facilitates transactions between buyers and sellers of floral products.

volume multimedia data. The Internet is a victim of its own success, its arteries so clogged that a user often crawls and stutters through cyberspace.

The "speed problem," as it is succinctly known, hangs like a cloud over all Internet transactions. A casual user may be merely annoyed by a delay as a site downloads. For serious users sending high volumes of data, the problem can be crippling. The speed problem affects every aspect of business on the Internet. Large companies that establish Internet sites on servers capable of handling thousands of concurrent visitors usually have a direct, high-speed connection to the Internet consisting of expensive T1, or even T3, leased lines. Smaller businesses have the option of connecting their server through an ISP using slower circuits or paying a company that has a high-speed connection to host their site. The choice would depend on the number of visitors expected and the activity generated.

Numerous solutions to the speed problem have been proposed. Still more are on the drawing table. Most solutions are aimed at increasing **bandwidth,** the measure of the data transfer capacity of a communications link. The idea is to expand "the pipes" so that more data can flow through. Some speedy alternatives to a 56 Kbps modem (discussed in Chapter 7) are satellite, ISDN, DSL and its variations, and cable modem (Table 9-1).

Satellite transmission is wireless and widely available. But this method is expensive and may be clogged during peak hours. **Integrated Services Digital Network,** usually known by its acronym, **ISDN,** transmits data at up to 128,000 bps. **Digital subscriber line (DSL)** service is up to 10 times faster than ISDN, but requires the user to be near a telephone company central office and to have copper wiring in place. In some areas the cable TV system is available for data transmission using **cable modems** at even higher speeds than DSL.

The speed problem is complicated by the fact that the Internet comprises many communication links, and no one "fix" can affect them all. The major links that tie servers across wide geographical areas are called the **backbone** of the Internet. Links that form the backbone may bear well-known commercial names, such as Sprint and MCI WorldCom, or names you might not know, such as CAIS and Exodus, and are noted for significant bandwidth. Suppose, however, that many users increase their home-access bandwidth. Widespread use of high-speed home-access systems will place even more demands on the backbone, and that could, in turn, slow everyone's access to the system. So far, though, advances in technology and investment in new facilities have allowed backbone capacity to increase at least as fast as demand. Whether this will continue is the subject of much debate.

Part of the reason for Internet congestion, and thus slower speeds, is that people have not been charged on the basis of their usage of the Internet. In forum after forum, experts predict that users are going to have to pay for Internet use. A heavy user, it is thought, should pay more than an occasional browser. Economists assert

TABLE 9-1	Internet Connection Options		
Connection	**Download Time, 10MB file**	**Pros**	**Cons**
56K modem	23 min.	In place now	Slow Must dial up
ISDN	10 min.	Easy to get Instant connection	Requires new equipment
DSL	50 sec.	Standard phone lines Simultaneous phone calls Always on	Limited availability Requires copper wire
Cable modem	20 sec.	Doesn't use phone line Simple, inexpensive setup Always on	Limited availability Expensive for business Neighborhood shares capacity
Satellite	3 min.	No wires Doubles as TV dish	Must buy dish Expensive hardware/service Slow at peak hours

GETTING PRACTICAL | Setting Up a Web Site

If you were setting up a physical store (commonly referred to as "bricks and mortar" to distinguish it from a retail Web site), you would need merchandise and sales-people. But that is just the beginning. You must have some mechanism for customers to gather merchandise to purchase; they may simply hold the goods in their hands, but a shopping cart is common. You must supply some way of charging customers—cash, check, credit card. You probably want to be able to ship goods to customers if they phone in an order.

A retail Web site, also referred to as a Web storefront, has similar activities, but they are handled in a different way, a way that is suitable to the physical gap between store and customer. You may have the expertise to set up a simple Web page, but including the software to handle sales transactions is much more complex. Fortunately, user-friendly "storefront" software can handle all aspects of a Web site retail operation.

A good example is iCAT Commerce Online, whose Chef's Catalog, customers are shown here. These are some of the functions that iCAT will handle:

- Create a storefront Web site that looks professional. This might not include fancy graphics or fonts, but it does mean that your site will be free of typos, easy to navigate, and clearly laid out.

- Set up an order- and payment-processing system. This includes letting customers add merchandise to their "shopping cart" and accepting payment by credit card in a secure environment.

- Market your site. To make sales, you need traffic. iCAT will see that you are listed with the major search engines.

Storefront software helps you get started by offering easy-to-use templates, basically fill-in-the-blank screens that the software converts to a site. You visit the company's Web site, fill in the options you want, and enter your product information. With iCAT there is no risk because there is a free trial period.

You may be interested in what iCAT considers the "hot" categories of online best-sellers in the immediate future. They include personal care products; sports paraphernalia; music-related theme merchandise; health- and nutrition-related products; home furnishing products; auto repair and home repair products; and patterned sets of china, glass, and silverware.

---

that, as in other segments of society, if people do not pay for what they consume, there will be no economic incentive to keep building the Internet.

Streaming

Perhaps the most notable bandwidth user is **streaming,** the downloading of active audio, video, and animation content. Users can hear and see the digitized content even as it is still being downloaded. Streamed sound and images usually appear via a browser plug-in, letting streaming begin within seconds of a user's click. But the price of that convenience is quality. Transmitting voluminous amounts of video and audio content over the network presents a serious bandwidth challenge, and the results are usually less than satisfactory. Still, it really is something to get even a limited version of radio and television capability on your computer. As with all aspects of data traveling over a network, performance will improve as bandwidth problems are alleviated.

A popular plug-in is RealPlayer, which can be downloaded free from the RealNetworks site (Figure 9-7a). Once you have downloaded and installed an audio-video plug-in into your browser, you can start streaming from sites that offer such data. Start with the free samples from the plug-in's Web site. Then move to other sites that specialize in video and sound.

One well-known site is Yahoo!Events, which presents live radio and some canned television shows (Figure 9-7b). When you indicate by a click that you want to receive some sort of streaming data, the site that has the data will immediately check your

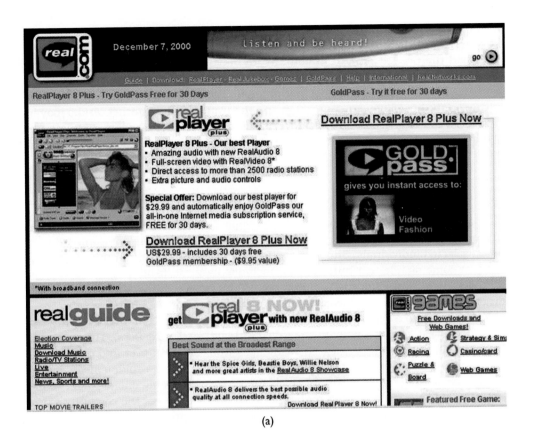

(a)

(b)

FIGURE 9-7

RealPlayer and Yahoo!Events.

(a) RealPlayer is a popular browser plug-in (add-on software) that can be downloaded free and then used to accept streaming—live—audio and video on your computer. (b) The site called Yahoo!Events presents live radio and video event coverage, as well as prerecorded audio and video events.

E-Speak

Just like any other specialized area, e-commerce has developed its own jargon. A few of the terms you might hear when talking with the movers and shakers of the e-business world are defined below:

● **Angel:** A wealthy private investor who is willing to provide financial backing to a start-up company.

● **Clicks and mortar:** A bricks-and-mortar company that develops an online operation.

● **First-mover advantage:** The advantage that goes to whoever gets their Web site online first, beating their competitors to the punch.

● **Gray-hairs:** Experienced executives hired by entrepreneurs to run the day-to-day operations of the business.

● **Halo effect:** The prestige and credibility gained by a start-up that receives funding from a prominent venture capitalist.

● **NDA:** Non-disclosure agreement—what you have someone sign so that you can discuss your plans without having them revealed to others.

● **OPM:** Other people's money. Using OPM keeps some entrepreneurs from worrying too much about failing.

● **Stealth mode:** Keeping your business plan a secret so that you can achieve the first-mover advantage.

browser for an audio-video plug-in. If you have none, it will tell you so and, most likely, give you an icon to click so that you can head to the appropriate site and download the needed plug-in. If you already have the plug-in, it will immediately spring into action in a separate window on your screen. In short order, you will hear or see, or perhaps both, the data you ordered. The quality you receive will depend greatly on the speed of your connection and the traffic on the Internet. Audio may be quite clear and could often be mistaken for an actual radio broadcast. Video can be herky-jerky for users other than those with very speedy connections. However, even these limited offerings can give a sense of the future of streaming media.

Multicasting

Suppose you work for a company that develops documentary packages. You have written a report that should be seen not by everyone in the company—only by a few dozen selected individuals. Suppose, further, that your computer-produced report is not just some simple text but, instead, includes bandwidth-hogging items such as graphics, sounds, and video clips. How would you proceed to send the report to the designated recipients over the company's computer network?

You could send a separate copy from your computer to the computer of each recipient on your list, one at a time; this is called **unicasting** (Figure 9-8a). This approach would waste bandwidth because the same files would be sent over and over, first to your company's server and then back out to the recipient. You could, instead, opt for **broadcast mode** (Figure 9-8b), in which the server sends only one copy of the file, but it is sent to every computer on the network, whether or not the computer's user should receive it. This too is wasteful—and possibly compromises security by placing the report in the hands of inappropriate people.

There is a third, and better, solution. **Multicasting** sends just one copy of each file and delivers it only to designated recipients (Figure 9-8c). Now expand the picture and imagine the impact of multicasting over the entire Internet. Multicasting network technology can reduce data traffic by delivering a single stream of data to thousands of recipients over whatever bandwidth is available. NASA space shuttle launchings and Rolling Stones concerts were some early multicasting events.

Push Technology

Businesses large and small have embraced the Internet. But businesses can find the Internet frustrating because they must sit idly by, so to speak, and hope that users will visit their sites. That is, in the jargon of the trade, they await users to *pull* data from their sites. The answer to this problem is the opposite approach: push technology.

Think of it this way: *Pull* is like going to the newsstand to pick up a paper; *push* is like having the paper delivered to your door. More precisely, **push technology** refers to software that automatically sends—pushes—information from the Internet to a user's personal computer. From the sender's point of view, this process is akin to TV broadcasting, so push technology is sometimes called **webcasting.** Proponents laud push technology as a time-saver for users: Instead of browsing and searching the Internet for what you want, customized information is gathered up for you from various sites and sent to you automatically. Detractors view push technology in less flattering terms, seeing it as marketing hype that will clog the Internet with frivolous graphics and unwanted advertising.

The pushing, however, begins only with the consent of the recipient. The concept was pioneered by PointCast, Inc., which has since been acquired by EntryPoint. It works like this: You download the free push software from the company's Web site and install it. Then, using the software, you select "channels" that you want to receive. The list of channels includes generic titles such as sports and business and brand names such as CNN and the *New York Times*. You can narrow your selections

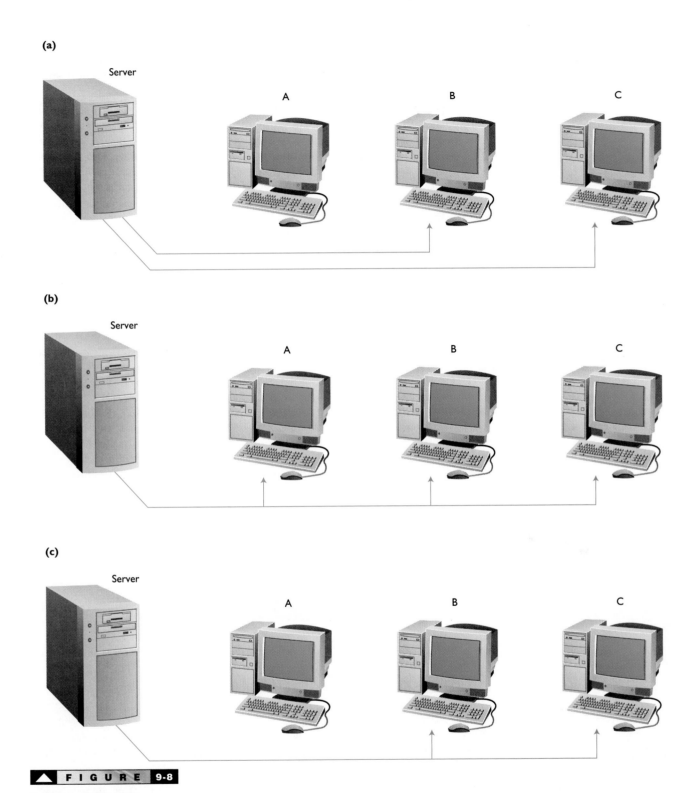

▲ **FIGURE** 9-8

Freeing up bandwidth.

(a) Wasteful: In the unicast model, the server sends multiple copies of the same multimedia stream, one to each designated user—in this case, users B and C. (b) Perhaps better, depending on the total number of users: In the broadcast model, the server sends one copy of the multimedia stream, dropping it off to every user on the network, whether or not they should receive it, in this case users A, B, and C. (c) Best: In the multicast model, the server sends one copy of the multimedia stream, delivering it only to designated users B and C.

further within the channels. Then the push software goes out to the Internet and retrieves, from various sites, information—and ads—related to your declared interests. These are presented on your screen, complete with stock quotes and sports scores flowing across the bottom of the screen, if desired.

This concept works best for users who have a permanent connection via the office computer network. The information is downloaded to a corporate server and then relayed to employees. News and information are updated throughout the day. For people using the software on a personal computer at home, the service can push information to you only when your computer is connected to the Internet. You click the push software's update button whenever you want the latest information; the push software will dial a connection, gather information from the Internet, disconnect itself, then display the new information on your screen. The software can even be set to connect and update automatically at regular intervals. Both the software and the information-gathering service are free. You must, of course, have the ability to connect to the Internet.

Push technology has been criticized in some quarters as being too bandwidth-hungry. In fact, some businesses have prohibited their employees from signing up for push technology. To address this concern, PointCast switched to a multicast model, sending files down the line just once for all users on the same server.

▶ INTRANETS

Although many businesses use the Internet to promote their products and services to the public, they are finding that an even more useful application is for their internal—company-only—purposes, hence the intranet.

Vendors promoting their intranet software products in magazine advertisements often make a play on the word—perhaps InTRAnet or even Intranet. They do not

---

▶ MAKING CONNECTIONS ◀ Buying a Car Online

The Internet has changed the way in which many people buy a new car. Although fewer than 1 percent of auto sales in 2000 were done completely over the Internet, J.D. Powers & Associates estimates that over 60 percent of car buyers use the Internet for research and price comparison. Many prospective buyers visit the manufacturers' Web sites for basic information, but most go to independent sites such as cars.com, autobytel.com, and Autoweb.com for the details.

So what strategy should you use in your search for that perfect car? If you know the make and model you want, start with the manufacturer's Web site first. If not, you might want to investigate the Web sites of magazines such as *Car & Driver, Road & Track,* or *Consumer Reports* for articles comparing and evaluating various vehicles. Once you have narrowed your search, you can visit the Web site of the

National Auto Dealer's Association (NADA) to determine the invoice prices that the dealer pays the manufacturer for the cars you're interested in. You will probably also want to visit one of the independent Web sites mentioned above to see what dealer incentives and holdbacks (money held in reserve by the manufacturer until the dealer sells a car) apply to your chosen vehicle.

After arming yourself with this information, you have two choices. One is to head to your local dealership prepared to do battle with the sales-person to work out the best deal possible. If you don't feel that you could hold your own in negotiations, you can visit a Web site such as CarsDirect.com, which will guarantee you a price for your new car, then buy it from a dealer and deliver it directly to your home or workplace.

want you to think that they are simply misspelling "Internet." In fact, an **intranet** is a private Internet-like network that is internal to a certain company. The number of intranets has been growing rapidly. Every Fortune 500 company either has an intranet or is planning one. Part of the reason for the phenomenal growth is the relative ease of setting up an intranet.

Setting Up an Intranet

It's fast, it's easy, it's inexpensive—relatively speaking, of course. The components of an intranet are familiar ones: the same ones that are used for the Internet. Hardware requirements include a server and computers used for access. These probably exist because most companies already have local area networks; this is why setting up an intranet is fast, easy, and inexpensive. The Internet TCP/IP protocols must be in place. The server, which will act as a clearinghouse for all data regardless of source, needs its own software. The server will process requests and also perhaps pull data from traditional sources such as a mainframe computer. As on the Internet, each access computer needs a browser.

The intranet developers will doubtless devote the most time and attention to writing the Web pages that employees will see and use. The pages must be well designed and easy to follow, opting for function over glitz. A typical opening page would probably have an attractive company logo and several clickable generic icons to represent functions. One click would lead to a more detailed page and so on. By presenting information in the same way to every computer, the developers can pull all the computers, software, and data files that dot the corporate landscape into a single system that helps employees find information wherever it resides.

Intranets at Work

A well-designed intranet can be used by most employees from day one. They can point and click and link to sites that contain information previously locked away behind functionaries and forms. Suppose, for example, that an employee needs to check on the status of her benefits. Traditionally, she would probably have to find the right form, fill it out correctly, submit it, and wait a few days for a response. Now all she has to do is point and click, give some identifying information such as Social Security number, and the information shows up on the screen and can be printed.

Employee information is just the beginning. Typical applications are internal job openings, marketing, vacation requests, corporate policy information, and perhaps company training courses. Some even include the local weather report and the daily cafeteria menu. Intranets even cut down on the flow of e-mail. Management can, instead of sending out mass e-mail to employees, post notices on a Web page and leave it to employees to check it regularly or use push technology to send information to them as needed.

The Internet Too

An intranet can remain private and isolated, but most companies choose to link their intranets to the Internet. This gives employees access to Internet resources and to other employees with their own intranets in geographically dispersed places. The employee access to the public Internet should not be confused with public access to the company intranet; the intranet is private.

However, companies may choose to provide access to their intranets to selected customers and suppliers. Such an arrangement is called an **extranet.** Some companies are finding that their long-standing relationships with customers and suppliers can be handled more easily and more inexpensively with an extranet than with more traditional electronic data interchange—EDI—systems.

◄► VIRTUAL PRIVATE NETWORKS

A **virtual private network (VPN)** provides technology that uses the public Internet as a channel for private data communication. A VPN essentially carves out a private passageway through the Internet. Thus a VPN allows remote offices, company road warriors, and even business partners or customers to use the Internet, rather than pricey private lines, to reach company networks. The idea of the VPN is to give the company the same capabilities at a much lower cost by sharing the public infrastructure.

Virtual private networks may be new, but the tunneling technology on which they are based is well established. **Tunneling,** also called **encapsulation,** is a way to transfer data between two similar networks over an intermediate network. Tunneling software encloses one type of data-packet protocol into the packet of another protocol. Although as yet there is no standard protocol for the packet that is doing the tunneling, Microsoft, 3Com, and several other companies have proposed a standard protocol called **Point-to-Point Tunneling Protocol (PPTP).** The original protocol, the one holding the tunnel, is the standard Internet TCP/IP protocol. Thus organizations can use the Internet to transmit data "privately" by embedding their own network protocol—PPTP technology—within the TCP/IP packets carried by the Internet.

VPN tunneling adds another dimension to the tunneling procedure. Before encapsulation takes place, the packets are encrypted—encoded—so that the data is unreadable to outsiders. The encapsulated packets travel through the Internet until they reach their destination; the packets are then separated and returned to their original format. Authentication technology is used to make sure the client has authorization to contact the server.

By replacing expensive private network bandwidth with relatively low-cost Internet bandwidth, a company can slash operating costs and simplify communications. No longer needed are the 800 lines and long-distance charges; employees simply place local or toll-free calls to Internet service providers (ISPs) to make the connection. VPNs also reduce in-house network management responsibilities because much of the remote communications burden is turned over to ISPs.

◄► CONSOLIDATION OF THE WEB

The World Wide Web started out as—and still is—a freewheeling environment in which anyone who could publish a Web page could participate. This participation meant that the Internet became the preferred medium for all kinds of ideological, political, cultural, and entertainment persuasions. A related notion is that the Internet is not owned by anyone; it is uncontrolled and uncontrollable.

But changes—business-related changes—have been in the wind for some time. The Internet, as it turns out, is not immune to the normal forces of consolidation, which bring efficiency and uniformity to new media and new industries. Indeed, the only thing different about the Web—a new trillion-dollar industry—is that the opportunities for consolidation are of such a large scale that it is occurring at warp speed, the Web's typical pace.

Ordinary Internet users first took notice of the consolidation process in 1999, when America Online bought Netscape. But less noticeable dealings have been proceeding apace. Although, for the great mass of consumers, the restructured Web will not look that different from prior communications media, a handful of well-known brands will determine the nature and content of the majority of what is seen and heard on a daily basis. The high-traffic, commercially viable sites will increasingly come into the hands of a few major conglomerates.

This process is not so different from what has happened in other industries in America. Mom-and-pop stores give way to regional and national chains. Then someone emerges to set a pace that everyone else must match—Wal-Mart Stores, Inc., in discount retailing or Blockbuster Entertainment in the video rental business. There always will be new players and lots of players. But there will also be defining players, players who consolidate. We cannot predict the players; we just know that they *are* there and they *will be* there—consolidating the Web.

▲

We have said that the Internet is interesting and fun, and it is. But it is much more than that. The Internet represents a new and important business model and, indeed, an entire new way of looking at industry and commerce.

CHAPTER REVIEW

▶ Summary and Key Terms

- The world of **electronic commerce,** or, more commonly, **e-commerce,** buying and selling over the Internet, represents a new economic order. Customers can buy just about anything on the Internet.

- Retail Web sites have begun adding **content** to attract visitors and boost sales.

- Some companies must settle for half measures in e-commerce because they fear that selling a product from their own Web site will alienate the sales representatives and stores with which they have established relationships.

- A Web site that is used as a gateway or guide to the Internet is called a **portal.** Portals and other sites collect money from **banner ads** and referrals to **affiliate** sites.

- Users who leave the current site for an advertised site are said to **click through;** to get business from users who will not click through, a **live banner,** which lets a user get more information about a product without leaving the current site, may be used.

- The most effective Web advertisements are **context-sensitive;** that is, the ad is related to the subject matter on the screen.

- E-commerce payments by credit card are probably safe over a secure server, especially if the site uses the **Secure Sockets Layer (SSL)** protocol.

- The **Internet Tax Freedom Act** imposed a three-year moratorium (which began in October 1998) on taxes imposed on the Internet and called for a committee to study the matter. The **Internet Non-Discrimination Act** extended the moratorium until 2005.

- Some primary entrepreneurial success factors are content, uniqueness, self-help, and community.

- **Business-to-consumer (B2C)** e-commerce refers to retail transactions between an online business and an individual. **Business-to-business (B2B)** e-commerce involves one business providing another business with the materials and supplies that it needs to conduct its operations.

- Numerous solutions to the speed problem have been proposed. Most solutions are aimed at increasing **bandwidth,** the measure of the capacity of a communications link. Satellite transmission, **Integrated Services Digital Network (ISDN), digital subscriber line (DSL)** service, and **cable modems** all provide faster access than standard modems, but cost more and might not be available at some sites.

- The major links that tie servers across wide geographical areas are called the **backbone** of the Internet.

- **Streaming** is the downloading of live audio, video, and animation content.

- **Unicasting** sends a copy of the data file from the server to the computer of each designated recipient. In **broadcast mode,** the server sends only one copy of the file, but it is sent to every computer on the network. **Multicasting** sends just one copy of each file and drops it off only with appropriate recipients.

- **Push technology,** also called **webcasting,** refers to software that automatically sends—pushes—information from the Internet to a user's personal computer.

- An **intranet** is a private Internet-like network that is internal to a specific company.

- An **extranet** provides customers and suppliers access to a company's intranet.

- A **virtual private network (VPN)** provides technology that uses the public Internet backbone as a channel for private data communication. **Tunneling,** also called **encapsulation,** is a way to transfer data between two similar networks over an intermediate network by enclosing one type of data packet protocol into the packet of another protocol. **Point-to-Point Tunneling Protocol (PPTP)** is a standard tunneling protocol.

► Critical Thinking Questions

1. Some established companies fret over whether or not to offer their goods and services over the Internet, possibly in competition with their traditional outlets. If the decision were up to you, at what point might you go forward with a complete retail site?

2. Consider an Internet business site that could be started by an entrepreneur. Some possibilities are for a series of children's books, an invention that instantly melts snow on sidewalks, or the rental of a small getaway cabin—or consider a business of your own choice. How would you introduce the success factors of content, uniqueness, self-help, and community into your Web site?

3. If you were on the committee decreed by the Internet Tax Freedom Act, what recommendations might you make about imposing taxes on Internet use? Do you see any comparisons with taxes that are already imposed on telephone use?

4. Sites that are heavy with graphics take longer to load than graphics-light sites. That is, a visitor must wait longer to view a graphics-rich site. Multimedia sites that include movement and sound take even longer to load. Which of these types of sites may be able to justify making visitors wait a bit longer to see the site: corporate presence, major retail, small entrepreneur, charitable organization, product demonstration, Web site designers, entertainment, personal home page, and games. Finally, how long should a visitor be expected to wait? How long are you personally willing to wait for a site to show up on your screen? Should the length of a reasonable wait time vary with the type of site?

5. What is your opinion of the advertisements that frequently appear on Web sites? The answer is not as simple as it may first appear. Keep in mind that just as commercials pay for free television, Web advertisements pay for the Internet. In answering this question, ignore the access fees—cable or satellite fees for television and ISP or online service fees for the Internet. In other words, would you be willing to pay a small fee every time that you visit a site that contains no advertisements? How do you think these fees would be charged and collected?

6. One of the important communication aspects of Internet commerce is the SSL protocol. What do the letters represent, and why is this protocol so important when making online purchases?

7. What does the term *streaming* mean when referring to media files such as audio or animation/video? What are the advantages and disadvantages of streaming media files compared to downloading these files? Name a "player" that can be used to listen to or watch streamed files. Have you ever heard or seen a streamed media file? If you have, comment on the audio and video quality of the media.

8. Some businesses, organizations, and educational institutions place information about themselves on the Internet as well as on their company, organizational, or institutional intranets. Describe the types of information that a company, organization, or institution might place on their Internet site, and the types of information that they would place on their intranet. Does your school use the Internet and have an intranet? If it has an intranet, can students, faculty, and staff access it from both on-campus computers as well as from off-campus computers?

▶ Student Study Guide

Multiple Choice

1. Another name for tunneling is
   a. portal
   b. cabling
   c. encapsulation
   d. bandwidth

2. Sending a file repeatedly, once for each recipient, is called
   a. webcasting
   b. unicasting
   c. broadcasting
   d. multicasting

3. The fastest communications link is via
   a. a cable modem
   b. a satellite
   c. a 56 K modem
   d. ISDN

4. Downloading live audio, video, and animation is called
   a. tunneling
   b. unicasting
   c. cabling
   d. streaming

5. Software that automatically sends information from the Internet to the user employs
   a. an affiliate
   b. a banner
   c. push technology
   d. an extranet

6. Which is *not* a key success factor for an entrepreneurial Web site?
   a. content
   b. uniqueness
   c. community
   d. streaming

7. A Web site that is used as a gateway or guide to the Internet is a(n)
   a. portal
   b. backbone
   c. ISDN
   d. extranet

8. The term that is used to describe the major communication circuits that link servers across wide geographical areas is
   a. encapsulation
   b. backbone
   c. tunneling
   d. e-commerce

9. A technology that uses the public Internet backbone as a channel for private data communications is known as
   a. e-commerce
   b. DSL
   c. VPN
   d. ISDN

10. DSL stands for
    a. digital subscriber line
    b. digital stream line
    c. digital self-help line
    d. digital service line

11. Users who leave the current site by clicking on a banner ad are said to
    a. push
    b. tunnel
    c. stream
    d. click through

12. When a single file is sent and delivered only to designated recipients, this is called
    a. broadcasting
    b. multicasting
    c. unicasting
    d. webcasting

13. An advertisement that is related to what is currently showing on the Web page is called
    a. encapsulation
    b. context-sensitive
    c. a portal
    d. the backbone

14. To attract visitors and increase sales, many retail sites have added
    a. VPN
    b. backbone
    c. content
    d. context

15. The measure of the capacity of a communication link is called its
    a. content
    b. transmission
    c. DSL
    d. bandwidth

16. When a computer sends just one copy of a file but delivers it to every computer on the network, whether or not the latter is a designated recipient, the sending computer is said to be
    a. unicasting
    b. multicasting
    c. webcasting
    d. broadcasting

17. A private Internet-like network within a company is called a(n)
    a. intranet
    b. extranet
    c. virtual private network
    d. ISDN

18. The general term for buying and selling on the Internet is
    a. click through
    b. e-commerce
    c. wholesale
    d. streaming

19. A network that allows a company's customers and suppliers to access it is called a(n)
    a. extranet
    b. VPN
    c. portal
    d. DSL

20. The type of e-commerce in which a business sells to individual consumers is
    a. B2I
    b. B2C
    c. B2B
    d. affiliate

True/False

T F 1. Bandwidth is the measure of the capacity of a communications link.
T F 2. Retail Web sites, by law, cannot include content other than products and services.
T F 3. Two companies associated with the Internet backbone are DSL and ISDN.
T F 4. An intranet is a public network and an extranet is a private network.
T F 5. Multicasting sends one copy of each file to every user on the network.
T F 6. A cable modem is slower than a traditional modem.
T F 7. A live banner ad lets a user see advertised information without leaving the current site.
T F 8. Encapsulation is related to virtual private network technology.
T F 9. Push technology is also called multicasting.
T F 10. E-commerce means downloading government-related Web sites.
T F 11. An ad that is related to the subject matter on the screen is said to be context-sensitive.
T F 12. Streaming is downloading live audio, video, and animation.
T F 13. One cost of establishing a Web site is the physical requirement for "bricks and mortar."
T F 14. E-commerce sites display their wares but do not permit actual purchases of goods via the Internet.
T F 15. Retail Web sites usually offer extra material, called content, that is totally unrelated to the product or service they sell.
T F 16. Some companies are nervous about actually selling a product or service on a Web site for fear of alienating their established contacts with stores and sales representatives.
T F 17. Items that are offered for sale via Web sites are limited to nonperishable goods such as CDs, books, and cameras.

T F 18. An affiliate site shares the profit from a sale with the site that made the referral.

T F 19. One problem with banner ads is that users are often reluctant to leave the current site to go to the advertised site.

T F 20. If a user invokes a search engine with the words "vacation" and "Maui" and the next screen includes a banner ad for a hotel in Maui, the ad is said to be context-sensitive.

T F 21. The most important success factor for an entrepreneurial Web site is the use of sophisticated graphics.

T F 22. When a Web site is visited, the advertisements are usually among the first elements to appear on the screen.

T F 23. A portal site has many offerings, mostly to encourage visitors to use that portal site as their guide to the Internet.

T F 24. B2B e-commerce has a much larger dollar volume than B2C e-commerce.

T F 25. An intranet allows a company's customers and suppliers to have access to the network.

Fill-In

1. The major links that tie Internet servers across wide geographical areas are called collectively the _____.

2. Another name for webcasting is _____.

3. Downloading live audio, video, and animation is called _____.

4. The capacity of a communications link is measured as its _____.

5. Sending the same file to everyone on the network is known as _____.

6. VPN stands for _____.

7. A private Internetlike network that is internal to a certain company is called a(n) _____.

8. An ad that matches the subject matter on the screen is said to be _____.

9. In the context of a VPN, another word for encapsulation is _____.

10. Sending just one copy of a file and delivering it only to designated recipients is called _____.

11. Portal sites collect money from sites to which they refer visitors; these sites are called _____.

12. Users who leave the current site to go to an advertised site are said to _____.

13. The short name for electronic commerce is _____.

14. When a computer sends a separate file to each designated recipient, this is known as _____.

15. To attract visitors, retail Web sites have added extra interesting information, called _____.

16. A Web site that is used as a gateway or guide to the Internet is called a(n) _____.

17. The primary entrepreneurial Web site success factors are
    a. _____.
    b. _____.
    c. _____.
    d. _____.

► Answers

Multiple Choice

1. c	6. d	11. d	16. d
2. b	7. a	12. b	17. a
3. a	8. b	13. b	18. b
4. d	9. c	14. c	19. a
5. c	10. a	15. d	20. b

True/False

1. T	8. T	14. F	20. T
2. F	9. F	15. F	21. F
3. F	10. F	16. T	22. T
4. F	11. T	17. F	23. T
5. F	12. T	18. T	24. T
6. F	13. F	19. T	25. F
7. T			

Fill-In

1. backbone
2. push technology
3. streaming
4. bandwidth
5. broadcasting
6. virtual private network
7. intranet
8. context-sensitive
9. tunneling
10. multicasting
11. affiliates
12. click through
13. e-commerce
14. unicasting
15. content
16. portal
17. a. content
    b. uniqueness
    c. self-help
    d. community

Planet Internet

Shopping Tour

Shopping conveniences have existed since catalogs were invented. Convenience is at a high point today because computer shopping offers goods and services handily bundled together.

Consolidation continues among the various shopping sites on the Web, with many sites opening and closing within a year, as often happens with small bricks-and-mortar businesses. While you may be interested in finding the absolute cheapest price for your product for a one-time purchase, you might want to consider paying a little more to support a site offering products you would like to purchase regularly in the future. (Again, just as you might support a local bricks-and-mortar specialty shop). If you really just want the best price, there are specialized price-comparison search engines, such as PriceWatch and Buy.com.

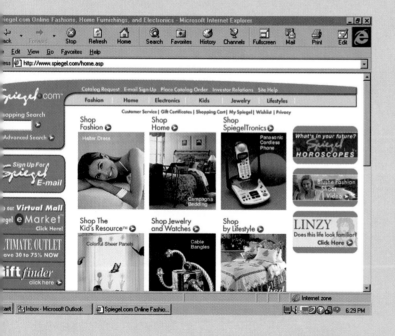

Electronic mall or specialty site? You know your shopping needs best. You can shop directly from AOL or Amazon for a wide variety of products. Your favorite mail order catalog may now have a Web site, which they update on a weekly basis to keep it current. If you don't know what's available on the Web, start with a search engine request, or check out vendor links on your favorite hobby Web site.

Is on-line shopping safe and secure? First, check to see if your site states that it handles secure transactions. If so, shoppers generally have few problems. Most major credit cards guarantee you the same "stolen number limits" as with any other credit card purchase. However, many sites also provide you with a phone number or even a printable mail order form if you feel more comfortable with either of those methods. Most now offer order confirmation and receipts via e-mail, and some will follow up with a hardcopy receipt. Your instructor could order reprints of a *Harvard Business Review* Case for the class, as a downloadable file, receive e-mail confirmation and a harcdopy receipt in the mail a week or so later. Web sites that expect to keep your business should provide accurate information about back-orders, shipping delays, and the like.

What about shipping charges and sales tax? Sites that offer goods at essentially the same basic price may differ greatly in shipping charges. There may be a minimum $10 shipping charge even for a $5 purchase (and if that's the only way to obtain your daughter's favorite stuffed toy for her birthday, you may be willing to pay $15 for a $5 toy). Not all specialized price comparison search engines include shipping charges in their charts, so be sure to check before purchasing. Some companies regularly collect sales tax, while many do not. The federal government has not decided how best to handle sales tax issues on the Internet on a national basis. Of course, you are responsible for state and local taxes as specified by your locale.

Do online merchants have special discounts for specific categories of customers, as happens sometimes with mail-order catalogs? It's possible, but it's likely that most will clearly specify the criteria for discounts and promotions as a result of the Amazon "pricing experiment." Amazon conducted a pricing experiment that was discovered by users and widely published, where the same customer pricing the same product at a different time of the day or using a different username was quoted (and sometimes charged) widely differing prices. Amazon refunded the difference between the lowest price and the sales price to affected customers and assured customers they would not conduct similar pricing experiments in the future.

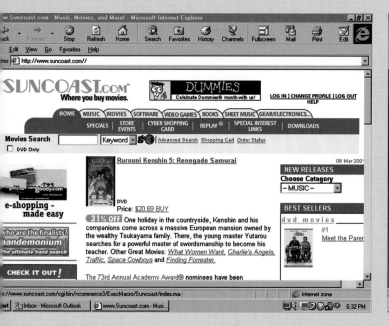

1. **Structured exercise.** Go to http://www.pren
   hall.com/capron, and use the links there to
   compare prices for a product using the specialized price-comparison sites provided.

2. **Freeform exercise.** Compare the price for a
   specified item on popular auction sites to the
   price for the same merchandise on another
   e-commerce site. What do you see as the most
   important differences between buying at auction
   sites versus buying from other e-commerce
   sites? Things to consider include price, availability, how long it takes to receive the item, payment and shipping options and security.

3. **Advanced exercise.** Working alone or with a
   group, make a short shopping list of familiar
   items. Compare prices and ease of shopping
   using an on-line retailer with those at local
   stores where you regularly shop. Be sure to log
   the time spent gathering information on-line and
   from the local stores (or from their sales flyers).
   Don't forget to include shipping and sales tax as
   appropriate.

Planet Internet

The Continuing Story of
the Computer Age:
Past, Present, and Future

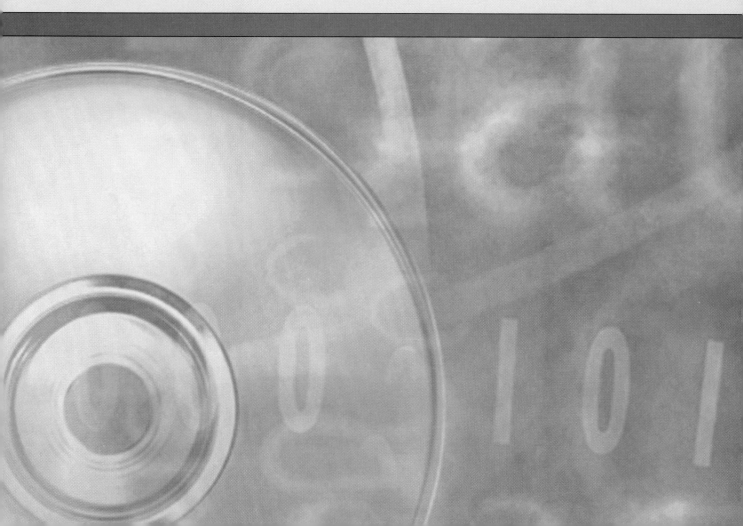

The Continuing Story of the Computer Age:
Past, Present, and Future

A P P E N D I X

LEARNING OBJECTIVES

Describe the generations of computer design leading up to the present

Describe the story of personal computer development

Explain the underlying concepts and terms of artificial intelligence

Explain the fundamentals of expert systems, robotics, and virtual reality

Give examples of the impact these fields have on business and everyday life

Anita Devine taught computer classes at Jackson Community College and worked on her master's degree in computer science on the side. She became quite interested in the artificial intelligence (AI) classes she was taking and thought her own students would be interested too. She did not want to teach a full-blown AI class but calculated that she could assemble an interesting introductory class that, for two Saturday sessions, would count as one credit.

Anita got the class approved. She then encouraged enrollment by posting flyers noting that there were no prerequisites and that the class included a demonstration of a home-built robot. She anticipated a good deal of interest and arranged for a large classroom but was amazed when 247 students enrolled. One of them was Alex Martinez, who was majoring in computer information systems. He figured it could not hurt to have a class called Introduction to Artificial Intelligence on his résumé. Rather to his surprise, he enjoyed the class and came away with some idea of what artificial intelligence was all about.

Eighteen months later, as he was interviewing for his first job, Alex was startled to hear the interviewer say, "I see that you took an artificial intelligence class. Do you know what an expert system is?" Alex's first impulse was to protest that he really knew nothing at all about artificial intelligence, that it was just a little nothing class, but then—all this was in less than 10 seconds—he remembered what an expert system is. So he said, as calmly as possible, "An expert system is a computer system that lets the computer be an expert on some topic." The interviewer responded, "Well, you probably know more than I do."

As it happened, one of the groups managed by this interviewer had just been tagged to develop an expert system for an insurance waiver process. The AI professionals were already in place, but some other technical folks were needed as a supporting cast. To his stunned delight, Alex was hired and added to the team. He was no more than a gofer for a while, but it became an interesting experience. By the end of a year he had moved within the company to a more traditional programming environment. But Alex remained bemused that artificial intelligence had been his ticket in the door.

► THE COMPUTER AGE BEGINS

The remarkable thing about the computer age is that so much has happened in so short a time. We have leapfrogged through four generations of technology in about 50 years—a span of time whose events are within the memory of many people today. The first three computer "generations" are pinned to three technological developments: the vacuum tube, the transistor, and the integrated circuit. Each has drastically changed the nature of computers. We define the timing of each generation according to the beginning of commercial delivery of the hardware technology. Defining subsequent generations has become more complicated because the entire industry has become more complicated.

The First Generation, 1951–1958: The Vacuum Tube

The beginning of the commercial computer age can be dated to June 14, 1951. This was the day the first **UNIVAC—Universal Automatic Computer**—was delivered to a client, the U.S. Bureau of the Census, for use in tabulating the previous year's census. The date also marked the first time that a computer had been built for a business application rather than for military, scientific, or engineering use. The UNIVAC was really the ENIAC in disguise and was, in fact, built by Mauchly and Eckert, who in 1947 had formed their own corporation.

In the first generation, **vacuum tubes**—electronic tubes about the size of light bulbs—were used as the internal computer components (Figure A-1). However, because thousands of such tubes were required, they generated a great deal of heat, causing many problems in temperature regulation and climate control. In addition, although all the tubes had to be working simultaneously, they were subject to frequent burnout, and the people operating the computer often did not know whether the problem was in the programming or in the machine.

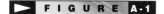
► FIGURE A-1

Vacuum tubes.

Vacuum tubes were used in the first generation of computers.

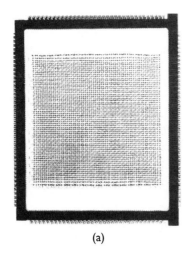
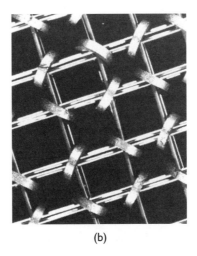

(a)   (b)

◄ **F I G U R E** **A-2**

Magnetic cores.

(a) A 6- by 11-inch magnetic core memory. (b) Close-up of magnetic core memory. A few hundredths of an inch in diameter, each magnetic core was mounted on wires. When electricity passed through a wire on which a core was strung, the core could be magnetized as either on or off.

Another drawback was that the language used in programming was machine language, which uses numbers. (Present-day higher-level languages are more like English.) Using numbers alone made programming the computer difficult and time-consuming. The UNIVAC used **magnetic cores** to provide memory. These consisted of small, doughnut-shaped rings about the size of pinheads, which were strung like beads on intersecting thin wires (Figure A-2). To supplement primary storage, first-generation computers stored data on punched cards. In 1957 magnetic tape was introduced as a faster, more compact method of storing data.

The Second Generation, 1959–1964: The Transistor

In 1947 three Bell Lab scientists—John Bardeen, Walter H. Brattain, and William Shockley—developed the **transistor,** a small device that transfers electronic signals across a resistor. (The name "transistor" began as a trademark concocted from "transfer" plus "resistor.") The scientists later received the Nobel Prize in Physics for their invention. The transistor revolutionized electronics in general and computers in particular. Transistors were much smaller than vacuum tubes, and they had numerous other advantages: They needed no warm-up time, consumed less energy, generated much less heat, and were faster and more reliable. In the late 1950s transistors were incorporated into computers.

During this generation another important development was the move from machine language to **assembly languages,** also called **symbolic languages.** Assembly languages use abbreviations for instructions (for example, L for LOAD) rather than numbers. This made programming less cumbersome.

After the development of symbolic languages came **high-level languages,** such as FORTRAN (1954) and COBOL (1959). Also, in 1962 the first removable disk pack was marketed. Disk storage supplemented magnetic tape systems and enabled users to have fast access to desired data.

Throughout this period computers were being used principally by business, university, and government organizations. They had not filtered down to the general public. The real part of the revolution was about to begin.

The Third Generation, 1965–1970: The Integrated Circuit

One of the most abundant elements in the earth's crust is silicon, a nonmetallic substance that is found in common beach sand as well as in practically all rocks and clay. The importance of this element to Santa Clara County, which is about 30 miles south of San Francisco, is responsible for the county's nickname: Silicon Valley. In 1965 Silicon Valley became the principal site for the manufacture of the so-called silicon chip: the integrated circuit.

An **integrated circuit (IC)** is a complete electronic circuit on a small chip of silicon. In 1965 integrated circuits began to replace transistors in computers. The

The Computer Museum

The Computer Museum in downtown Boston, Massachusetts, is the world's first museum devoted solely to computers and computing. The museum shows how computers have affected all aspects of life: science, business, education, art, and entertainment. Over half an acre of hands-on and historical exhibits, the museum chronicles the enormous changes in the size, capability, applications, and cost of computers over the past 40 years. Two minitheaters show computer classics as well as award-winning computer-animated films.

resulting machines were called third-generation computers. Integrated circuits are made of silicon because it is a **semiconductor.** That is, silicon is a crystalline substance that will conduct electric current when it has been "doped" with chemical impurities implanted in its latticelike structure.

The chips were hailed as a generational breakthrough because they had desirable characteristics: reliability, compactness, and low cost. Mass production techniques have made possible the manufacture of inexpensive integrated circuits.

The beginning of the third generation was trumpeted by the IBM 360 series (named for a full circle of service—360 degrees) in 1964. The System/360 family of computers, designed for both business and scientific use, came in several models and sizes. The "family of computers" concept made it possible for users to move to a more powerful machine without having to replace the software that already worked on the current computer. The equipment housing was blue, leading to IBM's nickname, Big Blue.

The 360 series was launched with an all-out, massive marketing effort to make computers business tools—to get them into medium-size and smaller business and government operations where they had not been used before. Perhaps the most far-reaching contribution of the 360 series was IBM's decision to **unbundle** the software, that is, to sell the software separately from the hardware. This approach led to the creation of today's software industry.

Software became more sophisticated during this third generation. Several programs could run in the same time frame, sharing computer resources. This approach improved the efficiency of computer systems. Software systems were developed to support interactive processing, which used a terminal to put the user in direct contact with the computer. This kind of access caused the customer service industry to flourish, especially in areas such as reservations and credit checks.

The Fourth Generation, 1971–Present: The Microprocessor

Through the 1970s computers gained dramatically in speed, reliability, and storage capacity, but entry into the fourth generation was evolutionary rather than revolutionary. The fourth generation was, in fact, an extension of third-generation technology. That is, in the early part of the third generation, specialized chips were developed for computer memory and logic. Thus all the ingredients were in place for the next technological development: the general-purpose processor-on-a-chip, otherwise known as the **microprocessor,** which became commercially available in 1971.

Nowhere is the pervasiveness of computer power more apparent than in the explosive growth in the use of the microprocessor. In addition to the common applications of the microprocessor in digital watches, pocket calculators, and personal computers, you can expect to find one in virtually every machine in the home or business— cars, copy machines, television sets, bread-making machines, and so on. Computers today are 100 times smaller than those of the first generation, and a single chip is far more powerful than ENIAC.

◢ THE STORY OF PERSONAL COMPUTERS

Personal computers are the machines you can "get closest to," whether you are an amateur or a professional. There is nothing quite like having your very own personal computer. Its history is very personal too, full of stories of success and failure and of individuals with whom we can readily identify.

Apple Leads the Way

The very first personal computer was the MITS Altair, produced in 1975. It was a gee-whiz machine, loaded with switches and dials but with no keyboard or screen. It took two teenagers, Steve Jobs and Steve Wozniak, to capture the public's imagination with the first Apple computer. They built it in that time-honored place of inventors, a garage, using the $1300 proceeds from the sale of an old Volkswagen. Designed for home use, the Apple was the first to offer an easy-to-use keyboard and screen. Founded in 1977, Apple Computer was immediately and wildly successful. (Figure A-3 shows the cover page of the user's manual for the first commercial Apple computer.)

The first Apple computer, the Apple I, was not a commercial success. It was the Apple II that anchored the early years of the company. In fact, it was the combination of the Apple II and the spreadsheet software called VisiCalc that caught the attention of the business community and propelled personal computers into the workplace.

The IBM PC Standard

Announcing its first personal computer in the summer of 1981, IBM proceeded to capture the top market share in just 18 months. Even more important, its machine became the industry standard (Figure A-4). The IBM machine included innovations such as an 80 character screen line, a full uppercase and lowercase keyboard, and the possibility of adding memory. IBM also provided internal expansion slots, so that peripheral equipment manufacturers could build accessories for the IBM PC. In addition, IBM provided hardware schematics and software listings to companies that wanted to build products in conjunction with the new PC. Many of the new products accelerated demand for the IBM machine. Even more important, many new companies sprang up just to support the IBM PC.

IBM made its computer from nonproprietary parts, opening the door for other manufacturers to do the same. Thus other personal computer manufacturers emulated the IBM standard, producing IBM **clones,** copycat computers that functioned identically to the IBM PC. The clones were able to run the large selection of software that had been designed for IBM computers. Almost all the major personal computer manufacturers today—Compaq, Dell, Gateway, and many more—continue to produce computers that are compatible with the IBM standard. In fact, IBM-compatible computers now dominate the personal computer market, leaving IBM with a market share that is small when compared with its original success.

The Microsoft/Intel Standard

In the history of the computer industry, the spotlight has been on the fast-changing hardware. However, personal computer users now focus more on the tremendous variety of software. The dominant force in personal computer software is the Microsoft Corporation.

Microsoft supplied the operating system—the underlying software—for the original IBM personal computer. This software, called MS-DOS, was used by IBM and by the IBM clones, permitting tiny Microsoft to grow quickly. Microsoft eventually presented more sophisticated operating systems, notably Windows. The Windows operating system is used on computers powered by a microprocessor from the Intel Corporation; this potent combination, nicknamed *Wintel,* has become the dominant force in personal computer sales.

Nevertheless, the Wintel standard is ever open to challenge. Efforts to offer computers that simply bypass Windows have not made significant inroads. It is noteworthy, however, that handheld models such as the Palm, which use neither Microsoft nor Intel products, are being used, to some degree, in lieu of personal computers. Furthermore, Linux, developed by Linus Torvalds at the University of Helsinki in Finland, offers personal computer users a graphical user interface operating system. Although copyrights are held by various creators of Linux's components, its distribution stipulations require that any copy be free. Despite its lack of a commercial marketing mechanism, Linux is making some inroads.

► THE INTERNET REVOLUTION

The word "revolution" is never far away when the discussion is about computers. But nothing in computer history has captured the attention of computer users as the

▲ FIGURE A-3

Apple manual.

Shown here is a collector's item: the very first manual for operation of an Apple computer. Unfortunately, the early manuals were a hodgepodge of circuit diagrams, software listings, and handwritten notes. They were hard to read and understand, enough to frighten away all but the hardiest souls.

▲ FIGURE A-4

The IBM PC.

Launched in 1981, this early IBM PC rose to the top of the best-seller list in just 18 months.

THE ENTREPRENEURS

Ever thought you'd like to run your own show? Make your own product? Be in business for yourself? Entrepreneurs are a special breed. They are achievement-oriented, like to take responsibility for decisions, and dislike routine work. They also have high levels of energy and a great deal of imagination. But perhaps the key is that they are willing to take risks.

Steve Jobs

Of the two Steves who formed Apple Computer, Steve Jobs was the true entrepreneur. Although both were interested in electronics, Steve Wozniak was the technical genius, and he would have been happy to have been left alone to tinker. But Steve Jobs would not let him alone for a minute; he was always pushing and crusading. In fact, Wozniak had hooked up with an evangelist, and they made quite a pair.

When Apple was getting off the ground, Jobs wanted Wozniak to quit his job so that he could work full-time on the new venture. Wozniak refused. His partner begged and cried. Wozniak gave in. While Wozniak built Apple computers, Jobs was out hustling, finding the best marketing person, the best venture capitalist, and the best company president. This entrepreneurial spirit paid off in a spectacular way as Apple rose to the top of the list of personal computer companies.

Bill Gates

When Bill Gates was a teenager, he swore off computers for a year and, in his words, "tried to act normal." His parents, who wanted him to be a lawyer, must have been relieved when Bill gave up on the computer foolishness and went off to Harvard in 1974. But Bill started spending weekends with his friend Paul Allen, dreaming about personal computers, which did not exist yet. When the MITS Altair, the first personal computer for sale, splashed on the market in January 1975, both Bill and Paul moved to Albuquerque to be near the action at MITS. But they showed a desire even then to chart their own course. Although they wrote software for MITS, they kept the rights to their work and formed their own company. It was called Microsoft.

When MITS failed, Gates and Allen moved their software company to their native Bellevue, Washington. They had 32 people in their employ in 1980 when IBM came to call. Gates recognized the big league when he saw it and put on a suit for the occasion. He was offered a plum: the chance to develop the operating system (a crucial set of software) for IBM's soon-to-be personal computer. Although he knew that he was betting the whole company, Gates never hesitated to take the risk. He purchased an existing operating system, which he and his crew reworked to produce MS-DOS—which stands for "Microsoft disk operating system." It was this product that sent Microsoft on its meteoric rise.

Michael Dell

The rise of the Dell Computer Corporation, founded by Michael Dell, is astonishing by any standard. It would be hard to say who is more pleased—customers, stockholders, or Mr. Dell himself. Customers, large and small, have learned that Dell personal computers are excellent and that company service is even better. Stockholders have enjoyed owning the fastest-rising stock of the 1990s. And Michael Dell? In addition to untold billions, he has the satisfaction of inventing a business model that is now copied worldwide.

The business began not in a fabled garage, but in a place just about as noteworthy for a good story line: Michael Dell's dorm room at the University of Texas. It was 1983, and he was 19 years old. He began with the premise of delivering high-performance computer systems directly to the end user. By not using resellers, Dell reduces both the cost of the computer and the time of delivery. Along the way, Dell adopted the Internet as a key sales tool. Dell generates millions in revenue every day from its Web site.

Internet has. Even the acceptance of the personal computer pales in comparison. "Revolution" is truly an appropriate word. Chapters 8 and 9 contain a more detailed discussion of the influence of the Internet on business and society in general.

There are two critical points to be understood regarding the history of the Internet. The first is that the Internet was started as ARPANet, a network of equal computers that was designed to survive a nuclear attack. Second, the Internet was made attractive to the average user by Dr. Tim Berners-Lee, who came up with the notion of hyperlinks, and Marc Andreesen, who produced the first graphical browser.

Unlike other parts of computer history, the Internet is well documented online. It makes sense to go to the source, rather than read an abbreviated version here. If you want to know more, submit words such as "Internet," "history," and "ARPANet" to a search engine, and numerous appropriate sites will be offered.

► THE FIFTH GENERATION: ONWARD

The term **fifth generation** was coined by the Japanese to describe the powerful, "intelligent" computers they wanted to build by the mid-1990s. Later the term evolved to encompass elements in several research fields related to computer intelligence: artificial intelligence, expert systems, and natural language.

But the true focus of this ongoing fifth generation is connectivity, the massive industry effort to permit users to connect their computers to other computers. The concept of the information superhighway has captured the imaginations of both computer professionals and everyday computer users.

► THE ARTIFICIAL INTELLIGENCE FIELD

Artificial intelligence (AI) is a field of study that explores how computers can be used for tasks that require the human characteristics of intelligence, imagination, and intuition. Computer scientists sometimes prefer a looser definition, calling AI the study of how to make computers do things that—at the present time—people can do better. The current definition is significant because artificial intelligence is an evolving science: As soon as a problem is solved, it is moved off the artificial intelligence agenda. A good example is the game of chess, once considered a mighty AI challenge. But now that most computer chess programs can beat most human competitors, chess is no longer an object of study by scientists and therefore no longer on the artificial intelligence agenda.

Today the term "artificial intelligence" encompasses several subsets of interests (Figure A-5):

- **Problem solving.** This area of AI includes a spectrum of activities, from playing games to planning military strategy.

- **Natural languages.** This facet involves the study of the person/computer interface in unconstrained native language.

- **Expert systems.** These AI systems present the computer as an expert on some particular topic.

- **Robotics.** This field involves endowing computer-controlled machines with electronic capabilities for vision, speech, and touch.

Although considerable progress has been made in these sophisticated fields of study, early successes did not come easily. Before examining current advances in these areas, let us pause to consider some moments in the development of artificial intelligence.

Early Mishaps

In the first days of artificial intelligence, scientists thought that the computer would experience something like an electronic childhood, in which it would gobble up the world's libraries and then begin generating new wisdom. Few people talk like this today because the problem of simulating intelligence is far more complex than just stuffing facts into the computer. Facts are useless without the ability to interpret and learn from them.

An artificial intelligence failure on a grand scale was the attempt to translate human languages via the computer. Although scientists were able to pour vocabulary

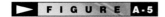

FIGURE A-5

The artificial intelligence family tree.

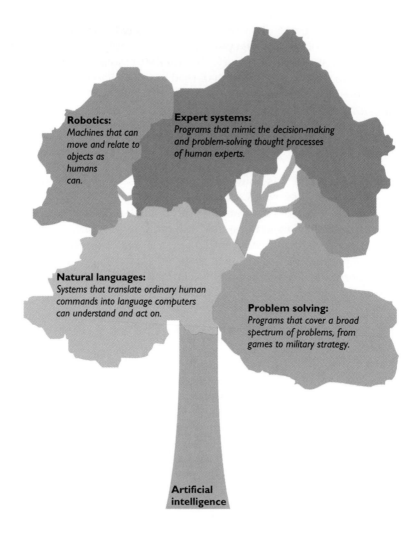

and rules of grammar into the computer, the literal word-for-word translations often resulted in ludicrous output. In one infamous example the computer was supposed to demonstrate its prowess by translating a phrase from English to Russian and then back to English. Despite the computer's best efforts, the saying "The spirit is willing, but the flesh is weak" came back "The vodka is good, but the meat is spoiled."

An unfortunate result of this widely published experiment was the ridicule of artificial intelligence scientists, who were considered dreamers who could not accept the limitations of a machine. Funding for AI research disappeared, plunging the artificial intelligence community into a slump from which it did not recover until expert systems emerged in the 1980s. Nevertheless, a hardy band of scientists continued to explore artificial intelligence, focusing on how computers learn.

How Computers Learn

The study of artificial intelligence is predicated on the computer's ability to learn and to improve performance on the basis of past errors. The two key elements of this process are the knowledge base and the inference engine. A **knowledge base** is a set of facts and rules about those facts. An **inference engine** accesses, selects, and interprets a set of rules. The inference engine applies the rules to the facts to make up new facts—thus the computer has learned something new. Consider this simple example:

FACT: Amy is Ken's wife.

RULE: If X is Y's wife, then Y is X's husband.

The computer—the inference engine—can apply the rule to the fact and come up with a new fact: Ken is Amy's husband. Although the result of this simplistic example may seem of little value, it is indeed true that the computer now knows two facts instead of just one. Rules, of course, can be much more complex and facts more plentiful, yielding more sophisticated results. In fact, artificial intelligence software is capable of searching through long chains of related facts to reach a conclusion—a new fact.

Further explanation of the precise way in which computers learn is beyond the scope of this book. However, the learning discussion can be used as a springboard to the question that most people ask about artificial intelligence: Can a computer really think?

The Artificial Intelligence Debate

To imitate the functioning of the human mind, a machine with artificial intelligence would have to be able to examine a variety of facts, address multiple subjects, and devise a solution to a problem by comparing new facts to its existing storehouse of data from many fields. So far, artificial intelligence systems cannot match a person's ability to solve problems through original thought instead of by using familiar patterns as guides.

There are many arguments for and against crediting computers with the ability to think. Some say, for example, that computers cannot be considered intelligent because they do not compose like Beethoven or write like Shakespeare. The response is that neither do most ordinary human musicians or writers—You do not have to be a genius to be considered intelligent.

Look at it another way. Suppose you rack your brain over a problem and then—aha!—the solution comes to you all at once. Now, how did you do that? You do not know, and nobody else knows either. A big part of human problem solving seems to be that jolt of recognition, that ability to see things suddenly as a whole. Experiments have shown that people rarely solve problems by using step-by-step logic, the very thing that computers do best. Most modern computers still plod through problems one step at a time. The human brain beats computers at "aha!" problem solving because it has millions of neurons working simultaneously.

Back to the basic question: Can a computer think or not? One possible answer: Who cares? If a machine can perform a task really well, does it matter whether it actually thinks? Still another answer is, yes, machines can really think, but not as humans do. They lack the sensitivity, appreciation, and passion that are intrinsic to human thought.

Data Mining

Computer brainpower can also be brought to bear on stores of data through **data mining,** the process of extracting previously unknown information from existing data. You might think that once data has been gathered and made available, you could know everything about it, but this is not necessarily so.

The information stored in hundreds of thousands of records on disk can be tallied, summarized, and perhaps even cross-referenced in some useful way by conventional computer programs. It is these traditional processes that produce the standard reports of business—bills, tax records, and annual reports. But conventional processes are unlikely to discover the hidden information that might give a competitive edge. The possible hidden information is just the sort of thing that a thinking person might uncover if the amount of data were of a manageable size. But no human can find nuances in massive data stores. Data mining, however, in a somewhat humanlike manner, might uncover data relationships and trends that are not readily apparent.

Companies are indeed using data-mining techniques to sift through their databases, looking for unnoticed relationships. Wal-Mart, for example, does this every day to optimize inventories. At the end of the day, all the sales data from every store comes into a single computer, which then interprets the data. The computer might notice, for example, that a lot of green sweaters have been selling in Boston and that,

in fact, the supplies were depleted. The same green sweater is hardly selling at all in Phoenix. A human can figure out the reason: It is St. Patrick's Day, and there are many more people of Irish descent in Boston than in Phoenix. For next St. Patrick's Day the computer will order a larger supply of green sweaters for the Boston stores.

The Natural Language Factor

The language that people use on a daily basis to write and speak is called a **natural language.** Natural languages are associated with artificial intelligence because humans can make the best use of artificial intelligence if they can communicate with computers in natural language. Furthermore, understanding natural language is a skill thought to require intelligence.

Some natural language words are easy to understand because they represent a definable item: "horse," chair," and "mountain," for example. Other words, however, are much too abstract to lend themselves to straightforward definitions: "justice," "virtue," and "beauty," for example. But this kind of abstraction is just the beginning of the difficulty. Consider the word "hand" in these statements:

- Morgan had a hand in the robbery.

- Morgan had a hand in the cookie jar.

- Morgan is an old hand at chess.

- Morgan gave Sean a hand with his luggage.

- Morgan asked Marcia for her hand in marriage.

- All hands on deck!

As you can see, natural language abounds with ambiguities; the word "hand" has a different meaning in each statement. In contrast, sometimes statements that appear to be different really mean the same thing: "Alan sold Jim a book for five dollars" is equivalent to "Jim gave Alan five dollars in exchange for a book." It takes sophisticated software to unravel such statements and see them as equivalent.

Feeding computers the vocabulary and grammatical rules they need to know is a step in the right direction. However, as you saw earlier in the account of the language translation fiasco, true understanding requires more: Words must be taken in context. Humans start acquiring a context for words from the day they are born. Consider this statement: Jack cried when Alice said she loved Bill. From our own context, several possible conclusions can be drawn: Jack is sad, Jack probably loves Alice, Jack probably thinks Alice doesn't love him, and so on. These conclusions might not be correct, but they are reasonable interpretations based on the context the reader supplies. On the other hand, it would *not* be reasonable to conclude from the statement that Jack is a carpenter or that Alice has a new refrigerator.

One of the most frustrating tasks for AI scientists is providing the computer with the sense of context that humans have. Scientists have attempted to do this in regard to specific subjects and found the task daunting. For example, a scientist who wrote software so that the computer could have a dialog about restaurants had to feed the computer hundreds of facts that any small child would know, such as the fact that restaurants have food and that people are expected to pay for it.

► EXPERT SYSTEMS

An **expert system** is a software package that is used with an extensive set of organized data that presents the computer as an expert on a particular topic. For example, a computer could be an expert on where to drill oil wells, on what stock purchase looks promising, or on how to cook soufflés. The user is the knowledge seeker, usually asking questions in a natural—that is, English-like—format. An expert system can respond to an inquiry about a problem with both an answer and an explanation of the answer. For example, an expert system specializing in stock purchases could be asked whether stocks of the Milton Corporation are currently a good buy. A possible answer is no, with backup reasons such as a very high price/earnings ratio or a recent change in top management. The expert system works by figuring out what the question means and then matching it against the facts and rules that it "knows" (Figure A-6). These facts and rules, which reside on disk, originally come from human experts.

But why go to all this trouble and expense? Why not just stick with human experts? Well, there are problems with human experts. They are typically expensive, they are subject to biases and emotions, and they may even be inconsistent. Finally, there have been occasions when experts have resigned or retired, leaving the company in a state of crisis. If there is just one expert, or even just a few experts, there might not be enough to satisfy the needs of the system. The computer, however, is ever present and just as available as the telephone.

Few organizations are capable of building an expert system from scratch. The sensible alternative is to buy an **expert system shell,** a software package that consists of the basic structure used to find answers to questions. It is up to the buyer to fill in the actual knowledge on the chosen subject. You could think of the expert system shell as an empty cup that becomes a new entity once it is filled—a cup of coffee, for instance, or a cup of sugar.

The most challenging task of building an expert system often is deciding who the appropriate expert is and then trying to pin down his or her knowledge. Experts often believe that much of their expertise is instinctive and therefore find it difficult to articulate just why they do what they do. However, the expert is usually following a set of rules, even if the rules are only in his or her head. The person ferreting out the information, sometimes called a **knowledge engineer,** must have a keen eye and the skills of a diplomat.

Once the rules are uncovered, they are formed into a set of IF-THEN rules. For example, IF the customer has exceeded a credit limit by no more than 20 percent and has paid the monthly bill on time for six months, THEN extend further credit. After the system is translated into a computerized version, it is reviewed, changed, tested, and changed some more. This repetitive process can take months or even years. Finally, it is put into the same situations as the human expert would face, where it should give equal or better service but much more quickly.

Aldo the Expert

The Campbell Soup Company has an expert system nicknamed Aldo, for Aldo Cimino, the human expert who knows how to fix the company's cooking machines. The human Aldo was getting on in years and was being run ragged, flying from plant to plant whenever a cooker went on the blink. Besides, how would the company manage when he retired? Now Aldo's knowledge has been distilled into an expert system that can be used by workers in any location.

◄ **F I G U R E A-6**

An expert system on the job.

This expert system helps Ford mechanics track down and fix engine problems.

► ROBOTICS

Many people smile at the thought of robots, perhaps remembering the endearing C-3PO *of Star Wars* fame and its "personal" relationship with humans. But vendors have not made even a small dent in the personal robot market—the much-heralded domestic robots who wash windows have not yet become household staples. So where are the robots today? Mainly in factories.

Robots in the Factory

Most robots are in factories, spray-painting and welding—and taking away jobs. The Census Bureau, after two centuries of counting people, has now branched out and today is counting robots as well. About 15,000 robots existed in 1985, a number that jumped to 50,000 just 10 years later. What do robots do that merits all this attention?

A **robot** is a computer-controlled device that can physically manipulate its surroundings. There are a wide variety of sizes and shapes of robots, each designed for a particular use. Often these uses are functions that would be tedious or even dangerous for a human to perform. The most common industrial robots sold today are mechanical devices with five or six directions of motion so that they can rotate into proper position to perform their tasks (Figure A-7).

Recently, **vision robots,** with the help of a TV camera eye, have been taught to see in living color—that is, to recognize multicolored objects solely from their colors. This is a departure from the traditional approach, whereby robots recognize objects by their shapes, and from vision machines that "see" only a dominant color. For example, a robot in an experiment at the University of Rochester was able to pick out a box of Kellogg's Sugar Frosted Flakes from 70 other boxes. Among the anticipated benefits of such visual recognition skills is supermarket checkout. You cannot easily bar code a squash, but a robot might be trained to recognize it by its size, shape, and color.

Field Robots

Think of some of the places you would rather not be: inside a nuclear power plant, next to a suspected bomb, at the bottom of the sea, on the floor of a volcano, or in the middle of a chemical spill. But robots readily go to all those places. Furthermore, they go there to do some dangerous and dirty jobs. These days, **field robots**—robots "in the field"—inspect and repair nuclear power plants, dispose of bombs, inspect oil rigs used for undersea exploration, explore steaming volcanoes, clean up chemical accidents, and even explore a battlefield in advance of soldiers. Field robots are also used to check underground storage tanks and pipelines for leaks and to clean up hazardous waste dumps. An undersea robot ventured into the icy waters off Finland and scanned the sunken ferry *Estonia*, sending back pictures of its weakened bow, which was thought to be a cause of the disaster. Newer undersea robots are being designed to swim like fish

► **FIGURE A-7**

Industrial robots.

(a) These standard robots are used in the auto industry to weld new cars. (b) This robot is not making breakfast. Hitachi uses the delicate egg to demonstrate that its visual-tactile robot can handle fragile objects. The robot's sensors detect size, shape, and required pressure, attaining sensitivity almost equal to that of a human hand.

(a)

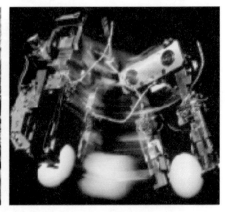

(b)

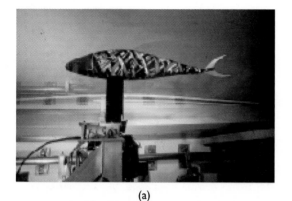

(a)

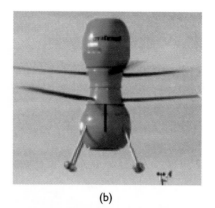

(b)

Field robots.

(a) Nicknamed Robotuna, this undersea robot will, scientists hope, be able to map the ocean floor, track schools of real fish, or detect pollution— and then swim home with the data. (b) Can a robot really fly? Yes. Flying robots have both military and civilian uses. This Sentinel robot can soar up to 10,000 feet to spy on an enemy, to inspect high-voltage wires, or to spot forest fires. (c) The robot called Spider checks gas tanks for cracks and sends computer images back to the ground, saving engineers from making a dangerous climb.

(c)

(Figure A-8a). Going in another direction, space researchers look forward to the day when "astrobots" can be stationed in orbit, ready to repair faulty satellites. Field robots may be equipped with wheels, tracks, legs, fins, or even wings (Figure A-8b). As a future goal, scientists hope to use robots to construct a space station and base on the moon.

Field robots have largely been overshadowed by factory robots, mainly because until recently, field robots have lacked the independence of their manufacturing counterparts, needing to be remotely controlled by human operators. Now, however, enough computer power can be packed into a field robot to enable it to make most decisions independently. Field robots need all the power they can get. Unlike factory robots, which are bolted to the ground and blindly do the same tasks over and over again, field robots must often contend with a highly unstructured environment, which may include features such as changing terrain and changing weather.

► VIRTUAL REALITY

The concept of **virtual reality,** sometimes called just **VR,** is to engage a user in a computer-created environment so that the user physically interacts with that environment. In fact, the user becomes so absorbed with the virtual reality interaction that the process is called **immersion.** Virtual reality alters perceptions partly by appealing to several senses at once—sight, hearing, and touch—and by presenting images that respond immediately to one's movements.

GETTING PRACTICAL | Robots in Our Lives

If you think robots are not practical in your own life, think again. Like computers before them, robots will soon be everywhere. Here are some examples.

● **Fill it up.** If filling your car's gas tank is not a favorite chore, you will be pleased to know that robots are taking over. Drivers pull up to a specially equipped station, swipe a plastic "tank card," and enter an identification number. The unit identifies the make and model of the auto, then guides the robotic arm to the car's fuel filler door. Once it is open, the robot then places the right grade and amount of gas in the tank and even replaces the cap.

● **My doctor the robot.** If you have orthopedic surgery, you might find that a key player alongside the surgeon is a robot. For example, to make room for a hip implant, a robotic arm drills a long hole in a thigh bone. Robotic precision improves the implant, reduces pain after surgery, and speeds healing.

● **Lending a hand.** Robots might soon be of significant use to the disabled. Researchers have already developed a robot for quadriplegics. The machine can respond to dozens of voice commands by answering the door, getting the mail, and even serving soup.

● **Road maintenance.** In California, road signs might soon say, "Robots at Work." Robots use lasers to spot cracks in the pavement and dispense the right amount of patch material. Soon robots will also be painting the road stripes.

● **Man's best friend.** The ultimate toy, a pet robot, can walk, lie down, and play games. Shown here, the Sony labs critter known as D21 is a prototype of things to come. The puppy weighs 2.8 pounds and packs a 64-bit microprocessor, 8 MB of memory, and a supersensitive camera eye. It knows commands too: Stick out your hand, and the pet will sit.

● **One cool clerk.** The very latest in modern technology and artificial intelligence has been used to create the Super RoboShop, the world's most convenient convenience store. Human store clerks have been replaced by the cheery little Robo, a computer-controlled bucket that does your shopping for you. Can't find batteries? Robo can, sparing the weary shopper from wandering the aisles or interacting with another human being. RoboShop is basically a gigantic vending machine delivering an eclectic mix of products—everything from cookies to comic books to cologne. Customers enter code numbers for desired products using an ATM-like keypad, pay the machine, and Robo whizzes into action, picking each item from the display cases without smashing so much as a single egg. This shop might not be in your life just yet: The first dozen RoboShops were in Japan and they are just now being developed in New York City.

● **Going bump in the night.** Chip, the chunky errand boy on the night shift at Baltimore's Franklin Square Hospital, fetches medicine, late meals, medical records, and supplies. A robot, Chip finds his way using sensitive whiskers and touch pads. Nurses love him because he saves them from having to run all over the hospital.

The visual part is made possible by sophisticated computers and optics that deliver to a user's eyes a three-dimensional scene in living color. The source of the scene is a database used by a powerful computer to display graphic images. The virtual reality system can sense a user's head and body movements through cables linked to the headset and glove worn by the user. That is, sensors on the user's body send signals to the computer, which then adjusts the scene viewed by the user. Thus the user's body movements can cause interaction with the virtual (artificial) world the user sees, and the computer-generated world responds to those actions (see Figure A-9).

Travel Anywhere, but Stay Where You Are

At the University of North Carolina, computer scientists have developed a virtual reality program that lets a user walk through an art gallery. The user puts on a head-mounted display, which focuses the eyes on a screen and shuts out the rest of the world. If the user swivels his or her head to the right, pictures on the right wall come into view; similarly, the user can view any part of the gallery just by making head movements. This action/reaction combination presents realistic continuing changes

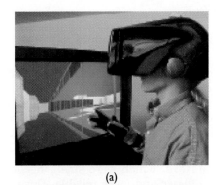

(a)

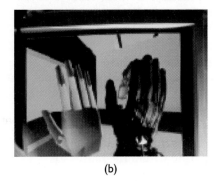

(b)

(c)

◄ **F I G U R E A-9**

Virtual reality.
(a) Users can "tour" a building by physically reacting—A turn of the head shows a different scene. (b) The data glove in the foreground has fiber-optic sensors to interact with a computer-generated world. (c) Virtual reality technology can be used to let people who are in wheelchairs design their own apartments.

to the user. Although actually standing in one place, the user feels as though he or she is moving and wants to stop short as a pedestal appears in the path ahead. It is as if the user is actually walking around inside the gallery.

In another example scientists have taken data about Mars, sent back by space probes, and converted it to a virtual reality program. Information about hills, rocks, and ridges of the planet are used to create a Mars landscape that is projected on the user's head screen.

The Promise of Virtual Reality

An embryonic technology such as virtual reality is filled with hype and promises. It is the practical commercial applications for real-world users that show where this technology might lead. Here are some applications that are under development:

● Wearing head mounts, consumers can browse for products in a "virtual showroom." From a remote location a consumer will be able to maneuver and view products along aisles in a warehouse.

● Similarly, from a convenient office perch a security guard can patrol corridors and offices in remote locations.

● Using virtual reality headsets and gloves, doctors and medical students will be able to experiment with new procedures on simulated patients rather than real ones.

Any new technology has its drawbacks. Some users experience "simulator sickness," even though they know the experience is not real. The developers of virtual reality are faced with daunting costs. Many hurdles remain in the areas of software, hardware, and even human behavior before virtual reality can reach its full potential.

▲

The immediate prospects for expert systems, robots, and virtual reality systems are growth and more growth. You can anticipate both increased sophistication and more diverse applications.

APPENDIX REVIEW

 Summary and Key Terms

- The first commercial computer generation dates to June 14, 1951, with the delivery of the **UNIVAC (Universal Automatic Computer)** to the U.S. Bureau of the Census. First-generation computers required thousands of **vacuum tubes,** electronic tubes about the size of lightbulbs. The main form of memory was **magnetic core,** small, doughnut-shaped rings about the size of pinheads, which were strung like beads on intersecting thin wires.

- Second-generation computers used **transistors,** which were small, needed no warm-up, consumed less energy, and were faster and more reliable. During the second generation, **assembly languages,** or **symbolic languages,** were developed. Later, **high-level languages,** such as FORTRAN and COBOL, were also developed.

- The third generation featured the **integrated circuit (IC)**—a complete electronic circuit on a small chip of silicon. Silicon is a **semiconductor,** a substance that will conduct electric current when it has been "doped" with chemical impurities.

- With the third generation, IBM announced the System/360 family of computers, which made it possible for users to move up to a more powerful machine without replacing the software that already worked on the current computer. IBM also **unbundled** the software, that is, sold it separately from the hardware.

- The feature of the fourth generation—the **microprocessor,** a general-purpose processor-on-a-chip—grew out of the specialized memory and logic chips of the third generation.

- The first personal computer, the MITS Altair, was produced in 1975. However, the first successful computer to include an easy-to-use keyboard and screen was offered by Apple Computer, founded by Steve Jobs and Steve Wozniak in 1977.

- IBM entered the personal computer market in 1981 and captured the top market share in just 18 months. Other manufacturers began to produce IBM **clones,** copycat computers that could run software designed for IBM computers.

- The leading software company worldwide is the Microsoft Corporation, which supplied the operating system for the original IBM personal computer and then went on to develop a variety of successful applications software.

- The term **fifth generation,** coined by the Japanese, evolved to encompass developments in artificial intelligence, expert systems, and natural languages. But the true focus of the fifth generation is connectivity, permitting users to connect their computers to other computers.

- **Artificial intelligence (AI)** is a field of study that explores how computers can be used for tasks that require the human characteristics of intelligence, imagination, and intuition. AI has also been described as the study of how to make computers do things that—at the present time—people can do better.

- Artificial intelligence is considered an umbrella term to encompass several subsets of interests, including **problem solving, natural languages, expert systems,** and **robotics.**

- In the early days of AI, scientists thought that it would be useful just to stuff facts into the computer; however, facts are useless without the ability to interpret and learn from them.

- An early attempt to translate human languages by providing a computer with vocabulary and rules of grammar was a failure because the computer could not distinguish the context of statements. This failure impeded the progress of artificial intelligence.

- The study of artificial intelligence is predicated on the computer's ability to learn and to improve performance on the basis of past errors.

- A **knowledge base** is a set of facts and rules about those facts. An **inference engine** accesses, selects, and interprets a set of rules. The inference engine applies rules to the facts to make up new facts.

- People rarely solve problems using the step-by-step logic that most computers use. The brain beats the computer at solving problems because it has millions of neurons working simultaneously.

- **Data mining** is the process of extracting previously unknown information from existing data.

- **Natural languages** are associated with artificial intelligence because humans can make the best use of artificial intelligence if they can communicate with the computer in human language. Furthermore, understanding natural language is a skill that is thought to require intelligence. A key function of the AI study of natural languages is to develop a computer system that can resolve ambiguities.

- An **expert system** is a software package that is used with an extensive set of organized data that presents the computer as an expert on a specific topic. The expert system works by figuring out what the question means and then matching it against the facts and rules that it "knows."

- For years, expert systems were the exclusive property of the medical and scientific communities, but in the early 1980s they began to make their way into commercial environments.

- Some organizations choose to build their own expert systems to perform well-focused tasks that can easily be crystallized into rules, but few organizations are capable of building an expert system from scratch.

- Some users buy an **expert system shell,** a software package that consists of the basic structure used to find answers to questions. It is up to the buyer to fill in the actual knowledge on the chosen subject.

- The person who works to extract information from the human expert is sometimes called a **knowledge engineer.**

- A **robot** is a computer-controlled device that can physically manipulate its surroundings. Most robots are in factories.

- **Vision robots** traditionally recognize objects by their shapes or else "see" a dominant color. But some robots can recognize multicolored objects solely from their colors.

- **Field robots** inspect and repair nuclear power plants, dispose of bombs, inspect oil rigs for undersea exploration, put out oil well fires, clean up chemical accidents, and much more.

- **Virtual reality,** sometimes called just **VR,** engages a user in a computer-created environment, so that the user physically interacts with the computer-produced three-dimensional scene. Because the user is so absorbed with the interaction, the process is called **immersion.**

Buyer's Guide:
How to Buy a
Personal Computer

▶ WHERE DO YOU START?

We cannot select a new computer system for you any more than we can choose a new car for you. But we can advise you on which features to look for and which features to avoid. We won't suggest a particular brand or model—so many new products are introduced every month that doing so would be impossible. If you are just beginning, however, we can help you to define your needs and ask the right questions.

Maybe you have already done some thinking and have decided that owning your own personal computer offers advantages. Now what? You can start by talking to other personal computer owners about how they got started and what pitfalls to avoid. You can also read some computer magazines, especially those with evaluations and ratings, to get a feel for what is available. Next locate several dealers. Most dealers are listed in the Yellow Pages, and many advertise in your local newspaper. Visit several. Don't be afraid to ask questions. You are considering a major purchase, so plan to take your time and shop around.

Finally, you might consider buying a computer system over the Internet or by direct mail. You can find advertisements in any computer magazine. Access the site (presumably, using someone else's computer) or call the listed toll-free number and ask them to send you a free brochure.

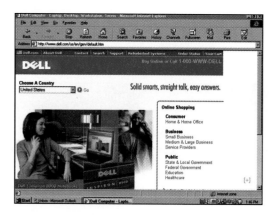

▶ ANTICIPATE YOUR SOFTWARE NEEDS FIRST

Before you buy a computer, it's important to know how you want to use it. This involves determining your software needs first and then buying the computer that runs the software you'll be using. What's the best way to determine your software needs? Research! Find out which software students in your area of study are using and which programs people working in your chosen career use. It's a good idea to interview friends, family, or people who work in your chosen field to find out what combination of software and hardware they prefer.

CHECK THE WEB SITE OR PHONE IT IN

These direct-mail dealers sell high-quality hardware at good prices. Check their Web sites or call these toll-free numbers to get free catalogs. You can also place an order via the Internet or by phone.

Dell Computer	IBM	Compaq Computer	Gateway 2000
www.dell.com	www.ibm.com	www.compaq.com	www.gateway.com
1-800-289-3355	1-800-426-3333	1-800-345-1518	1-800-846-2000

THE MAJOR CHOICES

The PC Standard?

Although computers are sold under many brand names, most offer the "PC standard," also referred to as the business standard. The PC standard is usually a computer that uses the Microsoft Windows operating system and an Intel microprocessor, a combination sometimes called "Wintel." If you will be using your computer for business applications and, in particular, if you need to exchange files with others in a business environment, consider sticking with the standard. However, the Apple iMac, noted for its ease of use, is an attractive alternative, especially for beginners.

Family Computer or Business Computer?

Although the basic machine is probably the same, many dealers offer a "family computer" and a "business computer." The family computer typically comes with a good modem and sound system, a joystick, and plenty of educational, financial, and entertainment software. The business computer will typically have a modest sound system and, most likely, one good suite of business software for such tasks as word processing and spreadsheets.

Desktop or Notebook?

Do you plan to use your computer in one place, or will you be moving it around? Notebook computers—also called laptop computers—have found a significant niche in the market, mainly because they are packaged to travel easily. A notebook computer is lightweight (most about 7 pounds and some as little as 2½ pounds) and small enough to fit in a briefcase or backpack. Today's notebook computers offer power and functionality that are equivalent to those of a desktop computer, but at a significantly higher cost.

Internet or In-Store?

Several reputable manufacturers sell reliable hardware via their Internet sites at good prices. However, they tend to be patronized by experienced users—businesses that order in bulk or individuals who are on their second or third computer and who know what they want. These buyers peruse the site and pick and choose the computer and options they want. They place an order via the site (or possibly over the phone) and have the new machine(s) delivered to the door. Because there is no retail middleman, they save money and also get the latest technology fast.

A first-time buyer, however, usually wants to kick the tires. You will probably be more comfortable looking over the machines, tapping the keyboard, and clicking the mouse. An in-store visit also gives you the opportunity to ask questions.

▶ WHAT TO LOOK FOR IN HARDWARE

The basic personal computer system consists of a central processing unit (CPU) and memory, a monitor (screen), a keyboard and a mouse, a modem, and assorted storage devices—probably a 3½-inch diskette drive, a CD-ROM or DVD-ROM drive, and a hard disk drive. Most people also want a printer, and many merchants offer package deals that include a printer. Unless you know someone who can help you out with technical expertise, the best advice is to look for a packaged system—that is, one in which the above components (with the exception of the printer) are assembled and packaged by the same manufacturer. This gives you some assurance that the various components will work together. Perhaps even more important, if something should go wrong, you will not have to deal with multiple manufacturers pointing fingers at one another.

Computer Housing

Sometimes called the computer case or simply "the box," the housing holds the electronic circuitry and has external receptors called ports to which the monitor, printer, and other devices are connected. It also contains the bays that hold the various disk drives. The monitor traditionally was placed on top of the computer case; there are still systems offered in that configuration. More common, however, is the minitower, in which the case stands on end and the monitor sits directly on the desk. The minitower was originally designed to be placed on the floor, conveniently out of the way. But the floor location turned out to be somewhat inconvenient, so many users keep their minitowers on the desk next to the monitor. The Apple iMac encloses all its internal equipment in a combination monitor-housing box; the see-through teal version is shown here.

Central Processing Unit

If you plan to purchase a PC-standard machine, you will find that most software packages run most efficiently on computers using a Pentium 4 microprocessor. Any lesser version of the Pentium should carry a bargain-basement price. A microprocessor's speed is expressed in megahertz (MHz) or gigahertz (GHz), and it is usually 750MHz and up. The higher the number, the faster—and more expensive—the microprocessor. If you enjoy 3D computer games, you'll want the fastest processor you can afford. Faster processors produce smoother, more realistic graphic animations.

Memory

Memory, or RAM, is measured in bytes, with each byte representing a character of data. The minimum memory threshold keeps rising, as software makers produce sophisticated products that run efficiently only with ever-larger amounts of memory. What is more, some users want or need to have several software programs open at the same time, to be able to switch conveniently among them. Lots of memory will help to keep everything running smoothly and speedily. We suggest a minimum of 64 megabytes of memory, 128 megabytes for serious users. It will make all the difference in the speediness of your computer. If you plan to work with digital photographs, you will need at least 128 megabytes, and if you need to edit video, consider 192 megabytes or even 256 megabytes.

Monitor

The monitor is a very important part of your computer system—you will spend all your computer time looking at it. Except in the case of the very cheapest personal computers, you can expect a monitor—in color—as standard equipment.

SCREEN SIZE   Monitors for home use usually have a screen display of between 15 and 19 inches, measured diagonally. Generally, a larger screen provides a display that is easier to read, so most monitors sold today have at least 15-inch screens.

However, the 17-inch screen reduces eyestrain and is well suited for displaying Internet Web pages, graphics, and large photos and illustrations.

SCREEN READABILITY   You might wish to compare the readability of different monitors. First, make certain that the screen is bright and has minimum flicker. Glare is another major consideration. Harsh lighting nearby can cause glare to bounce off the screen, and some screens seem more susceptible to glare than others. A key factor affecting screen quality is resolution, a measure of the number of dots, or pixels, that can appear on the screen. The higher the resolution—that is, the more dots there are—the more solid the text characters appear. For graphics, more pixels means sharper images. The most commonly available color monitors are Super VGA (SVGA) and Extended Graphics Array (XGA): XGA is best for graphic animations.

ERGONOMIC CONSIDERATIONS   Can the monitor swivel and tilt? If so, this will eliminate your need to sit in one position for a long period. The ability to adjust the position of the monitor becomes an important consideration when several users share the same computer, particularly people of different sizes, such as parents and children.

Input Devices

There are many input devices. We will mention only the two critical ones here: a keyboard and a mouse.

KEYBOARD   Keyboards vary in quality. To find what suits you best, sit down in the store and type. You might be surprised by the real differences in the feel of keyboards. Make sure the keys are not cramped together; you will find that your typing is error prone if your fingers are constantly overlapping more than one key. Assess the color and layout of the keyboard. Ideally, keys should be gray with a matte finish. The dull finish reduces glare.

Should you consider a wireless keyboard? A wireless keyboard uses infrared technology rather than wires to communicate with the computer. Thus you could use the keyboard at the far end of a conference table or on the kitchen table—any place within 50 feet of the computer. Furthermore, a touchpad—a mouse substitute—that can be used to drag the cursor or click on screen objects is built into the keyboard.

MOUSE   A mouse is a device that you roll on a tabletop or other surface to move the pointer on the screen. Since most software is designed to be used with a mouse, it is a necessary purchase and will likely come with any new desktop computer. Microsoft has introduced the IntelliMouse Explorer, shown here, whose IntelliEye operates by optical tracking technology rather than the traditional mouse ball on the bottom, making a smooth pointer movement.

Secondary Storage

You will need disk drives to read software into your computer and to store software and data that you wish to keep.

DISKETTE AND ZIP DRIVES   Some personal computer software today comes on diskettes, so you need a diskette drive to accept the software. Diskettes are also a common medium for exchange of data among computer users. Most computer systems today come with a 3½-inch diskette drive. A Zip drive is also an option for users who will be transporting large or numerous files.

CD-ROM AND DVD DRIVES   Most personal computer software comes on CD-ROM disks, which are far handier than multiple diskettes. But the main attraction is the use of high-capacity CD-ROMs for holding byte-rich images, sounds, and videos—the stuff of multimedia. The smoothness of a CD-ROM video presentation is indicated by the "X factor"—16X, 24X, 40X—the higher the better. However, CD-ROM is gradually being supplanted by even higher-capacity DVD-ROMs.

HARD DISK DRIVE   A hard disk drive is a standard requirement. A hard disk is fast and reliable and holds large amounts of data. Software comes on a set of several diskettes or on optical disk; it would be unwieldy to load these each time the software is used. Instead, the software is stored on the hard drive, where it is conveniently accessed from that point forward.

   All computer systems offer a built-in hard disk drive, with variable storage capacity—the more storage, the higher the price. Storage capacity is measured in terms of bytes—characters—of data. Keep in mind that software, as well as your data files, will be stored on the hard disk; just one program can take many millions of bytes. Hard disk capacity is measured in gigabytes—billions of bytes. The more the better, especially if you plan to save a lot of audio or video files.

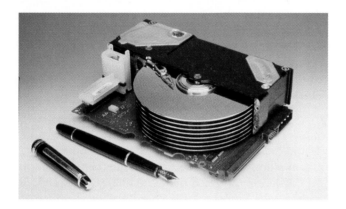

Printers

A printer is probably the most expensive peripheral equipment you will buy. Some inexpensive models are available, but those who have a great concern for quality output might pay a hefty price. When choosing a printer, consider speed, quality, and cost—not necessarily in that order.

Ink-jet printers, in which ink is propelled onto the paper by a battery of tiny nozzles, can produce excellent text and graphics. In fact, the quality of ink-jet printers approaches that of laser printers. The further attractions of low cost and quiet operation have made the ink-jet printer a current favorite among buyers, especially those who want color output.

Laser printers, which use technology similar to that of copying machines, are the top-of-the-line printers for quality and speed. The price of a low-end laser printer is within the budget of most users. Laser printers are particularly favored by desktop publishers to produce text and graphics on the same page. Affordable laser printers can produce output at 600 dots per inch (dpi), giving graphic images a sharpness that rivals that of photographs. At the high end, more expensive laser printers offer 1200 dpi. However, this rich resolution may be of little value to a buyer who plans to produce mostly text.

Affordable color printers are available for a few hundred dollars, although some are priced much higher. Even at a high price, color printers are not perfect. The rich color seen on the computer screen is not necessarily the color that will appear on the printed output. Furthermore, note that color printers often have fairly high operating costs for staples such as special coated paper and color ink cartridges. Still, color printers, once prohibitively expensive, are both attractive and affordable.

S Y S T E M
R E Q U I R E M E N T S

Make sure your hardware is compatible with the requirements of the software you are buying. You can find the requirements by reading the fine print on the software package. Here is a typical requirements blurb from a software package: Requires a personal computer with a Pentium or higher processor (Pentium III or higher recommended) running Microsoft Windows 98 or later operating system, 32 MB of memory (RAM) minimum, 64 MB recommended. Hard disk minimum installation 70 MB, typical installation 120 MB.

All-in-Ones

An all-in-one machine combines the capabilities of a full range of office equipment into one device: Printing, faxing, scanning, and copying abilities are all available on the same machine. There are certain advantages, such as installing and learning just one software package. Further, the all-in-one reduces the number of cables cluttering the floor and, perhaps most important, takes up less space than that required by multiple machines. The major disadvantage is that an equipment problem will disable all capabilities. You can purchase an adequate but somewhat limited all-in-one for a few hundred dollars. Businesses that want color capabilities, speedy printing, and all-day fax capabilities will pay a steeper price.

Portability: What to Look for in a Notebook

Generally, you should look for the same hardware components in a notebook computer as you would in a desktop computer: a fast microprocessor, plenty of memory, a clear screen, and diskette and hard drives. A CD-ROM or DVD-ROM drive is an option in most models.

Most models include an internal modem. Another option is a PC card modem that fits in a slot on the notebook. In either case you merely run a cord from the modem jack to the phone jack in the wall. Thus from your hotel room or from any place else that has a phone jack, you can be connected to online services, e-mail, and the Internet.

You will have to make some compromises on input devices. The keyboard will be attached, and the keys may be more cramped than those on a standard keyboard. Also, traveling users often do not have a handy surface for rolling a mouse, so the notebook will probably come with a built-in trackball or a touchpad. If you prefer a mouse, you can purchase one separately.

Other Hardware Options

There are a great many hardware variations; we will mention a few here. Note that, although we are describing the hardware, these devices may come with accompanying software, which must be installed according to directions before the hardware can be used.

COMMUNICATIONS CONNECTIONS   If you want to connect your computer via telephone lines to the office computer, to an online service such as America Online, or to the Internet or if you want to send and receive electronic mail, you need a communications device. Although the choices are many, the most common device, by far, is the modem. This device converts outgoing computer data into signals that can be transmitted over telephone lines and does the reverse for incoming data.

Most computers come with an internal modem, out of sight inside the computer housing. Furthermore, most people choose a fax modem, which serves the dual purpose of modem and fax. Using a fax modem, you can receive a fax and then print it out or send a fax if it originated in your computer (using, for example, word processing software) or was scanned into your computer. Most new computers come equipped with a fax modem.

OTHER INPUT DEVICES   If you are interested in action games, you might wish to acquire a joystick, which looks similar to the stick shift on a car. A joystick allows you to manipulate a cursor on the screen. A scanner is useful if you need to store pictures and typed documents in your computer. Scanners are often purchased by people who want to put their photographs on the computer or to use their computers for desktop publishing. Finally, you can purchase voice input hardware, which is basically a microphone.

SURGE PROTECTORS   Surge protectors protect against the electrical ups and downs that can affect the operation of your computer. In addition, a surge protector provides a receptacle for all power plugs and a handy switch to turn everything on or off at once. Some of the more expensive models, really uninterruptible power supply systems, provide up to 10 minutes of full power to your computer if the electric power in your home or office is knocked out. This gives you time to save your work on disk (so that the work will not be lost if the power fails) or to print out a report you need immediately.

► WHAT TO LOOK FOR IN SOFTWARE

You will use software that was written for the operating system software of that machine. Microsoft Windows is the most popular operating system, and almost all new PC-standard computers come with Microsoft Windows preinstalled. You'll find the Millennium Edition (ME) of Windows installed on most new computers. Windows users will want applications software written for the Windows environment. If you're using a Macintosh or an iMac, you will be running the Macintosh operating system (Mac OS). In this case, you will need application software written specifically for the Mac OS.

Hardware Requirements for Software

Identify the type of hardware required before you buy software. Under the heading System Requirements (sometimes called specifications) right on the software package, a list will typically include a particular kind of computer and operating system and a certain amount of memory and hard disk space.

Brand Names

In general, publishers of well-known software offer better customer support than lesser-known companies do. Support might be in the form of tutorials, classes by the vendor or others, and the all-important hotline assistance. In addition, makers of brand-name software usually offer superior documentation and upgrades to new and better versions of the product.

Where to Buy Software

Not very long ago, computer users bought their software at small specialty stores, where they hoped they could understand the esoteric language of the sales staff. In contrast, in enormous stores, buyers now pile software packages into their shopping carts like so many cans of soup. The choice of software vendors has expanded considerably.

COMPUTER SUPERSTORES   The computer superstores, such as CompUSA, sell a broad variety of computer hardware and software. Although their primary advantage is a vast inventory, they also offer on-site technical support.

WAREHOUSE STORES   Often billed as buyers' clubs, such as Sam's Club, the giant warehouse stores sell all manner of merchandise, including computer software.

MASS MERCHANDISERS   Stores such as Sears sell software along with their other various merchandise.

COMPUTER DEALERS   Some small retail stores sell hardware systems and the software that runs on them. Such a store usually has a well-informed staff and might be your best bet for in-depth consulting.

QUESTIONS TO ASK THE SALESPERSON AT THE STORE

- Can I expand the capabilities of the computer later?
- Whom do I call if I have a problem putting the machine together at home?
- Does the store offer classes on how to use the computer and software?
- What kind of warranty comes with the computer?
- Does the store or manufacturer offer a maintenance contract with the computer?

MAIL ORDER   Users who know what they want can get it conveniently and reasonably through the mail. Once an initial contact is made, probably from a magazine advertisement, the mail-order house will send catalogs of software regularly.

OVER THE INTERNET   Users who connect to the Internet often find it convenient to purchase software online. Each major software vendor has its own Web site and, among other things, offers its wares for sale. A buyer is usually given the choice of receiving the typical package—disks and documentation—through the mail or of downloading the software directly from the vendor's site to the buyer's computer.

► NOW THAT YOU HAVE IT, CAN YOU USE IT?

Once the proud moment has come and your computer system is at home or in the office with you, what do you do with it?

Documentation

Computer systems today come with extensive documentation, the written manuals and disk files that accompany the hardware. Usually, a simple brochure with detailed drawings will help you plug everything together. The installation procedure, however, is often largely (and conveniently) on disk. The same brochure that helps you assemble the hardware will guide you to the software on the diskette or CD-ROM. Using the software, the computer configures itself, mostly without any assistance from you.

Software documentation usually includes a user's guide, a reference manual for the various commands available with the software. Software tutorials are also common and are useful for the novice and experienced user alike. Software tutorials often come on a separate diskette or CD-ROM, and they guide you as you work through sample problems using the software.

Training

Can you teach yourself? In addition to the documentation supplied with your computer, numerous books and magazines offer help and answer readers' questions. Other sources are classes offered by computer stores and local colleges. These hands-on sessions may be the most effective learning method of all.

Maintenance Contract

Finally, when purchasing a computer, you might wish to consider a maintenance contract, which should cover labor. parts, and possibly advice on a telephone hotline. Such contracts vary in comprehensiveness. Some cover on-site repairs; others require you to pack up the computer and mail it back to the vendor. Another option is that the replacement part—say, a new monitor—is sent to you, and you then return the old monitor in the same packaging.

GLOSSARY

A

Accelerated Graphics Port (AGP) A bus that is designed to provide a dedicated connection between memory and an AGP graphics card.

Access arm A mechanical device that can access all the tracks of one cylinder in a disk storage unit.

Access time The time needed to access data directly on disk, consisting of seek time, head switching, and rotational delay.

Accumulator A register that collects the results of computations.

Acoustic coupler A modem that connects to a telephone receiver rather than directly to a telephone line.

Acquisition by purchase Buying an entire system for use by the organization, as opposed to designing a new system.

Active badge A badge that, embedded with a computer chip, signals the wearer's location by sending out infrared signals, which are read by computers distributed throughout a building.

Active cell The cell currently available for use in a spreadsheet. Also called the *current cell.*

Active-matrix LCD displays that produce a better image but use more power and are more expensive than passive-matrix displays.

Address A number used to designate a location in memory.

Affiliate A Web site whose owner has contracted with the owner of a web site that agrees to carry its banner ad.

Alpha A processor used in high-end workstations and servers.

Alphanumeric data Letters, digits, and special characters such as punctuation marks.

ALU See *Arithmetic/logic unit.*

America Online (AOL) A major online service that offers a variety of services.

Amplitude The height of the carrier wave in analog transmission. Amplitude indicates the strength of the signal.

Amplitude modulation A change of the amplitude of the carrier wave in analog data transmission to represent either the 0 bit or the 1 bit.

Analog transmission The transmission of data as a continuous electrical signal in the form of a wave.

Anchor tag In HTML, the command used to make a link. The key attribute of the anchor tag is HREF, which indicates a link destination. The anchor tag also includes the name of the word or words—the hypertext—that will be clicked to initiate the move to the new site.

ANSI American National Standards Institute.

Antivirus A computer program that stops the spread of a virus. Also called a *vaccine.*

AOL See *America Online.*

Applet A small program that can provide multimedia effects and other capabilities on Web pages.

Application service provider (ASP) A company that sets up and maintains applications software on its own systems and makes the software available for its customers to use over the Internet.

Applications software Programs designed to perform specific tasks and functions, such as word processing.

Arithmetic/logic unit (ALU) Part of the central processing unit, the electronic circuitry of the ALU executes all arithmetic and logical operations.

Arithmetic operations Mathematical calculations that the ALU performs on data.

ARPANet A network, established in 1969 by the Department of Defense, that eventually became the Internet.

Artificial intelligence The field of study that explores computer involvement in tasks requiring intelligence, imagination, and intuition.

ASCII (American Standard Code for Information Interchange) A coding scheme using 7-bit characters to repre-

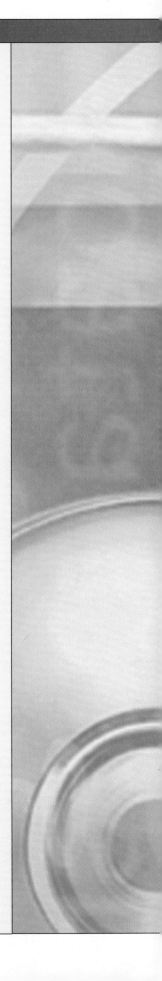

sent data characters. A variation of the code, called ASCII-8, uses 8 bits per character.

Assembler program A translator program used to convert assembly language programs to machine language.

Assembly language A second-generation language that uses abbreviations for instructions, as opposed to only numbers. Also called *symbolic language*.

Asynchronous transmission Data transmission in which data is sent in groups of bits, with each group of bits preceded by a start signal and ended with a stop signal. Also called *start/stop transmission*.

Attribute In object-oriented programming, a fact related to an object.

ATM See *Automated teller machine*.

Audio-response unit See *Voice synthesizer*.

Audit trail A method of tracing data from the output back to the source documents.

Automated teller machine (ATM) An input/output device connected to a computer used by bank customers for financial transactions.

Automatic recalculation In a spreadsheet, when one value or calculation is changed, all values dependent on the changed item are automatically recalculated to reflect the change.

Automatic reformatting In word processing, automatic adjustment of text to accommodate changes such as margin width.

Auxiliary storage Another name for secondary storage, which is storage for data and programs. Auxiliary storage is most often on disk.

Axis A reference line of a graph. The horizontal axis is the x-axis. The vertical axis is the y-axis.

B

Backbone The major communication links that tie Internet servers across wide geographical areas.

Background (1) In large computers, the memory area for running programs with low priorities. Contrast with *Foreground*. (2) On a Web site, the screen appearance behind the text and images.

Backup and restore Utility programs that facilitate making file back-ups and restoring damaged files.

Backup system A method of storing data in more than one place to protect it from damage or loss.

Bandwidth The range of frequencies that can fit on one communications line or link at the same time, or the capacity of the link.

Banner ad On a Web site, a clickable ad, often in the shape of a rectangle, that can take a user to the site of the advertiser.

Bar code A standardized pattern of vertical marks that represents the Universal Product Code (UPC) that identifies a product.

Bar code reader A stationary photoelectric scanner that inputs bar codes by means of reflected light.

Bar graph A graph made up of filled-in columns or rows that represent the change of data over time.

BASIC (Beginner's All-purpose Symbolic Instruction Code) A high-level programming language that is easy to learn and use.

Batch processing A data processing technique in which transactions are collected into groups, or batches, for processing.

Binary Regarding number systems, the binary number system uses exactly two symbols, the digits 0 and 1.

Binary system A system in which data is represented by combinations of 0s and 1s, which correspond to the two states off and on.

Biometrics The science of measuring individual body characteristics; used in some security systems.

Bit A binary digit.

Body tags In HTML, a pair of tags that enclose the content of the page.

Bomb An application that sabotages a computer by triggering damage—usually at a later date. Also called a *logic bomb*.

Boolean logic Regarding search engines on the Internet, a mathematical system that can be used to narrow the search through the use of operators such as AND, OR, and NOT.

Booting Loading the operating system into memory.

Bpi See *Bytes per inch*.

Broadcasting A method of file transmission that sends one copy of a file from one computer to every computer on the network.

Bridge A device that recognizes and transmits messages to be sent to other similar networks.

Browser Software used to access the Internet.

Bus or bus line An electronic pathway for data travel among the parts of a computer. Also called a *data bus*.

Bus network A network that has a single line to which each device is attached.

Button Clickable icons that represent menu choices or options.

Byte Strings of bits (usually 8) used to represent one data character—a letter, digit, or special character.

Bytes per inch (bpi) An expression of the amount (density) of data stored on magnetic tape.

C

C A sophisticated programming language invented by Bell Labs in 1974.

C++ An object-oriented programming language; an enhancement of C.

Cable modem A fast communications link that uses coaxial television cables already in place without interrupting normal cable TV reception.

Cache A relatively small amount of very fast memory that stores data and instructions that are used frequently, resulting in improved processing speeds.

CAD/CAM See *Computer-aided design/ computer-aided manufacturing*.

Candidates In systems analysis and design, alternative plans offered in the preliminary design phase of a project.

Carrier sense multiple access with collision detection (CSMA/CD) The line control method used by Ethernet. Each node has access to the communications line and can transmit if it hears no communication on the line. If two stations transmit simultaneously, they will wait and retry their transmissions.

Carrier wave An analog signal used in the transmission of electric signals.

Cathode ray tube (CRT) The most common type of computer screen.

CD-R A technology that permits writing on optical disks.

CD-ROM See *Compact disk read-only memory*.

Cell The intersection of a row and a column in a spreadsheet. Entries in a spreadsheet are stored in individual cells.

Cell address In a spreadsheet, the column and row coordinates of a cell. Also called the *cell reference*.

Cell contents The label, value, formula, or function contained in a spreadsheet cell.

Cell reference In a spreadsheet, the column and row coordinates of a cell. Also called the *cell address*.

Cellular modems Modems that can be used to transmit data over the cellular telephone system.

Central processing unit (CPU) Electronic circuitry that executes stored program instructions. It consists of two parts: the control unit and the arithmetic/logic unit. The CPU processes raw data into meaningful, useful information.

Centralized Description of a computer system in which hardware, software, storage, and computer access is in one location. Contrast with *Decentralized*.

CERN The name of the site of the particle physics lab where Dr. Tim Berners-Lee worked when he invented the World Wide Web; sometimes called the birthplace of the Web.

Change agent The role of the systems analyst in overcoming resistance to change within an organization.

Character A letter, number, or special character such as $.

Characters per inch (cpi) An expression of the amount (density) of data stored on magnetic tape.

Chief Information Officer (CIO) Top information systems in a company.

Circuit One or more conductors through which electricity flows.

CISC See *Complex instruction set computer.*

Class In object-oriented programming, an object class contains the characteristics that are unique to that class.

Click stream The set of a series of mouse clicks that link from site to site.

Click through Leaving the current Web site for an advertised site.

Client (1) An individual or organization contracting for systems analysis. (2) In a client/server network, a program on the personal computer that allows that node to communicate with the server.

Client/server A network setup that involves a server computer, which controls the network, and clients, other computers that access the network and its services. In particular, the server does some processing, sending the client only the portion of the file it needs or possibly just the processed results. Contrast with *File server.*

Clip art Illustrations already produced by professional artists for public use. Computerized clip art is stored on disk and can be used to enhance any kind of graph or document.

Clock A component of the CPU that produces pulses at a fixed rate to synchronize all computer operations.

Clone A personal computer that can run software designed for IBM personal computers.

CMOS See *Complementary metal oxide semiconductor.*

Coaxial cable Bundles of insulated wires within a shielded enclosure. Coaxial cable can be laid underground or undersea.

COBOL (Common Business-Oriented Language) An English-like programming language used primarily for business applications.

Cold site An environmentally suitable empty shell in which a company can install its own computer system.

Collaborative software See *Groupware.*

Collision The problem that occurs when two records have the same disk address.

Command A name that invokes the correct program or program segment.

Commercial software Software that is packaged and sold in stores. Also called *packaged software.*

Common carriers Companies that are licensed by the Federal Communications Commission to provide communications services to the public.

Communications medium The physical means of data transmission.

Compact disk read-only memory (CD-ROM) Optical data storage technology using disk formats identical to audio compact disks.

Compact disc-recordable (CD-R) A technology that permits writing on optical disks.

Compact disk-rewritable (CD-RW) A technology that allows you to erase and record over data multiple times.

Compare operation An operation in which the computer compares two data items and performs alternative operations based on the results of the comparison.

Compiler A translator that converts the symbolic statements of a high-level language into computer-executable machine language.

Complementary metal oxide semiconductor (CMOS) A semiconductor device that does not require a large amount of power to operate. CMOS is often found in devices that require low power consumption, such as portable computers.

Complex instruction set computer (CISC) A CPU design that contains a large number of instructions of varying kinds, some of which are rarely used. Contrast with *Reduced instruction set computer.*

Computer A machine that accepts data (input) and processes it into useful information (output). A computer system requires four main aspects of data handling—input, processing, output, and storage.

Computer Fraud and Abuse Act A law passed by Congress in 1984 to fight computer crime.

Computer Information Systems (CIS) The department responsible for managing a company's computer resources. Also called *Management Information Systems (MIS), Computing Services (CS),* or *Information Services.*

Computer literacy The awareness and knowledge of, and the capacity to interact with, computers.

Computer Matching and Privacy Protection Act Legislation that prevents the government from comparing certain records in an attempt to find a match.

Computer operator A person who monitors and runs the computer equipment in a large system.

Computer programmer A person who designs, writes, tests, and implements programs.

Computer-aided design/computer-aided manufacturing (CAD/CAM) The use of computers to create two- and three-dimensional pictures of products to be manufactured.

Computing Services The department responsible for managing a company's computer resources. Also called *Management Information Systems (MIS), Computer Information Systems (CIS),* or *Information Services.*

Concurrently With reference to the execution of computer instructions, in the same time frame but not simultaneously. See also *Multiprogramming.*

Conditional replace A word processing function that asks the user whether to replace text each time the program finds a particular item.

Consortium A joint venture to support a complete computer facility to be used as back up in an emergency.

Context sensitive In reference to an ad on a Web site, one that is related to the subject matter on the screen.

Continuous word system A speech recognition system that can understand sustained speech so that users can speak normally.

Control unit The circuitry that directs and coordinates the entire computer system in executing stored program instructions. Part of the central processing unit.

Cookie A small file stored on the user's hard drive that reflects activity on the Internet.

Coordinating In systems analysis, orchestrating the process of analyzing and planning a new system by pulling together the various individuals, schedules, and tasks that contribute to the analysis.

CPU See *Central processing unit.*

CRT See *Cathode ray tube.*

CSMA/CD See *Carrier sense multiple access with collision detection.*

Current cell The cell currently available for use in a spreadsheet. Also called the *active cell.*

Cursor An indicator on the screen; it shows where the next user-computer interaction will be. Also called a *pointer.*

Cursor movement keys Keys on the computer keyboard that allow the user to move the cursor on the screen.

Custom software Software that is tailored to a specific user's needs.

Cut and paste In word processing and some other applications, moving a block of text by deleting it in one place (cut) and adding it in another (paste).

Cylinder A set of tracks on a magnetic disk, one from each platter, vertically aligned. These tracks can be accessed by one positioning of the access arm.

Cylinder method A method of organizing data on a magnetic disk. This method organizes data vertically, which minimizes seek time.

D

DASD See *Direct-access storage device.*

DAT See *Digital audio tape.*

Data Raw input to be processed by a computer.

Data communications The process of exchanging data over communications facilities.

Data communications systems Computer systems that transmit data over communications lines, such as public telephone lines or private network cables.

Data compression Making a large data file smaller by temporarily removing nonessential but space-hogging items such as tab marks and double-spacing.

Data Encryption Standard (DES) The standardized public key system by which senders and receivers can scramble and unscramble messages sent over data communications equipment.

Data entry operator A person who keys data for computer processing.

Data flow diagram (DFD) A diagram that shows the flow of data through an organization.

Data item Data in a relational database table.

Data mining The process of extracting previously unknown information from existing data.

Data mirroring In RAID storage, a technique of duplicating data on a separate disk drive.

Data point Each dot or symbol on a line graph. Each data point represents a value.

Data striping In RAID storage, a technique of spreading data across several disks in the array.

Data transfer The transfer of data between memory and a secondary storage device.

Data transfer rate The speed with which data can be transferred between memory and a secondary storage device.

Database An organized collection of related files stored together with minimum redundancy. Specific data items can be retrieved for various applications.

Database management system (DBMS) A set of programs that creates, manages, protects, and provides access to the database.

DBMS See *Database management system.*

Debugging The process of detecting, locating, and correcting logic errors in a program.

Decentralized Description of a computer system in which the computer and its storage devices are in one place but devices that access the computer are in other locations. Contrast with *Centralized.*

Decision support system (DSS) A computer system that supports managers in nonroutine decision-making tasks. A DSS involves a model, a mathematical representation of a real-life situation.

Decision table A standard table of the logical decisions that must be made regarding potential conditions in a given system. Also called a *decision logic table.*

Default settings The settings automatically used by a program unless the user specifies otherwise, thus overriding them.

Delete key The key used to delete the text character at the cursor location or a text block that has been selected or marked.

Demodulation The process a modem uses to convert an analog signal back into digital form.

Density The amount of data stored on magnetic tape; expressed in number of characters per inch (cpi) or bytes per inch (bpi).

Dependent variable Output of a computerized model, particularly a decision support system. Called dependent because it depends on the inputs.

DES See *Data Encryption Standard.*

Desk-checking A programming phase in which a programmer manually steps through the logic of a program to ensure that it is error-free and workable.

Detail design A systems design subphase in which the system is planned in detail, including the details of output, input, files and databases, processing, and controls and backup.

Device drivers Utilities that allow the operating system to communicate with peripherals.

DFD See *Data flow diagram.*

Diagnostics Error messages provided by the compiler as it translates a program. Diagnostics inform the user of programming language syntax errors.

Digital subscriber line (DSL) A service that uses advances electronics to send data at very high speed over conventional copper telephone wires.

Digital transmission The transmission of data as distinct on or off pulses.

Digital versatile disk (DVD) A form of optical disk storage that has a double-layered surface and can be written on both sides, providing significant capacity. Also called DVD-ROM.

Digitizing tablet See *graphics tablet.*

Direct access Immediate access to a record in secondary storage, usually on disk.

Direct-connect modem A modem that is connected directly to the telephone line by means of a telephone jack.

Direct conversion A system conversion in which the user simply stops using the old system and starts using the new one.

Direct file organization An arrangement of records so that each is individually accessible.

Direct file processing Processing that allows the user to access a record directly by using a record key.

Direct-access storage device (DASD) A storage device, usually disk, in which a record can be accessed directly.

Disaster recovery plan Guidelines for restoring computer processing operations if they are halted by major damage or destruction.

Discrete word system A speech recognition system limited to understanding isolated words.

Disk cache An area of memory that temporarily stores data from disk that a program might need.

Disk drive A machine that allows data to be read from a disk or written on a disk.

Disk defragmenters Utilities that relocate disk files into contiguous locations.

Disk mirroring A concept associated with RAID that simply duplicates data on separate disk drives.

Disk pack A stack of magnetic disks assembled as a single unit.

Diskette A single disk, made of flexible Mylar, on which data is recorded as magnetic spots. A diskette is usually 3½ inches in diameter, with a hard plastic jacket.

Displayed value The calculated result of a formula or function in a spreadsheet cell.

Distributed data processing A computer system in which processing is decentralized, with the computers and storage devices and access devices in dispersed locations.

Documentation The instructions accompanying packaged software.

Documentation may be provided in a printed manual or in digital form on the distribution CD.

Document imaging A process in which a scanner converts papers to an electronic version, which can then be stored on disk and retrieved when needed.

Domain The name of the Internet service provider, as it appears in the Uniform Resource Locator.

Dot pitch The amount of space between dots on a screen.

Download In a networking environment, to receive data files from another computer, probably a larger computer or a host computer. Contrast with *Upload*.

DRAM See *Dynamic random-access memory*.

DSL See *Digital subscriber line*.

DSS See *Decision support system*.

Dual-boot system When booting an operating system, you are able to select which operating system will be loaded.

DVD See *Digital versatile disk*.

DVD-RAM A digital video disk format that enables users to record up to 2.6 GB of data.

DVD-ROM A digital video disk format capable of storing up to 4.7 GB of data, transferring data at higher speeds, and reading digital video disk and existing CD-ROM discs.

Dynamic random-access memory (DRAM) Memory chips that are periodically regenerated, allowing the chips to retain the stored data. Contrast with *Static random-access memory*.

E

EDI See *Electronic data interchange*.

EFT See *Electronic fund transfer*.

Electronic data interchange (EDI) A set of standards by which companies can electronically exchange common business forms such as invoices and purchase orders.

Electronic fund transfer (EFT) Paying for goods and services by transferring funds electronically. May also refer to the transfer of funds between financial institutions.

Electronic mail (e-mail) Sending messages from one terminal or computer to another.

Electronic mail client software Allows you to retrieve, create, send, store, print, and delete your e-mail messages.

Electronic software distribution Downloading software from the originator's site to a user's site, presumably for a fee.

Electronic spreadsheet A computerized worksheet used to organize data into rows and columns for analysis.

E-mail See *Electronic mail*.

Encapsulation (1) In object-oriented programming, the containment of both data and its related instructions in the object. (2) A way to transfer data between two similar networks over an intermediate network by enclosing one type of data packet protocol into the packet of another. Also called *tunneling*.

Encryption The process of encoding data to be transmitted via communications links, so that its contents are protected from unauthorized people.

Equal-to condition (=) A logical operation in which the computer compares two numbers to determine equality.

Erase head The head in a magnetic tape unit that erases any data previously recorded on the tape before recording new data.

Ergonomics The study of human factors related to computers.

ESS See *Executive support system*.

Ethernet A popular type of local area network that uses a bus topology.

E-time The execution portion of the machine cycle; E-time includes the execute and store operations.

Event-driven When one program is allowed to use a particular resource (such as the central processing unit) to complete a certain activity (event) before relinquishing the resource to another program.

Executive support system (ESS) A decision support system for senior-level executives who make decisions that affect an entire company.

Expansion slots The slots inside a computer that allow a user to insert additional circuit boards.

Expert shell Software having the basic structure to find answers to questions that are part of an expert system; the questions and supporting data must be added by the user.

Expert system Software that presents the computer as an expert on some topic.

External cache Cache (very fast memory for frequently used data and instructions) on chips separate from the microprocessor.

External modem A modem that is not built into the computer and can therefore be used with a variety of computers.

Extranet A network of two or more intranets.

F

Facsimile technology (fax) The use of computer technology to send digitized graphics, charts, and text from one facsimile machine to another.

Fair Credit Reporting Act Legislation that allows individuals access to their own credit records and gives them the right to challenge them.

Fax See *Facsimile technology.*

Fax modem A modem that allows the user to transmit and receive faxes without interrupting other applications programs, as well as performing the usual modem functions.

Feasibility study The first phase of systems analysis, in which planners determine if and how a project should proceed. Also called a system survey or a preliminary investigation.

Federal Privacy Act Legislation stipulating that government agencies cannot keep secret personnel files and that individuals can have access to all government files, as well as to those of private firms contracting with the government, that contain information about them.

Fiber optics Technology that uses glass fibers that can transmit light as a communications link to send data.

Field A set of related characters.

Field name In a database, the unique name describing the data in a field.

Field robot A robot that is used on location for such tasks as inspecting nuclear plants, disposing of bombs, cleaning up chemical spills, and other chores that are undesirable for human intervention.

Field type In a database, a category describing a field and determined by the kind of data the field will accept. Common field types are character, numeric, date, and logical.

Field width In a database or spreadsheet, the maximum number of characters that can be contained in a field.

File (1) A repository of data. (2) A collection of related records. (3) In word processing, a document created on a computer.

File compression utilities Programs that reduce the amount of space required by files.

File manager utilities Programs that organize and manage disk files in a directory structure.

File server A network relationship in which an entire file is sent to a node, which then does its own processing. Also, the network computer exclusively dedicated to making files available on a network. Contrast with *Client/server.*

File transfer protocol (FTP) Regarding the Internet, a set of rules for transferring files from one computer to another.

File transfer software In a network, software used to transfer files from one computer to another. See also *Download* and *Upload.*

Firewall A combination of hardware and software that prevents unauthorized traffic between a company's network and the Internet.

Flame An insulting or abusive e-mail message.

Flame war An exchange of flames.

Flaming Sending insulting e-mail messages, often by large numbers of people in response to spamming.

Flash memory Non-volatile memory chips.

Flatbed scanner A desktop scanner that scans a sheet of paper, thus using optical recognition to convert text or drawings into computer-recognizable form.

Flowchart The pictorial representation of an orderly step-by-step solution to a problem.

Font A complete set of characters in a particular size, typeface, weight, and style.

Font library A variety of type fonts stored on disk. Also called *soft fonts*.

Footer In word processing, the ability to place the same line, with possible variations such as page number, on the bottom of each page.

Footnote In word processing, the ability to make a reference in a text document to a note at the bottom of the page.

Foreground In large computers, an area in memory for programs that have a high priority. Contrast with *Background*.

Format (1) The process of preparing a disk to accept data. (2) The specifications that determine how a document or worksheet appears on the screen or printer.

Formula In a spreadsheet, an instruction placed in a cell to calculate a value.

FORTRAN (FORmula TRANslator) The first high-level programming language, introduced in 1954 by IBM; it is scientifically oriented.

Fourth-generation language A very high-level language. Also called a *4GL*.

Frames The capability of some browsers to display pages of a site in separate sections, each of which may operate independently.

Freedom of Information Act Legislation that allows citizens access to personal data gathered by federal agencies.

Freeware Software for which there is no fee.

Frequency The number of times an analog signal repeats during a specific time interval.

Frequency modulation The alteration of the carrier wave frequency to represent 0s and 1s.

Front-end processor A communications control unit designed to relieve the central computer of some communications tasks.

FTP See *File transfer protocol.*

Full-duplex transmission Data transmission in both directions at once.

Full justification In word processing, making both the left and right margins even.

Function A built-in spreadsheet formula.

Function keys Special keys programmed to execute commonly used commands; the commands vary according to the software being used.

G

Gantt chart A bar chart commonly used to depict schedule deadlines and milestones, especially in systems analysis and design.

Gateway A collection of hardware and software resources to connect two dissimilar networks, allowing computers in one network to communicate with those in the other.

GB See *Gigabyte.*

General-purpose register A register used for several functions, such as arithmetic and addressing purposes.

Gigabyte (GB) One billion bytes.

Graphical user interface (GUI) An image-based computer interface in which the user sends directions to the operating system by selecting icons from a menu or manipulating icons on the screen by using a pointing device such as a mouse.

Graphic artists People who use graphics software to express their ideas visually.

Graphics Pictures or graphs.

Graphics adapter board A circuit board that enables a computer to display pictures or graphs as well as text. Also called a *graphics card.*

Graphics card See *Graphics adapter board.*

Graphics tablet A rectangular board that contains an invisible grid of electronic dots.

Greater-than condition (>) A comparison operation that determines whether one value is greater than another.

Groupware Software that lets a group of people develop or track a project together, usually including electronic mail, networking, and database technology. Also called *collaborative software.*

GUI See *Graphical user interface.*

H

Hacker (1) An enthusiastic, largely self-taught computer user. (2) Currently, a person who gains access to computer systems illegally, usually from a personal computer.

Half-duplex transmission Data transmission in either direction, but only one way at a time.

Halftone In desktop publishing, a reproduction of a black-and-white photograph; it is made up of tiny dots.

Handheld scanner A small scanner that can be passed over a sheet of paper, thus using optical recognition to convert text or drawings into computer-recognizable form.

Hard copy Printed paper output.

Hard disk A rigid platter coated with magnetic oxide that can be magnetized to represent data. Hard disks are usually in a pack and are generally in a sealed module.

Hardware The computer and its associated equipment.

Head crash The result of a read/write head touching a disk surface and causing all data to be destroyed.

Header In word processing, the ability to place the same line, with possible variations such as page number, on the top of each page.

Head switching The activation of a particular read/write head over a particular track on a particular surface.

Hierarchy chart See *Structure chart.*

High-level language A procedural, problem-oriented programming language not tied directly to specific computer hardware.

Home page The first page of a Web site.

Host computer The central computer in a network, to which other computers, and perhaps terminals, are attached.

Hot list Regarding the Internet, a list of names and URLs of favorite sites.

Hot site For use in an emergency, a fully equipped computer center with hardware, communications facilities, environmental controls, and security.

HTTP See *HyperText Transfer Protocol.*

Hyperregion On a Web page, an icon or image that can be clicked to cause a link to another Web site; furthermore, the cursor image changes when it rests on the hyperregion.

Hypertext On a Web page, text that can be clicked to cause a link to another Web site; hypertext is usually distinguished by a different color and perhaps underlining; furthermore, the cursor image changes when it rests on the hypertext.

HyperText Transfer Protocol (HTTP) A set of rules that provide the means of communicating on the World Wide Web by using links. Note the http at the beginning of each Web address.

I

IC See *Integrated circuit.*

Icon A small picture on a computer screen; it represents a computer activity.

IEEE 1394 bus Also known as FireWire, a high-speed bus that is normally used to connect video equipment to a computer.

Imaging using A scanner to convert a drawing, photo, or document to an electronic version that can be stored and reproduced when needed. Once scanned, text documents may be processed by optical recognition software so that the text can be manipulated.

Immersion Related to virtual reality. When a user is absorbed by virtual reality interaction, the process is said to be immersion.

Impact printer A printer that forms characters by physically striking the paper.

Implementation The phase of a systems analysis and design project that includes training, equipment conversion, file conversion, system conversion, auditing, evaluation, and maintenance.

Independent variable Input to a computerized model, particularly a decision support system. Called independent because it can change.

Indexed file organization A method of file organization in which the records are stored in sequential order, but the file also contains an index of record keys. Data can be accessed both directly and sequentially.

Indexed processing See *Indexed file processing*.

Industry Standard Architecture (ISA) bus The oldest expansion bus still in common use. It is used for slow-speed devices such as the mouse and modem.

Inference engine Related to the field of artificial intelligence, particularly how computers learn; a process that accesses, selects, and interprets a set of rules.

Information Input data that has been processed by the computer; data that is organized, meaningful, and useful.

Information center A company unit that offers employees computer and software training, help in getting data from other computer systems, and technical assistance.

Information Services The department responsible for managing a company's computer resources. Also called *Management Information Systems (MIS)*, *Computer Information Systems (CIS)*, or *Computing Services*.

Information utility A commercial consumer-oriented communications system, such as America Online, that offers a variety of services, usually including access to the Internet.

Inheritance In object-oriented programming, the property meaning that an object in a subclass automatically possesses all the characteristics of the class to which it belongs.

Ink-jet printer A non-impact printer that forms output text or images by spraying ink from jet nozzles onto the paper.

Input Raw data that is put into the computer system for processing.

Input device A device that puts data in computer-understandable form and sends it to the processing unit.

Input requirements In systems design, the plan for input medium and content and forms design.

Instance In object-oriented programming, a specific occurrence of an object.

Instruction set The commands that a CPU understands and is capable of executing. Each type of CPU has a fixed group of these instructions, and each set usually differs from that understood by other CPUs.

Integrated circuit (IC) A complete electronic circuit on a small chip of silicon.

Integrated Services Digital Network (ISDN) A service that provides a digital connection over standard telephone lines. Although faster than using an analog modem, ISDN is much slower than DSL service.

Interlaced A screen whose lines are scanned alternatively, first the odd-numbered lines, and then the even-numbered lines. Although inexpensive, interlaced monitors are subject to flicker.

Internal cache Cache (very fast memory for frequently used data and instructions) built into the design of the microprocessor. Contrast with *External cache.*

Internal font A font built into the read-only memory (an ROM chip) of a printer.

Internal modem A modem on a circuit board. An internal modem can be installed in a computer by the user.

Internal storage The electronic circuitry that temporarily holds data and program instructions needed by the CPU.

Internet A public communications network once used primarily by businesses, governments, and academic institutions but now also used by individuals via various private access methods.

Internet service provider (ISP) An entity that offers, for a fee, a server computer and the software needed to access the Internet.

Internet Tax Freedom Act A federal law that imposes a three-year moratorium (beginning in October 1998) on taxes imposed on the Internet, and calls for a committee to study the matter.

Intranet A private Internet-like network internal to a certain company.

Interrupt In multiprogramming, a condition that temporarily suspends the execution of an individual program.

IP switches Internet protocol switches used to direct communications traffic among connected networks that have adopted the Internet protocol.

ISDN See *Integrated Services Digital Network.*

ISP See *Internet service provider.*

I-time The instruction portion of the machine cycle; I-time includes the fetch and decode operations.

J

Java A network-friendly programming language that allows software to run on many different platforms.

Joystick A graphics input device that allows fingertip control of figures on a monitor.

Justification In word processing, aligning text along the left or right margins, or both.

K

K or KB See *Kilobyte.*

Kernel Controls the entire operating system and loads into memory nonresident operating system programs from disk storage as needed.

Kerning In word processing or desktop publishing, adjusting the space between characters to create a more attractive or readable appearance.

Key A unique identifier for a record.

Key field In a database, a field that has been designated as a key can be used as the basis for a query of the database.

Keyboard A common computer input device similar to the keyboard of a typewriter.

Kilobyte (K or KB) 1024 bytes.

Knowledge base Related to the field of artificial intelligence, particularly how computers learn; a set of facts and rules about those facts.

Knowledge engineer Related to building an expert system, the person working to extract information from the human expert.

L

Label In a spreadsheet, data consisting of a string of text characters.

LAN See *Local area network.*

LAN manager A person designated to manage and run a computer network, particularly a local area network (LAN).

Landscape mode Orientation setting in which output is printed "sideways" on the paper.

Laptop computer A small portable computer, usually somewhat larger than a notebook computer.

Laser printer A non-impact printer that uses a light beam to transfer images to paper.

LCD See *Liquid crystal display*.

Leading In word processing or desktop publishing, the vertical spacing between lines of type.

Less-than condition < A logical operation in which the computer compares values to determine whether one is less than another.

Librarian A person who catalogs processed computer disks and tapes and keeps them secure.

Light pen A graphics input device that allows the user to interact directly with the computer screen.

Link (1) A physical data communications medium. (2) On the World Wide Web, clickable text or image that can cause a change to a different Web site.

Linkage editor A system program that combines an object module with prewritten modules from the system library to create an executable load module.

Link/load phase A phase that takes the machine language object module and adds necessary prewritten programs to produce output called the load module; the load module is executable.

Linux A Unix-like operating system that is freely available and not under control of any one company.

Liquid crystal display (LCD) A flat-panel monitor used on laptops and some desktop systems.

Live banner A type of Web site banner ad that lets a user get more information about a product without leaving the current site.

Load module An executable version of a program.

Local area network (LAN) A network designed to share data and resources among several computers, usually personal computers in a limited geographical area, such as an office or a building. Contrast with *Wide area network*.

Logic chip A central processing unit on a chip, generally known as a microprocessor but called a logic chip when used for some special purpose, such as controlling some under-the-hood action in a car.

Logic error A flaw in the logic of a program.

Logic flowchart A flowchart that represents the flow of logic in a program.

Logical field In a database, a field used to keep track of true and false conditions.

Logical operations Comparing operations. The ALU is able to compare numbers, letters, or special characters and take alternative courses of action depending on the result of the comparison.

Lurking Reading messages in newsgroups without writing any.

M

Mac OS Introduced with Apple's Macintosh computer in 1984, this operating system had the first generally available GUI. Its latest version, Mac OS X, is still considered easiest to use for beginners.

Machine cycle The combination of I-time and E-time, the steps used by the central processing unit to execute instructions.

Machine language The lowest level of language; it represents data and instructions as 1s and 0s.

Magnetic core A small, flat doughnut-shaped piece of metal used as an early memory device.

Magnetic disk An oxide-coated disk on which data is recorded as magnetic spots.

Magnetic tape A magnetic medium with an iron-oxide coating that can be magnetized. Data is stored on the tape as extremely small magnetized spots.

Magnetic tape unit A data storage unit used to record data on and retrieve data from magnetic tape.

Magnetic-ink character recognition (MICR) A method of machine-reading characters made of magnetized particles. A common application is checks.

Magneto-optical (MO) A hybrid disk that has the high-volume capacity of an optical disk but can be written over like a magnetic disk. It uses both a laser beam and a magnet to properly align magnetically sensitive metallic crystals.

Mail merge Adding names and addresses, probably from a database, to a prepared document, such as a letter prepared using word processing.

Main memory The electronic circuitry that temporarily holds data and program instructions needed by the CPU.

Main storage The electronic circuitry that temporarily holds data and program instructions needed by the CPU.

Mainframe A large computer that has access to billions of characters of data and is capable of processing large amounts of data very quickly. Notably, mainframes are used by such data-heavy customers as banks, airlines, and large manufacturers.

Management Information Systems (MIS) A department that manages computer resources for an organization. Also called *Computing Services* or *Information Services*.

Mark In word processing, one marks a certain section of text, called a block, by using some sort of highlighting, usually reverse video; the marked text is then copied, moved, or deleted.

Mark sensing See *optical mark recognition*.

Master file A file containing semipermanent data that must be updated to reflect business activity.

MB See *Megabyte*.

Mechanical mouse A mouse that has a ball on its underside that rolls as the mouse is moved.

Megabyte (MB) One million bytes. The unit often used to measure memory or storage capacity.

Megaflop One million floating-point operations per second. One measure of a computer's speed.

Megahertz (MHz) One million cycles per second. Used to express microprocessor speeds.

Memory The electronic circuitry that temporarily holds data and program instructions needed by the CPU.

Memory management The process of allocating memory to programs and keeping the programs in memory separate from one another.

Memory protection In a multiprogramming system, the process of keeping a program from straying into other programs in memory.

Message In object-oriented programming, a command telling what—not how—something is to be done, which activates the object.

Metasearch A search method that uses software to run queries on several search engines.

Method In object-oriented programming, instructions that tell the data what to do. Also called an operation.

MHz See *Megahertz*.

MICR See *Magnetic-ink character recognition*.

MICR inscriber A device that adds magnetic characters to a document, in particular, the amount of a check.

Microcomputer A relatively inexpensive type of computer, usually used by an individual in a home or office setting. Also called a *personal computer*.

Microprocessor A general-purpose central processing unit on a chip.

Microsecond One-millionth of a second.

Micro-to-mainframe link A connection between microcomputers and mainframe computers.

Microwave transmission Line-of-sight transmission of data signals through the atmosphere from relay station to relay station.

Millisecond One-thousandth of a second.

MIPS Millions of instructions per second. A measure of how fast a central processing unit can process information.

MIS See *Management Information Systems.*

MIS manager A person, familiar with both computer technology and the organization's business, who runs the MIS department.

MITS Altair Generally considered the first personal computer, offered as a kit to computer hobbyists in 1975.

Model (1) A type of database, each type representing a particular way of organizing data. The three database models are hierarchical, network, and relational. (2) In a DSS, an image of something that actually exists or a mathematical representation of a real-life system.

Modem Short for modulate/demodulate. A device that converts a digital signal to an analog signal or vice versa. Used to transfer data between computers over analog communications lines.

Modulation Using a modem, the process of converting a signal from digital to analog.

Monitor Hardware that features the computer's screen, includes housing for the screen's electronic components, and probably sits on a stand that tilts and swivels.

Monochrome A computer screen that displays information in only one color, usually green, on a contrasting background.

Monolithic Refers to the inseparable nature of memory chip circuitry.

Mosaic The first Web browser, invented in 1993 by Marc Andreessen, co-founder of Netscape, Inc.

Mouse A handheld computer input device whose rolling movement on a flat surface causes corresponding movement of the cursor on the screen. Also, a mouse button can be clicked to make selections from choices on the screen.

Motherboard Inside the personal computer housing, a board that holds the main chips and circuitry of the computer hardware, including the central processing unit chip.

Motion Picture Experts Group (MPEG) A set of widely accepted video standards.

MPEG See *Motion Picture Experts Group.*

Multicasting A method of file transmission that sends one copy of the file from one computer to the computer of each designated recipient.

Multimedia Software that typically presents information with text, illustrations, photos, narration, music, animation, and film clips—possible because the high-volume capacity of optical disks can accommodate photographs, film clips, and music. To use multimedia software, you must have the proper hardware: a CD-ROM drive, a sound card, and speakers. Multimedia also is offered on several Internet sites.

Multiplexer Combines the data streams from a number of slow-speed devices into a single data stream for transmission over a high-speed circuit.

Multiprocessing Using more than one central processing unit, a computer can run multiple programs simultaneously, each using its own processor.

Multiprogramming A feature of large computer operating systems under which different programs from different users compete for the use of the central processing unit; these programs are said to run concurrently.

N

Nanosecond One-billionth of a second.

Natural language A programming language that resembles human language.

Navigation bar A set of links on a Web page.

NC See *Network computer.*

Net box See *Net computer.*

Net computer A limited machine that has difficulty competing with cheap PCs.

Netiquette Appropriate behavior in network communications.

Network A computer system that uses communications equipment to connect two or more computers and their resources.

Network computer A computer used in conjunction with a television set to access the Internet. Also called a *net computer* or *net box* or *Web TV.*

Network interface card (NIC) A circuit board that can be inserted into a slot inside a personal computer to allow it to send and receive messages on a local area network (LAN).

Network manager A person designated to manage and run a computer network.

Network operating system An OS that's designed to let computers on a network share resources such as hard disks and printers.

Newsgroup An informal network of computers that allows the posting and reading of messages in groups that focus on specific topics. More formally called Usenet.

Newsreader software Software that's used to participate in newsgroups.

NIC See *Network interface card.*

Node A device, usually a personal computer, that is connected to a network.

Noise Electrical interference that causes distortion when a signal is being transmitted.

Non-impact printer A printer that prints without striking the paper.

Non-interlaced (NI) A description of screens that scan all lines in order, a procedure that is best for animated graphics. See *Interlaced.*

Notebook computer A small portable computer.

 O

Object In object-oriented programming, a self-contained unit that contains both data and related facts and functions—the instructions to act on that data.

Object linking and embedding (OLE) A Windows technology that lets you embed or link one document with another.

Object module A machine language version of a program; it is produced by a compiler or assembler.

Object-oriented programming (OOP) A programming approach that uses objects, self-contained units that contain both data and related facts and functions—the instructions to act on that data.

OCR See *Optical character recognition.*

OCR-A The standard typeface for characters to be input by optical character recognition.

Office automation The use of technology to help achieve goals in an office. Often associated with data communications.

OMR See *Optical mark recognition.*

Online In a data communications environment, a direct connection from a terminal to a computer or from one computer to another.

Online service A commercial consumer-oriented communications system, such as America Online or the Microsoft Network, that offers a variety of services, usually including access to the Internet. Also called an information utility.

OOP See *Object-oriented programming.*

Open source concept Something that is freely available and not under control of any one company.

Operating environment Software designed as a shell, an extra layer, for an operating system, so that the user does not have to memorize or look up commands.

Operating system A set of programs that lies between applications software and the computer hardware, through which a computer manages its own resources.

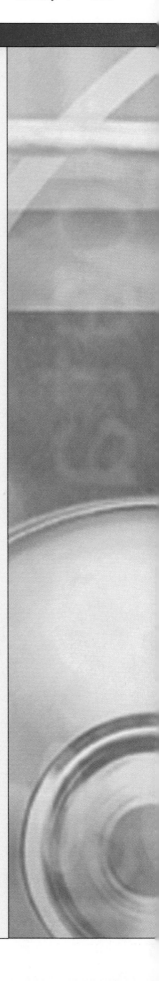

Operation In object-oriented programming, instructions that tell the data what to do. Also called a *method*.

Optical character recognition (OCR) A computer input method that uses a light source to read special characters and convert them to electrical signals to be sent to the computer.

Optical disk Storage technology that uses a laser beam to store large amounts of data at relatively low cost.

Optical mark recognition (OMR) A computer input method that uses a light source to recognize marks on paper and convert them to electrical signals to be sent to the computer.

Optical mouse A mouse that uses a light beam to monitor mouse movement.

Optical recognition system A category of computer input method that uses a light source to read optical marks, optical characters, handwritten characters, and bar codes and convert them to electrical signals to be sent to the computer.

Organization chart A hierarchical diagram depicting lines of authority within an organization, usually mentioning people by name and title.

Output Raw data that has been processed by the computer into usable information.

Output device A device, such as a printer, that makes processed information available for use.

Output requirements In systems design, the plan for output medium and content, types of reports needed, and forms design.

Outsourcing Assigning the design and management of a new or revised system to an outside firm, as opposed to developing such a system in-house.

P

Packaged software Software that is packaged and sold in stores. Also called *commercial software.*

Packet A portion of a message to be sent to another computer via data communications. Each packet is individually addressed, and the packets are reassembled into the original message once they reach their destination.

Page composition Adding type to a layout. In desktop publishing, the software may be called a page composition program.

Page frames Equal size portions of memory into which program pages are placed as needed for execution.

Page layout In publishing, the process of arranging text and graphics on a page.

Page table The index-like table with which the operating system keeps track of page locations.

Page template In word processing, a predesigned page that can contain page settings, formatting, and page elements.

Pages Equal-size blocks into which a program is divided to be placed into corresponding noncontiguous memory spaces called page frames. See also *Page frames.*

Pagination In word processing, options for placing the page number in various locations on the document page.

Paging The process of dividing a program into equal-size pages, keeping program pages on disk, and calling them into memory as needed.

Pan To move the cursor across a spreadsheet or a database to force into view fields that do not fit on the initial screen.

Parallel conversion A method of systems conversion in which the old and new systems are operated simultaneously until the users are satisfied that the new system performs to their standards; then the old system is dropped.

Parallel port External connector that transmits groups of bits together and is used for faster devices such as printers and scanners.

Parallel processing Using many processors, each with its own memory unit, that work at the same time to process data much more quickly than with the traditional single processor. Contrast with *Serial processing.*

Participant observation A form of observation in which the systems analyst temporarily joins the activities of the group.

Partition A separate memory area that can hold a program, used as part of a memory management technique that simply divides memory into separate areas. Also called a *region.*

Pascal A structured, high-level programming language named for Blaise Pascal, a seventeenth-century French mathematician.

Passie matrix Flat-panel monitor technology that is cheaper than active-matrix and uses less power, but isn't as bright. See *active-matrix.*

PC card A credit-card-sized card that slides into a slot in the computer, most often a modem, in which a cable runs from the PC card to the phone jack in the wall. Originally known as PCMCIA cards, named for the Personal Computer Memory Card International Association.

PC card bus A bus that accepts credit card-sized PC card devices and is normally found on laptops.

PDA See *Personal digital assistant.*

Peer-to-peer network A network setup in which there is no controlling server computer; all computers on the network share programs and resources.

Pen-based computer A small, portable computer that accepts handwritten input on a screen with a penlike stylus. Also called *personal digital assistant.*

Pentium A processor used in IBM-compatible PCs.

Peripheral Component Interconnect (PCI) bus A high-speed bus used to connect devices such as hard disks and network cards.

Peripheral equipment All of the input, output, and secondary storage devices attached to a computer.

Personal computer A relatively inexpensive type of computer, usually used by an individual in a home or office setting. Also called a *microcomputer.*

Personal digital assistant (PDA) A small, portable computer that is most often used to track appointments and other business information and that can accept handwritten input on a screen. Also called a *pen-based computer.*

Phase (1) In data transmission, the relative position in time of one complete cycle of a carrier wave. (2) In systems analysis and design, a portion of the systems development life cycle (SDLC).

Phased conversion A systems conversion method in which the new system is phased in gradually.

Picosecond One-trillionth of a second.

Pie chart A pie-shaped graph used to compare values that represent parts of a whole.

Pilot conversion A systems conversion method in which a designated group of users try the system first.

Pipelining A microprocessor design in which one instruction's actions—fetch, decode, execute, store—need not be complete before another instruction begins.

Pixel A picture element on a computer display screen; a pixel is merely one dot in the display.

Platform The hardware and software combination that comprises the basic functionality of a particular computer.

Plot area The area in which a graph is drawn, that is, the area above the x-axis and to the right of the y-axis.

Plug and Play A concept that lets the computer configure itself when a new component is added.

Plug-in Software that can be added to a browser to enhance its functionality.

PNG See *Portable Network Graphic.*

Pocket PC A PDA that can run stripped-down versions of some desktop software.

Point A typographic measurement equaling approximately 1/72 inch.

Pointer An indicator on a screen; it shows where the next user-computer interaction will be. Also called a *cursor.*

Point-of-sale (POS) terminal A terminal used as a cash register in a retail setting. It may be programmable or connected to a central computer.

Point-to-Point tunneling protocol (PPTP) A standard tunneling protocol.

Polymorphism In object-oriented programming, polymorphism means that when an individual object receives a message it knows how, using its own methods, to process the message in the appropriate way for that particular object.

Pop-up menu A menu of choices that appears, popping upward, when an initial menu choice is made.

Portable Network Graphic (PNG) A file format commonly used on Internet sites; PNG is non-proprietary and is replacing the GIF format.

Portal A Web site that is used as a gateway or guide to the Internet.

Portrait mode Paper output that is printed with the longest dimension up and down.

Ports External connectors that enable you to plug in peripherals such as a printer, a mouse, and a keyboard.

POS terminal See *Point-of-sale (POS) terminal.*

POTS (plain old telephone service) The most common dial-up system.

PowerPC A microprocessor used in the Apple Macintosh.

Preliminary design The subphase of systems design in which the new system concept is developed.

Preliminary investigation The first phase of the systems development life cycle, in which planners determine if and how a project should proceed. Also called a *feasibility study* or a *system survey.*

Primary memory The electronic circuitry that temporarily holds data and program instructions needed by the CPU. Also referred to as *memory* or *primary storage.*

Primary storage The electronic circuitry that temporarily holds data and program instructions needed by the CPU. Also referred to as *memory* or *primary memory.*

Printer A device for generating computer-produced output on paper.

Prompt A signal that the system is waiting for you to give an instruction to the computer.

Process (1) The computer action required to convert input to output. (2) An element in a data flow diagram that represents actions taken on data: comparing, checking, stamping, authorizing, filing, and so forth.

Processor The central processing unit (CPU) of a computer, a microprocessor.

Program A set of step-by-step instructions that directs a computer to perform specific tasks and produce certain results. More generically called software.

Programmable read-only memory (PROM) Chips that can be programmed with specialized tools called ROM burners.

Programmer/analyst A person who performs systems analysis functions in addition to programming.

Programming language A set of rules that can be used to tell a computer what operations to do. There are many different programming languages.

Project management software Software that allocates people and resources, monitors schedules, and produces status reports.

PROM See *Programmable read-only memory.*

Protocol A set of rules for the exchange of data between a terminal and a computer or between two computers.

Prototype A limited working system or subset of a system that is developed to test design concepts.

Pseudocode An English-like way of representing the solution to a problem.

Public domain software Software that is uncopyrighted, and thus may be altered.

Pull-down menu A menu of choices that appears, as a window shade is pulled down, when an initial menu choice is made.

Push technology Software that automatically sends—pushes—information from the Internet to a user's personal computer. Also called *webcasting*.

Q

Query languages A variation on fourth-generation languages that can be used to retrieve data from databases.

R

RAID See *Redundant array of inexpensive disks.*

RAM See *Random-access memory.*

Random-access memory (RAM) Memory that provides temporary storage for data and program instructions.

Range A group of one or more cells, arranged in a rectangle, that a spreadsheet program treats as a unit.

Raster-scan technology A video display technology. The back of the screen display has a phosphorous coating, which will glow whenever it is hit by a beam of electrons.

Read-only memory (ROM) Memory containing data and programs that can be read but not altered. Data remains in ROM after the power is turned off.

Read/write head An electromagnet that reads the magnetized areas on magnetic media and converts them into the electrical pulses that are sent to the processor.

Real storage That part of memory that temporarily holds part of a program pulled from virtual storage.

Real-time processing Processing in which the results are available in time to affect the activity at hand.

Record (1) A set of related fields. (2) In a database relation, one row.

Reduced instruction set computer (RISC) A computer that offers only frequently used instructions. Since fewer instructions are offered, this is a factor in improving the computer's speed. Contrast with *Complex instruction set computer.*

Redundant array of inexpensive disks (RAID) Secondary storage that uses several connected hard disks that act as a unit. Using multiple disks allows manufacturers to improve data security, access time, and data transfer rates.

Refresh To maintain an image on a CRT screen by reforming the screen image at frequent intervals to avoid flicker. The frequency is called the scan rate; 60 times per second is usually adequate to retain a clear image.

Register A temporary storage area for instructions or data.

Region A separate memory area that can hold a program, used as part of a memory management technique that simply divides memory into separate areas. Also called a *partition.*

Relation A table in a relational database model.

Relational database A database in which the data is organized in a table format consisting of columns and rows.

Relational model A database model that organizes data logically in tables.

Relational operator An operator (such as , or =) that allows a user to make comparisons and selections.

Removable hard disk cartridge A supplemental hard disk, that, once filled, can be replaced with a fresh one.

Resolution The clarity of a video display screen or printer output.

Resource allocation The process of assigning resources to certain programs.

Response time The time between a typed computer request and the response of the computer.

Retrovirus A virus that is powerful enough to defeat or even delete antivirus software.

Reverse video The feature that highlights on-screen text by switching the usual text and background colors.

Ring network A "circle" of point-to-point connections between computers at local sites. A ring network does not contain a central host computer.

RISC See *Reduced instruction set computer.*

Robot A computer-controlled device that can physically manipulate its surroundings.

ROM See *Read-only memory.*

ROM burner A specialized device used to program progammable read-only memory (PROM) chips.

Rotational delay For disk units, the time it takes for a record on a track to revolve under the read/write head.

Router A special computer that directs communications traffic when several networks are connected together.

S

Sampling In systems analysis, collecting a subset of data relevant to the system under study.

Sans serif A typeface that is clean, with no serif marks.

Satellite transmission Data transmission from earth station to earth station via communications satellites.

Scan rate The number of times a CRT screen is refreshed in a given time period. A scan rate of 60 times per second is usually adequate to retain a clear screen image.

Scanner A device that uses a light source to read text and images directly into the computer. Scanners can be of several varieties, notably handheld, sheetfeed, and desktop.

Screen A television-like output device that can display information.

Scrolling A feature that allows the user to move to and view any part of a document on the screen.

SDLC See *Systems development life cycle.*

Sealed module A disk drive containing the disks, access arms, and read/write heads sealed together.

Search engine Regarding the Internet, software that lets a user specify search terms that can be used to find Web sites that include those terms.

Secondary storage Additional storage, often on disk, for data and programs. Secondary storage is separate from the CPU and memory. Also called *auxiliary storage.*

Sector method A method of organizing data on a disk in which each track is divided into sectors that hold a specific number of characters. Data on the track is accessed by referring to the surface number, track number, and sector number where the data is stored.

Secure Sockets Layer (SSL) The protocol for online transaction payments.

Security A system of safeguards designed to protect a computer system and data from deliberate or accidental damage or access by unauthorized persons.

Seek time The time required for an access arm to move into position over a particular track on a disk.

Select In word processing, to mark a certain section of text, called a block, by some sort of highlighting, usually reverse video. The text is usually selected in advance of some other command upon the text, such as Move.

Semiconductor A crystalline substance that conducts electricity when it is "doped" with chemical impurities.

Semiconductor storage Data storage on a silicon chip.

Sequential file organization The arrangement of records in ascending or descending order by a certain field called the key.

Sequential file processing Processing in which records are usually in order according to a key field.

Serial port External connector that transmits data one bit at a time and is typically used for slow-speed devices such as the mouse and keyboard.

Serial processing Processing in which a single processor can handle just one instruction at a time. Contrast with *Parallel processing.*

Serif Small marks added to the letters of a typeface; the marks are intended to increase readability of the typeface. Contrast with *Sans serif.*

Server (1) In a client/server network arrangement, the computer that controls and manages the network and its services; the server usually has hard disks that hold files needed by users on the network. (2) A computer used to access the Internet; it has special software that uses the Internet protocol.

Shareware Software that is given away free, although the maker hopes that satisfied users will voluntarily pay for it.

Sheetfeed scanner A scanner that uses a motorized roller to feed a sheet of paper across the scanning head, thus using optical recognition to convert text or drawings into computer-recognizable form.

SIMM See *Single in-line memory module.*

Simplex transmission Transmission of data in one direction only.

Simulation The use of a computer model, particularly a decision support system, to reach decisions about real-life situations.

Single in-line memory module (SIMM) A board containing memory chips that can be plugged into a computer expansion slot.

Sink In a data flow diagram, a destination for data going outside the system.

Site license A license permitting a customer to make multiple copies of a piece of software.

Smalltalk An object-oriented language that supports a particularly visual system.

Smart terminal A terminal that has some processing ability.

Social engineering A tongue-in-cheek term for con artist actions, specifically, hackers persuading people to give away their passwords over the phone.

Soft copy Computer-produced output displayed on a screen.

Soft font A font that can be downloaded from the font library on disk with a personal computer to a printer.

Software Instructions that tell a computer what to do. Also called *programs.*

Software piracy The unauthorized copying of computer software.

SOHO Abbreviation for small office, home office, a designated group for which software is designed.

Source In a data flow diagram, a producer of data outside the system.

Source data automation The use of special equipment to collect input data as it is generated and send it directly to the computer.

Source document An instrument, usually paper, containing data to be prepared as input to a computer.

Source module A program as originally coded, before being translated into machine language.

Source program listing The printed version of a program as the programmer wrote it, usually produced as a byproduct of compilation.

Spamming Mass advertising on the Internet, usually done with software especially designed to send solicitations to users via e-mail.

Speech recognition Converting input data given as the spoken word to a form the computer can understand.

Speech recognition device A device that accepts the spoken word through a microphone and converts it into digital code that can be understood by a computer.

Speech synthesis The process of enabling machines to talk to people.

Spider A program that follows links throughout the Web.

Spooling A process in which files to be printed are placed temporarily on disk.

SRAM See *Static random-access memory.*

Star network A network consisting of one or more computers connected to a central host computer.

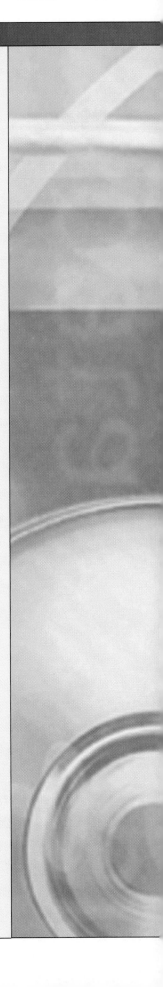

Start/stop transmission Asynchronous data transmission.

Static random-access memory (SRAM) A type of RAM that requires a continuous current to hold data. SRAM is usually faster but larger and more expensive than dynamic RAM. Contrast with *Dynamic random-access memory (DRAM)*.

Storage register A register that temporarily holds data taken from or about to be sent to memory.

Streaming The downloading of live audio, video, and animation content.

Structured interview In systems analysis, an interview in which only planned questions are used.

Structured programming A set of programming techniques that includes a limited number of control structures and certain programming standards.

Structured walkthrough A process by which a programmer's peers review the algorithm design and/or program code to verify correctness and offer suggestions for improvement.

Style In word processing, the way a typeface is printed—for example, in italic.

Suite A bundle of basic software designed to work together.

Supercomputer The largest and most powerful category of computers.

Supervisor program An operating system program that controls the entire operating system and calls in other operating system programs from disk storage as needed.

Supply reel A reel that has tape with data on it or on which data will be recorded.

Surge protector A device that prevents electrical problems from affecting data files.

SVGA (Super VGA) A superior screen standard with 800×600, 1024×768, 1280×1024, or 1600×1200 pixels. All SVGA standards support a palette of 16 million colors, but the number of colors that can be displayed simultaneously is limited by the amount of video memory installed in a system.

Symbolic address The meaningful name for a memory location. Instead of just a number, for example, a symbolic address should be something meaningful, such as NAME or SALARY.

Symbolic language A second-generation language that uses abbreviations for instructions. Also called *assembly language*.

Synchronous transmission Data transmission in which characters are transmitted together in a continuous stream.

Synonym The name for a record's disk address, produced by a hashing scheme, that is the same as a pre-existing address for a different record.

Syntax The rules of a programming language.

Syntax errors Errors in the use of a programming language.

Synthesis by analysis Speech synthesis in which a device analyzes the input of an actual human voice, stores and processes the spoken sounds, and reproduces them as needed.

Synthesis by rule Speech synthesis in which a device applies linguistic rules to create an artificial spoken language.

System An organized set of related components established to perform a certain task.

System journal A file whose records represent real-time transactions. Used to provide an audit trail recovery capabilities for online transaction-processing systems.

System requirements A detailed list of the things a particular system must be able to do, based on the results of the systems analysis.

System survey The first phase of systems analysis, in which planners determine if and how a project should proceed. Also called a feasibility study or a preliminary investigation.

System testing A testing process in which the development team uses test data to determine whether programs work together satisfactorily.

Systems analysis A phase of the systems development life cycle, involving studying an existing system to determine how it works and with an eye to improving the system.

Systems analyst A person who plans and designs computer systems.

Systems design A phase of the systems development life cycle, involving developing a plan for a new or revised system based on the results of the systems analysis phase.

Systems development The phase of the SDLC in which the system design is used to produce a functioning system. Activities include programming and testing.

Systems development life cycle (SDLC) The multiphase process required for creating or revising a computer system.

Systems flowchart A drawing that depicts the flow of data through some part of a computer system.

Systems software All programs related to coordinating computer operations, including the operating system, programming language translators, and service programs.

T

Tag In HTML, a command that performs a specific function.

Tape drive The device which reads data from and writes data on magnetic tape.

Target frame In a Web page with frames, the frame that holds the page currently referenced in the table of contents frame.

TCP/IP See *Transmission Control Protocol/Internet Protocol.*

Telecommuting Using telecommunications and computers at home as a substitute for working at an office outside the home.

Teleconferencing A system of holding conferences by linking geographically dispersed people together through computer terminals or personal computers.

Telnet A protocol that allows remote users to use their PC to log onto a host computer system over the Internet and use it as if they were sitting at a local terminal of that system.

Template (1) In desktop publishing, a predetermined page design that lets a user fill in text and art. (2) In a spreadsheet program, a worksheet that has already been designed for the solution of a specific type of problem, so that a user need only fill in the data. (3) In FrontPage, a predesigned page format.

Teraflop One trillion floating-point operations per second. One measure of a computer's speed, especially as related to parallel processors.

Terminal A device that consists of an input device (usually a keyboard), an output device (usually a screen), and a communications link to the computer.

Terminal emulation software Data communications software that makes a personal computer act like a terminal, so that it can communicate with a larger computer.

Text block A continuous section of text in a document that has been marked or selected.

Text editor Software that is somewhat like a word processing program, used by programmers to create a program file.

Theme A unified set of design elements and color schemes that can be applied to a Web page to give it a consistent and attractive appearance.

Thesaurus program With a word processing program, this program provides a list of synonyms and antonyms for a selected word in a document.

Thin client A computer that has no disk storage capability and is used basically for input/output.

Thrashing Occurs when the CPU spends all its time swapping pages in and out of real memory.

Time slice In time-sharing, a period of time—a fraction of a second—during which the computer works on a user's tasks.

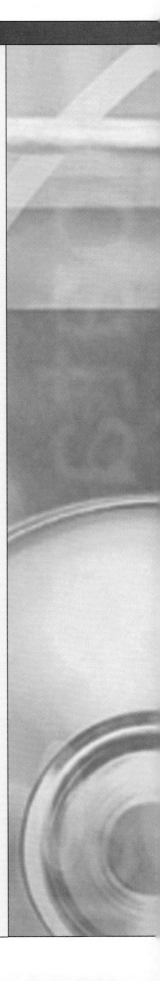

Time-sharing A special case of multi-programming in which several people use one computer at the same time.

Title The caption on a graph that summarizes the information in the graph.

Token passing The protocol for controlling access to a Token Ring network. A special signal, or token, circulates from node to node, allowing the node that "captures" the token to transmit data.

Token Ring network A network protocol that uses token passing to send data over the shared network cable. A computer that wants to send a message must capture the token before sending.

Top-level domain Regarding the Internet, in a Uniform Resource Locator (URL), the last part of the domain name, representing the type of entity, such as organization or education or country.

Topology The physical layout of a local area network.

Touchpad An input device that uses finger movement on its surface to control the pointer.

Touch screen A computer screen that accepts input data by letting the user point at the screen to select a choice. The finger touching the screen interrupts the light beams on the monitor's edge, pinpointing the selected screen location.

Track On a magnetic disk, one of many data-holding concentric circles.

Trackball A ball used as an input device; it can be hand-manipulated to cause a corresponding movement of the cursor on the screen. Trackballs are often built in on portable computers.

Transaction A business event that requires a business's records to be updated.

Transaction file A file that contains all changes to be made to the master file: additions, deletions, and revisions.

Transaction processing The technique of processing transactions one at a time, in the order in which they occur.

Transistor A small device that transfers electrical signals across a resistor.

Translator Software, typically a compiler, that converts a program into the machine language the computer can understand.

Transmission Control Protocol/Internet Protocol (TCP/IP) A standardized protocol permitting different computers to communicate via the Internet.

Transparent Computer activities of which a user is unaware even as they are taking place.

Transponder A device in a communications satellite that receives a transmission from earth, amplifies the signal, changes the frequency, and retransmits the data to a receiving earth station. The transponder makes sure that the stronger outgoing signals do not interfere with the weaker incoming signals.

Trojan horse An application that covertly places destructive instructions in the middle of a legitimate program but appears to do something useful.

Tunneling A way to transfer data between two similar networks over an intermediate network by enclosing one type of data packet protocol into the packet of another. Also called *encapsulation*.

Twisted pairs Wires twisted together in an insulated cable. Twisted pairs are frequently used to transmit data over short distances. Also called *wire pairs*.

Type size The size, in points, of a typeface.

U

Unbundle To sell software separately from the hardware on which it will run.

Unicasting A method of file transmission that sends a copy of a file from one computer to the computer of each designated recipient.

Uniform Resource Locator (URL) The unique address of a Web page or other file on the Internet.

Unit testing Testing an individual program by using test data.

UNIVAC I (Universal Automatic Computer I) The first computer built for business purposes.

Universal Product Code (UPC) A code number unique to a product. The UPC code is the bar code on the product's label.

Universal serial bus (USB) An external bus architecture that connects peripherals such as keyboards, mice, and digital cameras.

Unix A multiuser, time-sharing operating system that runs on all types of computers.

Unstructured interview In systems analysis, an interview in which questions are planned in advance, but the questionnaire can deviate from the plan.

UPC See *Universal Product Code.*

Update To keep files current by changing data as appropriate.

Updating in place The ability to read, change, and return a record to its same place on the disk.

Upload In a networking environment, to send a file from one computer to another, usually to a larger computer or a host computer. Contrast with *Download.*

URL See *Uniform Resource Locator.*

Usenet An informal network of computers that allows the posting and reading of messages in newsgroups that focus on specific topics. Also called *newsgroups.*

User-friendly A term to refer to software that is easy for a novice to use.

User involvement The involvement of users in the systems development life cycle.

Utility programs (utilities) Programs that perform many common tasks for users.

V

Vaccine A computer program that stops the spread of a virus. Also called an *antivirus.*

Vacuum tube An electronic tube used as a basic component in the first generation of computers.

Value In a spreadsheet, data entered into a cell.

Variable (1) On a graph, the items that the data points describe. (2) In a program, a name assigned to a memory location, whose contents can vary.

Vector An arrow—a line with directional notation—used in a data flow diagram.

Vertical market A market consisting of a group of similar customers, such as dentists, who are likely to need similar software.

Very high-level language A fourth-programming generation language.

Video graphics Computer-produced animated pictures.

Video Privacy Protection Act Legislation that prohibits video vendors from revealing what videos their customers rent.

Videoconferencing Computer conferencing combined with cameras and wall-size screens.

Virtual memory See *Virtual storage.*

Virtual private network (VPN) Technology that uses the public Internet backbone as a channel for private data communication.

Virtual reality (VR) A system in which a user is immersed in a computer-created environment, so that the user physically interacts with the computer-produced three-dimensional scene.

Virtual storage A technique of memory management in which part of the application program is stored on disk and is brought into memory only as needed. The secondary storage holding the rest of the program is considered virtual storage.

Virus A set of illicit instructions that passes itself on to other programs with which it comes into contact.

Vision robot A robot that can recognize an object by its shape or color.

Voice input Using the spoken word as a means of entering data into a computer.

Voice output device See *Voice synthesizer.*

Voice synthesizer A device that converts data in main storage to vocalized

sounds understandable to humans. Also called an *audio-response unit* and *voice output device.*

Volatile Subject to loss when electricity is interrupted or turned off. Data in semiconductor storage is volatile.

Volume testing The testing of a program or a system by using real data in large amounts.

VPN See *Virtual private network.*

VR See *Virtual reality.*

W

WAN See *Wide area network.*

Wand reader An input device that scans the special letters and numbers on price tags in retail stores and sends that input data to the computer. Often connected to a point-of-sale terminal in a retail store.

Web See *World Wide Web.* Also, using FrontPage software, a set of Web pages.

Web site An individual location on the World Wide Web.

Web TV See *Network computer.*

Webcasting Software that automatically sends—pushes—information from the Internet to a user's personal computer. Also called *push technology.*

Weight In word processing or desktop publishing, the variation in the visual heaviness of a typeface; for example, words look much heavier when in boldface type.

"What-if" analysis The process of changing one or more spreadsheet values and observing the resulting calculated effect.

Wide area network (WAN) A network of geographically distant computers and terminals. Contrast with *Local area network.*

Windows CE An operating system for palmtop and personal digital assistant computers developed by Microsoft Corporation.

Windows Me The latest in the Win9x series.

Windows NT A 32-bit operating system developed by Microsoft Corporation for use in corporate client/server networks.

Windows 95 An operating system developed for IBM-compatible PCs developed by Microsoft Corporation. Windows 95 is a true operating system that introduced numerous improvements over its predecessors.

Windows 98 A 32-bit operating system developed for IBM-compatible PCs by Microsoft Corporation as the successor to Windows 95.

Windows 2000 The latest generation in the NT series.

Windows XP The latest generation of Windows that incorporates and extends the consumer-oriented features of Windows Me into the stable, dependable Windows 2000 environment.

Wire pairs Wires twisted together in an insulated cable. Wire pairs are frequently used to transmit data over short distances. Also called *twisted pairs.*

Wireless Transmitting data over networks using infrared or radio wave transmissions instead of cables.

Wireless Application Protocol (WAP) A protocol used by wireless access providers to format Web pages for viewing on mobile handheld devices.

Wireless mouse A mouse that uses an infrared beam rather than a cord to send signals to the computer.

Word The number of bits that constitute a common unit of data, as defined by the computer system.

Word processing Computer-based creating, editing, formatting, storing, retrieving, and printing of a text document.

Word wrap A word processing feature that automatically starts a word at the left margin of the next line if there is not enough room for it on the current line.

Worksheet Another name for an electronic spreadsheet, a computerized version of a manual spreadsheet.

Workstation A computer that combines the compactness of a desktop computer with power that almost equals that of a mainframe.

World Wide Web (the Web) An Internet subset of sites with text, images, and sounds; most Web sites provide links to related topics.

WORM See *Write-once, read-many media.*

Worm A program that spreads and replicates over a network.

Write-once, read-many media (WORM) Media that can be written on only once; then they become read-only media.

WYSIWYG An acronym meaning what you see is what you get; in FrontPage WYSIWYG refers to the fact that you see the page as it will look as you create it.

X

XGA (extended graphics array) A high-resolution graphics standard that provides high resolutions, supports more simultaneous colors than SVGA, and can be non-interlaced. Contrast with SVGA.

Z

Zone recording Involves dividing a disk into zones to take advantage of the storage available on all tracks, by assigning more sectors to tracks in outer zones than to those in inner zones.

CREDITS

Brief Table of Contents
vi:Courtesy Sun Microsystems.

Table of Contents
viii:©Mark Harmel/Tony Stone Images;
ix:©David Hanover/Tony Stone Images;
ix:©Don Smetzer/Tony Stone Images;
xix:Courtesy of Hewlett Packard;
xxiii:Courtesy Wacom Technology Corp.

Chapter One
MN01-01:2000 and Beyond:Courtesy of
Levi Strauss and Co.; MRC Box:Wired
Campus:©C/B Productions/The Stock
Market;01-03a:©1998 PhotoDisc, Inc;
01-03b:©Shambroom/Photo
Researchers, Inc; MN01-02:"Gemstar
eBook™, model RCA REB 1200,
manufactured by Thomson Consumer
Electronics under license from
Gemstar."; 01-04a:©The Stock Solution;
01-04b:Courtesty of Hewlett Packard;
01-05a:©David R. Frazier/Photo
Researchers, Inc.; MN01-03:Move Over
Kid.©Llewellyn/Uniphoto; 01-07:©Will
and Deni McIntyre/Photo Researchers;
01-08a:Courtesy of International
Business Machines Corporation/
Unauthorized use not permitted.

Chapter Two
02-04:Courtesy of Microsoft
Corporation. All right reserved;
02-05:Courtesy of Microsoft Corporation.
All rights reserved; 02-06:Courtesy of
Microsoft Corporation. All rights
Reserved; 02-07:Courtesy of Microsoft
Corporation. All rights reserved;
02-08:Courtesy of Microsoft; GP02-
01a:Courtesy of Microsoft Corporation.
All right reserved; GP02-01b:Courtesy
of Microsoft Corporation. All rights
reserved; 02-12:Courtesy of Microsoft
Corporation. All rights reserved;
02-13:Courtesy of Microsoft Corporation.
All rights reserved; PI02-01:Reprinted
with permission from
www.internet.com.©2001 internet com
Corporation. All rights reserved
Internet.com is the exclusive
Trademark of internet.com Corporation;
PI02-02:Courtesy of Yahoo!
Corporation.

Chapter Three
03-02:TurboTax, a product of
Intuit/Used courtesy of Intuit;
03-03:©National Geographic; MN03-
02:Disney Magic. ©Disney Enterprises,
Inc; 03-08:Courtesy of Microsoft
Corporation. All rights reserved;
03-09:Courtesy Lotus Development
Corporation. Used with permission of
Lotus Development Corporation. Lotus
Notes is a registered trademark of Lotus
Development Corporation; MRC03-
01:©Greg Martin/Wired Magazine; PI03-
02:©2001 Sierra On-line, Inc. All Rights
reserved. Tribes and the Tribes logo are
trademarks of Sierra On-Line. Used with
permission.

Chapter Four
04-08:Courtesy Giga-Byte Technology;
PI04-01:Courtesy of PC Media, Inc;
PI04-03:©2001 by
hardwaremasters.com; PI04-
04:Courtesy of www.dependable IT.com.
All rights reserved.

Chapter Five
MRC05-01:Courtesy of Intel;
05-01a:Courtesy of Compaq;
05-01b:Courtesy of International
Business Machines Corporation.
Unauthorized use not permitted;
05-03b:Courtesy Logitech Corporation;
05-04a:©Vikki Hart/The Image Bank;
05-04b:Courtesy of Microsoft;
05-11a:Courtesy of Visioneer;
05-11b:Courtesy of Logitech;
05-13a:Courtesy of Spectra Physics;
05-13b:©Jeff Greenberg/Omni;
05-16:Courtesy of International
Business Machines Corporation.
Unauthorized use not permitted;
GP05-01:Courtesy of Hewlett Packard;
05-17:Courtesy of MidiLand;
05-21a:Courtesy of Hewlett Packard;
PI05-01:Used with permission; PI05-02:
Courtesy of www.northernwebs.com.

Chapter Six
06-03a:Courtesy of Ancodyne, Inc;
06-03c:Courtesy of Seagate Technology
Corporation; 06-04a:Courtesy of
Quantum Corporation; 06-09:Courtesy

of International Business Machines Corporation. Unauthorized use not permitted;MN06-03:Courtesy of Domino's Pizza; 06-12:courtesy OF International Business Machines Corporation. Unauthorized use not permitted;PI06-01:courtesy of Benedict Mahoney; PI06-02:Courtesy of Carol Kunze.

Chapter Seven

07-01:©Jose Louis Pelaes/Stock Market; 07-04:©Photodisc 1999; 07-08:©Hiroyuki Matsumoto/TSI; GP07-01:©2001 America Online, Inc; 07-14:©Jim Cummings/FPG; 07-15:©Joe Cornish/TSI; 07-16:America Online Software and screens ©2001 America Online, Inc. Used with permission.

Chapter Eight

08-02:Reprinted with permission from www.internet.com. ©2001 internet.com Corp. All rights reserved. Internet.com is the exclusive Trademark of internet.com Corporation; 08-03:Courtesy of Netscape Communications; 08-07:Courtesy of techtarget.com; MRC08-01:Courtesy of Microsoft Corporation; PI08-02:Used with permission; PI08-03:Used with permission.

Chapter Nine

09-01d:Used with permission. The OfficeMax.com stylized logo and any other related trademarks are the property of OMX, Inc; 09-03:Courtesy of Yahoo! Corporation; 09-04a:©2000 Lycos, Inc. Lycos® is a registered trademark of Carnegie Mellon University. All rights reserved; 09-04b:HotBot® is a registered service mark of Wired Ventures, Inc., a subsidiary of Lycos, Inc. All rights reserved; 09-05:©1996-2001 The Motley Fool. All rights reserved; 09-07b:Courtesy of Yahoo! Corporation; PI09-02:Used with permission; PI-09-03:Used with permission.

A

Accelerated Graphics Port (AGP) bus, 4-115

access arms, 6-166, 6-167

accessibility, 1-11, 2-45, 5-148

access speed, 6-171

accounting software, 3-81–82

active-matrix technology, 5-145

ActiveX, 8-237

addressable pixels, 5-144

addresses, 4-105, 4-106, 6-179, 8-244

Adobe Acrobat Reader, 8-237

advertising, 3-82, 5-138, 9-264–266

affiliates, 9-263

AGP (Accelerated Graphics Port) bus, 4-115

agriculture, 1-9

algorithm, 6-179

Allen, Paul, 296

all-in-one machines, 316

Altair computer, 296

AltaVista, 8-239, 8-240

ALU (arithmetic/logic unit), 4-101–102

AMD, 4-111

America Online (AOL), 7-213, 9-264, 9-269

amplitude, 7-199

analog transmission, 7-198, 7-199

Andreessen, Marc, 8-229, 8-230, 297

angel, 9-273

animation, streaming, 9-272–273

anonymous FTP, 8-242

AOL (America Online), 7-213, 9-264, 9-269

Apple Computer, 3-74, 294–296

Apple II, 295

applets, 8-237

application service provider (ASP), 3-73

applications software, 3-68–73

   ethics, 3-83–84

   Linux, 2-47

   Windows, 2-36, 2-44

Arecibo Radio Telescope, 4-110

arithmetic/logic unit (ALU), 4-101–102

Army education, 8-228

ARPANet, 8-228–229, 296–297

artificial intelligence (AI), 297–300

   data mining, 299–300

   debate on, 299

   defined, 297

   history of, 297–298

   how computers learn, 298–299

   natural languages, 300

   robotics, 302–304

   virtual reality, 304–305

ASCII code, 4-107, 4-108

assembly languages, 293

asynchronous transmission, 7-201

ATM (automated teller machine), 7-214

audio, streaming, 9-272–273

automated teller machines (ATMs), 7-214

auxiliary storage. *See* secondary storage

B

backbone, 9-271

background memory, 2-50

backup utility, 2-52

bandwidth, 9-271, 9-275

banner ads, 9-264–265

bar-code readers, 1-14–15, 5-139–140, 5-149

bar codes, 5-139–140

Bardeen, J., 293

batch processing, 6-180–181, 6-182–183

Bell Laboratories, 2-45

Berners-Lee, Tim, 8-229, 297

binary system, 4-105–108

bits, 4-107

bits per second (bps), 7-200

Bluetooth, 7-207

Boeing Company, 3-78–79

bookmarks, 2-62

books on computer, 1-16

Boolean logic, 8-240

booting, 2-36–37

bpi (bytes per inch), 6-175

bps (bits per second), 7-200

Brattain, H. W., 293

bridges, 7-209

broadcast mode, 9-273, 9-275

browser control panel, 8-233

browsers, 1-19, 2-63, 3-74, 3-77, 8-229, 8-232

   buttons, 8-233–234

   and competition, 8-236–237

   frames, 8-236

   functions and features, 8-233–237

   Java, 8-237

   menus, 8-233–234

   moving from site to site, 8-238

   plug-ins, 8-237

   URLs, 8-234–235

embedded systems, 2-44–45
encapsulation, 9-278
end-users, 1-12
energy companies, 1-8
entrepreneurs, 9-267–269, 296
EntryPoint, 9-276
equal-to condition, 4-101
erase head, 6-175
ergonomics, 313
Ethernet, 7-202, 7-211
ethics
    and applications software, 3-83–84
    and data, 5-150–151
    domain names, 7-215
    investment scheme, 9-265
    multimedia presentations, 6-174
    and operating systems, 2-38
E-time, 4-105
European Union, 7-224
event-driven multiprogramming, 2-48–49
Excite, 8-239, 8-243, 9-264
execution time, 4-105
expansion buses, 4-114–116
expert systems, 297, 298, 300–301
expert system shells, 301
Exploria, 9-261
Extended Binary Coded Decimal
    Interchange Code (EBCDIC), 4-107–108
external cache, 4-117
external modems, 7-199
extranets, 9-278

F

facsimile technology, 7-212
FAQs, 5-158
favorites, 2-62
faxing, 7-212
fax modems, 7-212
FBI, 1-20
Federal Communications Commission
    (FCC), 7-206–207
Federal Trade Commission (FTC), 7-223
FedEx, 5-140
fiber optics, 7-202
field robots, 302–303
fields, 6-176–177
fifth generation, 297
file compression, 2-52–53
file manager, 2-52

file names, 2-40
file organization, 6-177–180
files, 6-176
file servers, 7-209–210
file transfer protocol (FTP), 8-242
file transfer software, 7-208
filter software, 8-244
FireWire, 4-115
first-mover advantage, 9-273
flame, 8-242
flash memory, 4-117–118
flatbed scanners, 1-14, 5-138, 5-139
flat-panel screens, 5-145, 5-146
Ford Motor Company, 9-270, 301
foreground memory, 2-50
frames, 8-236
fraud. *See* security and privacy
Free Software Foundation, 6-190
freeware, 3-70, 6-190
frequency, 7-199
front-end processors, 7-208
FTP (file transfer protocol), 8-242

G

games, 5-135
Gardner, David, 9-267–268
Gardner, Tom, 9-267–268
Gates, Bill, 2-40, 296
Gateway 2000, 310
gateways, 7-209
GB (gigabytes), 4-107
General Motors (GM), 9-270
gigabytes (GB), 4-107
gigahertz (GHz), 4-116
Global Positioning System (GPS), 4-113
GNU Project, 6-190
Go Network, 9-264
Google, 8-239
government
    computer usage, 1-9
    Internet regulation, 8-224, 9-266–267
GPS (Global Positioning System), 4-113
graphical user interface (GUI), 2-37,
    2-39, 5-133
graphic artists, 3-77
graphics. *See also* images
    business graphics, 1-8, 5-149
    CAD/CAM software, 5-150
    digital cameras, 5-133, 5-143
    software for, 3-77
    video graphics, 5-150